2019
The Supreme Court Review

"Judges as persons, or courts as institutions, are entitled to no greater immunity from criticism than other persons or institutions . . . [J]udges must be kept mindful of their limitations and of their ultimate public responsibility by a vigorous stream of criticism expressed with candor however blunt."
—*Felix Frankfurter*

". . . while it is proper that people should find fault when their judges fail, it is only reasonable that they should recognize the difficulties. . . . Let them be severely brought to book, when they go wrong, but by those who will take the trouble to understand them."
—*Learned Hand*

THE LAW SCHOOL
THE UNIVERSITY OF CHICAGO

Volume 2019

The Supreme Court Review

EDITED BY
DAVID A. STRAUSS
GEOFFREY R. STONE
AND JUSTIN DRIVER

THE UNIVERSITY OF CHICAGO PRESS
CHICAGO AND LONDON

The Supreme Court Review, Volume 2019

Published annually by The University of Chicago Press.
www.journals.uchicago.edu/SCR/

© 2020 by The University of Chicago

All rights reserved. No part of this book may be reproduced in any form by any electronic or mechanical means (including photocopying, recording, or information storage and retrieval) without permission in writing from the publisher. Chapters may be copied or otherwise reused without permission only to the extent permitted by Sections 107 and 108 of the U.S. Copyright Law. Permission to copy articles for personal, internal, classroom, or library use may be obtained from the Copyright Clearance Center (www.copyright.com). For all other uses, such as copying for general distribution, for advertising or promotional purposes, for creating new collective works, or for resale, please contact Permissions Coordinator, Journals Division, University of Chicago Press, 1427 E. 60th Street, Chicago, IL 60637 USA. Fax: (773) 834-3489. E-mail: journalpermissions@press.uchicago.edu.

Subscriptions: Individual subscription rates are $84 print + electronic and $67 e-only. Institutional print + electronic and e-only rates are tiered according to an institution's type and research output: $106 to $185 (print + electronic), $92 to $161 (e-only). For additional information, including back-issue sales, classroom use, rates for single copies, and prices for institutional full-run access, please visit www.journals.uchicago.edu /SCR/. Free or deeply discounted access is available in most developing nations through the Chicago Emerging Nations Initiative (www.journals.uchicago.edu/ceni/).

Please direct subscription inquiries to Subscription Fulfillment, 1427 E. 60th Street, Chicago, IL 60637-2902. Telephone: (773) 753-3347 or toll free in the United States and Canada (877) 705-1878. Fax: (773) 753-0811 or toll-free (877) 705-1879. E-mail: subscriptions@press.uchicago.edu.

Standing orders: To place a standing order for this book series, please address your request to The University of Chicago Press, Chicago Distribution Center, Attn. Standing Orders/Customer Service, 11030 S. Langley Avenue, Chicago, IL 60628. Telephone toll free in the U.S. and Canada: 1-800-621-2736; or 1-773-702-7000. Fax toll free in the U.S. and Canada: 1-800-621-8476; or 1-773-702-7212.

Single-copy orders: In the U.S., Canada, and the rest of the world, order from your local bookseller or direct from The University of Chicago Press, Chicago Distribution Center, 11030 S. Langley Avenue, Chicago, IL 60628. Telephone toll free in the U.S. and Canada: 1-800-621-2736; or 1-773-702-7000. Fax toll free in the U.S. and Canada: 1-800-621-8476; or 1-773-702-7212. In the U.K. and Europe, order from your local bookseller or direct from The University of Chicago Press, c/o John Wiley Ltd. Distribution Center, 1 Oldlands Way, Bognor Regis, West Sussex PO22 9SA, UK. Telephone 01243 779777 or Fax 01243 820250. E-mail: cs-books@wiley.co.uk.

The University of Chicago Press offers bulk discounts on individual titles to Corporate, Premium, and Gift accounts. For information, please write to Sales Department—Special Sales, The University of Chicago Press, 1427 E. 60th Street, Chicago, IL 60637 USA or telephone 1-773-702-7723.

This book was printed and bound in the United States of America.

ISSN: 0081-9557
E-ISSN: 2158-2459
ISBN: 978-0-226-70856-0 (cloth)
E-ISBN: 978-0-226-70873-7 (ebook)

IN MEMORIAM

KENNETH KARST

CONTENTS

THE ROBERTS COURT AND ADMINISTRATIVE LAW   1
    Gillian E. Metzger

MISSISSIPPI GODDAMN: FLOWERS v MISSISSIPPI'S CHEAP
    RACIAL JUSTICE   73
    Paul Butler

THE ANTI-CAROLENE COURT   111
    Nicholas O. Stephanopoulos

TRADEMARKS, HATE SPEECH, AND SOLVING A PUZZLE
    OF VIEWPOINT BIAS   183
    Kent Greenfield

THE INSIDE-OUT CONSTITUTION:
    DEPARTMENT OF COMMERCE v NEW YORK   231
    Jennifer M. Chacón

ESTABLISHMENT CLAUSE APPEASEMENT   271
    Micah Schwartzman and Nelson Tebbe

PRECEDENT AND DISCRETION   313
    William Baude

THE SUPREME COURT'S CHALLENGE TO CIVIL SOCIETY   335
    Linda Greenhouse

TO PROMOTE THE GENERAL WELFARE:
    WHY MADISON MATTERS   355
    James T. Kloppenberg

GILLIAN E. METZGER

THE ROBERTS COURT
AND ADMINISTRATIVE LAW

Administrative law today is marked by the legal equivalent of mortal combat, where foundational principles are fiercely disputed and basic doctrines are offered up for "execution."[1] Several factors have led to administrative law's currently fraught status. Increasingly bold presidential assertions of executive power are one, with President Trump and President Obama before him using presidential control over administration to advance controversial policies that failed to get congressional sanction.[2] In the process, they have deeply enmeshed administrative agencies in political battles—indeed, for President Trump, administrative agencies *are* the political battle, as his administration has waged an all-out war on parts of the national bureaucracy.[3] These bold assertions of administrative authority stem in part from Congress's

---

Gillian E. Metzger is Harlan Fiske Stone Professor of Constitutional Law, Columbia Law School.

AUTHOR'S NOTE: Special thanks to Jessica Bulman-Pozen, Olati Johnson, Tom Merrill, Daphna Renan, and David Strauss for extremely helpful comments and to Dustin Graber and Charles See for excellent research assistance, including acquiring knowledge of the Chicago citation style.

[1] *Kisor v Wilkie*, 139 S Ct 2400, 2425 (2019).

[2] For examples of "bold attempts to accrete executive power" in both the Obama and Trump administrations, see Jerry L. Mashaw and David Berke, *Presidential Administration in a Regime of Separated Powers: An Analysis of Recent American Experience*, 35 Yale J Reg 549, 550 (2018).

[3] See Evan Osnos, *Trump vs. the "Deep State,"* New Yorker (May 14, 2018), at https://www.newyorker.com/magazine/2018/05/21/trump-vs-the-deep-state.

© 2020 by The University of Chicago. All rights reserved.
978-0-226-70856-0/2020/2019-0001$10.00

inability to address pressing problems, with political polarization, intense partisanship, and near parity between the main parties often leading to legislative gridlock.[4] The contemporary political climate also means that fights over administrative actions have become fierce and unrelenting. Moreover, the combination of these two developments—aggressive administrative advancement of presidential agendas in a deeply partisan and polarized world—has spurred a significant uptick in politically charged administrative law litigation, epitomized by the dramatic expansion in red state and blue state lawsuits challenging executive branch actions they oppose.[5] In addition, conservative groups have put sustained efforts into fostering academic attacks on core features of administrative government, efforts that have provided the intellectual scaffolding for today's doctrinal disputes.[6] And, finally, there is the Trump administration's emphasis on selecting judges who are receptive to these conservative attacks on administrative governance in court.[7]

A particularly important contributor to administrative law's contested status is the Roberts Court. The replacement of Chief Justice Rehnquist and Justice O'Connor with Chief Justice Roberts and Justice Alito brought a new skepticism about administrative government to the Supreme Court. Meanwhile, Justice Scalia and Justice Thomas did 180 degree turns in their approaches to administrative law, penning attacks on administrative law decisions they themselves had authored just a few years earlier.[8] Justice Gorsuch's elevation to

---

[4] See Gillian E. Metzger, *Agencies, Polarization, and the States*, 115 Colum L Rev 1739, 1748–49, 1757–58 (2015); see also Jody Freeman and David B. Spence, *Old Statutes, New Problems*, 163 U Pa L Rev 1, 17–63 (2014) (providing detailed examples of how congressional gridlock may prompt agencies to use their authority under preexisting statutes to address newly emerging regulatory challenges).

[5] See *Lawsuits*, State Energy & Environmental Impact Center (July 31, 2019), at https://www.law.nyu.edu/centers/state-impact/ag-actions/active-lawsuits (listing 63 active law suits against the Trump administration, with 34 filed or joined by California and 26 by New York); Neena Satija, *Texas vs. the Feds—a Look at the Lawsuits*, Texas Tribune (Jan 17, 2017), at https://www.texastribune.org/2017/01/17/texas-federal-government-lawsuits/ (highlighting that the state of Texas sued the Obama administration 48 times during his two Terms).

[6] See, for example, Jane Mayer, *Dark Money: The Hidden History of the Billionaires Behind the Rise of the Radical Right* 2–10 (Doubleday, 2016) (describing Charles and David Koch's extensive funding of anti-administrative political organizations).

[7] See Jason Zengerie, *How the Trump Administration Is Remaking the Courts*, NY Times Mag (Aug 22, 2018), at https://www.nytimes.com/2018/08/22/magazine/trump-remaking-courts-judiciary.html (describing the judicial appointment process under Trump and the role played by the Federalist Society).

[8] Compare *Michigan v EPA*, 135 S Ct 2699, 2712 (2015) (Thomas, J, concurring) (*Chevron* deference unconstitutionally requires courts to defer to agencies' interpretations of ambiguous

the Court added another strident administrative skeptic to the mix,[9] and by his final Term on the Court even Justice Kennedy had joined the ranks of administrative law's critics.[10]

This judicial skepticism of administrative government, which I have elsewhere labeled anti-administrativism, is heavily constitutional, marked by a formalist and originalist approach to the separation of powers, a deep distrust of bureaucracy, and a strong turn to the courts to protect individuals against administrative excess and restore the original constitutional order.[11] Several opinions demonstrated these traits in the lead-up to the 2018 Term, from the Court's decision in *Free Enterprise Fund v PCAOB* striking down double-for-cause removal protection, to Justice Thomas's concurrence in *Department of Transportation v Association of American Railroads* attacking modern delegation, to Chief Justice Roberts's dissent in *City of Arlington v FCC* rejecting deference to agency jurisdictional determinations, to the many concurrences in *Perez v Mortgage Bankers Association* calling deference to agency regulatory interpretations into question.[12] But perhaps the clearest example is the ongoing debate over *Chevron* deference, or the doctrine that a court should defer to a reasonable interpretation of an ambiguous statutory provision offered by the agency charged with its implementation.[13] The most cited administrative law decision for decades, *Chevron* has been under full-blown assault at the Supreme Court since 2015, when Justice Thomas condemned the practice of courts

---

statutes) with *National Cable & Telecommunications Association v Brand X Internet Services*, 545 US 967, 982–83 (2005) (Thomas, J) (requiring courts to defer to reasonable agency interpretations of ambiguous statutes, even if the court has already interpreted the statute differently). For Justice Scalia's changed view on his *Auer* opinion, see text accompanying notes 30–33.

[9] *Gutierrez-Brizuela v Lynch*, 834 F3d 1142, 1158 (10th Cir 2016) (Gorsuch, J, concurring) (arguing that *Chevron* deference is unconstitutional).

[10] *Pereira v Sessions*, 138 S Ct 2105, 2120 (2018) (Kennedy, J, concurring) (finding the "reflexive deference" exhibited in certain applications of *Chevron* deference "troubling").

[11] Gillian E. Metzger, *The Supreme Court 2016 Term—Foreword: 1930s Redux: The Administrative State Under Siege*, 131 Harv L Rev 1, 3–4, 33–46 (2017).

[12] *Free Enterprise Fund v Public Company Accounting Oversight Board*, 561 US 477, 495–99 (2010); *Department of Transportation v American Railroads*, 135 S Ct 1225, 1246, 1251 (2015) (Thomas, J, concurring in the judgment); *City of Arlington v FCC*, 569 US 290, 314–16 (2013) (Roberts, CJ, dissenting); *Perez v Mortgage Bankers Association*, 135 S Ct 1199, 1210–25 (2015) (concurrences by Alito, Scalia, and Thomas, JJ).

[13] *Chevron v Natural Resources Defense Council, Inc*, 467 US 837, 842–43 (1984). See also *United States v Mead*, 533 US 218, 226–27 (2001) (limiting *Chevron* deference in addition to instances where the agency has the power to issue rules with the force of law and exercised that authority in issuing the interpretation in question).

deferring to agency statutory interpretations as violating Article III and creating unconstitutional delegations.[14] Although Thomas made his argument in an opinion concurring in the judgment that no one else joined, by *Pereira v Sessions* three years later there appeared to be at least four Justices who considered *Chevron* deference to be constitutionally problematic,[15] and the Court itself has not relied on *Chevron* deference since 2014.[16]

Still, a striking feature of the Roberts Court's anti-administrativism before the 2018 Term was its largely rhetorical character. Although several Justices waxed expansively about an out-of-control national bureaucracy, the most dramatic attacks on the administrative state's constitutionality and administrative law were largely restricted to concurrences and dissents. The occasional majority opinions invalidating administrative arrangements on constitutional grounds were notably narrow, cabining their analysis with carve-outs and remedial minimalism.[17] And the Court was adept in its avoidance tactics, for example, repeatedly determining that statutes were unambiguous and thereby sidestepping the need to take on the debate over *Chevron*'s constitutionality.[18] In short, for all of its alarmism about bureaucrats running amok and assertions that the contemporary administrative state violates the constitutional order, the Roberts Court hadn't yet pulled back significantly on administrative governance in practice.

Thus, the increasingly burning question was whether the Roberts Court was willing to put its might where its mouth was on administrative law, even at the cost of destabilizing long-standing governance regimes. Or would its anti-administrativism continue to live mainly at the margins, tamping down perceived administrative law excesses

---

[14] *Michigan*, 135 S Ct at 2712 (2015) (Thomas, J, concurring).

[15] 138 S Ct at 2120–21 (Kennedy, J, concurring), id at 2129 (Alito, J, dissenting) (both voicing concerns with the Court's treatment of *Chevron*); *Gutierrez-Brizuela*, 834 F3d at 1154–56 (Gorsuch, J, concurring) (questioning whether *Chevron* violates separation of powers).

[16] See *Cuozzo Speed Technologies, LLC v Lee*, 136 S Ct 2131, 2142 (2016) (applying *Chevron* deference to validate Patent and Trademark Office rules for *inter partes* review).

[17] See Metzger, 131 Harv L Rev at 47–48 & n 278 (cited in note 11).

[18] See, for example, *Wisconsin Central Ltd. v United States*, 138 S Ct 2067, 2074 (2018); *Epic Systems Corp. v Lewis*, 138 S Ct 1612, 1630 (2018); see also *Pereira*, 138 S Ct at 2121 (Alito, J, dissenting) ("Here, a straightforward application of *Chevron* requires us to accept the Government's construction of the provision at issue. But the Court rejects the Government's interpretation in favor of one that it regards as the best reading of the statute. I can only conclude that the Court, for whatever reason, is simply ignoring *Chevron*").

without forcing radical changes in administrative law doctrines or received wisdom about the structural constitution? Justice Kavanaugh's track record on the D.C. Circuit—the nation's leading administrative law court—suggested that he would be amenable to further narrowing and retraction in core administrative law doctrines of deference and delegation.[19] Moreover, the Court granted certiorari in several cases that raised pointed challenges to basic administrative law precepts, suggesting that it was finally willing to put its anti-administrativism into action.[20]

Yet administrative law's denouement did not come. After a Term rife with important administrative law decisions, established administrative law remains in force, albeit narrowed. Thus, in *Kisor v Wilkie*,[21] the Court did not overturn the *Auer* doctrine of deference to agency regulatory interpretations, although it tempered such deference in significant ways. Similarly, in *Department of Commerce v New York*,[22] the Court ultimately reaffirmed and arguably expanded administrative law's core requirement of reasoned decision making to include a prohibition on pretextual explanations of agency decisions. In several other cases, the Court hewed to existing administrative law frameworks. The case in which the anti-administrativist view gained the most traction was *Gundy v United States*,[23] where four Justices signaled sympathy for a full-bore assault on the constitutionality of broad delegations. Even so, a plurality upheld the measure in question applying the Court's well-established doctrine on delegation, and as of this writing it remains unclear (and in my view unlikely) whether a majority will materialize for a major doctrinal recalibration on delegation that would call the constitutionality of the administrative state into question.

The 2018 Term cases demonstrate that the Roberts Court is deeply divided on administrative law. These divisions track clear ideological

---

[19] Christopher J. Walker, *Judge Kavanaugh on Administrative Law and Separation of Powers*, SCOTUSBlog (July 26, 2018), at https://www.scotusblog.com/2018/07/kavanaugh-on-administrative-law-and-separation-of-powers (summarizing Justice Kavanaugh's D.C. Circuit opinions on separation of powers and agency deference).

[20] See Petition for Writ of Certiorari, *Kisor v Wilkie*, 18-15, *i (US filed June 29, 2018); Petition for Writ of Certiorari, *Gundy v United States*, 17-6086, *i (US filed Sept 20, 2017).

[21] 139 S Ct 2400 (2019).

[22] 139 S Ct 2551 (2019).

[23] 139 S Ct 2116 (2019).

lines. Justice Gorsuch emerged as the voice of the four more conservative Justices this Term, intent on overturning established administrative law doctrines and pulling back on administrative government. Meanwhile Justice Kagan led the four liberal Justices in a defensive effort, seeking to deter or at least mitigate the conservative assault. In the middle was Chief Justice Roberts, sharing the conservatives' suspicion of government and bureaucracy yet resistant to the dramatic disruption and potential institutional costs to the Court that Gorsuch's approach might yield. The cases, particularly *Kisor* and *Department of Commerce*, also illuminate several core analytic themes and tensions in the Roberts Court's administrative law jurisprudence. These include recently reemerged philosophical disputes over the distinction between law and policy as well as more longstanding constitutional disagreements about separation-of-powers formalism, functionalism, and minimalism. Another central development is an increased historical focus, a development evident in Roberts Court administrative law opinions from all quarters. This increased historicism surfaced notably in revived debates over the meaning of the 1946 Administrative Procedure Act (APA), with originalist and textualist interpretation of the APA squaring off against a more evolving, common law approach to the statute and administrative law writ large. Although important, these analytic disagreements are unable on their own to explain the direction of Roberts Court administrative law. Among other issues, they map the Court's ideological divides imperfectly, with some trends spanning both camps and inconsistencies on both sides.

Taking a further step back, two contrasting frames emerge from the Roberts Court's administrative law opinions from the 2018 Term, building on these analytic tensions. The first is formalist in the extreme, insisting on sharp demarcations among the branches and between law and policy. It is also insistently originalist, condemning contemporary judicial review doctrines as at odds with traditional understandings of the judicial power and the meaning of the APA. With its categorical and uncompromising stance, commitment to limited government and aggressive judicial review, this approach has the potential to radically transform American governance. That seems in part its purpose, as this radical frame is accompanied by deep skepticism about administrative government.

The second frame encompasses Justices with a broader range of views about constitutional structure and administrative government.

Most are functionalist and accepting of constitutional evolution, but at least the Chief Justice (a sometime adherent) is more formalist and originalist. They also disagree on the extent to which administrative government poses a serious problem at all, and if it does whether the concern is the potential for arbitrary agency action or a politically unaccountable bureaucracy. But what unites them is that they are unwilling to radically disrupt existing governance regimes, at least not all at once. Instead, they share a commitment to addressing whatever problems exist with administrative government by gradually fine-tuning doctrine. The central characteristic of this approach is therefore its incremental, common law character. The impact of this incrementalist approach is harder to discern, given both the variation within its ranks and the longer time horizon needed to assess incremental change. It also leaves lower courts greater room to apply administrative law as they see fit, which could yield more pullback in administrative law or its continued preservation, depending on the orientations of lower court judges. Like its radical cousin, this incrementalist frame could result in a substantial pullback in administrative power, but it would have this effect through a more subconstitutional and statutory interpretation guise and over a longer period of time.

In assessing the future impact of Roberts Court administrative law, the most important factor may be this tension between radicalism and incrementalism. Which of these analytic frames will ultimately prevail still remains an open question, but incrementalism was plainly the victor in the 2018 Term's administrative law decisions. That is significant, but should also not obscure that there was unity across the Court in urging greater judicial scrutiny of administrative action. Moreover, despite invocations of the importance of bureaucratic expertise, these decisions share the concerns with unaccountable, aggrandized, and arbitrary administrative power that characterize the Roberts Court's administrative jurisprudence more widely.

That administrative power is expansive is indisputable, as is the possibility that such power can be abused. Yet the Roberts Court's portrayal of administrative government is strikingly incomplete. Notably lacking is reference to the ways that the administrative state operates to constrain power, render it accountable, and advance individual liberty. The lack of such an affirmative account reinforces the sense that the goal of Roberts Court administrative law may be to pull back on government for its own sake, rather than to better achieve constitutional values. Absent a more balanced view of the administrative state, the Roberts Court is unlikely to develop a coherent approach to administrative law.

Part I of what follows discusses the 2018 Term's administrative law cases, looking in detail at the two decisions addressing judicial review of agency decision making, *Kisor v Wilkie* and *Department of Commerce v New York*. Part II then elucidates several key analytic tensions underlying these decisions and the Roberts Court's administrative law jurisprudence writ large, while Part III assesses what the 2018 Term decisions portend for the future of administrative law.

I. Administrative Law in the 2018 Term

Administrative law took center stage in the 2018 Term. A range of cases presented the Court with opportunities to remake doctrine, opportunities that the Court for the most part declined. In some instances, the Court took a minimalist approach, invoking established doctrine to resolve relatively noncontroversial issues and punting the difficult questions back to the lower courts.[24] In others, the Court engaged more forthrightly with contentious administrative law issues, albeit ultimately sidestepping dramatic changes.[25]

Two administrative law decisions deserve special attention: *Kisor v Wilkie* and *Department of Commerce v New York*. Both were prominent cases that centered on the core and much disputed issue of judicial deference to administrative determinations. Both also involved a majority affirming the principle of deference as well as existing deference doctrines, and thus they too are instances in which the Court

---

[24] See *Weyerhaeuser Co. v Fish & Wildlife Service*, 139 S Ct 361, 369, 371–72 (2018) (remanding question of whether property requiring some modification to support a species can count as habitat and whether the Secretary had acted arbitrarily in assessing the costs and benefits of designing property not currently occupied by frog species as habitat); see also *PDR Network v Carlton & Harris Chiropractic*, 139 S Ct 2051, 2055–56 (2019) (remanding for court of appeals to determine whether the FCC order at issue was a legislative or interpretive rule and whether the petitioner had a "prior" and "adequate" opportunity to obtain judicial review of the order).

[25] *Gundy v United States*, 139 S Ct 2116 (2019), is a prime example. There, Justice Kagan, id at 2129–30 (Kagan, J) (plurality), and Justice Gorsuch, id at 2133–37, 2143–45 (Gorsuch, J, dissenting), battled directly over the constitutionality of congressional delegations of policymaking authority to administrative agencies. The radical potential of the case lies in the fact that Chief Justice Roberts and Justice Thomas joined Gorsuch's dissent and Justice Alito penned a concurrence indicating his willingness to reconsider nondelegation doctrine, id at 2130 (Alito, J, concurring in the judgment). But these were, in the end, a dissent and a concurrence, and a majority upheld the specific delegation challenged there under the existing intelligible-principle test.

avoided dramatic change. Together, these two cases offer an illuminating window on recurring themes and tensions in the Roberts Court's approach to administrative law.

A. KISOR V WILKIE

Factually, *Kisor* arose from a veteran's repeated efforts to get disability benefits from the Department of Veterans Affairs. Jurisprudentially, the background to *Kisor* lay in a 2011 concurrence by Justice Scalia, where he criticized the practice of giving deference to agency interpretations of their own regulations.[26] Known as either *Seminole Rock* deference (after a 1945 decision setting out the doctrine[27]) or more recently as *Auer* deference (after a 1997 decision reaffirming the doctrine[28]), this doctrine provides that courts should defer to an agency's interpretation of its own regulation unless the interpretation is "plainly erroneous or inconsistent with the regulation" or there is some other "reason to suspect that the interpretation does not reflect the agency's fair and considered judgment on the matter in question."[29] Despite having authored *Auer* for a unanimous Court fourteen years earlier, Justice Scalia argued in 2011 that "it seems contrary to fundamental principles of separation of powers to permit the person who promulgates a law to interpret it as well" and expressed concern "that deferring to an agency's interpretation of its own rule encourages the agency to enact vague rules which give it the power, in future adjudications, to do what it pleases."[30] A majority of the Court cited Justice Scalia's concerns the next year in *Christopher v SmithKline Beecham Corporation*, when it refused to grant *Auer* deference to the Department of Labor's (DOL) new interpretation of Fair Labor Standards Act regulations, an interpretation DOL had offered in amicus briefs without prior notice to regulated parties.[31]

Justice Scalia reiterated and expanded his criticism of the doctrine in 2013 in *Decker v Northwest Environmental Defense Center*, where he picked up two additional votes (Chief Justice Roberts and Justice Alito)

---

[26] *Talk America Inc. v Michigan Bell Co.*, 564 US 50, 67–68 (2011) (Scalia, J, concurring).
[27] *Bowles v Seminole Rock & Sand Co.*, 325 US 410, 413–14 (1945).
[28] *Auer v Robbins*, 519 US 452 (1997).
[29] Id at 461–62.
[30] *Talk America*, 564 US at 68 (Scalia, J, concurring).
[31] 567 US 142, 159–61 (2012).

for his call to reconsider *Auer* deference.[32] And in 2015, in *Perez v Mortgage Bankers Association*, Justice Scalia further argued that *Auer* deference also violated the Administrative Procedure Act.[33] Justice Thomas, now fully on board, wrote an even longer opinion arguing that *Auer* was unconstitutional because it "represents a transfer of judicial power to the Executive Branch, and . . . amounts to an erosion of the judicial obligation to serve as a 'check' on the political branches."[34] Justice Alito also signaled his sympathy with these views, describing them as "offer[ing] substantial reasons why the *Seminole Rock* doctrine may be incorrect."[35] But the focus of *Perez* was on invalidating, as "contrary to the clear text of the [APA]," the D.C. Circuit's requirement that agencies undertake notice-and-comment rulemaking before significantly changing a definitive interpretation of a rule.[36] The *Perez* majority was content to relegate the *Auer* issue to a footnote, responding simply that "[e]ven in cases where an agency's interpretation receives *Auer* deference, . . . it is the court that ultimately decides whether a given regulation means what the agency says. Moreover, *Auer* deference is not an inexorable command in all cases."[37]

Perez sparked concerted efforts by business groups and conservative organizations to get a case seeking to overrule *Auer* before the Court.[38] In one such case, involving the Department of Education's interpretation of its rules to require public schools to allow transsexual students to use the gender bathroom of their choice, certiorari was granted but ultimately dismissed when the Trump administration rescinded the interpretation.[39] Finally, however, with *Kisor* they scored the legal vehicle of their dreams. *Kisor* involved about as sympathetic a plaintiff as one could find: a former Marine, still suffering from his

---

[32] 568 US 597, 615 (2013) (Scalia, J, concurring in part and dissenting in part).

[33] 135 S Ct 1199, 1211–12 (2015) (Scalia, J, concurring in the judgment).

[34] Id at 1217 (Thomas, J, concurring in the judgment).

[35] Id at 1210 (Alito, J, concurring in part and concurring in the judgment).

[36] Id at 1206.

[37] *Perez*, 135 S Ct at 1208 n 4.

[38] See Brief Amici Curiae of the Chamber of Commerce of the United States of America, *Garco Construction Inc. v Secretary of the Army*, No 17-225, *2–3 (US filed Sept 11, 2017) (cert denied) (requesting the Court to reconsider *Auer*); Brief Amici Curiae of American Action Forum et al, *United States Aid Inc. v Bible*, No 15-861, *3 (US filed Feb 3, 2016) (cert denied) (calling for the overruling of *Auer*); Brief Amici Curiae of Cato Institute et al, *Gloucester County School Board v GG*, No 16-273, *4 (US filed Sept 27, 2016) (case resolved on other grounds) (taking no position on the merits but urging the Court to overrule *Auer*).

[39] *Gloucester County School Board v GG*, 137 S Ct 1239 (2017) (mem).

service in Vietnam, wrongly denied disability benefits when he first applied in 1982 and then subsequently unable to recoup benefits retroactively because the agency deemed the new service records he supplied not "relevant" for purposes of a VA regulation governing when the agency could reconsider an earlier benefits denial.[40] Moreover, the Court granted certiorari solely on the question of whether *Auer* deference should be overruled.[41] The general consensus from both *Auer*'s critics and its defenders was that the Court was poised to overrule the doctrine.[42]

But that didn't happen. Instead, the Court, by a 5–4 vote, declined to overrule *Auer*. Justice Kagan's majority opinion defending *Auer* deference was joined in full by the three other liberal Justices, but Chief Justice Roberts—who provided the crucial fifth vote—joined only in part. Meanwhile Justice Gorsuch, concurring only in the judgment and joined by the three other conservative Justices, assumed the role of *Auer*'s prime attacker, complaining that "[i]t should have been easy for the Court to say goodbye to *Auer*."[43] Justice Kavanaugh, joined by Justice Alito, also wrote separately.

1. *Justice Kagan and the limits on Auer deference.* At first glance, Justice Kagan's opinion has a slightly schizophrenic air. She led with *Auer*'s virtues, emphasizing several reasons why it makes sense to presume that Congress, having delegated power to an agency to implement a statute through rulemaking, would also intend to delegate power to resolve ambiguities in those rules. "In part, that is because the agency that promulgated a rule is in the 'better position to reconstruct' its original meaning";[44] in part, it is because agencies are more expert and politically accountable than courts; and in part, it is

---

[40] 38 CFR § 3.156(c)(1).

[41] *Kisor*, 139 S Ct at 2408–09.

[42] See, for example, Gillian Metzger, *The Puzzling and Troubling Grant in Kisor*, SCOTUSblog (Jan 30, 2019), at https://www.scotusblog.com/2019/01/symposium-the-puzzling-and-troubling-grant-in-kisor/ (describing the grant in *Kisor* as part of a conservative effort to overrule *Auer* and "troubling for what the case may portend about how the Roberts Court, with its newly cemented conservative majority, views the administrative state"); Kimberly Hermann, *The Supreme Court and the Forgotten "Three Ring Government,"* SCOTUSblog (Jan 29, 2019), at https://www.scotusblog.com/2019/01/symposium-the-supreme-court-and-the-forgotten-three-ring-government/ (stating that "[t]he Supreme Court granted certiorari to decide whether it should overrule *Auer* and *Seminole Rock*" and that "[a] number of Supreme Court opinions ... suggest that the court will answer that question with a 'yes'").

[43] *Kisor*, 139 S Ct at 2425 (Gorsuch, J, concurring in the judgment).

[44] Id at 2412 (plurality) (quoting *Martin v Occupational Safety & Health Review Commission*, 499 US 144, 152 (1991) (internal additions omitted)).

because deferring to agency interpretations yields greater uniformity and consistency in interpretations than having courts exercising independent judgment.[45] But her most central point—what Kagan termed "the core theory of *Auer* deference"[46]—was that "sometimes the law runs out and policy-laden choice is what is left over."[47] And "Congress ... is attuned to the comparative advantages of agencies over courts in making such policy judgments."[48] Moreover, she emphasized that ambiguity in regulations is inevitable; although at times the result of "careless drafting," ambiguity often instead "reflects the well-known limits of expression or knowledge."[49]

Justice Kagan then ended her opinion by rebutting at length the many attacks made against *Auer* deference. One such attack, raised by Kisor and by Justice Gorsuch in dissent, was that judicial deference to agency regulatory interpretations violates § 706 of the APA, which provides that "the reviewing court shall decide all relevant questions of law ... and determine the meaning or applicability of the terms of an agency action."[50] Kagan argued that courts comply with § 706 even when they grant *Auer* deference, both because they apply extensive independent review before deciding to defer and because courts are determining the meaning of a rule by deferring when they conclude that Congress delegated authority to interpret the rule to the agency which promulgated it.[51] She further defended *Auer*'s constitutionality by insisting that courts still "retain a firm grip on the interpretive function," agencies exercise executive power rather than judicial power when they interpret, and the combination of legislative, judicial, and executive functions in agencies had long been upheld.[52] She also dismissed the claim that *Auer* deference creates poor agency incentives "to issue vague and open-ended regulations," maintaining that it

---

[45] Id at 2410–14 (Kagan, J) (plurality).

[46] Id at 2415 (Kagan, J) (plurality).

[47] *Kisor*, 239 S Ct at 2415 (Kagan, J) (plurality).

[48] Id at 2413 (Kagan, J) (plurality).

[49] Id at 2410 (Kagan, J) (plurality).

[50] 5 USC § 706.

[51] *Kisor*, 139 S Ct at 2419–20 (Kagan, J) (plurality). She further insisted that deference does not give an interpretive rule the binding effect that the APA limits to legislative rules for which § 553 demands notice-and-comment procedures, emphasizing again the independent review that courts undertake before deciding to defer and the restriction of *Auer* deference to "an agency's authoritative and considered judgments" served § 553 values. Id at 2420–21 (Kagan, J) (plurality).

[52] Id at 2421–22 (Kagan, J) (plurality).

"does not survive an encounter with reality."[53] Finally, Kagan argued strongly for retaining *Auer* deference on stare decisis grounds.[54]

In between these powerful defenses of *Auer* deference, however, Justice Kagan elaborated a multitude of limits that significantly constrain when *Auer* deference applies. First, *Auer* deference is only triggered in cases of "genuin[e] ambigu[ity]," which means not just surface ambiguity but the type of ambiguity that remains after a court has rigorously applied the traditional tools of statutory interpretation. In addition, the agency must offer a reasonable interpretation, and the interpretation must be one that represents the agency's "authoritative" view, "implicates its substantive expertise," reflects its "fair and considered judgment," and does not "create unfair surprise to regulated parties."[55] This long list closely parallels the "significant limits" on *Auer* deference that the Solicitor General advocated in his *Kisor* brief.[56] And it led Justice Gorsuch, in concurring in the judgment, to chastise the majority for retaining *Auer* deference only in a "maimed," "enfeebled," and "zombified" form.[57] That may go too far, but Chief Justice Roberts and Justice Kavanaugh have a point in claiming that the distance between Justice Kagan's opinion retaining *Auer* and Justice Gorsuch's dispensing with it "is not as great as it may initially appear."[58] Certainly that was true in the case at hand, for Kagan ultimately concluded that the lower court "jumped the gun in declaring the [VA's] regulation ambiguous" and suggested that the nonprecedential agency interpretation at issue—one of 80,000 issued by 100 judges sitting singly each year—might well not be the type of considered, authoritative interpretation needed for *Auer* deference to apply.

A reader is left wondering whether *Auer* deference is really as beneficial as Justice Kagan makes it out to be—and if it is, why on earth the majority doesn't let it have broader sway. One obvious

---

[53] Id at 2421 (Kagan, J) (plurality) (noting not only the lack of empirical evidence to support this claim, but also that agencies have all sorts of practical incentives to be clear).

[54] Id at 2422 (Kagan, J) (plurality).

[55] *Kisor*, 139 S Ct at 2414–18 (internal quotations and citations omitted).

[56] Brief for the Respondent in Opposition, *Kisor v Wilkie*, No 18-15, *12 (US filed Feb 25, 2019).

[57] *Kisor*, 139 S Ct at 2425 (Gorsuch, J, concurring in the judgment).

[58] Id at 2424 (Roberts, CJ, concurring in part); see also id at 2448 (Kavanaugh, J, concurring in the judgment).

explanation for this tension in Justice Kagan's opinion is Chief Justice Roberts. He concurred only in the parts of Kagan's opinion setting out *Auer*'s limits, arguing that *Auer* deference should be retained on stare decisis grounds, and reversing for reconsideration of whether *Auer* deference should be applied here. Put differently, only four Justices were willing to state that *Auer* deference yields benefits or conforms to Congress's expectations and the APA. Why Roberts was unwilling to join more of Kagan's opinion is difficult to explain, given that he had previously argued that the courts' law-declaring role under the Constitution and the APA can be compatible with deference to agency legal interpretations.[59] But in light of his stance, the limits *Kisor* imposed on *Auer* deference appear to be the necessary price to have *Auer* retained by a majority at all.

Although the need to secure Roberts's vote no doubt played an important role in shaping the majority opinion, it would be a mistake to view Kagan's cabining of *Auer* as simply strategic. To begin with, Kagan herself offered a different account, arguing that the limits are prerequisites for securing the benefits of *Auer* deference and not impediments to that goal. As she put it, the presumption that Congress would want a court to defer to an agency's interpretation would not be justified absent ambiguity or "when a court concludes that an interpretation does not reflect an agency's authoritative, expertise-based, fair or considered judgment."[60] In addition, Kagan contended that these limits were ones that the Court had already recognized in its prior *Auer* jurisprudence. Moreover, as a legal academic Justice Kagan had argued strongly in favor of limiting deference to interpretations meaningfully reviewed and personally offered by the agency official to whom Congress had delegated authority over the relevant administrative action.[61] Kagan wrote there about *Chevron* deference, but an obvious linkage exists to her argument here that *Auer* deference should be limited to "authoritative" and "considered" agency regulatory interpretations. Indeed, in many ways *Kisor* represents the importation of *Chevron/Mead* analysis into the *Auer* context: The *Kisor* limits add a

---

[59] See *City of Arlington*, 569 US at 316–17 (Roberts, CJ, dissenting) (arguing that deference is compatible with the court's law-declaring role provided Congress had delegated interpretive authority to agencies).

[60] *Kisor*, 139 S Ct at 2414 (Kagan, J) (plurality) (internal additions and citations omitted).

[61] David J. Barron and Elena Kagan, *Chevron's Nondelegation Doctrine*, 2001 Supreme Court Review 201, 235, 238–39 (2001).

Mead Step Zero, identifying certain contexts in which *Auer* deference is not even potentially available, and also a rigorous *Chevron* Step One inquiry, in which a court must determine if sufficient ambiguity exists to trigger *Auer* deference.[62]

These defenses of *Kisor*'s limits are only partially successful. It is true that the Court already had "cabined *Auer*'s scope in varied and critical ways,"[63] but the Court certainly expanded on these limits in *Kisor*. More importantly, Kagan papered over the evident tensions between the limits she articulated and the justifications she offered for *Auer* deference. Take, for example, Kagan's argument that agencies are more expert and politically accountable than courts, and thus Congress would likely consider agencies better positioned to make the policy judgments that resolving regulatory ambiguity requires.[64] Surely this institutional competency argument for deference also extends to instances in which agencies change their interpretations, even at the cost of unfair surprise, provided agencies provide a reasoned explanation for the change. Yet Kagan rejected deference in such circumstances. And while a good case can be made that Congress would not intend deference when the text of a rule is clear, it is hardly obvious that Congress would want courts to work hard to resolve seeming ambiguities on their own, rather than to defer to agencies once some ambiguity becomes apparent. After all, agencies' greater expertise and knowledge of the rule likely makes them better positioned to determine when ambiguity actually exists, as well as to resolve that ambiguity once identified. Kagan also downplayed the costs that *Auer*'s limits may carry, in particular the way that a more case-by-case assessment of relevant factors increases uncertainty for regulated parties and agencies alike. Gorsuch underscored this point,[65] and it is

---

[62] *Kisor*, 139 S Ct at 2414–18 (listing limits and noting the parallel to *Chevron/Mead*); see Thomas W. Merrill, *The Mead Doctrine: Rules and Standards, Meta-Rules and Meta-Standards*, 54 Admin L Rev 807, 812–19 (2002) (outlining the *Chevron/Mead* framework and describing the multiple factors *Mead* identified as relevant in determining if deference applies); see also Kristin E. Hickman and Mark R. Thomson, *The Chevronization of Auer*, 103 Minn L Rev Headnotes 103, 107 (2019) (arguing, pre-*Kisor*, that "[a] multi-step *Auer* doctrine is emerging ... that mirrors the several steps and complexity of ... *Chevron* deference").

[63] *Kisor*, 139 S Ct at 2418. Along with other administrative law professors, I made this point in a brief to the Court in *Kisor*. See Brief of Administrative Law Scholars in Support of Affirmance, *Kisor v Wilkie*, No 18-15, *11–13 (US filed Mar 4, 2019).

[64] *Kisor*, 139 S Ct at 2413 (Kagan, J) (plurality).

[65] Id at 2445 (Gorsuch, J, concurring in the judgment).

one that Kagan had previously acknowledged,[66] yet she largely ignored it here.

This is not to say that the limits Justice Kagan imposed on *Auer* deference are indefensible, but rather that their underlying rationale does not and cannot lie solely in congressional intent. Instead, these limits stem from normative and functional concerns—in particular, fairness to regulated parties, the need for a check on agency power, ensuring expert decision making, and encouraging political accountability. In her past life as an academic, Kagan was open about how deference doctrines "arise from and reflect candid policy judgments ... about the allocation of interpretive authority."[67] But in *Kisor* she avoided forthright engagement with the conflicting concerns at work in constructing deference doctrines. Take again the example of changed agency interpretations: Such interpretations often reflect transformations in administrative policy stemming from change in political control of the executive branch, yet they risk undercutting legitimate reliance. In *Kisor*, Justice Kagan plainly prioritized reliance over electoral accountability, but we are left to wonder why.[68]

2. *Justice Gorsuch's contrasting vision.* Justice Gorsuch provided a very different take on *Auer* deference, recounting in detail what had become the standard litany of *Auer*'s sins. He maintained that *Auer* deference was a historical aberration plainly at odds with the APA's judicial review and procedural requirements. In his view, § 706's "unqualified command requires the court to determine legal questions—including questions about a regulation's meaning—by its own lights." Hence, a "court that, in deference to an agency, adopts something other than the best reading of a regulation ... is abdicating the duty Congress assigned to it."[69] And *Auer* "effectively nullifies the distinction" Congress drew between notice-and-comment rules that carry the force of law and interpretive rules that do not.[70] In the face

---

[66] Barron and Kagan, 2001 Supreme Court Review at 225–27 (cited in note 61) (emphasizing burdens that a case-by-case approach to *Chevron* deference impose on agencies).

[67] Id at 203.

[68] One possible reason is that agencies can still achieve policy change; they simply must change the underlying legislative rule through notice-and-comment rulemaking to do so. Justice Gorsuch offered this argument. See *Kisor*, 139 S Ct at 2442 (Gorsuch, J, concurring in the judgment). But Kagan rejected such a procedural requirement on the ground (also articulated in *Perez*) that the APA does not impose notice-and-comment rulemaking requirements on interpretive rules. Id at 2420 (Kagan, J) (plurality).

[69] Id at 2432 (Gorsuch, J, concurring in the judgment).

[70] Id at 2434 (Gorsuch, J, concurring in the judgment).

of such "clear statutory commands," he argued, it made no sense to presume that Congress "really, secretly, wanted courts to treat agency interpretations as binding."[71] He argued equally forcefully that *Auer* violates Article III and the separation of powers "by coopt[ing] the judicial power," and uniting "the powers of making, enforcing and interpreting the laws ... in the same hands," thereby compromising "a cornerstone of the rule of law."[72] Underlying these statutory and constitutional arguments was Gorsuch's rejection of Kagan's equation of law and policy. Such an equation "contradicts a basic premise of our legal order: that we are governed not by the shifting whims of politicians and bureaucrats, but by written laws whose meaning is fixed and ascertainable."[73] Left out of this portrayal is the possibility that the alternative to agency deference might actually be governance by the shifting whims of life-tenured federal judges, as they struggle to give meaning to complicated and indeterminate laws.

A particularly notable contrast lies in the two opinions' views of agencies. For Justice Kagan, agencies are expert bodies assigned public responsibilities by Congress and inevitably confronted with regulatory ambiguity.[74] For Justice Gorsuch, they are biased actors who are no different than self-interested private parties and will exploit ambiguity to their own advantage.[75] For Kagan, agencies' political aspect is a positive feature, helping to ensure that the administrative state remains accountable; for Gorsuch, it means that *Auer* deference threatens the constitutional structure by elevating "raw political executive power" over the Constitution's promise of an independent and impartial judiciary.[76] These divergent views suggest very different understandings of the administrative state. Implicit in Kagan's opinion is a positive account of administrative government and the benefits of expert and accountable regulation; the image she repeatedly referred to was of the FDA and its expertise when it comes

---

[71] Id at 2435 (Gorsuch, J, concurring in the judgment).

[72] *Kisor*, 139 S Ct at 2439–40 (Gorsuch, J, concurring in the judgment) (emphasis omitted).

[73] Id.

[74] Id at 2410, 2413, 2421 (Kagan, J) (plurality).

[75] Compare id at 2425–26; see also id 2442–43 (Gorsuch, J, concurring in the judgment) (noting agency expertise as a basis for taking agency views seriously, but not for deference because agencies may be wrong).

[76] Compare *Kisor*, 139 S Ct at 2413 (Kagan, J) (plurality), with id at 2439–40 (Gorsuch, J, concurring in the judgment).

to identifying active moieties.⁷⁷ Justice Gorsuch explicitly articulates a darker vision, one under which the "explosive growth of the administrative state [and regulations] over the last half-century" means that the "mischief" and "cost" of *Auer* deference have "increased dramatically."⁷⁸

In addition, where Justice Kagan's defense of *Auer* is qualified and cabined, Justice Gorsuch's attack on the doctrine is uncompromising and absolute. Yet at times Gorsuch's arguments seem overdone. From his opinion it is hard to understand how the Court could ever have been so benighted to adopt *Auer* deference in the first place, let alone adhere to it for decades and preserve it for the future. Or take Gorsuch's attack on "the majority's attempt to remodel *Auer*'s rule into a multi-step, multifactor inquiry [that] guarantees more uncertainty and much litigation."⁷⁹ Although the uncertainty generated by *Kisor* is a valid point, Gorsuch insisted in the same breath that the better approach would be to apply the notoriously fuzzy doctrine of *Skidmore* deference—under which the weight given an agency's interpretation of a regulation would depend on the factors that give it "power to persuade."⁸⁰ On a clarity and certainty scale, *Kisor*'s domesticated version of *Auer* and *Skidmore* deference are hardly worlds apart.

Ultimately, Gorsuch insisted that *Kisor*'s affirmance of *Auer* is "more a stay of execution than a pardon," all but inviting future challenges until the Court "find[s] the nerve . . . [to] inter *Auer* at last."⁸¹ By thus vowing continued resistance, Gorsuch may have done more to guarantee ongoing uncertainty and dispute than the majority's new limits did. And with the disruptive stakes of efforts to

---

⁷⁷ Id at 2410, 2413 (plurality). Under an FDA regulation, pharmaceutical companies receive exclusive rights to drug products if they contain "no active moiety that has been approved by FDA in any other" new drug application. 21 CFR § 314.108(a) (2010). Kagan emphasized the difficult questions that interpreting this regulation entails, such as whether "[a company has] created a new 'active moiety' by joining a previously approved moiety to lysine through a non-ester covalent bond." *Kisor*, 139 S Ct at 2410 (Kagan, J) (plurality). Speaking with conviction, she added that "[i]f you are a judge, you probably have no idea of what the FDA's rule means." Id at 2413 (Kagan, J) (plurality).

⁷⁸ *Kisor*, 139 S Ct at 2446–47 (Gorsuch, J, concurring in the judgment).

⁷⁹ Id at 2447 (Gorsuch, J, concurring in the judgment).

⁸⁰ Id at 2447–48 (Gorsuch, J, concurring in the judgment); *Skidmore v Swift & Co.*, 323 US 134, 140 (1944) (listing relevant factors for extending deference); Richard W. Murphy, *A New Counter-Marbury: Reconciling Skidmore Deference and Agency Interpretive Freedom*, 56 Admin L Rev 1, 41 (2004) (describing the "fuzzy" nature of *Skidmore* analysis).

⁸¹ *Kisor*, 139 S Ct at 2425–26 (Gorsuch, J, concurring in the judgment).

overturn *Auer* thus clarified, it is not surprising that stare decisis became the decisive issue in the case.

3. *Stare decisis, Auer deference, and Chevron*. *Kisor* was one of many cases in the 2018 Term in which stare decisis emerged as a central point of contention among the Justices.[82] What made *Kisor* unusual is that stare decisis concerns carried the day here—and even more, did so over the contention that stare decisis was categorically inapplicable to deference doctrines.

Both Justice Kagan and Justice Gorsuch offered standard stare decisis arguments. Kagan's main stare decisis claim was that overruling *Auer* deference would cause great disruption because the doctrine represents a "long line of precedents ... going back 75 years or more" and "pervades the whole corpus of administrative law. . . . It is the rare overruling that introduces so much instability into so many areas of law, all in one blow."[83] Kagan's argument on this score was helped by the fact that both Kisor's attorney and the Solicitor General had acknowledged that overturning *Auer* would open up many precedents to reconsideration.[84] She also emphasized that Congress was free to overrule *Auer* but had not done so, suggesting that *Auer* deference should enjoy the same high level of stare decisis accorded statutory constructions.[85] Gorsuch, for his part, drew on a litany of established grounds for rejecting stare decisis, insisting that *Auer* deference was accidental, never justified, unworkable, at odds with norms of legal interpretation, and not a doctrine on which private parties had relied.[86]

But their main bone of contention centered on how *Auer* deference should be viewed. Justice Kagan framed *Auer* deference as a substantive doctrine and inseparable (at least categorically) from the results reached in specific cases where it is applied.[87] Justice Gorsuch did not seriously dispute the disruptive impact of overruling *Auer* if

---

[82] Stare decisis to Supreme Court precedent was discussed in five cases in the 2018 Term, including *Kisor*. See *Knick v Township of Scott*, 139 S Ct 2162 (2019); *Franchise Tax Board v Hyatt*, 139 S Ct 148 (2019); *Gamble v United States*, 139 S Ct 1960 (2019); *Stokeling v United States*, 139 S Ct 544 (2019).

[83] *Kisor*, 139 S Ct at 2422.

[84] Id.

[85] Id.

[86] Id at 2445–47 (Gorsuch, J, concurring in the judgment).

[87] Id at 2410–14 (Kagan, J) (plurality).

viewed in substantive terms. But he rejected this framing, arguing that the better analogy is to see *Auer* as an interpretive methodology, like the "proper weight to afford to historical practice in constitutional cases or legislative history in statutory cases," which the Court does not regard as "binding future Justices with the full force of horizontal *stare decisis*."[88] Gorsuch based this claim on the fact that *Auer* does not "purport to settle the meaning of a single statute or resolve a particular case" but instead claims "to prescribe an interpretive methodology governing every future dispute."[89]

Neither Justice Kagan's nor Justice Gorsuch's arguments on this front are fully satisfying. As Randy Kozel has maintained, deference doctrines fall somewhere in between decisions addressing specific substantive interpretations and interpretive methodologies.[90] It is analytically possible, if smacking of *ipse dixit*, to overrule *Auer* while still according stare decisis effect to specific decisions reached in reliance on *Auer*. In addition, Gorsuch has a point in arguing that *Auer*'s breadth of application means that applying stare decisis here has a greater constraining effect on judges than granting stare decisis to specific interpretations.[91] On the other hand, Gorsuch's further suggestion that congressional efforts to tell courts how to review agency interpretations may unconstitutionally intrude on judicial independence is a more radical proposition than he acknowledged and unsupported by current case law.[92] It would call much of § 706 of the APA into question, for example, as that provision consists entirely of congressional instructions to courts on how to review agency action.[93]

---

[88] Id at 2444 (Gorsuch, J, concurring in the judgment). Whether interpretive methodologies are as optional as Gorsuch claims is debatable; Gorsuch himself suggests that one reason to get rid of *Auer* is that the doctrine is at odds with currently governing norms of interpretation that give little weight to congressional intent. Id at 2442 (Gorsuch, J, concurring in the judgment). Whether they should be optional is debatable as well. Compare Abbe Gluck, *The States as Laboratories of Statutory Interpretation: Methodological Consensus and the New Modified Textualism*, 119 Yale L J 1750 (2010), with Evan J. Criddle and Glen Staszewski, *Against Methodological Stare Decisis*, 102 Georgetown L J 1573 (2014).

[89] *Kisor*, 139 S Ct at 2444 (Gorsuch, J, concurring in the judgment).

[90] Randy J. Kozel, *Statutory Interpretation, Administrative Deference, and the Law of Stare Decisis*, 97 Tex L Rev 1125, 1128 (2019).

[91] *Kisor*, 139 S Ct at 2444 (Gorsuch, J, concurring in the judgment) (claiming that stare decisis in the *Auer* context would dictate "the interpretive inferences that future Justices must draw in construing statutes and regulations that the Court has never engaged").

[92] Id at 2439–40 (Gorsuch, J, concurring in the judgment).

[93] See 5 USC § 706; Merrill, 54 Admin L Rev at 823 (cited in note 62) (explaining that the Court's precedents in *Christensen v Harris County*, 529 US 576 (2000), and *United States v*

On the whole, Kagan's identification of *Auer* as a substantive doctrine is more persuasive than Gorsuch's effort to analogize it to a method of interpretation. To begin with, Gorsuch's effort to equate *Auer* with an interpretive methodology is hard to square with the Court's practice of treating deference doctrines as mandatory. Prior to the current attack on *Auer* and *Chevron*, the Court did not debate whether or not those frameworks governed its review of agency regulatory and statutory interpretations; instead, the Justices' disagreements centered on questions internal to the frameworks, such as whether the relevant regulatory or statutory texts were ambiguous.[94] And while vertical stare decisis raises issues about the Supreme Court's superintendence of lower federal courts that are absent from horizontal stare decisis, it merits note that the Court does not portray deference doctrines as optional for lower courts to follow. To the contrary, the Court has reversed lower courts for mistakes in their application of these doctrines.[95] Of course, that an approach represents the Court's current practice does not immunize it from criticism and change, but current practice should carry particular weight in stare decisis assessments.

In addition, Gorsuch's suggestion that transsubstantive doctrines should not trigger stare decisis would have a dramatic impact on administrative law. Administrative law is transsubstantive to its core. Although many of its transsubstantive doctrines are ultimately rooted in the APA or another statute, they frequently represent substantial judicial development from that statutory basis.[96] As a result, rejecting stare decisis for transsubstantive doctrines could open up the field to fundamental transformation. That links Gorsuch's rejection of stare

---

Mead, 533 US 218 (2001), "make it clear that Congress has the authority to turn *Chevron* deference on and off"). For an argument that Congress lacks power to enact mandatory rules of statutory interpretation, see Larry Alexander and Saikrishna Prakash, *Mother May I? Imposing Mandatory Prospective Rules of Statutory Interpretation*, 20 Const Comm 97, 99–100 (2003).

[94] See, for example, *MCI Telecommunications Corp. v American Telephone & Telegraph Co.*, 512 US 218 (1994), where the majority and dissent disagreed over whether the phrase "modify any requirement" was sufficiently ambiguous to warrant *Chevron* deference.

[95] *Decker*, 568 US 597 (2013) (reversing the Ninth Circuit for failing to apply *Auer* deference to an agency interpretation of a rule); *Entergy Corp. v Riverkeeper Inc.*, 556 US 208 (2009) (reversing the Second Circuit for failing to grant *Chevron* deference to the EPA's choice to use cost-benefit analysis).

[96] Gillian E. Metzger, *Embracing Administrative Common Law*, 80 Geo Wash L Rev 1293, 1295–97 (2012).

decisis to the rest of his opinion and its broad invocation of constitutional first principles to oppose *Auer* deference. It also supports Kagan's insistence that rejection of *Auer* deference would be profoundly disruptive; the arguments for overturning *Auer* are not easily cabined to the context of agency regulatory interpretations but would extend to other deference contexts and other instances in which agencies combine legislative, executive, and adjudicatory functions.

The potential implications of *Kisor* for other administrative law doctrines was driven home by Chief Justice Roberts and Justice Kavanaugh, both of whom insisted in their concurrences that the decision in *Kisor* did not resolve the propriety of *Chevron* deference to agency statutory interpretations.[97] These statements are puzzling. Stare decisis should be at least as much of a concern for *Chevron* deference, if not more so, given *Chevron*'s greater centrality to administrative law.[98] Moreover, it is hard to see why the formalist argument that granting agencies interpretive power unconstitutionally intrudes on the judicial power would be any different between *Auer* and *Chevron*. Indeed, Justice Thomas and then-Judge Gorsuch have penned opinions castigating *Chevron* deference in exactly the same terms.[99] Given that this argument failed to obtain majority support in *Kisor*, logically it should also fail to get majority support in a case addressing *Chevron*. Further reinforcing the parallels between the two deference doctrines, the Court already has curtailed *Chevron* deference in ways similar to the limits imposed on *Auer* deference in *Kisor*, such as requiring more evidence that an interpretation is authorized and more judicial probing before concluding that ambiguity exists.[100]

Perhaps Roberts and Kavanaugh simply did not want to be read as answering the question of *Chevron*'s status in a case addressing *Auer*,

---

[97] *Kisor*, 139 S Ct at 2425 (Roberts, CJ, concurring in part); id at 2449 (Kavanaugh, J, concurring in the judgment).

[98] Indeed, in *Perez*, 135 S Ct at 1212–13 (Scalia, J, concurring in the judgment). Justice Scalia argued that stare decisis counted more strongly for retaining *Chevron* deference than *Auer* deference.

[99] See *Michigan v EPA*, 135 S Ct 2699, 1712–14 (2015) (Thomas, J, concurring); *Gutierrez-Brizuela v Lynch*, 834 F3d 1142, 1149–52 (10th Cir 2016) (Gorsuch, J, concurring).

[100] See, for example, *Mead*, 533 US at 226–27 (emphasizing limits on *Chevron*'s applicability, in particular that "Congress [have] delegated authority to the agency generally to make rules carrying the force of law, and that the agency interpretation claiming deference was promulgated in the exercise of that authority") and *Wisconsin Central Ltd. v United States*, 138 S Ct 2067, 2074 (2018) (concluding that the statutory text in question was "clear enough . . . , leaving no ambiguity for the agency to fill"). Indeed, Justice Kagan noted this similarity. See *Kisor*, 139 S Ct at 2414 (Kagan, J) (plurality) (citing *Mead*, 533 US at 229–31).

but were not signaling they would reach a different result. Alternatively, they may have wanted to preserve room to pull back further on *Chevron*'s across-the-board presumption of implied congressional delegation of authority to agencies to fill gaps and resolve ambiguities in the statutes they administer. This would fit their prior jurisprudence; in particular, Roberts has argued that questions addressing jurisdiction or matters of "deep economic and political significance" should not receive *Chevron* deference, and Kavanaugh has rejected *Chevron* deference for agency authority to issue major rules.[101] If so, they might continue to support *Chevron* deference to agency interpretations when expressly authorized by Congress or when they view statutory terms as plainly granting deference. Another possible reason for their statements is that, unlike *Auer*, *Chevron* deference grants an agency interpretive authority over Congress's handiwork and not the agency's own regulations. Although Justice Scalia viewed this feature as making *Auer* deference more suspect because it allowed agencies to self-delegate power,[102] one could argue that the opposite is true. On this view, *Chevron* is the greater threat to the constitutional order because it elevates agencies over Congress and in the process removes statutes as critical external checks on agencies' claims to power. If adopted, this argument would most strongly call *Chevron* deference into question, but for that reason it is hardest to square with both Justices' willingness to grant *Chevron* deference in the past.

B. DEPARTMENT OF COMMERCE V NEW YORK

Judicial deference to agency decision making was also at the heart of *Department of Commerce*. But that was where the parallels between these two cases ended. *Department of Commerce* lacked a Supreme Court jurisprudential lead-up akin to that in *Kisor*. Similarly lacking were calls for a fundamental reconsideration of existing doctrine; to the contrary, the different opinions in *Department of Commerce* sought to outdo each other with their adherence to governing frameworks.

---

[101] See *King v Burwell*, 135 S Ct 2480, 2489 (2015) (refusing to apply *Chevron* deference to a question of deep economic and political significance absent express indication from Congress that it wanted the agency to have such interpretive authority); *United States Telecom Association v FCC*, 855 F3d 381, 417–18 (DC Cir 2017) (Kavanaugh, J, dissenting from denial of rehearing en banc) (arguing that there must be clear congressional authorization for major agency rules).

[102] See *Decker*, 568 US at 619–21 (Scalia, J, concurring and dissenting in part).

Most striking, however, was the changed position of the different Justices, with the Justices who urged overturning *Auer* here arguing for substantial deference to agency policy choices, and those who defended *Auer* here advocating subjecting agency decision making to greater scrutiny.

At issue in *Department of Commerce* was Commerce Secretary Wilbur Ross's decision in March 2018 to add a question about citizenship to the 2020 census. Doing so went against the strong advice of the Census Bureau in the Department of Commerce. Ever since 1950, the bureau has argued against adding a citizenship question to the census form that went to most households, out of concern that the question would lower response rates and generate false claims of citizenship that would undercut the census's accuracy. Moreover, bureau officials maintained that better citizenship data were available from other administrative records, including the American Community Survey, which the bureau sends every year to a small percentage of U.S. households on a rotating basis.[103] Ross ultimately opted for an approach that would include a citizenship question on the census as well as draw on administrative records. In explaining his decision to add the question—and in testifying to Congress—Ross repeatedly emphasized that the Department of Justice (DOJ) needed census-block citizenship data to enforce the Voting Rights Act and had submitted a letter asking for the question's inclusion.[104]

Litigation immediately followed, with two of the lawsuits being consolidated in federal district court in New York City. The case was unusual from the start. It quickly became evident that the initial administrative record submitted to the court was, to put it kindly, sparse. On its own initiative, the government supplemented the record with a brief memo from Ross indicating not only that Ross had sought to include a citizenship question well before DOJ's request, but also that DOJ had only made the request at Commerce's prodding. These revelations caused the district court to order the government to complete the administrative record, which led to over 12,000 pages of new

---

[103] *Department of Commerce*, 139 S Ct at 2562; Joint Appendix Volume I, *Department of Commerce v New York*, No 18-966, *104–06 (US filed Mar 6, 2019) (Memo of John M. Abowd); Brief of Former Census Bureau Directors, *Department of Commerce v New York*, No 18-966, *2–4 (US filed Apr 1, 2019).

[104] Joint Appendix Volume III, *Department of Commerce v New York*, No 18-966, *956 (US filed Apr 1, 2019) (Ross testimony to Congress); Joint Appendix Volume I, *Department of Commerce v New York*, No 18-966, *546 (US filed Mar 6, 2019).

material being added.¹⁰⁵ In addition, the district court granted the plaintiffs' motion for extra-record discovery and depositions, including of Secretary Ross, after concluding that the new record material strongly suggested that the plaintiffs would find evidence showing that Ross acted in bad faith.¹⁰⁶ These discovery disputes were the basis for the case's first appearance at the Supreme Court in October 2018, where the Court stayed Ross's deposition but let the rest of the extra-record development go forward, over a dissent by Justices Gorsuch and Thomas.¹⁰⁷ The district court proceeded to issue a mammoth 178-page opinion just three months later, enjoining addition of the citizenship question on the grounds that Secretary Ross's decision violated the Census Act and was arbitrary and capricious, and further that the Secretary's explanation for why he had added the question was pretextual.¹⁰⁸ The Supreme Court immediately jumped back in, taking the uncommon step of granting the government's request for certiorari before the court of appeals heard the case and making the case a late addition to the 2018 Term.¹⁰⁹

Much of this speed and early Supreme Court involvement can be put down to fast-approaching deadlines for printing the census, but also reflected the case's high-profile status and clear political ramifications. The states and localities challenging the decision to add a citizenship question were blue jurisdictions with substantial noncitizen populations that stood to lose representation and funds from undercounting minorities. Those supporting the administration were red jurisdictions that would gain from an undercount elsewhere.¹¹⁰ In addition, adding the citizenship question echoed strongly with the Trump administration's harsh stance on unlawful immigration and

---

¹⁰⁵ *Department of Commerce*, 139 S Ct at 2564; Appendix to Petition for Writ of Certiorari, *Department of Commerce v New York*, No 18-966, *546a (US filed Jan 25, 2019).

¹⁰⁶ See *New York v Department of Commerce*, 333 F Supp 3d 282, 285–86 (SDNY 2018); *New York v Department of Commerce*, 2018 WL 5260467 *2 (SDNY 2018).

¹⁰⁷ *In re Department of Commerce*, 139 S Ct 16 (Oct 22, 2018).

¹⁰⁸ *New York v Department of Commerce*, 351 F Supp 3d 502, 515–16 (SDNY 2019).

¹⁰⁹ For a discussion of the Solicitor General's recent efforts to get cases to the Supreme Court extremely quickly, including in *Department of Commerce*, see Stephen I. Vladeck, *The Solicitor General and the Shadow Docket*, 133 Harv L Rev 123 (2019).

¹¹⁰ Brief Amici Curiae of the State of California, *Department of Commerce v New York*, No 18-966, *2–3 (US filed Apr 1, 2019) (arguing for the Court to uphold the district court decision); Brief Amici Curiae of Oklahoma et al, *Department of Commerce v New York*, No 18-966, *1–4 (US filed Mar 6, 2019) (urging the Court to reverse the district court decision).

with Republican efforts to draw electoral districts based on citizenship voting age population—a move that a leading Republican redistricting strategist described as "advantageous to Republicans and Non-Hispanic Whites" and argued "would clearly be a disadvantage for the Democrats."[111] Fittingly, the drama surrounding the case reached an even greater pitch once it was revealed after oral argument that this same strategist had urged Ross to add the question and ghostwritten the DOJ letter. That the strategist's involvement emerged only because his estranged daughter happened to find the documents in his files after his death was just icing on the cake.[112]

1. *Chief Justice Roberts's split opinion.* Chief Justice Roberts was again the pivotal vote in the case but here wrote the majority opinion. Like Kagan's opinion in *Kisor*, Roberts's majority opinion has a split personality. Roberts was joined by four Justices—Thomas, Alito, Gorsuch, and Kavanaugh—in concluding that Secretary Ross's decision to add the question was not arbitrary and capricious and did not violate the Census Act. And he was also joined by four Justices, but a different four—Ginsburg, Breyer, Sotomayor, and Kagan—in concluding that the decision nonetheless had to be remanded because the explanation Ross provided was pretextual.[113]

The split character of Roberts's opinion shows even more in his tone and reasoning. Most of the opinion treated Ross's decision as a perfectly reasonable and historically grounded policy choice. Roberts began with a brief description of the role and history of the census, emphasizing that "[e]very census between 1820 and 2000 (with the exception of 1840) asked at least some of the population about their citizenship or place of birth."[114] Roberts proceeded to give Secretary Ross every possible benefit of the doubt and then some. For example,

---

[111] Letter of Respondents New York Immigration Coalition et al Notifying Court of New Proceedings in the District Court, *Department of Commerce v New York*, No 18-966 (US filed May 30, 2019); The Use of Citizen Voting Age Population in Redistricting, *New York v Department of Commerce*, No 1:18-cv-02921-JMF, Exhibit D *6, 9 (SDNY filed May 30, 2019) (Hofeller Letter), https://www.commoncause.org/wp-content/uploads/2019/05/2019-05-30-Letter-Motion-dckt-587_1.pdf. See also Justin Levitt, *Citizenship and the Census*, 119 Colum L Rev 1355 (2019).

[112] Michael Wines, *Deceased G.O.P. Strategist's Hard Drives Reveal New Details on the Census Citizenship Question*, NY Times (May 30, 2019), at https://www.nytimes.com/2019/05/30/us/census-citizenship-question-hofeller.html. See also *La Union Del Pueblo Entero v Ross*, 771 F Appx 323 (4th Cir 2019) (remanding to the district court for further proceedings in light of the Hofeller Letter).

[113] *Department of Commerce*, 139 S Ct at 2555.

[114] Id at 2561.

where the district court and Justice Breyer's partial dissent criticized Ross for failing to take into account the Census Bureau's assessment that adding a citizenship question would harm the accuracy of the census, Roberts underscored uncertainties in the bureau's analysis. Roberts even went so far as to suggest that it was "inconclusive" whether adding the question would depress census response rates at all, despite the Census Bureau's own conclusions to the contrary. This framing allowed Roberts to portray Ross's decision as a paradigmatic example of the type of "value-laden decision making and the weighing of incommensurables under conditions of uncertainty" to which courts owe deference.[115] Not only was "the choice between reasonable policy alternatives in the face of uncertainly... the Secretary's to make," but also Ross's choice was "reasonable and reasonably explained, particularly in light of the long history of the citizenship question on the census."[116]

Then in the final Part V of his opinion, Roberts dramatically changed his tune. Here Roberts took the evidentiary record at face value and rejected the government's entreaties to exclude the extra-record material, concluding that ultimately the district court was justified in adding it. Far from being a reasonable decision maker in the face of uncertainty, Ross was now portrayed as having a closed mind from the get-go: "Th[e] evidence showed that the Secretary was determined to reinstate a citizenship question from the time he entered office ... [and] instructed his staff to make it happen."[117] Worse, that evidence showed that Ross's "VRA enforcement rationale—the sole stated reason [for adding the citizenship question]—seems to have been contrived,"[118] was "incongruent with ... the record,"[119] and simply "a distraction."[120] Or, put with less finesse, the record showed that Ross had lied. By definition, that meant he had acted unreasonably, for "[a]ccepting contrived reasons would defeat the purpose" of courts requiring agencies to provide reasoned explanations for their actions.[121]

---

[115] Id at 2571.
[116] Id.
[117] *Department of Commerce*, 139 S Ct at 2574.
[118] Id at 2575.
[119] Id.
[120] Id at 2576.
[121] Id.

Roberts's invalidation of Ross's decision as pretextual stands in sharp contrast to his majority opinion just a year before in *Trump v Hawaii*.[122] There, Roberts wrote for a 5–4 Court sustaining a ban on travel to the United States from a number of countries, almost all of which were majority Muslim, despite substantial evidence suggesting the ban was animated by anti-Muslim bias. This evidence included the proverbial smoking gun—numerous statements by President Trump and his advisors demonstrating such bias and arguing for a Muslim ban or identifying the travel ban as a Muslim ban—as well as a process used in issuing the initial version of the ban that deviated substantially from usual practice.[123] Yet other than recounting this history, Roberts limited his analysis to the face of the ban and the process used to produce the version of the ban that was before the Court.[124] In *Hawaii*, Roberts emphasized that the travel ban implicated national security matters over which courts owed the President particular deference, and the absence of such matters in *Department of Commerce* may help explain his greater scrutiny here. Yet as both Justices Thomas and Alito argued, the census is also a context in which the executive branch enjoys substantial discretion, but that did not preclude Roberts from invalidating on pretext grounds.

On the other hand, the split character of Roberts's opinion in *Department of Commerce* brings to mind another Roberts opinion, the one he wrote in 2012 in *NFIB v Sebelius*. There, too, Roberts alternated between his conservative and liberal colleagues, agreeing with the former that the individual mandate of the Affordable Care Act (ACA) fell outside the constitutional scope of Congress's commerce or necessary and proper powers but joining with the latter to hold that the ACA nonetheless was a constitutional tax.[125] And the same institutional legitimacy concerns that motivated Roberts in *NFIB*[126] appear to have played a role here, as signaled by Roberts's statement that the Court did not have to "exhibit a naivete from which ordinary citizens are free" in concluding that Ross's claimed rationale

---

[122] 138 S Ct 2392 (2018).

[123] Id at 2435–40 (Sotomayor, J, dissenting).

[124] Id at 2420–23.

[125] *National Federation of Independent Business v Sebelius*, 567 US 519 (2012).

[126] Joan Biskupic, *The Chief: The Life and Turbulent Times of Chief Justice John Roberts* 248 (Basic Books, 2019) (claiming that concerns for the institutional legitimacy of the Court helped persuade Roberts to switch his vote).

of wanting to support VRA enforcement was pretextual.[127] To sanction Ross's decision in the face of such evident deception and partisanship risked the Court being viewed as simply a political institution, much the way invalidating the signal Democratic political achievement in a generation might have done.[128] Reports that Roberts changed his stance on pretext after oral argument, while the drama surrounding the case was growing outside the Court, adds support to the conclusion that institutional legitimacy concerns animated his position.[129]

Yet this legitimacy account does not really explain the split character of Roberts's opinion. Why risk having the Court appear political by defending the Trump administration's decision to add a citizenship question, only to conclude that this decision was pretextual and therefore invalid? If Roberts's goal was to give each side something to mute criticism of the Court, he was no more successful here than in *NFIB*; in both cases his opinions sparked strong partial dissents and critical public response.[130] An alternative explanation for Roberts's split opinion is that he believed the pretextual problem with Ross's decision was curable. This explanation fits with Roberts's decision to remand and his emphasis that the Court was "not hold[ing] that the agency decision here was substantively invalid."[131] But it is harder to square with Roberts's conclusion that the only reason Ross had offered for adding the question—enhanced VRA enforcement—was not an actual reason for his decision. That conclusion, pivotal to Roberts's determination that Ross's explanation was pretextual, made it very hard to see how the pretext problem could be cured without undertaking an entirely new decision-making process.[132] But the

---

[127] *Department of Commerce*, 139 S Ct at 2575 (quoting *United States v Stanchich*, 550 F2d 1294, 1300 (2d Cir 1977) (Friendly, J)).

[128] Biskupic, *The Chief* at 233 (cited in note 126) (noting that Roberts disliked the initial partisan lineup to strike down the ACA).

[129] See Joan Biskupic, *How John Roberts Killed the Census Citizenship Question*, CNN (Sept 12, 2019), at https://www.cnn.com/2019/09/12/politics/john-roberts-census-citizenship-supreme-court/index.html.

[130] Both opinions prompted conservative calls for his impeachment. See Tim Mak, *Blog Chatter: Impeach Roberts*, Politico (June 28, 2012), at https://www.politico.com/story/2012/06/bloggers-say-impeach-roberts-077947 (noting calls for Chief Justice Roberts's impeachment post-*NFIB*); Josh Gerstein, *Conservatives Blast Roberts as Turncoat*, Politico (June 27, 2019), at https://www.politico.com/story/2019/06/27/conservatives-blast-roberts-1386124 (highlighting identical demands post–*Department of Commerce*).

[131] *Department of Commerce*, 139 S Ct at 2576.

[132] Id at 2575–76; *SEC v Chenery*, 332 US 194, 196 (1947) ("[A] simple but fundamental rule of administrative law . . . is . . . that a reviewing court, in dealing with a determination or

Solicitor General had long maintained that the census form had to be finalized by the end of June to meet the deadlines for conducting the census in 2020, which would not allow leeway for anything more than a pro forma stamp on remand.[133] Not only would such a pro forma approach fail to cure the pretext the Court had identified, but upholding such a pro forma process after remand would make the Court look worse than if it had just upheld the decision initially. As a result, the pretext ruling meant the end of the Trump administration's effort to add a citizenship question to the 2020 census, as DOJ attorneys soon concluded and ultimately so did the Attorney General and the President.

2. *The administrative record, pretext, and arbitrary and capriciousness review.* Reflecting the split nature of Roberts's opinion, there were strong partial dissents from the other Justices on each side, as well as from Justice Alito, who argued that judicial review was inappropriate because the content of the census was "committed to agency discretion by law."[134] Put together, the *Department of Commerce* opinions represent an administrative law smorgasbord, addressing a range of difficult questions concerning pretext in administrative contexts, the nature of the administrative record, the scope of arbitrary and capriciousness review, and the proper balance of politics and expertise in administrative contexts. Yet, strikingly, none of the opinions acknowledged the difficulty of the issues addressed and instead treated the answers they gave as dictated by existing precedent and indisputable.

Justice Thomas, joined by Justices Gorsuch and Kavanaugh, condemned the Court's invalidation of Ross's decision on pretext grounds as "unprecedented" and a dangerous "departure from our deferential review of discretionary agency decisions."[135] He insisted that pretext was simply not a relevant inquiry under arbitrary and capriciousness review and that the record did not establish pretext in any event. Thomas also chastised the Court for "proceeding beyond the administrative record," warning that the effect of doing so was to provide a

---

judgment which an administrative agency alone is authorized to make, must judge the propriety of such action solely by the grounds invoked by the agency.").

[133] See Petition for Writ of Certiorari, *Department of Commerce v New York*, No 18-966, *13–14 (US filed Jan 25, 2019).

[134] 5 USC § 701(a)(2); *Department of Commerce*, 139 S Ct at 2598 (Alito, J, concurring in part and dissenting in part).

[135] Id at 2576 (Thomas, J, concurring in part and dissenting in part).

new "avenue of attack" for opponents of executive branch actions, which would "allow partisans to use the courts to harangue executive officers through depositions, discovery, delay, and distraction."[136]

Thomas's concerns about courts going outside the record resonate in existing case law. A venerable line of administrative law jurisprudence emphasizes that "the focal point of judicial review should be the administrative record already in existence, not some new record made initially in the reviewing court."[137] After initially allowing court supplementation in instances when more formal findings were lacking, the Court's past case law had quickly moved to the view that when a reviewing court considers the agency record to be inadequate in some way, "the proper course, except in rare circumstances, is to remand to the agency for additional investigation of explanation."[138] Thomas's sudden solicitude for effective governance is surprising, given the extent to which he has dismissed similar functionality concerns in his recent administrative law opinions.[139] Still, his point on this score is well taken. In an era in which litigation is the prime means by which partisans on both sides seek to derail executive branch actions they oppose, allowing extra-record supplementation risks further hampering of effective government administration.

Yet the issue of the district court's extra-record supplementation was largely a sideshow here. Neither the discovery nor the depositions that the district court ordered in *Department of Commerce* ended up mattering all that much.[140] Instead, what was pivotal was the material the government supplied to complete the administrative record per a stipulation with the plaintiffs. The district court found that this material alone demonstrated that Ross's decision was arbitrary and capricious and pretextual.[141] Although Roberts invoked the wider universe of both completed-record and extra-record material, he too

---

[136] Id at 2580, 2583 (Thomas, J, concurring in part and dissenting in part).

[137] *Camp v Pitts*, 411 US 138, 142 (1973); accord, *Florida Power & Light v Lorion*, 470 US 729, 743–44 (1985); *Citizens to Protect Overton Park v Volpe*, 401 US 402, 421 (1971).

[138] Compare *Florida Power & Light*, 470 US at 744, with *Overton Park*, 401 US at 421.

[139] *Department of Transportation*, 135 S Ct at 1247–48 (Thomas, J, concurring in the judgment) (arguing that the President cannot exercise explicit "policy discretion," which would represent an impermissible delegation of legislative power).

[140] This extra-record evidence was most discussed by Justice Breyer, who quoted in passing from the deposition of the DOJ official who wrote the DOJ letter. *Department of Commerce*, 139 S Ct at 2595 (Breyer, J, concurring in part and dissenting in part).

[141] *New York*, 351 F Supp 3d at 660–61.

emphasized that the completed-record material on its own created the "strong showing of bad faith or improper behavior" sufficient to justify extra-record supplementation under the Court's restrictive precedents.[142]

Notably, neither Roberts's majority opinion nor Thomas's partial dissent address the question of what should be included in the administrative record in the first place. The proper answer to this question is not clear in informal proceedings such as the decision making here, where agencies are not limited to considering materials in a formal record.[143] The APA states that judicial review should be undertaken based on the "whole record" without defining what counts as the record: Is it the record provided to the court, the record that the agency considered or relied upon in making its decision, or the record of all the material before the agency? Lower courts take different approaches to this question.[144] Moreover, practical and functional concerns point in different directions. Limiting judicial review to the record provided to a court or that the agency relied on risks giving agencies incentives to include and consider only materials supporting their decisions, but including all the material before the agency or all the material the agency considered risks producing a massive record that is highly burdensome to generate, overwhelms courts, and obscures the main bases of the agency's decision making.[145] Roberts avoided this issue by relying on the fact that the government had not challenged the district court's conclusion that the administrative record was incomplete and stipulated to the addition of substantial new

---

[142] *Department of Commerce*, 139 S Ct at 2574–76.

[143] The requirement of on-the-record decision making means that identifying the record is not an issue with respect to formal proceedings. See 5 USC § 556(e); Jeffrey S. Lubbers, *A Guide to Federal Agency Rulemaking* 287–302 (ABA, 5th ed 2012).

[144] See Travis O. Brandon, *Reforming the Extra-Record Evidence Rule in Arbitrary and Capricious Review of Informal Agency Actions: A New Procedural Approach*, 21 Lewis & Clark L Rev 981, 997–98, 1000–01, 1008–09 (2017); Aram A. Gavoor and Steven A. Platt, *Administrative Records and the Courts*, 67 Kansas L Rev 1, 62–69 (2018). In 2013, the Administrative Conference of the United States issued a report and recommendations on best practices for the compilation, preservation, and certification of administrative records and also guidance on when courts can seek supplementation. See Recommendation 2013-14—Administrative Record in Informal Rulemaking, 78 Fed Reg 41352, 41358 (July 10, 2013), at https://www.acus.gov/research-projects/administrative-record-informal-rulemaking.

[145] See Brandon, 21 Lewis & Clark L Rev at 1012–17 (cited in note 144) (arguing in favor of supplementing the record provided "the plaintiff provides reasonable proof that the agency considered the evidence" as "practical and workable"); Gavoor and Platt, 67 Kansas L Rev at 69–75 (cited in note 144) (listing negative consequences to allowing supplementation with other evidence considered by the agency).

material.¹⁴⁶ Yet the result in *Department of Commerce* may make the government less willing to do so in the future.

Justice Thomas's insistence that pretext inquiries are strangers to administrative law is also only partially correct. It's true that arbitrary and capriciousness review does not usually speak in terms of pretext and the Supreme Court had not previously held agency action arbitrary and capricious on pretext grounds.¹⁴⁷ But Thomas downplays the way that arbitrary and capriciousness review serves to identify pretextual decision making without calling it such. Take, for instance, *Motor Vehicle Association v State Farm Mutual Automobile Insurance*, the case that set out the modern arbitrary and capriciousness standard. There, the National Highway Traffic and Safety Administration had justified rescinding its automotive passive restraint rule entirely on the grounds that the rule would not achieve predicted safety benefits. In overturning that rescission, the Court emphasized obvious regulatory alternatives that should have been explored if the agency really were trying to advance safety, as the governing statute required.¹⁴⁸ The Court did not put its holding in terms of pretext, instead concluding that the agency was not acting reasonably to achieve its safety goals. However, an implicit corollary of concluding that an agency's policy undercuts its stated goals is that those goals probably weren't really motivating the agency in the first place. Chief Justice Rehnquist's partial dissent in *State Farm* highlighted this point, accusing the majority of going too far in overturning the agency out of a concern that the agency's decision was actually driven by political considerations.¹⁴⁹ Moreover, approaching pretext as part of a general

---

¹⁴⁶ *Department of Commerce*, 139 S Ct at 2574.

¹⁴⁷ Lower courts had, albeit rarely. See, for example, *Texas v United States*, 809 F3d 134, 171–76 (5th Cir 2015) (upholding the district court's determination that justification given for Department of Homeland Security's Deferred Action for Parents of Americans and Lawful Permanent Residents was "pretext"); *James Madison Ltd. v Ludwig*, 82 F3d 1085, 1096 (DC Cir 1996) (bad faith is "material to determining whether the Government acted arbitrarily"); *Tummino v Hamburg*, 936 F Supp 2d 162, 188, 194–97 (EDNY 2013) (concluding FDA denial of citizen petition was arbitrary and capricious because agency acted in bad faith and provided pretextual explanation).

¹⁴⁸ *Motor Vehicle Association v State Farm Mutual Mobile Insurance*, 463 US 29, 46–47 (1983) (stating that the agency could not abandon the mandatory passive-restraint requirement without first considering an airbag-only requirement).

¹⁴⁹ Id at 59 (Rehnquist, CJ, concurring in part and dissenting in part) ("The agency's changed view of the standard seems to be related to the election of a new President of a different political party."). Jennifer Nou notes that pretext, in the form of "rationales masking the genuine motivations for decisions," especially political motivations, are common in administrative

arbitrary and capriciousness review has the advantage of forestalling the need for an extra-record investigation into a decision maker's subjective motivations, thereby addressing Thomas's concerns about such inquiries. It similarly avoids the need for courts to specify the extent to which political considerations can legitimately affect agency action, a notoriously difficult line to draw and one courts have long evaded.[150]

Of course, approaching pretext as part of general arbitrary and capriciousness review will fail to police against pretextual rationales in contexts where the agency's action is otherwise well supported.[151] Yet that seems a worthwhile trade-off; at least absent allegations that the undisclosed rationale is invidious, the burdens of extra-record investigation into pretext are harder to defend when the agency action is independently supportable. The real risk in this context is that this independent support will turn out to be manufactured or insubstantial. But that risk can be mitigated by subjecting stated agency rationales to more skeptical and probing scrutiny in the face of evidence of pretextual decision making.

Hence, this surrogate role of arbitrary and capriciousness review highlights again the oddity of Chief Justice Roberts's split opinion, combining highly deferential review of the substantive basis for adding the citizenship question with invalidation of the decision on pretextual grounds. Justice Breyer's partial dissent provided the skeptical scrutiny that Roberts's opinion lacked, closely examining evidence in the record about the impact of the question on different groups. He concluded that the administrative record established that adding the question would only impose costs and yield no benefits; it would "diminish the accuracy of the enumeration of population" while at the same time "produce citizenship data that is *less* accurate, not more."[152]

---

contexts. See Jennifer Nou, *Census Symposium: A Place for Pretext in Administrative Law?*, SCOTUSBlog (June 28, 2019), at https://www.scotusblog.com/2019/06/census-symposium-a-place-for-pretext-in-administrative-law/.

[150] Nou, *A Place for Pretext* (cited in note 149); *Sierra Club v Costle*, 697 F2d 298, 407 (DC Cir 1981) (refusing to require disclosure of White House ex parte communications relating to informal rulemaking, noting that to survive judicial review the rule "must have the requisite factual support in the rulemaking record").

[151] See *Sierra Club*, 697 F2d at 408 (acknowledging and accepting the risk that "undisclosed Presidential prodding may direct an outcome that is factually based on the record, but different from the outcome that would have obtained in the absence of Presidential involvement").

[152] *Department of Commerce*, 139 S Ct at 2584 (Breyer, J, concurring in part and dissenting in part).

And he rejected the Secretary's use of uncertainty as a basis for discounting the Census Bureau's estimates of harmful effects, arguing that uncertainty is endemic in regulatory contexts and does not excuse an agency from not at least explaining why it decided to "tak[e] action without 'engaging in a search for further evidence.'"[153]

Despite their very different applications of arbitrary and capriciousness review, both Roberts and Breyer, as well as Thomas and Alito, invoked *State Farm* as guiding their analyses. Whether *State Farm* and the Court's arbitrary and capriciousness precedents require searching scrutiny is a matter of scholarly dispute,[154] and there are many decisions in which courts stress uncertainty and take a more forgiving stance, as the Supreme Court did here.[155] The broader point is that arbitrary and capriciousness scrutiny is malleable, with judges able to dial their scrutiny up and down based on their assessments of contextual factors in a particular case. For his part, Breyer underscored this malleability, insisting that "[c]ourts do not apply these principles of administrative law mechanically. Rather, they take into account . . . the nature and importance of the particular decision, the relevance and importance of missing information, and the inadequacies of a particular explanation in light of their importance."[156]

3. *Politics, deference, and discretion.* What then led some Justices in *Department of Commerce* to dial down their scrutiny of the substantive reasonableness of Ross's decision making and others to dial it up? Several factors appeared to be in play, most centrally politics and discretion.

Politics surfaced most prosaically in Justice Thomas's opinion, with Thomas repeatedly accusing the district court of invalidating the citizenship question out of bias against the Trump administration. Thomas insisted that only bias could explain the district court's

---

[153] Id at 2590 (quoting *State Farm*, 463 US at 52).

[154] Jacob Gersen and Adrian Vermeule, *Thin Rationality Review*, 114 Mich L Rev 1355, 1358–59 (2016) (arguing that the Supreme Court overwhelmingly applies a much less searching scrutiny under arbitrary and capriciousness review than is generally acknowledged).

[155] See Adrian Vermeule, *Law's Abnegation* 158 (Harvard, 2016) (identifying *FCC v Fox*, 566 US 502 (2009) and *Baltimore Gas & Electric Co. v Natural Resource Defense Council, Inc.*, 462 US 87 (1983) as instances when the Court applied lenient review); see generally Gersen and Vermeule, 114 Mich L Rev at 1355 (cited in note 154) (arguing that the claim that courts apply hard-look review is a myth).

[156] *Department of Commerce*, 139 S Ct at 2585 (Breyer, J, concurring in part and dissenting in part) (concluding that the importance of this topic to the functioning of a democratic society warranted searching review).

detailed record review and findings of pretext: "I do not deny that a judge predisposed to distrust the Secretary or the administration could arrange those facts [from the record] on a corkboard and—with a jar of pins and a spool of string—create an eye-catching conspiracy web."[157] That three Supreme Court Justices signed onto such a pointed attack on the impartiality of a lower court judge is extraordinary, all the more so given that five of their colleagues agreed with the district court's analysis, at least in part. It is also deeply ironic, for by launching this attack these Justices were themselves embedding a partisan message in the pages of the U.S. Reports. After all, the prime expositor of the claim that lower court judges who rule against the Trump administration's actions are doing so out of bias is President Trump himself.[158]

But politics also appeared in a more principled form, in differing views of the relationship between political accountability and deference to agency policy-making. For Roberts, such deference rests fundamentally on principles of political accountability. Provided the policy choices of an agency's political leaders are at least plausible, they should be respected. Contrary views of career bureaucrats should get little weight, if not be viewed with outright suspicion. As he put it, "the Census Act authorizes the Secretary, not the [Census] Bureau, to make policy choices within the range of reasonable options."[159] Indeed, a desire to reaffirm the importance of judicial deference to the policy choices of agencies' political leadership seems the best explanation of Roberts's decision that adding the citizenship question per se was not arbitrary and capricious, even as he invalidated Ross's decision as pretextual. Roberts also made a point of underscoring the legitimacy of political influence in his discussion of pretext, insisting that "a court may not set aside an agency's policymaking decision solely because it might have been influenced by political considerations or prompted by an Administration's priorities."[160] One benefit

---

[157] Id at 2582 (Thomas, J, concurring in part and dissenting in part); see also id at 2576 (Thomas, J, concurring in part and dissenting in part) ("[T]he decision of the district court ... was transparently based on the application of an administration-specific standard. . . . The law requires a more impartial approach.").

[158] Adam Liptak, *Trump Takes Aim at Appeals Court, Calling It a "Disgrace,"* NY Times (Nov 20, 2018), at https://www.nytimes.com/2018/11/20/us/politics/trump-appeals-court-ninth-circuit.html?module=inline.

[159] *Department of Commerce*, 139 S Ct at 2571 (claiming that Breyer "subordinat[ed] the Secretary's policymaking discretion to the Bureau's technocratic expertise").

[160] Id at 2573.

of Roberts's split vote is that it allowed him to reinforce this structural principle of political control of policy while still protecting the Court from sanctioning blatant manipulations and falsehoods.

Justice Breyer, by contrast, tied deference for discretionary agency decisions closely to expertise and carefully reasoned explanation. He treated the fact that Ross deviated from the recommendations of the agency's in-house experts, the Census Bureau, as grounds for a probing judicial reception.[161] Breyer did not deny that an agency head's "policy choice between two reasonable but uncertain options" would deserve deference.[162] But he argued that the Census Bureau's memos showed that the option of adding the question was not reasonable and the extent of uncertainty was exaggerated.[163] Indeed, far from viewing political accountability as compelling deference here, Breyer argued that letting Ross's decision stand risked "undermining public confidence in the integrity of our democratic system itself," given the importance of an accurate census for political representation.[164] Interestingly, Justice Breyer and the liberal Justices concurring with him appeared far more amenable to connecting politics and deference in *Kisor*. There, they joined Kagan's opinion tying deference to authoritative interpretations by agency heads and identifying political accountability as a basis for deference. This divergence is potentially explainable on the grounds that *Kisor* did not involve a conflict between political accountability and expertise, but unfortunately the contrast was never addressed by Breyer—leaving the impression that opposition to adding the citizenship question may have animated his more stringent scrutiny here.

Similarly, the conservative Justices' emphasis on political accountability as grounds for deference seems in tension with Justice Gorsuch's identification of the political nature of agency decision making as counting strongly against deference in *Kisor*. Justice Thomas explained the difference between the two cases as lying in the nature of the agency decision at issue: a discretionary policy choice versus an interpretation of law.[165] Whereas deference to agency legal

---

[161] Id at 2589–92 (Breyer, J, concurring in part and dissenting in part).

[162] Id at 2593 (Breyer, J, concurring in part and dissenting in part).

[163] *Department of Commerce*, 139 S Ct at 2592–93 (Breyer, J, concurring in part and dissenting in part).

[164] Id at 2585 (Breyer, J, concurring in part and dissenting in part).

[165] Id at 2578 n 3 (Thomas, J, concurring in part and dissenting in part).

interpretations violated Article III, deference to agency discretionary decisions reflected "a 'presumption of regularity'" for the Executive out of "respect for a coordinate branch of government whose officers not only take an oath to support the Constitution, as we do, . . . but also are charged with faithfully executing our laws."[166] Justice Alito went even further, arguing that the broad discretion Congress gave the Secretary of Commerce over the content of the census meant that courts had no jurisdiction to review the Secretary's decision making at all.[167]

Although this emphasis on discretion helped align the conservative Justices' stances in *Department of Commerce* and *Kisor*, it highlighted a conflict between *Department of Commerce* and *Gundy*. In *Gundy*, Justice Gorsuch's dissent—joined by Chief Justice Roberts and Justice Thomas—argued strongly that broad congressional delegations of authority to the executive branch were unconstitutional: Congress can delegate to the executive power to "fill up the details" once "Congress had announced the controlling general policy"; Congress can also delegate fact-finding responsibilities and assign "wide discretion" over matters in which the executive independently enjoys broad authority, such as foreign affairs.[168] But what Congress cannot do is delegate to the executive power to "make the policy judgments" incorporated in "generally applicable rules of conduct governing future actions by private persons."[169] Plainly, the responsibilities delegated to the Secretary under the Census Act are far more policy laden than just fact-finding, and decades of dispute over including a question on citizenship make clear that adding it cannot be seen as just filling up the details of the census either. Responsibility for the census is constitutionally assigned to Congress and not an area of inherent executive authority. Moreover, private persons are required to fill out the census, and the fact that not responding to the census is considered a misdemeanor[170] creates another parallel to *Gundy*, though the criminal consequences of violating the statute at issue there were far

---

[166] Id at 2579–80 (Thomas, J, concurring in part and dissenting in part) (internal quotations omitted). See also *Michigan*, 135 S Ct at 2712 (Thomas, J, concurring) (arguing that deference on legal questions violates Article III).

[167] Id at 2597 (Alito, J, concurring in part and dissenting in part).

[168] *Gundy*, 139 S Ct at 2136–37 (Gorsuch, J, dissenting).

[169] Id at 2133, 2141 (Gorsuch, J, dissenting).

[170] 13 USC § 221.

more severe. In short, the breadth of discretion given to the Secretary that the conservative Justices relied on to justify deference in *Department of Commerce* appears to be precisely the kind of delegation that several of them would have held unconstitutional in *Gundy*.[171] Yet they never acknowledged, let alone explained, this inconsistency.

II. THE MANY ISMS OF ROBERTS COURT ADMINISTRATIVE LAW

The Roberts Court is clearly conflicted when it comes to administrative law. *Kisor* and *Department of Commerce* showcase a Court divided on administrative law substance and methodology, with the Justices diverging notably even when they ostensibly agree on the governing legal framework. Moreover, these divides frequently map the growing ideological and partisan divides on the Court: The 2018 Term found Justice Kagan often leading the liberal Democratic-appointed Justices in defending established administrative law, while Justice Gorsuch was often at the forefront of the conservative Republican-appointed Justices in attacking existing doctrine and Chief Justice Roberts stood squarely in the middle.[172] Given that administrative law cases frequently carry high political stakes, such a stark ideological and partisan divide should be particularly troubling for those worried about the Court being seen as a politicized actor.[173] The Justices' flipped stances on deference between these two cases reinforce that politicized appearance.

Drill further down, and several analytic tensions become apparent. These are familiar analytic divides from public law more broadly, but their appearance in the administrative law context is more recent. These tensions—between formalism and anti-formalism, originalism and more general historicism, textualism and common law development—provide the intellectual underpinnings for today's battles over administrative law. Yet it is hard to see these divisions as driving

---

[171] Justice Alito did not join Gorsuch's opinion in *Gundy*, and Justice Kavanaugh did not participate in the case.

[172] On the growing ideological and partisan divide, see generally Neal Devins and Lawrence Baum, *Split Definitive: How Party Polarization Turned the Supreme Court into a Partisan Court*, 2016 Supreme Court Review 301 (2016).

[173] See Claire Brockway and Bradley Jones, *Partisan Gap Widens in Views of the Supreme Court*, Pew Research Center (Aug 7, 2019) ("[T]hree-quarters of Republicans and Republican-leaning independents have a favorable opinion of the Supreme Court, compared with only about half (49%) of Democrats and Democratic leaners.").

Roberts Court administrative law. In particular, these analytic tensions do not consistently map onto the Justices' line-ups in administrative law cases or the ideological divisions on the Court.

A. FORMALISM AND NONFORMALISM

The first clearly evident conceptual divide centers on formalism. One group of Justices is deeply formalist in approach across a range of administrative law issues, while another is resolutely nonformalist. Nonformalism on the Roberts Court is hard to define specifically; it encompasses a range of approaches from legal realism, to pragmatism, functionalism, and minimalism. The 2018 Term decisions suggest that while formalism has a greater presence on the Court now than for many decades, it has yet to secure a committed majority.

1. *Legal realism versus legal formalism.* Underlying current disputes over deference to administrative determinations lies a fundamental disagreement on the nature of legal interpretation and the relationship of law and policy.[174] This is clearest in *Kisor*. There, Justice Gorsuch portrayed law as fixed, determinate, and categorically distinct from policy.[175] This categorical distinction between law and policy, and correspondingly between legal interpretation and policy choice, was essential for his argument that deference to agency regulatory interpretations violates Article III. That argument hinged on the *Marbury* claim that "[i]t is emphatically the province and duty of the judicial department to say what the law is,"[176] along with an insistence that courts must exercise independent judgment in order to adequately perform this law-declaring function.[177] But if regulatory interpretation constitutes policy choice to a significant degree, such interpretation appears less the type of law-declaring activity that on

---

[174] See Jeffrey A. Pojanowski, *Neoclassical Administrative Law*, 133 Harv L Rev 852, 861–84 (2020).

[175] See text accompanying note 73.

[176] *Marbury v Madison*, 5 US (1 Cranch) 137, 177 (1803).

[177] *Kisor*, 139 S Ct at 2437–38 (Kagan, J) (plurality). Whether declaring the law necessarily entails exercising independent judgment is much disputed. Justice Kagan argued in *Kisor* that judges also can declare the meaning of law by determining that the law assigns primary interpretive responsibility to another institution of government. But the Court has come to read *Marbury* as standing for a requirement of independent judgment and judicial supremacy in constitutional interpretation. See *Cooper v Aaron*, 358 US 1, 18 (1958); Henry P. Monaghan, *Marbury and the Administrative State*, 83 Colum L Rev 1, 9–10 (1983).

Gorsuch's account is constitutionally assigned to the courts' independent purview and into which the political branches may not intrude.[178]

Justice Kagan's statement in *Kisor* that "sometimes . . . law runs out," leaving "policy-laden choice,"[179] might at first suggest a similar view of law and policy as distinct entities. But her argument was actually the opposite. Her insistence that regulatory ambiguity is inevitable, and that law is incomplete and cannot resolve all legal disputes, painted law and legal interpretation as intrinsically linked to policy choice. And she moved from arguing that legal interpretation in the context of regulatory ambiguity involves policy choice to the claim that in many instances Congress would likely want that policy choice to rest in the hands of an expert, experienced agency. From there, *Auer* deference followed.

The classical image of law as fixed, determinate, and categorically distinct from policy is highly formalist, whereas the view of law as indeterminate and inevitably entailing policy choice typifies legal realism.[180] The terms of this debate are thus familiar, but its surfacing today is more surprising. The legal realist view of law has dominated administrative law ever since the cementing of the administrative state in the 1940s.[181] Adrian Vermeule has described the ensuing years as a time of law's ever-growing abnegation, with law pushed to the margins as more and more decisions appeared in a policy guise better fit for agencies than courts.[182] Even when formalism made a comeback in related public law fields, as occurred with the advent of textualism in statutory interpretation in the 1980s,[183] ordinary administrative law retained its realist orientation. After all, it was in 1984 that

---

[178] Not surprisingly, therefore, Justice Thomas has articulated a similarly firm divide between law and policy in his opinions arguing that deference to agency statutory and regulatory interpretations is unconstitutional. See *Michigan v EPA*, 135 S Ct 2699, 2712 (2015) (Thomas, J, concurring).

[179] *Kisor*, 139 S Ct at 2415 (Kagan, J) (plurality).

[180] See Frederick Schauer, *Formalism*, 97 Yale L J 509, 510–15 (1988); see also Frederick Schauer, *Legal Realism Untamed*, 91 Tex L Rev 749, 754–56 (2013); see also Brian Z. Tamanaha, *Understanding Legal Realism*, 87 Tex L Rev 731, 732 (2009).

[181] See Cass R. Sunstein, Essay, *Beyond Marbury: The Executive's Power to Say What the Law Is*, 115 Yale L J 2580, 2593–95, 2598 (2006); see also Richard Pildes, *Institutional Formalism and Realism in Constitutional and Public Law*, 2013 Supreme Court Review 1, 21–30 (describing movement between institutional realism and institutional formalism in administrative law); Pojanowski, 133 Harv L Rev at 857 (cited in note 174) (noting "the working, moderate legal realism that characterizes much mainstream administrative law").

[182] Vermeule, *Law's Abnegation* at 10 (cited in note 155).

[183] William N. Eskridge, Jr., *The New Texualism*, 37 UCLA L Rev 621, 646–47 (1989).

the *Chevron* Court justified deference to reasonable agency interpretations of ambiguous statutory provisions, arguing that in those contexts interpretation entails a policy choice implicitly delegated to the agency.[184]

In its current incarnation in Roberts Court administrative law, legal realism surfaces in a domesticated legal process guise.[185] Law is not portrayed as entirely or necessarily indeterminate; even realist-inclined Justices often conclude that agency statutory interpretations fail *Chevron* and are not deserving of deference.[186] Moreover, Justice Kagan's arguments for deference in *Kisor* echo legal process's focus on a rational Congress and the institutional capacities of courts and agencies. Critically, moreover, Kagan ties deference not to abstract institutional features, but instead to judicial determinations of whether particular decisions reflect agencies' comparative institutional advantages.[187] Richard Pildes has used the term "institutional realism" to capture this sensitivity to "how these institutions actually function in, and over, time."[188] Justice Breyer's opinion in *Department of Commerce* is to the same effect: Deference turns on whether a specific agency decision shows expertise and informed, thorough consideration; it does not follow automatically from the fact that the decision represents a policy question or was made by a politically accountable actor.[189]

By contrast, legal formalism in Roberts Court administrative law takes a categorical approach to policy questions as well as legal questions. Two distinct formalist approaches to policy are evident in this Term's decisions. On the one hand, there is Justice Gorsuch's separation-of-powers formalism in *Gundy*, which classifies broad policy determinations as categorically legislative and constitutionally excluded from agencies' ambit. On the other, there is Justice Thomas's

---

[184] *Chevron v National Resources Defense Council*, 467 US 837, 843–45, 865–86 (1984).

[185] See William N. Eskridge, Jr. and Philip P. Frickey, *The Making of the Legal Process*, 107 Harv L Rev 2031, 2042–45 (1994) (arguing that legal process was a synthesis of legal realism and other pre–World War II intellectual traditions, and describing legal process's core intellectual commitments as "the reasoned elaboration of purposive law," "law as an institutional system," and "the centrality of process") (capitalization omitted).

[186] See, for example, *Sturgeon v Frost*, 139 S Ct 1066, 1080 n 3 (2019) (Kagan, J) ("Because we see ... no ambiguity as to Section 103(c)'s meaning, we cannot give deference to the Park Service's contrary construction" under *Chevron*).

[187] *Kisor*, 139 S Ct at 2416 (Kagan, J) (plurality).

[188] Pildes, 2013 Supreme Court Review at 2 (cited in note 181).

[189] *Department of Commerce*, 139 S Ct at 2595 (Breyer, J, concurring in part and dissenting in part).

effort in *Department of Commerce* to preserve an arena for administrative policy judgments largely immune from judicial review, at the same time as he would banish policy from the world of law. Justice Kavanaugh signaled a similar effort in *Kisor* when he urged courts to "engage in appropriately rigorous scrutiny of an agency's interpretation of a regulation, and ... simultaneously be appropriately deferential to an agency's reasonable policy choices within the discretion allowed by a regulation."[190] Jeffrey Pojanowski has offered a sustained analytic defense of such a conjoined approach, which he terms neoclassical administrative law. The aim is precisely "to sharpen the line between law and policy in administrative law, with the consequence of increasing judicial responsibility on questions of law while decreasing it on matters [of] policymaking discretion."[191]

At first glance, a neoclassical approach might seem to offer a happy compromise of formalism and realism, respecting constitutional lines and also comparative institutional strengths. But combining legal formalism and policy deference in this fashion is unlikely to succeed. Any sharp demarcation between questions of law and questions of policy is implausible—as a practical as well as a conceptual matter. In an increasingly statutory and regulatory world such as ours, policy choices rarely surface in law-free zones. The choices judges will make in construing law will inevitably significantly curtail the space left for policy. Although Kavanaugh argued that "open-ended terms like 'reasonable,' 'appropriate,' 'feasible' or 'practicable' ... afford agencies broad policy discretion,"[192] courts accustomed to definitively resolving interpretive ambiguity on their own may find these terms to have definite legal content as well.[193] Moreover, the arguments for deference to agencies on fact and policy matters—such as agencies'

---

[190] *Kisor*, 139 S Ct at 2449 (Kavanaugh, J, concurring in the judgment). See also Brett M. Kavanaugh, *Fixing Statutory Interpretation*, 129 Harv L Rev 2118, 2153–54 (2016) ("This very important principle sometimes gets lost: a judge can engage in appropriately rigorous scrutiny of an agency's statutory interpretation and simultaneously be very deferential to an agency's policy choices within the discretion granted to it by the statute.").

[191] Pojanowski, 133 Harv L Rev at 884 (cited in note 174).

[192] *Kisor*, 139 S Ct at 2448 (Kavanaugh, J, concurring in the judgment).

[193] See, for example, *Michigan*, 135 S Ct at 2707–08 (reading "appropriate" in provision of the Clean Air Act as requiring EPA to consider costs in making initial decision to regulate); *MetLife v Financial Stability Oversight Council*, 177 F Supp 3d 219, 239–41 (DDC 2016) (statutory provision requiring agency to consider "any other risk-related factor" it deems "appropriate" required agency to consider costs to company of being subject to regulation).

greater political accountability, expertise, or congressional authorization—also push toward deference in law application, which easily spills over into law interpretation.[194] As Vermeule has put it, "[l]ogically, there [is] no necessary contradiction" between courts according deference to agencies on ordinary fact questions and exercising independent judgment on questions of law, but "the deep premises and attitude of each [a]re inconsistent with the deep premises and attitude of the other."[195] In like vein, Kristin Hickman and Nicholas Bednar contend that recognition of the institutional benefits of agency policymaking make something akin to *Chevron* deference inevitable.[196] Even on a more theoretical plane, legal formalism and broad policy deference to agencies do not easily combine. Legal formalism goes hand in hand with a broader separation-of-powers formalism that, as noted, views agency policy determinations as executive branch usurpation of the legislative power.

2. *Formalism, functionalism, and remedial minimalism in separation-of-powers analysis.* Although legal determinacy formalism was largely absent on the Court until recently, formalism has had a steady presence in separation-of-powers analysis. separation-of-powers formalism evinces the same commitment to categorical lines, with the relevant lines here being constitutional distinctions among legislative, executive, and judicial power, each of which is viewed as formally vested in one branch of government with intermixing limited to those instances expressly sanctioned in the Constitution. By contrast, a more functionalist analysis views powers as overlapping, emphasizes the overall balance among the branches, and focuses on the benefits of a particular governmental structure and that structure's impact on a branch's ability to perform its core functions.[197] As many commentators have argued, formalism and functionalism should not be viewed as opposed approaches in the separation-of-powers context; most decisions have elements of both orientations, and both approaches share

---

[194] Cass Sunstein argues that pre-*Chevron* decisions granting deference to agency statutory interpretations represented such law application. Cass R. Sunstein, *Chevron as Law*, 107 Georgetown L J 1613, 1649 (2019); see, for example, *NLRB v Hearst Publications, Inc.*, 322 US 111, 130 (1944); *Gray v Powell*, 314 US 402, 412 (1941).

[195] Vermeule, *Law's Abnegation* at 28 (cited in note 155).

[196] Nicholas R. Bednar and Kristin Hickman, *Chevron's Inevitability*, 85 Geo Wash L Rev 1392, 1397–98 (2017).

[197] M. Elizabeth Magill, *Beyond Powers and Branches in Separation of Powers Law*, 150 U Pa L Rev 603, 608–09 (2001); see also John F. Manning, *Separation of Powers as Ordinary Interpretation*, 124 Harv L Rev 1939, 1950–62 (2011) (discussing formalism and functionalism).

key elements, such as a concern about aggrandized power.[198] Yet still, they represent discrete stances between which the Court alternates in its separation-of-powers jurisprudence.

These formalist and functionalist orientations were clearly on display this Term. Justice Gorsuch's opinions in *Gundy* and *Kisor* were paradigms of formalist separation-of-powers analysis, arguing that the Constitution's text draws clear lines between the distinct categories of executive, legislative, and judicial power.[199] Yet he ultimately justified strict enforcement of the Constitution's distribution of powers in teleological terms, in particular as essential to protecting individual liberty and guarding against "arbitrary use of governmental power."[200] Kagan barely engaged Gorsuch's lengthy constitutional attack on *Auer*, but her dismissive response was largely functionalist, noting that the Court had long upheld mixing of executive and judicial functions in agencies and emphasizing that judges were able to check agency regulation interpretations under *Auer*.[201] Functionalism also dominated Kagan's constitutional defense of delegation in *Gundy*, where she offered a vision of separation of powers that stressed flexibility, practicality, and effectiveness before reframing the case as being about statutory interpretation rather than constitutional structure.[202] And Chief Justice Roberts elevated realism over formalism in *Department of Commerce*, when he insisted that the Court was not naive and would not fall for Ross's contrived VRA justification.[203]

Although in the 2018 Term formalist arguments fell short, at other times the Roberts Court has taken a formalist approach to separation of powers and constitutional structural analysis generally.[204]

---

[198] See Magill, 150 U Pa L Rev at 609–11 (cited in note 197); see also Manning, 124 Harv L Rev at 1971–73 (cited in note 197) (arguing that both represent free-floating and purposivist forms of separation-of-powers analysis). For a critique of the formalism-functionalism framing of separation of powers and an argument that it should be recast as a cycling between rules and standards, see Aziz Z. Huq and Jon D. Michaels, *The Cycles in Separation-of-Powers Jurisprudence*, 126 Yale L J 346, 354–56 (2016).

[199] *Gundy*, 139 S Ct at 2133 (Gorsuch, J, dissenting).

[200] *Kisor*, 139 S Ct at 2348 (Gorsuch, J, concurring in the judgment); *Gundy*, 139 S Ct at 2133–35, 2142 (Gorsuch, J, dissenting).

[201] *Kisor*, 139 S Ct at 2421–22 (Kagan, J) (plurality).

[202] *Gundy*, 139 S Ct at 2123 (Kagan, J) (plurality).

[203] *Department of Commerce*, 139 S Ct at 2576.

[204] See Ronald J. Krotoszynski, Jr., *Cooperative Federalism, the New Formalism, and the Separation of Powers Revisited: Free Enterprise Fund and the Problem of Presidential Oversight of State-Government Officers Enforcing Federal Law*, 61 Duke L J 1599, 1607 (2012).

Examples include two leading opinions written by Chief Justice Roberts: *Free Enterprise Fund*, which imposed a categorical prohibition on double-for-cause removal protection; and *Stern v Marshall*, which drew a bright-line distinction between public and private rights for purposes of determining when adjudication outside of the Article III courts is constitutional.[205] Yet there have also been notable instances when the Court has taken a more functionalist stance. In *NLRB v Noel Canning*, the Court took a pragmatic approach to interpreting the scope of the Recess Appointments Clause, justifying its reading as necessary to serve the clause's purpose and supported by long-standing practice.[206] And in *Wellness International Network v Sharif*, the Court held that consent of the parties can make some forms of non-Article III adjudication constitutional, insisting that analysis of this "question must be decided not by 'formalistic and unbending rules,' but 'with an eye to the practical effect that the' practice 'will have on the constitutionally assigned role of the federal judiciary.'"[207] Even the Court's more formalist decisions can have a heavy functionalist component; a key driver of *Free Enterprise*, for example, is "the Court's own functional assessment of how much accountability executive officers properly owe to the President."[208]

As important, even the Roberts Court's formalistic separation-of-powers decisions are often cabined in ways that suggest concern with minimizing their practical impact. *Free Enterprise Fund* and *Stern* are again good examples of this phenomenon. In *Free Enterprise*, Roberts's majority opinion took a minimalist approach to remedying its finding that double-for-cause removal protection for members of the Public Company Accounting Oversight Board was unconstitutional,

---

[205] *Free Enterprise Fund*, 561 US at 492; *Stern v Marshall*, 564 US 462, 483–84 (2011). Although the Court's formalism often leads to invalidation of the challenged measure, that result is not universal. Recently, in *Oil States Energy Services, LLC v Greene's Energy Group, LLC*, the Court adhered to a formalist distinction between private and public rights, yet nonetheless upheld the non–Article III method of administrative adjudication at issue. 138 S Ct at 1365, 1373 (2018). And on occasion a more functionalist analysis leads to invalidation, as in *Lucia v SEC*, when the Court focused on the specific functions and responsibilities of administrative law judges at the SEC in concluding that they were inferior officers. 138 S Ct at 2044, 2052–54 (2018).

[206] 573 US at 513, 532, 540–43 (2014).

[207] 135 S Ct at 1932, 1944–45 (2015) (quoting *Commodity Futures Trading Commission v Schor*, 478 US 833, 851 (1986)).

[208] See John F. Manning, *The Supreme Court 2013 Term—Foreword: The Means of Constitutional Power*, 128 Harv L Rev 1, 47 (2014).

signaling in the process that it was not calling single-for-cause protection into question. Insisting that the unconstitutional double-for-cause provision could be severed while leaving the Board otherwise intact, the Court rejected greater "blue-pencil[ing]" of Sarbanes-Oxley Act provisions as a job "belong[ing] to the Legislature, not the Judiciary."[209] In a similar vein, Roberts's majority opinion in *Stern* not only suggested a carve-out for administrative adjudication, but also retained a broad definition of public right and reaffirmed precedents that sanctioned a broad role for non-Article III adjudication.[210] The question of whether to continue with this minimalist approach to remedying separation-of-powers violations is now before the Court, with the Justices adding a question on severability to their consideration of the constitutionality of the Consumer Financial Protection Bureau's single-director structure.[211]

Such remedial minimalism might seem at first to be functionalist, insofar as it tailors constitutional remedies to limit disruption and preserve as much of Congress's work as possible. Formalist separation-of-powers decisions are famous for casting aside analogous concerns of convenience, efficiency, and utility in service of upholding separation-of-power principles.[212] On the other hand, rejection of greater remedial creativity as outside of the judicial role sounds in a formalist register. More significantly, remedial minimalism is likely critical for the success of separation-of-powers formalism in practice. Otherwise, adoption of separation-of-powers formalism might well entail substantial transformation in the national administrative state, as Justice Gorsuch suggested in his *Kisor* and *Gundy* opinions—a result that might make a majority of the Court less willing to sustain formalist arguments. From this perspective, remedial minimalism appears primarily as a strategic device, one that makes separation-of-powers formalism more palatable, even if analytically more aligned with functionalism.

* * *

---

[209] *Free Enterprise Fund*, 561 US at 495–96, 509–10.

[210] *Stern*, 564 US at 488–93.

[211] See *Seila Law LLC v Consumer Financial Protection Bureau*, No 19-7, 2019 WL 5281290, at *1 (US Oct 18, 2019) (directing the parties to address whether "[i]f the Consumer Financial Protection Bureau is found unconstitutional on the basis of the separation of powers, can 12 USC § 5491(c)(3) be severed from the Dodd-Frank Act?").

[212] See *INS v Chadha*, 462 US 919, 944 (1983).

In short, the Roberts Court is simultaneously formalist and nonformalist in its approach to administrative law. Greater coherence exists within the two ideological camps, with conservatives often taking a more formalist view and the liberals being more nonformalist and specifically functionalist in orientation. Even here, however, there are noteworthy inconsistencies. Several conservative Justices have signed onto opinions stating that deference to agency legal interpretations can be constitutional,[213] as well as taken a minimalist or even functionalist approach to separation of powers.[214] And the same is true of the Roberts Court liberals, who at times have been willing to pull back on deference or adopt formalist approaches to separation of powers.[215] These inconsistencies in part reflect the fact that antiadministrativist views have been gradually emerging, as well as strategic defensive compromises. But the overall effect is to suggest a court deciding cases on a somewhat ad hoc basis.

B. ORIGINALISM AND HISTORICISM

A second prominent feature of many Roberts Court administrative law opinions is their focus on the past. To some extent, this is simply a manifestation of originalism's increased role in Roberts Court constitutional analysis, combined with the heavy constitutional flavor of attacks on established administrative law.[216] The historical lens often extends beyond the Founding, however, to include consideration of

---

[213] See, for example, *Pereira*, 138 S Ct at 2121 (Alito, J, dissenting) (criticizing the Court for not adhering to *Chevron*); *City of Arlington*, 569 US at 317–18 (Alito and Kennedy, JJ, joining dissent by Roberts, CJ, arguing that deference to agency legal interpretations is compatible with courts' law-declaring role if Congress has delegated such authority).

[214] See text accompanying notes 209–12; *Wellness Networks*, 135 S Ct at 1949 (Alito, J, concurring in the judgment in part); *PHH Corp. v Consumer Financial Protection Bureau*, 839 F3d 1, 30–36 (2016) (Kavanaugh, J, dissenting from decision en banc) (making the functionalist argument that an agency headed by a single director with for-cause removal protection lacks the checks on abuse of power of multimember-headed independent agencies and is unconstitutional).

[215] See, for example, *Kisor*, 139 S Ct at 2414–18 (Kagan, J) (plurality) (limiting *Auer* deference); *Oil States*, 138 S Ct at 1379–80 (Breyer, Ginsburg, and Sotomayor, JJ, concurring in opinion upholding administrative adjudication on purely originalist public rights grounds; Kagan, J, concurred without separate opinion); *Noel Canning*, 573 US at 550 (adopting bright-line rule that "the Senate is in session when it says it is, provided that, under its own rules, it retains the capacity to transact Senate business").

[216] See Larry Solum, *Legal Theory Lexicon 019: Originalism*, Legal Theory Blog (as revised on Aug 11, 2019), at https://lsolum.typepad.com/legal_theory_lexicon/2004/01/legal_theory_le_1.html (originalism on Roberts Court).

judicial precedent and sometimes governmental practice over the nineteenth century. This wider scope reflects broader trends in constitutional interpretation and originalist scholarship, in particular emphasis on political branch practices as constructing constitutional meaning or liquidating constitutional meaning over time.[217] As Sophia Lee has suggested, this wider historical orientation also reflects antiadministrativists' view of the nation's first century as a period of limited administrative government and judicial ascendancy in enforcing the law.[218]

In prior Terms, Justice Thomas has most consistently and comprehensively developed the originalist attack on modern administrative law. In the 2018 Term, this role fell to Justice Gorsuch. Originalism underlies Gorsuch's formalist account of law and the judicial power in *Kisor*, but especially dominates his *Gundy* dissent, which opens with a lengthy discussion of the Framers' views of constitutional structure, legislative power, and their fear of excessive lawmaking.[219] Gorsuch also takes a wider historical lens, however. In *Kisor*, he examined the Court's precedents on deference over the nineteenth and early twentieth centuries to show that *Auer* was a historical aberration.[220] Similarly, in *Gundy* he reviewed the Court's delegation jurisprudence over time to show that, even if the Court upheld delegations, it nonetheless adhered to his account of the narrow bounds of constitutional delegation until the 1940s. Indeed, in both opinions Gorsuch portrays the post-New Deal era of the 1940s as a period of sharp break from long-standing traditions.[221]

No doubt, Justice Gorsuch's engagement with nineteenth- and early twentieth-century jurisprudence is in part a strategic effort to rebut what on the surface appear to be strong stare decisis arguments for retaining current administrative law doctrines. Yet this engage-

---

[217] For discussion of these trends in originalist thinking, see Lawrence B. Solum, *The Fixation Thesis: The Role of Historical Fact in Original Meaning*, 91 Notre Dame L Rev 1, 3–16 (2015). For discussion of constitutional liquidation and its relationship to interpretive approaches that emphasize historical practice, see Willam Baude, *Constitutional Liquidation*, 71 Stan L Rev 1 (2019), and Curtis A. Bradley and Neil S. Seigel, *Historical Gloss, Madisonian Liquidation, and the Originalism Debate*, Va L Rev (forthcoming 2020), at https://papers.ssrn.com/sol3/papers.cfm?abstract_id=3331588.

[218] Sophia Z. Lee, *Our Administered Constitution: Administrative Constitutionalism from the Founding to the Present*, 168 U Pa L Rev 1699, 1702–03 (2019).

[219] *Gundy*, 139 S Ct at 2133–36 (Gorsuch, J, dissenting).

[220] *Kisor*, 139 S Ct at 2426–30 (Gorsuch, J, concurring in the judgment).

[221] *Gundy*, 139 S Ct at 2137–39 (Gorsuch, J, dissenting); *Kisor*, 139 S Ct at 2426–29 (Gorsuch, J, concurring in the judgment).

ment is also evidence of the limited sway originalism actually has in Roberts Court opinions attacking the administrative state. Indeed, despite its frequent invocation, originalism often has a superficial cast in these opinions, surfacing primarily in claims that administrative government is at odds with the general separation-of-powers principles and concerns of the Framers, rather than in evidence of originalist rejection of specific practices.[222] A prime example is Gorsuch's opinion in *Gundy*, which based its nondelegation arguments on abstract accounts of the Framers' views of constitutional structure and legislative power, rather than focusing on actual delegations from the period.[223]

Interestingly, the historical lens is not limited to administrative law's opponents. Administrative law's judicial defenders often adopt a historicist stance as well. To be sure, they give more weight to recent history than their anti-administrative colleagues, but recent history for these purposes often stretches back eighty to ninety years. Thus, in *Kisor* and *Gundy* Justice Kagan emphasized lines of precedents dating back to the 1940s and before that upheld deference to agencies' regulatory interpretations and broad delegations.[224] Perhaps the starkest historicist defense of established administrative arrangements came in Justice Breyer's 2014 majority opinion in *NLRB v Noel Canning*. In that case, Breyer drew on political branch practices going back to the Founding as well as the post–World War II period to hold that the recess appointment power could be used during an intrasession recess and with respect to vacancies that existed before the recess commenced.[225] Moreover, Breyer expressly justified historical practice as particularly important in separation-of-powers challenges, a marked contrast to his view four years earlier in *Free Enterprise Fund* that historical practices at the time of the Founding did not offer "significant help" in assessing a separation-of-powers challenge to removal protections.[226]

---

[222] See Metzger, 131 Harv L Rev at 45–46 (cited in note 11). An exception is *Oil States*, where both Justice Thomas's majority opinion and Justice Gorsuch's dissent discussed original practices relating to the granting and rescinding of patents in detail. 138 S Ct at 1377; id at 1381–83 (Gorsuch, J, dissenting).

[223] *Gundy*, 139 S Ct at 2133–37; Julian Davis Mortenson and Nicholas Bagley, Delegation at the Founding *20–21 (unpublished manuscript, Dec 2019), at https://papers.ssrn.com/sol3/papers.cfm?abstract_id=3512154.

[224] *Kisor*, 139 S Ct at 2411–12 & nn 2–3 (Kagan, J) (plurality); *Gundy*, 139 S Ct at 2129–30 (Kagan, J) (plurality).

[225] *Noel Canning*, 573 US at 524–26, 528–33, 543.

[226] *Free Enterprise Fund*, 561 US at 517.

In short, Justices of all stripes are increasingly looking to past practices and historical precedents in administrative law cases. *Department of Commerce* showcased this trend too. There, both Chief Justice Roberts and Justice Thomas emphasized the long historical practice of including a citizenship question on the census as far back as 1782, with Roberts holding that this "early understanding ... and long practice" meant that asking about citizenship did not violate the Enumeration Clause.[227] Justice Breyer similarly relied on the history of the census, but the historical account he offered put prime emphasis on transformations in how the census was conducted after 1950, in response to concerns about high undercounting rates.[228]

Historical battles also dominate recent administrative law scholarship. Prominent attacks on administrative government by Philip Hamburger, Joseph Postell, and others argue that current national administrative government marks a stark departure from expectations and practices at the Founding through the nineteenth century.[229] Their accounts are disputed by historians offering numerous studies of administrative governance dating back just as far.[230] The extent of judicial deference to administrative legal interpretations is an issue of particular historical dispute. In an article cited by Justice Gorsuch in *Kisor*, Aditya Bamzai contends that before the 1940s the Supreme Court did not have a tradition of deferring to executive interpretations, as Justice Scalia among others had maintained. Instead, the Court "'respected' longstanding and contemporaneous *executive* interpretations of law as part of a practice of deferring to longstanding and contemporaneous interpretation *generally*."[231] Disagreeing with Bamzai, Craig Green maintains that the Court's jurisprudence is more varied and supportive of deference to executive actors, identifying instances in which the Court suggested that "the construction

---

[227] 139 S Ct at 2567, 2577.

[228] Id at 2585–87 (Breyer, J, concurring in part and dissenting in part).

[229] See generally, for example, Philip Hamburger, *Is Administrative Law Unlawful?* (Chicago, 2014); Joseph Postell, *Bureaucracy in America: The Administrative State's Challenge to Constitutional Government* (Missouri, 2017); see also Richard Epstein, *The Dubious Morality of the Modern Administrative State* (Manhattan Institute, 2019).

[230] See, for example, Brian Balough, *A Government Out of Sight* (Cambridge, 2009); Jerry Mashaw, *Creating the Administrative Constitution* (Yale, 2012); William Novak, *The Myth of the "Weak" American State*, 113 Am Hist Rev 752, 752–53 (2008).

[231] Aditya Bamzai, *The Origins of Judicial Deference to Executive Interpretation*, 126 Yale L J 908, 916, 965 (2017).

given to a statute by those charged with the duty of executing it is always entitled to the most respectful consideration."[232] And Lee argues that early administrative agencies "had the first and often final word on the Constitution's meaning" such that "reinstating the 19th century constitutional order ... would all but eliminate judicial review of [agency] actions' constitutionality."[233]

This historical scholarship holds important lessons for current debates over administrative law and the administrative state more broadly. The extensive history of administrative agencies operating from the nation's beginnings to today undercuts efforts to paint contemporary administrative government as a fundamental deviation from the Constitution. To be sure, the extent of administrative authority existing before the twentieth century is disputed. In addition, much of the early national administrative state was developmental and distributional, with many administrative agencies operating in the territories or implementing administrative regimes that involved matters of public right.[234] Still, too many early examples exist of broad administrative discretion, coercive administrative actions targeting private rights, and limited judicial review to justify accounts that portray administrative government and administrative law as twentieth-century aberrations.[235]

Moreover, it is unclear why the public right focus and territorial operation of early administrative regimes should limit their historical significance. Those were the primary contexts in which the national

---

[232] *United States v Moore*, 95 US 760, 763 (1877); Craig Green, *Deconstructing the Administrative State: Constitutional Debates over Chevron and Political Transformation in American Law* 128–34 (Temple University Beasley School of Law Research Paper No 2018-35, Nov 2018), at https://papers.ssrn.com/sol3/papers.cfm?abstract_id=3264482.

[233] Lee, 168 U Pa L Rev at 1707 (cited in note 218).

[234] Samuel DeCanio, *Democracy and the Origins of the American Regulatory State* 21–22 (Yale, 2015); see also Hamburger, *Is Administrative Law Unlawful?* at 193–203 (cited in note 229) (early administration involved benefits and privileges); Aditya Bamzai, *Delegation and Interpretive Discretion: Gundy, Kisor, and the Formation and Future of Administrative Law*, 133 Harv L Rev 164, 177–82 (2019) (distinguishing early precedent sustaining broad delegations as relating to public rights).

[235] Some examples from Jerry Mashaw include the 1807–09 embargo, operation of the Land Office, and steamship regulation in the 1850s. Mashaw, *Creating* at 91–143, 192–208, 216–18 (cited in note 230). Ann Woolhandler maintains that the "[u]sing the right/privilege theory to explain older patterns in judicial review is problematic," noting that "the Court sometimes reviewed government exactions affecting private rights under the deferential res judicata model. At other times, the Court accorded rigorous judicial review in cases seeking remedies for denials of government benefits or largesse." *Judicial Deference to Administrative Action*, 43 Admin L Rev 197, 231–34 (1991).

government of the time was active, and its actions had tremendous importance for the individuals affected.[236] Although some administrative skeptics view this history as suggesting that administrative power to regulate and adjudicate private rights is limited,[237] an alternative lesson to draw is that the national government has always relied on agencies when it decides to act. And it is possible to understand many forms of contemporary regulation, particularly those involving permits and licenses or that create statutory rights and obligations, as modern-day versions of public rights—indeed, for many decades the Supreme Court has taken just such an approach.[238] Thus, even if this history is viewed as limited to public rights, it would still carry substantial relevance in establishing the historical legitimacy of administrative governance.

Hence, originalism and historicism may turn out to be powerful tools in administrative government's defense. At the same time, framing the defense of administrative law and administrative government in historical terms has the downside of suggesting that the acceptable bounds and forms of administrative action are set by what has been done before. This leads to novelty and innovation being viewed as indications that an administrative arrangement is constitutionally suspect, a position advanced in several Roberts Court opinions.[239] But as the D.C. Circuit recently stated, such a view is at odds with the Court's separation-of-powers jurisprudence, which has often sustained measures that were novel in their day.[240] Nor is such a

---

[236] For a discussion of the importance of the territories to contemporary debates over administrative law and to the lives of many Americans in the nation's early years, see Gregory Ablavsky, *Administrative Constitutionalism in the Northwest Territory*, 167 U Pa L Rev 1631, 1633–36 (2019).

[237] See, for example, Hamburger, *Is Administrative Law Unlawful?* at 198–202 (cited in note 229) (acknowledging the historical administrative adjudication of patent rights but distinguishing them from other private rights); Gary Lawson, *Appointments and Illegal Adjudication: The America Invents Act Through a Constitutional Lens*, 2018 Geo Mason L Rev 26, 38–50 (describing nineteenth-century cases rejecting the administrative adjudication of land patents and contrasting them with "case law from the past eight decades systematically upholding administrative actions that adjudicate private vested rights").

[238] See *Stern*, 564 US at 490 (noting "the Court rejected the limitation of the public rights exception to actions involving the Government as a party" but has "limit[ed] the exception to cases in which the claim at issue derives from a federal regulatory scheme, or in which resolution of the claim by an expert Government agency is deemed essential to a limited regulatory objective within the agency's authority").

[239] Leah M. Litman, *Debunking Antinovelty*, 66 Duke L J 1407, 1415–21 (2017).

[240] *PHH Corp. v Consumer Financial Protection Bureau*, 881 F3d 75, 102–03 (DC Cir 2018) (en banc) (noting that the independent counsel, the FTC, and the Sentencing Commission all represented new arrangements but where upheld as constitutional).

constraint easily squared with the Constitution's text, which gives Congress broad power to structure government as it sees fit.²⁴¹

A historical lens can also stand in tension with efforts to rethink constitutional and administrative law to better fit current realities.²⁴² This tension is particularly acute when the historical lens is an originalist one, as the worlds of 1789 and 2020 are far apart when it comes to the shape and responsibilities of national government. But even a more limited backward-looking gaze may ill fit efforts to address the governance crises of today. Two of the most salient characteristics of contemporary national government are the deep political polarization that has stymied congressional action on pressing issues and increasingly bold assertions of presidential power that undercut established administrative practices and legal regimes.²⁴³ Although both have surfaced in earlier eras, their combination and intensity today create governance challenges that did not exist even a generation ago, and their resolution may necessitate experimenting with structural arrangements at odds with traditional governmental models.

C. APA TEXTUALISM, APA ORIGINALISM, AND ADMINISTRATIVE COMMON LAW

A third analytic contrast in Roberts Court administrative law concerns the different stances the Justices take toward the APA and other administrative law statutes. The Roberts Court is often described as textualist in its approach to statutory interpretation, including by the Justices themselves.²⁴⁴ Whether this is a wholly accurate description is a matter of debate; the Court has deviated from textualism in several prominent statutory interpretation cases.²⁴⁵ In the administrative

---

²⁴¹ See Manning, 128 Harv L Rev at 5–7 (cited in note 208).

²⁴² For an effort to rethink administrative government's constitutionality along these lines, emphasizing the constitutional implications of the broad delegations that characterize contemporary government, see Metzger, 131 Harv L Rev at 87–94 (cited in note 11).

²⁴³ Id at 75–76; Sarah Blinder, *The Dysfunctional Congress*, 18 Ann Rev Pol Sci 85, 91–97 (2015).

²⁴⁴ See Manning, 128 Harv L Rev at 22–29 (cited in note 208); Anton Metlisky, *The Roberts Court and the New Textualism*, 38 Cardozo L Rev 671, 672 (2016). Justice Kagan famously stated "we are all textualists now" during a lecture she gave at Harvard Law School. *Justice Elena Kagan, The Scalia Lecture: A Dialogue with Justice Kagan on the Reading of Statutes* 8:29 (Harvard Law School, Nov 18, 2015), at http://today.law.harvard.edu/in-scalia-lecture-kagan-discusses-statutory-interpretation.

²⁴⁵ Compare Metlsky, 38 Cardozo L Rev at 672–74 (cited in note 244), with Abbe R. Gluck, *Imperfect Statutes, Imperfect Courts: Understanding Congress's Plan in the Era of Unorthodox*

law context, at least, the Roberts Court has equivocated between textualist and common law approaches to major administrative law statutes.

Textualism was supreme in *Perez v Mortgage Bankers Association* in 2015.[246] Although the APA expressly exempts interpretive rules from notice-and-comment rulemaking requirements, D.C. Circuit doctrine had held that once an agency issued a definitive interpretation of a regulation, the agency had to use notice-and-comment rulemaking to change that interpretation.[247] As noted above, the Roberts Court unanimously reversed, with the majority opinion emphasizing that the D.C. Circuit's approach was "contrary to the clear text of the APA's rulemaking provisions."[248] Textualism also dominated the Court's approach to the Freedom of Information Act (FOIA) in *Food Marketing Institute v Argus Leader*, a 2018 Term decision rejecting a widely followed lower court interpretation of FOIA's Exemption 4 as protecting confidential information from disclosure only when disclosure would cause competitive harm. That interpretation, according to Justice Gorsuch's majority opinion for a 6–3 Court, ignored that "[i]n statutory interpretation disputes, a court's proper starting point lies in a careful examination of the ordinary meaning and structure of the law itself. Where ... that examination yields a clear answer, judges must stop."[249]

Text also featured in *Kisor*, with Justice Kagan and Justice Gorsuch battling over the meaning of § 706. This battle took an originalist cast, focusing on what the APA's text was understood to mean when originally adopted. Gorsuch drew on the APA's legislative history and contemporaneous scholarly accounts to argue that the APA was originally understood to require de novo judicial review of legal questions, while Kagan countered with evidence that the APA's enactors

---

Lawmaking, 129 Harv L Rev 62, 80–96 (2015). For the interesting suggestion that the Court's turn to purposivism is linked to its move away from *Chevron*, see Note, *The Rise of Purposivism and the Fall of Chevron*, 130 Harv L Rev 1227 (2017).

[246] 135 S Ct 1199 (2015).

[247] See 5 USC § 553(b)(A); *Paralyzed Veterans of America v DC Arena LP*, 117 F3d 579, 586 (1997).

[248] See text accompanying note 36; *Perez*, 135 S Ct at 1206.

[249] 139 S Ct 2356, 2364, 2366 (2019). In so holding, the Court echoed an earlier Roberts Court decision interpreting FOIA's Exemption 2, where Justice Kagan's majority opinion denied that its interpretation was at odds with long-standing lower-court doctrine, but added that even if it were in conflict, "we have no warrant to ignore clear statutory language on the ground that other courts have done so." *Milner v Department of the Navy*, 562 US 562, 569–72, 576 (2011).

had intended § 706 to restate the existing common law approach to judicial review.[250] Chief Justice Roberts's narrow join left this debate over the APA's meaning in a 4–4 tie. Yet *Kisor* is fundamentally a reaffirmation of administrative common law. Kagan's refinement of *Auer*'s limits for a majority of the Court was the epitome of common law doctrinal elaboration, and upholding the doctrine on stare decisis gave ultimate priority to judicial precedent. For all his textualism with respect to § 706, even Justice Gorsuch left room for some judicial development of judicial review doctrine in his embrace of *Skidmore* and his insistence that *Auer* violates § 553's notice-and-comment requirements because of its practical effects, despite the section's express exception for interpretive rules.[251]

Common law development of judicial review doctrine was further on display in *Department of Commerce*. Indeed, administrative common law was a constant baseline in the case, with all the Justices relying on *State Farm* despite that decision's expansion of arbitrary and capriciousness review beyond its original meaning.[252] But administrative common law was even more prominent in Chief Justice Roberts's elaboration of a prohibition on pretext for a majority of the Court—a prohibition that, as mentioned above, was implicit in existing case law but not expressly developed.[253] Moreover, despite taking a textual approach to statutory interpretation in other contexts, Roberts never stopped to respond to Justice Thomas's complaint that such a pretext inquiry and adding extra-record materials had no basis in the APA's text.[254] Instead, he simply invoked the Court's precedents for going beyond the record if a strong showing of bad faith is made and the APA's requirement of reasoned decision making.[255]

Viewing the 2018 Term opinions along with earlier precedent, it becomes clear that the Justices' views on textualist versus common

---

[250] *Kisor*, 139 S Ct at 2419–20 (Kagan, J) (plurality); id at 2435–36 (Gorsuch, J, concurring in the judgment).

[251] 139 S Ct at 2434–35, 2442–43 (Gorsuch, J, concurring in the judgment).

[252] See Metzger, 80 Geo Wash L Rev at 1299–1300 (cited in note 96). But see Evan D. Bernick, *Envisioning Administrative Procedure Act Originalism*, 70 Admin L Rev 807, 847–49 (2018) (arguing that hard-look review fits within the "vague contours" of "arbitrary [and] capricious" as originally understood in the APA).

[253] See text accompanying notes 147–48.

[254] See *Department of Commerce*, 139 S Ct at 2578–79 (Thomas, J, concurring in part and dissenting in part).

[255] Id at 2574, 2576.

law interpretations of administrative law statutes do not track their ideological divisions or overall stance on administrative government. Instead, many individual Justices oscillate between administrative law textualism and a more common law stance, as does the Court as a whole.[256] To some extent, this oscillation may reflect the specific administrative law measures at issue. For example, FOIA's text is far more detailed and more recently amended than the APA, which helps explain the contrast between *Argus Leader*, on the one hand, and *Kisor* and *Department of Commerce* on the other, all decided in the 2018 Term. And the Court's notably greater textualism in *Perez* than *Kisor* and *Department of Commerce* may result from the fact that *Perez* involved the APA's procedural requirements rather than its provisions for judicial review. Not only are the APA's procedural requirements more detailed and specific than its judicial review provisions, but the Court has allowed courts more leeway to develop the latter.[257]

Significantly, however, such oscillation between APA textualism and administrative common law is not a new phenomenon. For many decades, the Court has periodically rejected administrative common law as being at odds with the APA while simultaneously developing new administrative common law doctrines. Despite this oscillation, the common law approach to the APA has dominated, especially in the area of judicial review.[258] The paradigm example is *Chevron*, which never referenced § 706's text at all and justified its two-step approach to deference on a combination of imputed congressional intent, precedent, pragmatic factors, and constitutional structure.[259]

---

[256] There are exceptions. Justice Breyer fairly consistently adopts a common law approach. See *Argus Leader*, 139 S Ct at 2368–69 (Breyer, J, concurring in part and dissenting in part); *Milner*, 562 US at 585–90 (Breyer, J, dissenting), and Justices Thomas and Gorsuch have been more consistently textualist (see, for example, text accompanying note 254); *Gutierrez-Brizuela v Lynch*, 834 F3d 1142, 1151 (10th Cir 2016) (Gorsuch, J, concurring).

[257] Compare *Vermont Yankee Nuclear Power Corp. v Natural Resources Defense Council*, 435 US 519, 524, 542–49 (1978) (insisting that "[a]gencies are free to grant additional procedural rights [beyond those in the APA] . . . but reviewing courts are generally not free to impose them"), with *Chevron*, 467 US at 842–43 (setting out a two-step standard for judicial review of agency statutory interpretations without referencing the APA).

[258] See Metzger, 80 Geo Wash L Rev at 1298–1310 (cited in note 96). At the same time, courts are "reluctant to be open about their use of common law in the administrative law arena." Jack M. Beermann, *Common Law and Statute Law in Administrative Law*, 63 Admin L Rev 1, 2–3 (2011).

[259] John F. Duffy, *Administrative Common Law in Judicial Review*, 77 Tex L Rev 113, 189–93 (1999).

A growing number of scholars now argue for APA originalism and critique the common law approach to the APA.[260] The arguments against administrative common law range from defenses of textualist statutory interpretation writ large to attacks on the legitimacy of judicial lawmaking to concerns about the harmful effects of specific common-law-developed doctrines.[261] Notably, these critiques are offered by scholars with a range of views about judicial deference to agencies and administrative government more broadly. In particular, prominent defenders of the administrative state have advocated that courts should follow the APA's original meaning and text.[262] Critiques of administrative common law also are not limited to the APA; John Brinkerhoff has defended the Roberts Court's recent FOIA textualism on the grounds that lower courts' common law interpretations of FOIA wrongly downplayed FOIA's pro-disclosure orientation and instead imposed a "strong pro-government gloss over nearly all of FOIA."[263]

This growing scholarship underscores the potential pitfalls of administrative common law. But as I have argued elsewhere, it is important to separate out the merits and demerits of particular common law doctrines from the general enterprise of administrative common law.[264] I am skeptical of efforts to broadly replace administrative common law with a textual and originalist approach to the APA. The APA's text often supports alternative readings, as made clear by the dueling accounts of § 706 in *Kisor* and the strong and weak forms of arbitrary and capriciousness review in *Department of Commerce*. Moreover, the original meaning of the APA was and remains contested.[265] George

---

[260] See, for example, Bernick, 70 Admin L Rev at 809 & n 11 (cited in note 252) (providing examples). John Duffy started this trend, writing the first sustained attack on common law approaches to judicial review under the APA twenty years ago. See Duffy, 77 Tex L Rev at 120 (cited in note 259).

[261] See, for example, Nicholas Bagley, *The Puzzling Presumption of Reviewability*, 127 Harv L Rev 1285, 1287–89, 1303–09 (2014) (arguing that the APA's text does not support the presumption of reviewability that the Court has identified and that the presumption illegitimately intrudes on congressional policy choices); Kathryn E. Kovacs, *Superstatute Theory and Administrative Common Law*, 90 Ind L J 1207, 1254–60 (2015) (applying superstatute theory to the APA and critiquing administrative common law on public deliberation grounds).

[262] See Sunstein, 107 Georgetown L J at 1642–57 (cited in note 194); see also Bagley, 127 Harv L Rev at 1287–89, 1303–09 (cited in note 261) (arguing that APA textualism and originalism lead to greater agency freedom from intrusive judicial review).

[263] John C. Brinkerhoff, Jr., *FOIA's Common Law*, 36 Yale J Reg 575, 578–79 (2019).

[264] Metzger, 80 Geo Wash L Rev at 1355 (cited in note 96).

[265] For a detailed articulation of this view with respect to § 706, see Sunstein, 107 Georgetown L J at 1642–57 (cited in note 194).

Shepherd has described "the fight over the APA" as "a pitched political battle for the life of the New Deal." This battle meant that key provisions of the APA were left intentionally ambiguous so that agreement on the APA could be reached. And it meant that the APA's legislative history was intentionally manipulated by both sides to advance their cause, leaving contradictory sources for future interpreters.[266] One clear data point, however, is that the Supreme Court never viewed the APA as overturning administrative common law or its judicial review precedents, other than imposing a more searching version of substantial evidence review.[267]

As important, administrative common law is an inevitable and legitimate phenomenon in our constitutional separation-of-powers system.[268] It is inevitable given the difficulties Congress faces in legislating and the practical impossibility of specifying answers to newly emergent administrative law issues in advance. The result is that courts end up tasked with policing agency actions under statutory constraints that increasingly are out of step with administrative realities. Of course, courts could leave the necessary updating to Congress, and sometimes do. But experience shows that—at least with a capaciously worded statute—courts feel a practical imperative to perform that updating role rather than simply apply administrative constraints ill suited to serving congressional purposes in the face of changed realities.[269] Administrative law's transsubstantive nature, which means that the effects of not gap-filling or updating would mean inadequate administrative controls across a wide range of executive branch activities, reinforces judges' inclinations for common law development. A similar reinforcing effect comes from administrative law's focus on the structures and procedures that lie at the heart of the administrative state,

---

[266] George B. Shepherd, *Fierce Compromise: The Administrative Procedure Act Emerges from New Deal Politics*, 90 Nw U L Rev 1557, 1560, 1662–63 (1996) ("As the bill's enactment became imminent, each party to the negotiations over the bill attempted to create legislative history—to create a record that would cause future reviewing courts to interpret the new statute in a manner that would favor the party.").

[267] See Sunstein, 107 Georgetown L J at 1653–56 (cited in note 194) (discussing the Court's adherence to such as *Gray v Powell*, 314 US 402 (1941) and *NLRB v Hearst Publications*, 322 US 111 (1944)); Green, *Deconstructing* at 134–38 (cited in note 232).

[268] This paragraph and the next draw on ideas I set out at length in Metzger, 80 Geo Wash L Rev at 1320–55 (cited in note 96).

[269] A prime example is judicial development and elaboration of judicial review of rulemaking in the face of the explosion of social regulation in the 1960s and 1970s. See Robert L. Rabin, *Federal Regulation in Historical Perspective*, 38 Stan L Rev 1189, 1301–09 (1986).

such as the court-agency relationship. Not only is this relationship difficult to capture comprehensively in statutes,[270] but also courts may view elaboration of judicial review doctrines as especially within their bailiwick.

This structural character of administrative law closely relates to a third feature that underlies the development of administrative common law: the quasi-constitutional character of ordinary administrative law. Administrative law plays a critical role in building out the administrative state, and even more in domesticating the administrative state within the constitutional order. Although rarely judicially acknowledged, the primary means by which courts have addressed constitutional concerns about agencies' powers has been through subconstitutional administrative law requirements, such as the requirement of reasoned decision making, rather than direct constitutional scrutiny.[271] Judicial development of administrative common law reflects this use of administrative law to address the constitutional tensions raised by the modern administrative state.

To be sure, that administrative common law may be practically inevitable does not render it legitimate. But unlike earlier instances of federal court lawmaking, administrative common law does not displace state law or alter the primary rules that govern private behavior. Instead, it shares the focus on uniquely federal interests that marks many legitimate forms of federal common law.[272] Equally central, most administrative common law has a statutory basis to which it is at least loosely tethered, such as the judicial review provisions of the APA. And, critically, to the extent it serves to implement separation-of-powers concerns, administrative common law is part of the elaboration of constitutional requirements seen as lying at the core of the judicial role today.

---

[270] See Lisa Schultz Bressman, *Procedures as Politics in Administrative Law*, 107 Colum L Rev 1749, 1772–73 (2009).

[271] For further development of this argument, see generally Gillian E. Metzger, *Ordinary Administrative Law as Constitutional Common Law*, 110 Colum L Rev 479 (2010); see also Emily S. Bremer, *The Unwritten Administrative Constitution*, 66 Fla L Rev 1217, 1218–19, 1234–48 (2014) (arguing that "administrative law has evolved into an unwritten constitution that governs the administrative power not contemplated by the U.S. Constitution"). To Justice Gorsuch's credit, he acknowledged the role that subconstitutional doctrines play in policing discretion in *Gundy*, 139 S Ct at 2141–42 (Gorsuch, J, dissenting) (discussing vagueness and major questions doctrines as surrogates for delegation doctrine).

[272] *Texas Industries v Radcliffe Materials, Inc.*, 451 US 630, 640–41 (1981).

III. Whither Roberts Court Administrative Law?

Focusing simply on these analytic themes and tensions, it is hard to discern a clear direction for the Roberts Court on administrative law. The Court is at times formalist and at times nonformalist; at times textualist and at times more common law in orientation. And while its administrative law opinions have turned consistently more historicist over recent years, that backward focus has encompassed a range of approaches, from originalism to an emphasis on historical practice and precedent. Greater coherence becomes apparent when the Justices are viewed in their overall ideological groupings, and some individual Justices are particularly consistent. But the Court as a whole seems to vacillate in ways that resist principled explanation. Instead, the factor that best explains Roberts Court administrative law seems to be the varied administrative law jurisprudence of Chief Justice Roberts himself.

Taking a step back, two broader frames emerge from the 2018 Terms decisions and the Roberts Court's administrative law jurisprudence writ large. One is radical and could portend dramatic changes in existing doctrine; the other is incrementalist and seemingly more modulated in its reforms. The incrementalist approach dominated the 2018 Term administrative law decisions, and there are reasons to think that may continue. But although these two approaches are analytically distinct, in practice both may result in similar pullbacks on administrative authority. Moreover, both frames are united in one key regard: increasing judicial supervision of administrative government. And both convey the sense that the administrative state must be cabined to guard against unaccountable, aggrandized, and arbitrary administrative power. Notably absent across both is an affirmative argument for the potential benefits of administrative government, other than recognition on the incrementalist side of the value of bureaucratic expertise.

The lack of a more robust defense of the administrative state represents a substantial hole in Roberts Court administrative law jurisprudence. Failure to invoke the full range of potential benefits from administrative government makes Roberts Court administrative law jurisprudence appear increasingly one-sided and political. Moreover, a fuller picture of administrative government is needed if the Roberts Court's interventions are to yield a coherent approach to administrative law.

A. RADICALISM AND INCREMENTALISM IN ROBERTS COURT ADMINISTRATIVE LAW

Viewing the analytic tensions described above in broader perspective, two methodological frames emerge from the Roberts Court's 2018 administrative law decisions. What stands out in Justice Gorsuch's *Kisor* opinion is the absolutist and categorical nature of his argument. He insists on the need for clear rules and rejects altogether any claims of stare decisis.[273] A similar absolutist and categorical character typifies Gorsuch's approach in *Gundy*, with his insistence on reviving direct constitutional barriers to delegation and unwillingness to address delegation concerns through more indirect and subconstitutional means.

This uncompromising commitment to formalism, originalism, and textualism—evident in Justice Thomas's opinions as well—has potential to radically reshape existing doctrine and administrative institutions. It would require overruling *Chevron* and *Auer* deference, as both Justices openly acknowledge, but the implications of this approach would extend well past deference doctrines. Taken categorically, without acceptance of patterns of governance that have emerged over time, a formalist insistence on strict lines dividing legislative, executive, and judicial power calls into question the combination of rulemaking, enforcement, and adjudication that lies at the heart of modern administrative agencies.[274] Applying such a division, Gorsuch's and Thomas's prior opinions have suggested they would pull administrative adjudication back to only covering matters of public right, defined in originalist terms.[275] Asserting that original understandings so require, they would also deem a broad swath of federal government personnel to be principal or inferior officers, thereby rendering a large

---

[273] Compare *Kisor*, 139 S Ct at 2443–48 (Gorsuch, J, concurring in the judgment) (arguing that stare decisis does not require retention of *Auer*), with *Perez*, 135 S Ct at 1212 (Scalia, J, concurring in the judgment) (acknowledging that *Chevron* may be too established to be overturned).

[274] See Cass R. Sunstein and Adrian Vermeule, *The Unbearable Rightness of Auer*, 84 U Chi L Rev 297, 298, 312 (2017).

[275] See *Oil States Energy Services, LLC v Greene's Energy Group, LLC*, 138 S Ct 1365, 1381–82 (2018) (Gorsuch, J, dissenting) (arguing that system for administrative review of granted patents was unconstitutional because granted patents were not considered matters of public right at the founding); *B&B Hardware, Inc. v Hargis Industries, Inc.*, 135 S Ct 1293, 1316 (2015) (Thomas, J, dissenting) ("Because federal administrative agencies are part of the Executive Branch, it is not clear that they have power to adjudicate claims involving core private rights.").

number unconstitutionally appointed.[276] Meanwhile, requiring the APA to be applied in accordance with its enacted text and original meaning would not just overturn *Chevron* and *Auer* and entail a pullback in arbitrariness review; it would also throw into doubt long-standing doctrines that developed the procedural requirements of notice-and-comment rulemaking and access to judicial review.[277]

By contrast, Justice Kagan's *Kisor* opinion is above all else incrementalist. Far from absolute, it instead emphasizes case-by-case analysis and a commitment to developing precedent and existing practice rather than dramatic change. Such contextualized, precedent and practice-based analysis has long characterized Justice Breyer's administrative law opinions.[278] And incrementalism was also on display in Justice Kagan's decision in *Lucia v SEC*, which ruled that ALJs at the Securities and Exchange Commission were unconstitutionally appointed inferior officers. In so holding, Kagan wrote about as narrowly as possible, closely following existing precedent and refusing to define inferior officer more broadly or consider the scope of the judges' removal protection.[279] Perhaps more importantly given his role as the fulcrum of the Court on administrative law, Chief Justice Roberts's administrative law opinions are often incrementalist as well. Although the Chief Justice has advanced formalist principles with a categorical edge, he has applied them in a minimalist manner that substantially circumscribes their impact.[280] Roberts's penchant for minimalism was particularly clear with his limited and selective join in *Kisor*, which left the law versus policy and APA debates in the case unresolved and instead focused on addressing his concerns about *Auer* deference with minimal disruption to existing doctrine.

---

[276] See *Lucia v SEC*, 138 S Ct 2044, 2056 (2018) (Thomas, J, concurring) ("The Founders likely understood the term 'Officers of the United States' to encompass all federal civil officials who perform an ongoing, statutory duty—no matter how important or significant the duty.") (citation omitted).

[277] See note 252 and its accompanying text (discussing arbitrary and capriciousness review); *American Radio Relay League v FCC*, 524 F3d 227, 245–47 (DC Cir 2008) (Kavanaugh, J, concurring) (arguing that current notice-and-comment requirements are not compatible with the APA's text as originally understood).

[278] See *Noel Canning*, 573 US 513, 524 (2014) (Breyer, J) (emphasizing that "in interpreting the [Recess Appointments] Clause, we put significant weight upon historical practice"); *Barnhart v Walton*, 535 US 212, 222 (2002) (Breyer, J) (arguing that *Chevron* deference is appropriate based on consideration of multiple factors).

[279] *Lucia*, 138 S Ct at 2051 (Kagan, J) ("The *sole question* here is whether the Commission's ALJs are 'Officers of the United States' or simply employees of the Federal Government.") (emphasis added).

[280] See text accompanying notes 209–10.

In the contest between radicalism and incrementalism during the 2018 Term, incrementalism was the victor. This could in part be a reflection of the fact that the 2018 Term was a transition year, with Justice Kennedy's resignation and Justice Kavanaugh replacing him to create a solid conservative majority on the Court. Popular criticism of the Court in response may have made Roberts in particular unwilling to adopt more radical positions, and fears that the new majority will overturn contentious precedents fueled the repeated debates over stare decisis.[281] If this pattern continues in future Terms, then the most radical attacks on the constitutionality of administrative governance may not gain majority support.

The counter is *Gundy* and the constitutionality of broad congressional delegations of authority to the executive branch. Despite his incrementalism elsewhere, the Chief Justice signed onto Justice Gorsuch's constitutional attack on broad delegations of authority to the executive branch in *Gundy*—an attack that Justice Kagan described as meaning that "most of Government is unconstitutional."[282] Each of the five conservative Justices has now signaled willingness to reconsider the Court's lenient nondelegation doctrine.[283] Were the Court to support significant constitutional barriers to delegation, that would be a sign of radicalism ascendant in Roberts Court administrative law. However, it remains to be seen how far Roberts, Alito, and Kavanaugh are actually willing to go reviving limits on delegation. Their same-Term endorsement of broad executive branch policy discretion in *Department of Commerce* may signal that they will not go very far. Previously, both Roberts and Kavanaugh have addressed excessive-delegation concerns through a statutory interpretation lens rather than broad-scale constitutional invalidation, and they may opt to continue with such subconstitutional approaches going forward.[284]

---

[281] Cf. Joan Biskupic, *Chief Justice John Roberts Is Exercising the Power He's Craved*, CNN Politics (June 27, 2019), at https://www.cnn.com/2019/06/27/politics/john-roberts-supreme-court/index.html.

[282] 139 S Ct at 2130 (Kagan, J) (plurality).

[283] See id at 2131 (Gorsuch, J, joined by Roberts, CJ, and Thomas, J, dissenting) (arguing for stricter constitutional limits on delegation); id at 2131 (Alito, J, concurring in the judgment) (signaling support for reconsidering "the approach we have taken [to nondelegation] for the past 84 years"); *Paul v United States*, 140 S Ct 342 (2019) (Kavanaugh, J, statement on denial of certiorari) ("Justice Gorsuch's scholarly analysis of the Constitution's nondelegation doctrine ... may warrant further consideration in future cases.").

[284] See *King v Burwell*, 135 S Ct 2480, 2483 (2015) (refusing to apply *Chevron* deference on the grounds that "had Congress wished to assign" "a question of deep 'economic and political

Chief Justice Roberts's past practice of building up to overruling precedents over time rather than in one fell swoop also merits note.[285] This might suggest that radical changes in administrative law may yet occur, notwithstanding the 2018 Term's incrementalism. Yet Roberts has had opportunities to push for more radical administrative law outcomes in the past and not pursued them—despite describing administrative government in stark terms that would seem to merit a more dramatic response.[286] Put differently, when it comes to bottom-line results, Roberts's anti-administrativism has often lost out to his Burkean and common law instincts.

Crucially, however, even incrementalism can have a significant impact on existing administrative law and administrative institutions. One need look no further than the aftermath of *Kisor* to see this effect. In the four-month period after *Kisor*'s issuance, the courts of appeals directly considered whether to apply *Auer* deference in light of *Kisor* in thirty cases and deferred to the agency's approach in only ten of those. In an additional five cases, the court declined deference but ultimately upheld the agency's interpretation, for an overall rate of the government prevailing 50 percent of the time.[287] By comparison, studies of the years leading up to *Kisor* have identified the courts as granting *Auer* deference or the government as prevailing 71 percent of the time.[288] Similarly, despite their bottom-line minimalism, the Court's decisions on removal, the status of administrative law judges,

---

significance'" to an agency "it surely would have done so expressly"); *United States Telecommunications Association v FCC*, 855 F3d 381, 419 (Kavanaugh, J, dissenting from denial of en banc review) (arguing that for an agency to have authority to issue a "major agency rule[ ] of great economic and political significance . . . Congress must clearly authorize the agency to do so"). Kavanaugh has noted that Gorsuch's view would preclude the approach that Kavanaugh had previously articulated, of allowing Congress to delegate authority to an agency "to decide [a] major policy question" if Congress does so "expressly and specifically." *Paul*, 140 S Ct at *1.

[285] For a discussion of Chief Justice Roberts's minimalism in this vein, see generally Jamal Greene, *Maximinimalism*, 38 Cardozo L Rev 623 (2016).

[286] See Metzger, 131 Harv L Rev at 36, 47–48 (cited in note 11).

[287] These numbers come from examining court of appeals and district court cases in the Westlaw citing decisions database that cited *Kisor* between June 26, 2019 to October 26, 2019. A total of sixty-two cases cited *Kisor*, but only thirty directly considered whether to apply *Auer* deference.

[288] See Cynthia Barmore, *Auer in Action: Deference After Talk America*, 76 Ohio St L J 813, 825–27 (2015) (studying deference rates in the court of appeals between 2011 to 2014 and finding deference rates fell from 82 percent in 2011–12 to 71 percent in 2013–14); Richard J. Pierce, Jr. and Joshua Weiss, *An Empirical Study of Judicial Review of Agency Interpretations of Agency Rules*, 63 Admin L Rev 515, 519–20 (2011) (finding that across 219 cases between 1999 and 2007, district and appellate courts granted *Auer* deference at a 76 percent rate); William Yeatman, Note, *An Empirical Defense of Auer Step Zero*, 106 Geo L J 515, 547 (2018) (finding

and the constitutionality of administrative adjudication have sparked a slew of challenges to well-established features of the administrative state.[289] And, if widespread, statutory narrowing of delegated authority in response to background delegation concerns could lead to a significant pullback in agency authority. Hence, over time both the radical and incrementalist approaches may yield substantial change to existing administrative law and a significant pullback in administrative governance.

A final important factor determining the shape of administrative law going forward is what happens in the federal appellate courts. That is the level where most administrative law decisions are issued, and where the ultimate impact of the Court's interventions will be determined. *Chevron* is the leading example; more than the decision itself, it was subsequent actions by lower courts and Justice Scalia that made *Chevron* canonical.[290] Similarly, it will be how the lower courts apply *Kisor*—whether they continue to treat it as significantly narrowing but preserving *Auer*, or instead as essentially doing away with *Auer* deference or only tweaking *Auer* at the margins—that will establish *Kisor*'s impact on administrative law in practice. The same is true of *Department of Commerce*'s emphasis on weaker arbitrary and capriciousness review of agency decision making. As a result, the Trump administration's efforts to stock the federal courts with anti-administrativist judges may well prove more important than Supreme Court doctrine in transforming the shape of administrative law.

B. CONSTRAINING THE ADMINISTRATIVE STATE

It is also worth highlighting a central feature that, despite their differences, the radical and incrementalist approaches share: Both

---

that the government prevailed at an overall rate of 74 percent in cases when the court invoked *Auer* in the period 1993 to 2013, but only at a 71 percent rate after 2006).

[289] See, for example, *Seila Law LLC v Consumer Protection Bureau*, 2019 WL 5281290 at *1 (US Oct 18, 2019) (asking the parties to address the severability of the CFPB from Dodd-Frank should it be found unconstitutional); *Arthrex, Inc. v Smith & Nephew, Inc.*, 2019 WL 5616010, *1 (Fed Cir 2019) (holding that Administrative Patent Judges were improperly appointed principal officers); *Collins v Mnuchin*, 938 F3d 553, 563 (5th Cir 2019) (en banc) (holding that the FHFA "for cause" removal protection was unconstitutional); *Cochran v SEC*, 2019 WL 1359252, at *1 (ND Tex 2019) (up on appeal before the 5th Circuit) (challenging the constitutionality of the SEC's ALJ's removal protection. The 5th Circuit issued a preliminary injunction on the administrative proceedings until the case is resolved).

[290] See Gary Lawson and Stephen Kam, *Making Law out of Nothing at All: The Origins of the Chevron Doctrine*, 65 Admin L Rev 1, 33–73 (2013); Thomas W. Merrill, *The Story of Chevron: The Making of an Accidental Landmark*, in Peter L. Strauss, ed, *Administrative Law Stories* 399 (Foundation, 2006).

involve an assertion of greater judicial control over the administrative state and justify that greater role for courts on concerns about the dangers of expanding administrative power. Indeed, skepticism about administrative government may well be the consistent driver animating Roberts Court administrative law, albeit given full sway under Justice Gorsuch's radicalism and tamped down under Justice Kagan's incrementalism.

A striking characteristic of many Roberts Court administrative law opinions is their sharp rhetorical attack on the administrative state and bureaucracy. Chief Justice Roberts deserves the top award for the most pointed prose in this regard. His reference in *Free Enterprise* to a "vast and varied federal bureaucracy" that "wields vast power and touches almost every aspect of daily life" is a prime example, and his description in *City of Arlington v FCC* of "hundreds of federal agencies poking into every nook and cranny of daily life" is equally evocative.[291] Several other Justices have made disparaging remarks about the bureaucracy as well, often quoting Roberts's language in *Free Enterprise*. Justice Gorsuch in particular repeatedly positions judges as the protectors of "the unpopular and vulnerable" against "bureaucrats"[292] and "a bureaucrat's caprice."[293] He echoed these sentiments to some extent in *Kisor*, invoking the administrative state's "explosive growth," and "self-interested" bureaucrats with shifting whims."[294] But the 2018 Term decisions were relatively tame and balanced on the rhetorical front, with Chief Justice Roberts in particular holding his fire. Perhaps the attacks on the "deep state" that currently dominate the political arena convinced the Justices that similar bureaucracy bashing by the Court would be inappropriate.[295]

Instead, what surfaced clearly in the 2018 Term opinions was a more principled debate over the relevance of bureaucratic expertise. As noted above, both Justice Kagan in *Kisor* and Justice Breyer in *Department of Commerce* portrayed expertise as a central benefit of administrative government and one that administrative law doctrine

---

[291] *Free Enterprise Fund*, 561 US at 499; *City of Arlington*, 569 US at 315.

[292] *Oil States*, 138 S Ct at 1381 (Gorsuch, J, dissenting).

[293] *Biestek v Berryhill*, 139 S Ct 1148, 1163 (2019) (Gorsuch, J, dissenting).

[294] *Kisor*, 139 S Ct at 2432, 2442, 2446 (Gorsuch, J, dissenting).

[295] For a description of that political battle, which has become even more prominent in the impeachment inquiry, see Peter Baker et al, *Trump's War on the "Deep State" Turns Against Him*, NY Times (Oct 23, 2019), at https://www.nytimes.com/2019/10/23/us/politics/trump-deep-state-impeachment.html.

should be tailored to foster. Thus, Kagan precluded *Auer* deference from applying to administrative interpretations of regulations that did not "in some way implicate its substantive expertise" while Breyer relied heavily on the contrary and documented views of agency experts in concluding that Ross's decision was arbitrary and capricious.[296] By contrast, Justice Gorsuch elevated judicial expertise over that of bureaucrats, arguing that it was ultimately for courts to weigh "the expert agency's views" against "competing expert and other evidence supplied in an adversarial setting."[297] And Chief Justice Roberts insisted on the primacy of an agency's political officials over its experts, emphasizing that agency decisions are legitimately driven by political priorities. This is a point Roberts has made before, most notably arguing in *Free Enterprise* that "[o]ne can have a government that functions without being ruled by functionaries, and a government that benefits from expertise without being ruled by experts."[298] Justice Thomas also has voiced skepticism of arguments for deference based on administrative expertise, identifying them as misplaced and historically rooted in the progressives' "belief that bureaucrats might more effectively govern the country than the American people."[299]

Yet these disagreements over bureaucratic expertise should not obscure the similarities in these accounts. All the Justices ended up supporting greater judicial scrutiny of administrative decision making in some form, whether by restricted deference to agency interpretations, heightened scrutiny of agency policy determinations, or both. As significant, they did so invoking the need to guard against the danger of excessive administrative power. Even Justice Kagan in *Kisor* argued "that administrative law doctrines must take account of the far-reaching influence of agencies and the opportunities such power carries for abuse."[300] Granted, what the Justices view as the danger posed by expanded administrative government varies in important ways. As I have previously argued, at times Justices stress the danger of aggrandized administrative power threatening individual liberty, and at others the fear is that administrative power is politically

---

[296] *Kisor*, 139 S Ct at 2417 (Kagan, J) (plurality); *Department of Commerce*, 139 S Ct at 2587–93 (Breyer, J, concurring and dissenting in part).

[297] *Kisor*, 139 S Ct at 2442–43 (Gorsuch, J, concurring in the judgment).

[298] *Free Enterprise Fund*, 561 US at 499.

[299] *Perez*, 135 S Ct at 1223 n 6 (Thomas, J, concurring).

[300] *Kisor*, 139 S Ct at 2423 (Kagan, J) (plurality).

unaccountable.[301] In *Department of Commerce* Justice Breyer suggested a different account, implying that the real danger was too much political control of administrative power,[302] while the Chief Justice focused on the traditional concern that exercise of administrative power must be reasoned and not arbitrary.[303] And in *Kisor* and *Gundy*, Justice Gorsuch repeatedly portrayed administrative power as biased as well as aggrandized, worsening the threat to individual liberty.[304] Despite these differences, the consistent theme is of the potential dangers of administrative government.

Notably lacking from the 2018 Term decisions, and from Roberts Court administrative law generally, is a robust defense of the administrative state. The contribution that bureaucratic expertise makes to better decision making and effective government is a central benefit of administrative agencies.[305] But administrative agencies serve other critical functions too. Bureaucracy works to constrain as well as empower government, through close supervision and enforcement of legal controls on government actors. Administrative government is also essential for ensuring political accountability; it is agencies implementing statutes through regulations and enforcement that put democratically adopted policy into operation.[306] And administrative agencies are equally important to securing individual liberty, by protecting individuals against abuses of private power and ensuring access to the basic goods (safe food, a clean environment, protection against private exploitation, and so on) needed for a full and free life. The D.C. Circuit underscored this point recently in its en banc majority opinion in *PHH Corporation v CFPB*. There, in rejecting the claim that a single-headed agency with removal protection posed a greater threat to individual liberty than a multimember commission, Judge Pillard emphasized the liberty benefits of financial regulation:

---

[301] Metzger, 131 Harv L Rev at 36–38 (cited in note 11).

[302] *Department of Commerce*, 139 S Ct at 2589–90, 2592–93, 2595 (Breyer, J, concurring in part and dissenting in part).

[303] Id at 2575–76.

[304] *Kisor*, 139 S Ct at 2425, 2432, 2439, 2446–47 (Gorsuch, J, concurring in the judgment); *Gundy*, 139 S Ct at 2131 (Gorsuch, J, dissenting).

[305] It is also an administrative feature under increased threat. See Brad Plumer and Coal Davenport, *Science Under Attack: How Trump Is Sidelining Researchers and Their Work*, NY Times (Dec 28, 2019), at https://www.nytimes.com/2019/12/28/climate/trump-administration-war-on-science.html.

[306] Metzger, 131 Harv L Rev at 77–87 (cited in note 11).

> It remains unexplained why we would assess the challenged removal restriction with reference to the liberty of financial providers, and not more broadly to the liberty of individuals and families who are their customers.... Congress understood that markets' contribution to human liberty derives from freedom of contract, and that such freedom depends on market participants' access to accurate information, and on clear and reliably enforced rules against fraud and coercion.[307]

For that matter, financial regulation also advances liberty interests of regulated parties, for example by guarding against abusive tactics that can wreak financial havoc or destroy consumer trust in an industry.

What would a fuller defense of administrative government have looked like in the 2018 Term administrative law decisions? In *Department of Commerce*, more emphasis could have been put on how the Census Bureau's actions represented an internal bureaucratic effort to reinforce democracy and the rule of law. Policy setting by top political appointees is certainly an important form of political accountability, as Chief Justice Roberts insisted. But there is surely also a political accountability benefit to resisting actions by political leaders that threaten the basic representative structure of our political system, as well as an important rule-of-law value in ensuring that political leaders do not abuse government power for partisan gain. In *Kisor*, it could have meant more of an argument for interpretive deference precisely because such deference allows agencies to interpret ambiguous regulations in ways that they believe will best advance their regulatory goals. Although for Gorsuch this amounts to self-serving and liberty-threatening bias, that assumes that public agencies are no different than private parties. A more robust defense of administrative government would reject that equation, and instead emphasize how effective implementation of statutes and regulations can be liberty enhancing and in the public interest. The same liberty-enhancing argument could have been developed in defense of broad delegations in *Gundy*; such delegations can enhance liberty by ensuring that government is able to respond quickly and effectively to new private abuses of power as they arise. In fairness, Justice Breyer's and Kagan's opinions hinted at these arguments, with Breyer mentioning the importance of an accurate census to democracy and

---

[307] *PHH Corp. v Consumer Financial Protection Bureau*, 881 F3d 75, 106 (DC Cir 2018) (en banc); see also id at 105–06 (arguing in addition that if "a removal restriction leaves the President adequate control of the executive branch's functions," courts do not undertake a separate inquiry into the restriction's impact on liberty).

Kagan underscoring agencies' knowledge and value to Congress.[308] But for the most part they emphasized neutral-sounding administrative expertise and did not develop a broader account of how the administrative state reinforces the constitutional order.

Failing to note these potential benefits leads to a one-sided portrayal of the administrative state as inherently a threat to democracy, rule of law, and liberty. And this one-sidedness in turn suggests that the ultimate goal of Roberts Court administrative law may be to pull back on government on ideological and political grounds, rather than because doing so advances constitutional values or some other principled basis. That perception should be a concern even for conservative Justices who are deeply skeptical of administrative government. As important, a more balanced account of agencies' strengths and weaknesses is needed for the Roberts Court to develop a coherent approach to administrative law. Absent a more sophisticated and nuanced understanding of administrative government, the Roberts Court's administrative law decisions are unlikely to rise above the level of ad hoc and occasionally inconsistent interventions.

---

[308] *Department of Commerce*, 139 S Ct at 2584–85, 2595 (Breyer, J, concurring in part and dissenting in part); *Kisor*, 139 S Ct at 2413 (Kagan, J) (plurality); *Gundy*, 139 S Ct at 2130 (Kagan, J) (plurality).

PAUL BUTLER

MISSISSIPPI GODDAMN: FLOWERS v MISSISSIPPI'S CHEAP RACIAL JUSTICE

> Alabama's gotten me so upset
> Tennessee made me lose my rest
> And everybody knows about *Mississippi Goddamn*.
> (Nina Simone, *Mississippi Goddamn*)

Flowers v Mississippi is a Supreme Court case about a man who was tried six times for the same crimes.[1] The trials took place over a span of twenty-one years. In four of the trials, there was a conviction, but appellate courts reversed because of prosecutorial misconduct. In the other two trials, the jury was unable to reach a unanimous verdict, and the judge declared a mistrial.

Curtis Flowers was charged with murdering four people—Robert Golden, Carmen Rigby, Bertha Tardy, and Derrick Stewart—in a small town in Mississippi. Mr. Flowers is African American. Doug Evans, the district attorney who was the lead prosecutor in all six trials, is white. Winona, Mississippi, where the killings occurred, is roughly 53 percent black and 46 percent white.

Paul Butler is Albert Brick Professor of Law, Georgetown University Law Center.

AUTHOR'S NOTE: I am grateful to Justin Driver for superb editing and thoughtful comments that significantly advanced this piece. Much appreciation for helpful comments to Michael Dreeben, Thomas Frampton, Sheri Lynn Johnson, Vida Johnson, Justin Murray, Abbe Smith, Gerry Spann, and Rod Wilkins. I also thank the participants in a Georgetown University Law Center faculty workshop. Imani Gunn and Jasdeep Kaur provided exemplary research assistance.

[1] *Flowers v Mississippi*, No 17-9572, slip op at 5 (US June 21, 2019). All of the facts in this introduction are taken from the Supreme Court's decision in this case.

© 2020 by The University of Chicago. All rights reserved.
978-0-226-70856-0/2020/2019-0002$10.00

The issue in *Flowers* was whether, in Mr. Flowers's sixth trial, the prosecutor improperly struck African American potential jurors in violation of *Batson v Kentucky*. In criminal trials each side has a limited number of peremptory strikes by which it can remove prospective jurors. Traditionally, peremptory strikes could be exercised "for any reason or no reason at all," but *Batson* and its progeny prohibit race- and gender-based strikes.[2] In Mr. Flowers's sixth trial, the state had exercised peremptory strikes against five of the six black prospective jurors. In the six trials combined, the prosecution employed its peremptory challenges to strike forty-one of forty-two African American prospective jurors.

In the sixth trial Mr. Flowers was convicted and sentenced to death. In a 7–2 decision, the Supreme Court reversed the conviction. Justice Brett Kavanaugh wrote the majority opinion, which found that the trial judge erred when he ruled that the prosecution's strike of one African American prospective juror, Carolyn Wright, was not "motivated in substantial part by discriminatory intent."[3]

Justice Clarence Thomas, joined for the most part by Justice Neil Gorsuch, dissented. Thomas wrote that Ms. Wright "would have been stricken by any competent attorney."[4] In a part of the opinion not joined by Gorsuch, Thomas wrote, "[*Batson*] was suspect when it was announced, and I am even less confident of it today."[5] Thomas believes that African American defendants would be advantaged by the ability to strike white prospective jurors because "the racial composition of a jury matters because racial biases, sympathies, and prejudices still exist. This is not a matter of 'assumptions' as *Batson* said. It is a matter of reality."[6]

Flowers v Mississippi raises complex questions about what the law can and should do to remedy race discrimination, what should happen when the constitutional rights of jurors are in tension with the constitutional rights of accused persons, and how far the United States has progressed in eradicating white supremacy from the criminal legal process.

---

[2] *Hernandez v New York*, 500 US 352, 374 (1991) (O'Connor, J, concurring).

[3] *Flowers*, slip op at 3.

[4] Id at 3 (Thomas, J, concurring).

[5] Id at 33.

[6] Id at 41.

In contrast, the six trials of Curtis Flowers were painfully simple. Here are the most essential facts.

In the first trial, with an all-white jury, Mr. Flowers was convicted.

In the second trial, with a jury of eleven whites and one black, Mr. Flowers was convicted.

In the third trial, which also had a jury of eleven whites and one black, Mr. Flowers was convicted.

In the fourth trial, with a jury of seven whites and five blacks, a mistrial was declared, because the jurors could not agree on a verdict.

In the fifth trial, with a jury of nine whites and three blacks, another mistrial was declared, because the jury was unable to reach a verdict.

In the six trial, with a jury of eleven whites and one black, Mr. Flowers was convicted.

The race of the jurors thus determined the outcome of each trial. If there was an all-white jury or a jury with only one African American, there was a conviction. In juries that had three or more African Americans, there was a mistrial, because the jurors could not arrive at a unanimous decision.

You would not learn this most important fact from a casual read of the majority opinion. Kavanaugh extolled the virtues of colorblindness in a case where color meant everything. The majority opinion is an interracial group fantasy, joined by all the Court's moderates and all but two of its conservatives.[7]

One might have expected that the four moderate Justices knew better. Dissenting in *Utah v Strieff*, Justice Sotomayor wrote the most powerful racial critique of the U.S. criminal legal process ever to appear in the Supreme Court Reporter.[8] Citing Michelle Alexander's *The New Jim Crow* and works by James Baldwin and Ta-Nehisi Coates, Sotomayor wrote that "people of color are disproportionate victims" of police abuse, and that "[u]ntil their voices matter too, our justice system will continue to be anything but."[9] Last Term, commenting on the denial of a cert, Sotomayor stated, "racial bias [by jurors] is a familiar and recurring evil . . . racism can and does seep in the jury system."[10]

---

[7] David A. Strauss, *The Myth of Colorblindness*, 1986 Supreme Court Review 99 (1986).

[8] *Utah v Strieff*, 136 S Ct 2056 (2016) (Sotomayor, J, dissenting).

[9] Id at 12.

[10] *Tharpe v Warden*, No 14-12464, slip op (11th Cir 2018), cert denied, *Tharpe v Ford*, No 18-6819, slip op at 4–5 (US Mar 18, 2019).

Yet in *Flowers*, only Justice Thomas was grounded in the "reality" that bias by white jurors can undermine a fair process for a black accused person.[11] On the constitutionality of race-consciousness, the liberal Justices and Clarence Thomas "switch sides."[12]

I want to defend a portion of Thomas's dissent, which has been widely ridiculed. I also want to question the contention that District Attorney Evans is a racist, based simply on his exercise of peremptory challenges against African Americans. My analysis stems, in part, from my own exercise of peremptory challenges when I was a prosecutor. There are cases in which it would come close to legal malpractice for either the prosecutor or the defense to ignore race. Nobody in *Flowers* can or does, not even Justice Kavanaugh in his fantasia about how race does not matter.

Mississippi has particularly vexing issues with regard to racial justice. Mississippi is where, in 1955, Emmet Till, after being falsely accused of flirting with a white woman, was kidnapped from his home by two white men, pistol-whipped, shot, and then dumped into the Tallahatchie River. After two trials and two acquittals, the accused men gave *Look* magazine a detailed story on how they had done the killing.[13] Mississippi is where, in 1963, NAACP leader Medgar Evers was assassinated by Byron De La Beckwith, a member of the White Citizens' Council.[14] Mississippi is where, in 1964, civil rights activists James Chaney, Andrew Goodman, and Michael Schwerner were abducted and murdered.[15] Mississippi is where, in 1970, the police opened fire on a group of Jackson State University students protesting segregation at a local bowling alley. Two students were killed, and twelve were injured.[16]

Mississippi's population is 40 percent African American, the highest of any state, but it has not elected a black person to a statewide

---

[11] *Flowers*, slip op at 41 (Thomas, J, concurring).

[12] Tania Tetlow, *Solving Batson*, 56 Wm & Mary L Rev 1859 (2015).

[13] Charles Payne, *I've Got the Light of Freedom: The Organizing Tradition and the Mississippi Freedom Struggle* 54 (California, 1995).

[14] Andrew Glass, *Medgar Evers Laid to Rest, June 19, 1963*, Politico (June 19, 2014), at https://www.politico.com/story/2014/06/medgar-evers-la-108023.

[15] John Dittmer, *Local People: The Struggle for Civil Rights in Mississippi* 247 (Illinois, 1994).

[16] Whitney Blair Wyckoff, *Jackson State: A Tragedy Widely Forgotten*, NPR (May 3, 2010), https://www.npr.org/templates/story/story.php?storyId=126426361.

office in 129 years.[17] Mississippi prisons are likely the worst in the country, and they are filled with African Americans.[18]

But the concerns about race and the criminal legal process that this article raises are national. Mississippi is only a particularly egregious example of a broader phenomenon. This was, I think, Nina Simone's meaning when, after noting substantial problems in Alabama and Tennessee, she wrote "Mississippi Goddamn."[19] *Flowers* can be understood to mean that, even by the usual standards of exercising peremptory strikes, an out-of-control district attorney in Winona, Mississippi, went several bridges too far. But this understanding of *Flowers* is troubling because it permits less egregious instances of racial mischief to go unchecked.

This essay proceeds in four parts. Part I describes the majority opinion. Part II contends that the Supreme Court's outcome in *Flowers* is correct based on precedent, but notes that the majority opinion reflects a conservative "color-blind" ideology that impedes racial justice. Part III rehabilitates, to a degree, Justice Thomas's widely critiqued dissenting opinion. Part IV situates *Flowers* as part of a post-race discourse that submerges and discounts the continuing significance of race.

I. Flowers for Flowers

In his 2019 Year End Report on the Federal Judiciary, Chief Justice John Roberts wrote,

> When judges render their judgments through written opinions that explain their reasoning, they advance public understanding of the law. Chief Justice Earl Warren illustrated the power of a judicial decision as a teaching tool in *Brown v. Board of Education*, the great school desegregation case. His unanimous opinion on the most pressing issue of the era was a mere 11 pages—short enough that newspapers could publish all or almost all of it and every citizen could understand the court's rationale.[20]

---

[17] John A. Tures and Seth Golden, *African Americans Haven't Won Office in Mississippi in 129 Years*, Salon (June 21, 2019), https://www.salon.com/2019/06/21/no-african-american-has-won-office-in-mississippi-in-129-years_partner/.

[18] Associated Press, *Legal Group Seeks Federal Inquiry Into Mississippi Prisons*, NY Times (Jan 7, 2020), https://apnews.com/5425d96a098d68e7ea7365e1329ddf4d.

[19] Nina Simone, *Mississippi Goddamn* (Philips Records, 1964).

[20] Chief Justice's Year-End Reports on the Federal Judiciary, *2019 Year-End Report* (Supreme Court of the United States, 2019), https://www.supremecourt.gov/publicinfo/year-end/2019year-endreport.pdf.

In the report, Roberts called on his judicial colleagues "to continue their efforts to promote public confidence in the judiciary, both through their rulings and through civic outreach."

Justice Kavanaugh's majority opinion in *Flowers* exemplifies the civic education that Chief Justice Roberts advocated. At thirty-one pages, the opinion is significantly longer than *Brown*, but it is clear and well written. Kavanaugh describes how jury selection works, noting that "[o]ther than voting, serving on a jury is the most substantial opportunity that most citizens have to participate in the democratic process."[21]

For people concerned about discrimination in the criminal legal process, Kavanaugh's opinion serves "to promote public confidence in the judiciary," as Chief Justice Roberts's 2019 Year End Report recommended all federal judges attempt to do in their opinions. *Flowers* waxes eloquently on the importance of "a criminal trial free of racial discrimination in the jury selection process."[22] There is a lengthy description of the Court's holding in *Batson v Kentucky*, a case decided in 1986 in which the court ruled that prosecutors who use peremptory challenges to strike prospective jurors on the basis of race violate the right of the jurors, under the Fourteenth Amendment's Equal Protection Clause.[23]

Kavanaugh makes a bold and far-reaching claim about *Batson*'s transformation of the American legal system. He writes,

> *Batson* ended the widespread practice in which prosecutors could (and often would) routinely strike all black prospective jurors in cases involving black defendants. . . . *Batson* immediately revolutionized the jury selection process that takes place every day in federal and state criminal courtrooms throughout the United States.[24]

Kavanaugh's high appraisal of *Batson*'s import includes the observation: "By taking steps to eradicate racial discrimination from the jury selection process, *Batson* sought to protect the rights of defendant and jurors, and to enhance public confidence in the fairness of the criminal justice system."[25] Lest there be any doubt about the Court's

---

[21] *Flowers v Mississippi*, No 17-9572, slip op at 7 (US June 21, 2019).

[22] Id at 15.

[23] *Batson v Kentucky*, 476 US 79 (1986).

[24] *Flowers*, slip op at 15–16.

[25] Id.

vigilance in eradicating discrimination in the jury selection process, Kavanaugh states: "In the decades since *Batson*, this Court's cases have vigorously enforced and reinforced the decision, and guarded against any backsliding."[26]

In the way that some historians have described *Brown* as having a purpose larger than simply adjudicating a dispute about what public school Linda Brown was allowed to attend, *Flowers* also is expressive.[27] The Court intended to deliver a loud message that it will not tolerate racism in the criminal legal process. Though many people would probably not think of criminal justice reform as "the most pressing issue of the era," as Chief Justice Roberts described school desegregation in 1954, concerns about racism in the criminal legal process have become prominent in national discourse.[28] In determining whether the Mississippi prosecutor violated *Batson*, *Flowers* is an easy case, and Kavanaugh's opinion treats it as such.

At Mr. Flowers's sixth trial, twenty-six people—six black and twenty white—were presented as potential jurors. The state exercised a total of six peremptory strikes, and used five of the six against black prospective jurors, leaving one black juror to be seated and eleven whites. The trial court concluded that the state had offered race-neutral reasons for each of the five strikes against five black prospective jurors. Mr. Flowers was convicted, and sentenced to death.[29]

On appeal, Flowers argued that the state violated *Batson* in exercising peremptory strikes against black prospective jurors. In a 5–4 decision, the Mississippi Supreme Court affirmed the conviction, agreeing with the trial court that the state's race-neutral reasons were not pretextual.[30]

---

[26] Id at 16.

[27] Mary L. Dudziak, *Brown as a Cold War Case*, 91 J Am Hist 32 (June 2004).

[28] See Katie Park and Jamilies Larty, *2020: The Democrats on Criminal Justice*, Marshall Project (Jan 13, 2020), https://www.themarshallproject.org/2019/10/10/2020-the-democrats-on-criminal-justice; Timothy Williams and Thomas Kaplan, *The Criminal Justice Debate Has Changed Drastically. Here's Why*, NY Times (Aug 20, 2019), https://www.nytimes.com/2019/08/20/us/politics/criminal-justice-reform-sanders-warren.html; Frank Leon Roberts, *How Black Lives Matter Changed the Way Americans Fight for Freedom*, ACLU (July 13, 2018), https://www.aclu.org/blog/racial-justice/race-and-criminal-justice/how-black-lives-matter-changed-way-americans-fight; Tom Jacobs, *Racism Declined During the Black Lives Matter Campaign*, Pacific Standard (April 3, 2018), https://psmag.com/social-justice/racism-declined-during-the-black-lives-matter-campaign.

[29] *Flowers*, slip op at 6–7.

[30] Id at 7 (citing *Flowers v State*, 158 So3d 1009, 1058 (2014)).

The Supreme Court granted certiorari, vacated, and remanded in light of the decision in *Foster v Chatman*.[31] On remand, the Mississippi Supreme Court, by a 5–4 decision, again upheld Flowers's conviction. The Supreme Court again granted certiorari on the *Batson* question, and reversed.

The Court found four facts, taken together, to require reversal: (1) in the six trials combined, the state employed its peremptory challenges to strike forty-one of forty-two black prospective jurors that could have been struck; (2) in the sixth trial, the state exercised peremptory strikes against five of the six black prospective jurors; (3) at the sixth trial, in an apparent effort to find pretextual reasons to strike black prospective jurors, the state engaged in dramatically disparate questioning of black and white prospective jurors; and (4) the state then struck at least one black prospective juror, Carolyn Wright, who was similarly situated to white prospective jurors who were not struck by the state.[32] All these relevant facts and circumstances established "that the trial court committed clear error in concluding that the State's peremptory strike of black prospective juror Carolyn Wright was not 'motivated in substantial part by discriminatory intent.'"[33]

Early in the opinion, Kavanaugh noted that the Court was not holding that "any one of those four facts alone would require reversal."[34] Indeed, he took pains to state that *Flowers* does not create any new antidiscrimination doctrine, or extend *Batson* in any way. Also early in the opinion, Kavanaugh noted, "We break no new legal ground. We simply enforce and reinforce *Batson* by applying it to the extraordinary facts of this case."[35]

In the opinion's concluding paragraphs, Kavanaugh returned to his early exhortations on how modest the Court's holding is. In fact, he repeated it virtually verbatim, stating, "To reiterate, we need not and do not decide that any one of those four facts alone would require reversal,"[36] and "we break no new legal ground. We simply enforce

---

[31] *Foster v Chatman*, 136 S Ct 1737 (2016) (holding that the defendant had established a *Batson* violation).

[32] *Flowers*, slip op at 2–3.

[33] Id at 3.

[34] Id.

[35] Id.

[36] *Flowers*, slip op at 21.

and reinforce *Batson* by applying it to the extraordinary facts of this case."³⁷ As the old joke goes, "it sounded so nice, he had to say it twice."

Justice Samuel Alito's concurrence underscores this point. The reason that Alito wrote separately is preemptive: he sought to limit *Flowers*'s future import. Alito's opinion opened: "As the Court takes pains to note, this is a highly unusual case. Indeed, it is likely one of a kind."³⁸ The next four paragraphs observe that Mr. Flowers was tried six different times by the same prosecutor in a small town and that "many of those trials were marred by racial discrimination in the selection of jurors and prosecutorial misconduct."³⁹ Alito then stated that "[w]ere it not for the unique combinations of circumstances present here," he would have "no trouble" finding that *Batson* had not been violated.⁴⁰

The message that the Kavanaugh and Alito opinions sent to anyone hoping that *Flowers* might signal a more progressive race or criminal jurisprudence from the Roberts Court is, "Move on. There is nothing to see here."

Justice Clarence Thomas's dissent, on the other hand, contained plenty to see. It is longer than Kavanaugh's majority opinion and Alito's concurrence combined. Thomas signaled his interest at oral argument, when he asked his first question in three years.⁴¹ His writing in this case is substantial enough to merit its own analysis, which appears in Part III of this essay.

II. STILL COLOR-BLIND AFTER ALL THESE YEARS

Flowers was an easy case, and Justice Kavanaugh properly applied the *Batson* framework. The Roberts Court got the law right, and in equal protection cases with minority appellants, that is a significant, and all too rare, achievement. District Attorney Doug Evans was the rare public official whose conduct was so blatant that it met

---

³⁷ Id at 31.

³⁸ Id at 1 (Alito, J, concurring).

³⁹ Id.

⁴⁰ *Flowers*, slip op at 2 (Alito, J, concurring).

⁴¹ Robert Barnes, *Supreme Court Examination of Jury Discrimination Prompts Rare Question from Clarence Thomas*, Wash Post (Mar 20, 2019), https://www.washingtonpost.com/politics/courts_law/in-supreme-court-case-about-jury-discrimination-a-surprise-from-thomas/2019/03/20/d9c67b80-4b23-11e9-93d0-64dbcf38ba41_story.html.

the extraordinarily high standards for proof of intentional discrimination of conservatives like Roberts and Alito.[42] The evidence that the prosecutor was exercising race-based peremptory challenges was overwhelming.

Nevertheless, three substantial problems plague the majority opinion. First, as a practical matter, the decision will have virtually no impact, other than as an abstract expression of the Court's commitment to racial justice. Second, if Kavanaugh actually believes, as he writes, that "equal justice under law requires a criminal trial free of racial discrimination in the jury selection process," he missed a key opportunity to strengthen *Batson*, which is widely regarded as ineffectual.[43] Third, ironically in an opinion that all but called a prosecutor a racist, the Court was willfully blind about the role of race in the criminal legal process. *Flowers* maps on to conservative jurisprudence about equal protection that requires official color-blindness. This mandate is not in the best interests of racial minorities. As Dorothy Roberts wrote, "By appealing to formal racial equality, the [Supreme Court] Justices issue rulings that appear to be neutral and fair when they actually not only ignore the material harms inflicted by systems that are structured by white supremacy, but also shield those systems from efforts to dismantle them."[44]

I am not the only scholar who has been critical of *Flowers* and *Batson* from a racial justice perspective. Thomas Ward Frampton cited *Flowers* as an example of "the whiggish tone that dominates the Court's recent pronouncements on race and the jury."[45] Dorothy Roberts observed, "By misidentifying the relationship between jury selection and white supremacy, the Court in *Flowers* went off track. Justice Kavanaugh's opinion did nothing to invalidate all-white juries as violations of the Fourteenth Amendment's antislavery ideals. To the contrary, Justice Kavanaugh made it clear that the Court's aim was the opposite—to maintain the current jury selection system."[46] Writing about *Batson* and its progeny, Tania Tetlow stated, "The

---

[42] Contrast *Flowers v Mississippi*, No 17-9572, slip op (US June 21, 2019), with *Parents Involved in Community Schools v Seattle School District No. 1*, 551 US 701 (2007).

[43] *Flowers*, slip op at 15.

[44] Dorothy E. Roberts, *Supreme Court, 2018 Term—Foreword: Abolition Constitutionalism*, 133 Harv L Rev 1, 79 (2019).

[45] Thomas Ward Frampton, *What Justice Thomas Gets Rights About Batson*, 72 Stan L Rev Online 1, 6 (2019).

[46] Roberts, 133 Harv L Rev at 98 (cited in note 44).

Court also relied on the rather circular logic that the idea that race and gender matter to jury deliberations is 'the very stereotype the law condemns.' The court does not want race or gender to matter, so it pretends that they do not."[47]

A. RACIAL JUSTICE RHETORIC WITHOUT RACIAL JUSTICE

The *Flowers* Court's holding is so limited, even on its own terms, that it will not help other victims of discrimination. If not a one-off, a *Bush v Gore* for Curtis Flowers, it suggests that relief is going to be granted in only the most overt, highly unusual circumstances.[48] In fact, a reasonable inference from Justice Alito's concurrence is that the Court might have decided the case differently if prosecutors had used the peremptory challenges in exactly the same way but Mr. Flowers had "only" been tried four or five times rather than six, or if different prosecutors had tried the six cases rather than one prosecutor, or if the trial occurred in a big city rather than a small town.[49] It seems safe to predict that judges will invoke *Flowers* far more frequently to reject *Batson* challenges than to grant those challenges.

Thus the Court obtains the public relations/"civic education" benefit of demonstrating how it cracked down on a "racist" prosecutor, but with virtually no impact on the millions of black and brown people who are subject to the criminal legal process. In dissent, Justice Thomas observed that *Flowers* can be viewed primarily as an effort to "boost [the Court's] self-esteem."[50] He is right. The Supreme Court gets to look good on racial justice while doing next to nothing.

This effect is exemplified by *Slate*'s coverage of the case, a few days after it was decided. The headline read, "Brett Kavanaugh's Latest Opinion Protects Black Defendants Against Racist Prosecutors."[51] As

---

[47] Tetlow, 56 Wm & Mary L Rev at 1877 (cited in note 12) (quoting *Powers v Ohio*, 499 US 400, 410 (1995)).

[48] *Bush v Gore*, 531 US 98, 109 (2000) ("Our consideration is limited to the present circumstances, for the problem of equal protection in election processes generally presents many complexities."); *Snyder v Louisiana*, 552 US 472 (2008).

[49] See *Flowers*, slip op at 1–2 (Alito, J, concurring).

[50] *Flowers*, slip op at 42 (Thomas, J, dissenting).

[51] Mark Joseph Stern, *Brett Kavanaugh's Latest Opinion Protects Black Defendants Against Racist Prosecutors*, Slate (June 21, 2019), https://slate.com/news-and-politics/2019/06/brett-kavanaugh-clarence-thomas-racist-juries-mississippi.html.

rehearsed above, the Court's decision, on its own terms, did not protect "black defendants" but rather reversed the conviction of one black man who had been tried six times, in the face of overwhelming evidence that the prosecutor had violated *Batson*. Kavanaugh did not even "protect" Mr. Flowers from a "racist" prosecutor because, as Justice Thomas noted in his dissenting opinion, "If [the Kavanaugh] opinion today has a redeeming quality, it is this: The State is perfectly free to convict Curtis Flowers again."[52]

The *Slate* article states, "To Kavanaugh's credit, his opinion . . . bolsters constitutional safeguards against prosecutorial attempts to purge minorities from juries."[53] Justice Kavanaugh himself would have to disagree that his opinion "bolsters constitutional safeguards" because of his twice-stated disclaimer that "we break no new legal ground."

B. MISSED OPPORTUNITY

Perhaps the Court's failure to break new legal ground would be justified if *Batson* actually worked. But not only has the case been remarkably ineffective at protecting African American jurors from discrimination, virtually everyone in the criminal justice community agrees with this assessment. This disjuncture raises questions about what Kavanaugh's actual project is in *Flowers*, beyond the aforementioned "public confidence in the judiciary" one.

Recall Kavanaugh's bold claims about the impact of *Batson*. He asserts it "ended the wide-spread practice in which prosecutors could (and often would) routinely strike all black prospective jurors in cases involving black defendants" and that it "immediately revolutionized the jury selection process."[54] This assertion is ludicrous. Kavanaugh cites no evidence to support these contentions because no evidence exists.[55] In fact, Justice Thomas's dissenting opinion provides

---

[52] *Flowers*, slip op at 42 (Thomas, J, dissenting). In fact, Mr. Flowers remains under indictment. He has been released on bail pending the state's decision about whether to re-try him a seventh time. Doug Evans decided, on his own volition, to recuse himself from a seventh trial. Mihir Zaveri, *White Prosecutor, Doug Evans, Asks to Recuse Himself From Curtis Flowers Case*, NY Times (Jan 7, 2020), https://www.nytimes.com/2020/01/07/us/doug-evans-curtis-flowers.html.

[53] Stern, *Brett Kavanaugh's Latest Opinion* (cited in note 51).

[54] *Flowers*, slip op at 16.

[55] Radley Balko, *There's Overwhelming Evidence that the Criminal-Justice System Is Racist. Here's the Proof*, Wash Post (June 24, 2019), https://www.washingtonpost.com/news

substantial evidence that prosecutors post-*Batson* have continued to discriminate against African American prospective jurors.[56] As I will explain in the next section, this discrimination is rational, and thus unlikely to be halted without strong sanctions against prosecutors who engage in it.

I believe Justice Kavanaugh must have known that he was, at minimum, overstating *Batson*'s significance for three distinct reasons. First, there is a glaring lack of support for these claims in the paragraph of the opinion where he makes them. It is as though Kavanaugh asked his law clerks to find support for his propositions about the effectiveness of *Batson*, and they came back with nothing. But the Court was not going to permit the grim reality to undercut the lofty rhetoric. I understand that Kavanaugh was trying to, and succeeded in, writing an opinion that would be joined by Justices ranging the ideological gamut from Alito to Sotomayor.[57] But that does not explain why he would make a claim that is demonstrably false, and not appreciate the significance of the lack of evidentiary support for the claim. By contrast, the next paragraph of the opinion, addressing how the Court's subsequent cases have "enforced and reinforced" *Batson*, contains nine citations.[58]

Second, it's a commonplace among lawyers, judges, and scholars that *Batson* is underenforced and easy to evade. At the time of his *opinion* in *Flowers*, Kavanaugh had been on the bench for thirteen years. Within legal circles, believing that *Batson* "immediately revolutionized" juries is like believing that *Brown* immediately revolutionized segregated schools.[59]

/opinions/wp/2018/09/18/theres-overwhelming-evidence-that-the-criminal-justice-system-is-racist-heres-the-proof/#section4 ("Though the Supreme Court made it illegal for prosecutors to exclude prospective jurors because of race in the 1986 case *Batson v Kentucky*, that ruling has largely gone unenforced. The *New Yorker* reported in 2015 that in the approximately 30 years since the ruling, courts have accepted the flimsiest excuses for striking black jurors and that prosecutors have in turn trained subordinates how to strike black jurors without a judicial rebuke.").

[56] *Flowers*, slip op at 41–42 (Thomas, J, dissenting).

[57] See Frank H. Easterbrook, *Ways of Criticizing the Court*, 95 Harv L Rev 802, 804–05 (1982) ("Moreover the Justices believe that a show of agreement is beneficial to the institution—witness the efforts to achieve unanimity in *Brown v. Board of Education* and *United States v. Nixon*—and collegial work and compromise are essential to the ability of the Justices to agree.").

[58] *Flowers*, slip op at 16.

[59] See Shari Seidman Diamond et al, *Realistic Responses to the Limitations of Batson v. Kentucky*, 7 Cornell J L & Pub Pol 77 (1997); David D. Hopper, *Batson v. Kentucky and the*

Third, Kavanaugh is not an ordinary jurist with merely a passing familiarity with *Batson*. As a law student, he wrote a thoughtful and sophisticated note on *Batson* that was published in the *Yale Law Journal*.[60] The note, published in 1989, three years after the Court had handed down the decision, focused on the problem of enforcing *Batson*. It opened with this quotation from Justice Marshall's concurring opinion in the case: "Any prosecutor can easily assert facially neutral reasons for striking a juror, and trial courts are ill-equipped to second-guess those reasons."[61]

In the note, Kavanaugh argued that when a defendant makes a prima facie case that a prosecutor has engaged in purposeful discrimination, the defendant has a constitutional right to hear and rebut the prosecutor's argument that he is not discriminating. Kavanaugh further argued that the judge should have the discretion to conduct the proceeding as "a full-scale evidentiary hearing in which the prosecutor is a witness, testifies to the reasons for his peremptories, and is subjected to cross-examination by the defense counsel."[62]

Thus it is quite plausible that Kavanaugh knows that *Batson* did not actually "end" race-based peremptory challenges or "immediately revolutionize" the jury-selection process. As I will discuss in Part III, I am skeptical that *Batson* can accomplish this goal. My more limited point here is, since the seven Justices in the majority evidently do not share my skepticism, it is revealing that they did not use *Flowers* as an opportunity to strengthen *Batson*, or otherwise reduce prosecutorial discrimination against prospective minority jurors. Were the Court so inclined, there is a cottage industry of legal scholarship exploring how that might be done.[63]

Prosecutorial Peremptory Challenge: Arbitrary and Capricious Equal Protection?, 74 Va L Rev 811 (1988).

[60] See Brett M. Kavanaugh, *Defense Presence and Participation: A Procedural Minimum for Batson v. Kentucky Hearings*, 99 Yale L J 187 (1989); Stern, *Brett Kavanaugh's Latest Opinion* (cited in note 51).

[61] Kavanaugh, 99 Yale L J at 187 (cited in note 60).

[62] Id at 189.

[63] Thomas Ward Frampton, *The Jim Crow Jury*, 71 Vand L Rev 1593 (2019); Tetlow, 56 Wm & Mary L Rev (cited in note 12); Nancy S. Marder, *Batson Revisited*, 97 Iowa L Rev 1585 (2012); Wendy Lynn Trugman, *The Representative Jury Standard: An Alternative to Batson v. Kentucky*, 23 Am Crim L Rev 403 (1985–86); William T. Pizzi, *Batson v Kentucky: Curing the Disease but Killing the Patient*, 1987 Supreme Court Review 97 (1987); Eric L. Muller, *Solving the Batson Paradox: Harmless Error, Jury Representation, and the Sixth Amendment*, 106 Yale L J 93 (1996).

C. WILLFUL COLOR-BLINDNESS

There is a perception, widely shared by conservative jurists, that color-blindness creates racial justice, and is required, in most cases, by the Fourteenth Amendment's Equal Protection Clause.[64] Many progressives, in contrast, argue that race-consciousness is a necessary element of any racial justice project.[65] The tension is evidenced in famous lines in opinions written by Justice Harry Blackmun and Chief Justice John Roberts. In *Regents of the University of California v Bakke*, in an opinion endorsing affirmative action in college admissions, Blackmun argued: "In order to get beyond racism, we must first take race into account. There is no other way."[66] In *Parents Involved in Community Schools v Seattle School District*, in an opinion striking down a school desegregation plan, Roberts contended: "The way to get beyond race is to get beyond race."[67]

Batson and *Flowers* are "get beyond race" cases disguised as progressive civil rights interventions. They endorse color-blindness as the route to "equal protection" and fairness for racial minorities. They perpetuate the illusion that pretending not to notice race resolves problems of racial subordination. As both history and present experience reveal, this strategy fails.

Indeed, the first time the concept of color-blindness appeared in a Supreme Court opinion, it was pitched as a way to preserve white supremacy. Dissenting in *Plessy v Ferguson*, Justice Harlan stated:

> The white race deems itself to be the dominant race in this country. And so it is, in prestige, in achievements, in education, in wealth, and in power. So, I doubt not, it will continue to be for all time, if it remains true to its great heritage, and holds fast to the principles of constitutional liberty. But in view of the constitution, in the eye of the law, there is in this country no superior, dominant, ruling class of citizens. There is no caste here. Our

---

[64] See Ian F. Haney Lopez, *Is the Post in Post-Racial the "Blind" in Colorblind?*, 32 Cardozo L Rev 807 (2011); R. Richard Banks, *Race-Based Suspect Selection and Colorblind Equal Protection Doctrine and Discourse*, 48 UCLA L Rev 1075 (2001); Andrew Kull, *The Color-Blind Constitution?*, 106 Harv L Rev 2027 (June 1993); *Parents Involved in Community Schools v Seattle School District No. 1*, 551 US 701 (2007).

[65] Kimberle Williams Crenshaw, *Race, Reform, and Retrenchment: Transformation and Legitimation in Antidiscrimination Law*, 101 Harv L Rev 1331 (May 1988); Reva B. Siegel, *Discrimination in the Eyes of the Law: How Color Blindness Discourse Disrupts and Rationalizes Social Stratification*, 88 Cal L Rev 77 (2000); Bryan K. Fair, *Foreword: Rethinking the Colorblindness Model*, 13 Natl Black L J 1 (1993).

[66] *Regents of the University of California v Bakke*, 438 US 265, 407 (1978).

[67] *Parents Involved*, 551 US at 748.

constitution is color-blind, and neither knows nor tolerates classes among citizens.[68]

Prior to *Batson*, the Supreme Court had recognized that a juror's racial identity might influence her work as a juror. In order to understand how the Court's jurisprudence evolved to a requirement of color-blindness, a deeper exploration is required into the vexing problem of exclusion of African Americans from jury service.

The Civil Rights Act of 1875 made it a criminal offense for state officials to bar individuals from jury service on account of their race. In 1880, in *Strauder v West Virginia*, the Supreme Court held that a West Virginia law that restricted jury service to whites violated the Fourteenth Amendment.[69] Significantly, *Strauder* acknowledged that white and black jurors might have different perspectives; one of the harms of the West Virginia law was that it excluded the "black" perspective, in a way that might disadvantage African American litigants. As the Court put it, "[i]t is well known that prejudices often exist against particular classes in the community, which sway the judgment of jurors, and which, therefore, operate in some cases to deny persons of those classes the full enjoyment of that protection which others enjoy."[70]

Although *Strauder* invalidated a statute that facially excluded black jurors, the Court also informed legislators that nothing in its opinion meant that "a State may not prescribe the qualifications of its jurors, and in so doing make discriminations. It may confine the selection to males, to freeholders, to citizens, to persons within certain ages, or to persons having educational qualifications."[71]

The lesson of *Strauder*, like the lessons of *Batson* and *Flowers*, was that discrimination against African American jurors should not be blatant. If bias can be disguised as a nonracial "qualification" or "race neutral" explanation it is permissible. In the *Batson* context, how lax the standard is for race neutral was demonstrated in *Hernandez v New York*, in which a Latinx man claimed that prosecutors had struck him because he is Hispanic. The Supreme Court accepted the prosecutor's response—Mr. Hernandez was struck not because he was Hispanic but because he spoke Spanish—as race neutral.[72]

---

[68] *Plessy v Ferguson*, 163 US 537, 559 (1896) (Harlan, J, dissenting).

[69] *Strauder v West Virginia*, 100 US 303 (1880).

[70] Id at 309.

[71] Id at 310.

[72] *Hernandez v New York*, 500 US 352 (1991).

In the aftermath of *Strauder*, jurisdictions routinely turned to more covert methods of discrimination, including peremptory challenges in individual courtrooms rather than wholesale legal barriers to their service. Since blacks typically were a minority of the population, often the number of peremptory strikes available to prosecutors exceeded the number of prospective black jurors, ensuring all-white juries.

Eighty-five years after *Strauder*, in 1965, the Court decided *Swain v Alabama*.[73] Mr. Swain, an African American defendant, had been sentenced to death. He presented evidence that no black juror had served on a jury in the county where he was tried in over a decade, and the prosecutor had struck all six qualified black jurors in that case. The Court held that under *Strauder*, Swain had not established unconstitutional discrimination, and that a defendant could not object to the state's use of peremptory strikes in an individual case. A prosecutor could permissibly strike a prospective juror for any reason, including the assumption that a black prospective juror would be favorable to a black defendant or unfavorable to the state because of race.

Like *Strauder*, *Swain* acknowledged the reality that a juror's race might be relevant to how she decides a case. Both *Strauder* and *Swain* focused on the defendant's rights, rather than the rights of the prospective juror. According to *Swain*, the peremptory "challenge is one of the most important of the rights secured to the accused."[74] Thus, "In the quest for an impartial and qualified jury, Negro and white, Protestant and Catholic, are alike subject to being challenged without cause."[75] The *Swain* Court did not think prospective jurors were denied equal protection by peremptory challenges because any potential juror was subject to the challenges "whether they be Negroes, Catholics, accountants or those with blue eyes."[76]

---

[73] *Swain v Alabama*, 380 US 202 (1965).

[74] Id at 219.

[75] Id at 221.

[76] Id at 212. The Court allowed that there might be a point at which a prosecutor's use of race-based peremptories might violate the Constitution: "[W]hen the prosecutor in a county, in case after case, is responsible for the removal of Negroes who have been selected as qualified jurors by the jury commissioners and who have survived challenges for cause, with the result that no Negroes ever serve on petit juries, the Fourteenth Amendment takes on added significance. . . . If the State has not seen fit to leave a single Negro on any jury in a criminal case, the presumption protecting the prosecutor may well be overcome." Id at 223–24. Justin Driver observed that, in the era between *Swain* and *Batson*, no court ever found a violation using this test. Driver also noted that "[c]ommentators repeatedly condemned

Twenty-one years later in *Batson*, the Court reversed *Swain*, holding that upon a defendant's showing of prima facie discrimination, the prosecution was required to prove race-neutral reasons for its peremptory strikes.

Batson established the following principles: (1) A defendant need not demonstrate a history of racially discriminatory strikes to make out a claim of race discrimination, and such requirement could impose an insurmountable burden. In the eyes of the Constitution, one racially discriminatory strike is one too many. (2) A prosecutor cannot strike a black juror based on an assumption or belief that that juror would favor a black defendant. (3) Discrimination against one defendant or juror on account of race is not remedied by discrimination against other defendants or jurors on account of race; the argument that race-based peremptories should be permissible because they are visited upon defendants and jurors of all races is not valid. (4) Race-based peremptories are not permissible because both prosecution and defense could employ them and balance things out. Black prospective jurors, where blacks typically make up a minority of the population, are often outnumbered by the amount of peremptory strikes available to the prosecutor.[77]

Batson focused on the constitutional rights of the prospective juror, rather than the defendant. In doing so, the Court not only rejected any contention that the race of a juror might be relevant to how she would decide a case, it suggested that it would be unconstitutional for a prosecutor to act on such an assumption. Justice Powell wrote, for the majority, "Just as the Equal Protection Clause forbids the States to exclude black persons from the venire on the assumption that blacks as a group are unqualified to serve as jurors, so it forbids the States to strike black veniremen on the assumption that they will be biased in a particular case simply because the defendant is black."[78]

Dissenting in *Batson*, Justice Rehnquist observed that race-based peremptory strikes may be "based upon seat-of-the-pants instincts, which are undoubtedly crudely stereotypical and may in many cases be hopelessly mistaken."[79] Rehnquist went on to acknowledge,

---

Swain's standard because they believed that it stemmed from a perhaps willful naiveté regarding the realities of Southern justice." Justin Driver, *The Constitutional Conservatism of the Warren Court*, 100 Cal L Rev 1101, 1132–34 (2012).

[77] *Batson*, 476 US at 79–82.

[78] Id at 97.

[79] Id at 138 (Rehnquist, J, dissenting).

> The use of group affiliations, such as age, race, or occupation, as a "proxy" for potential juror partiality, based on the assumption or belief that members of one group are more likely to favor defendants who belong to the same group, has long been accepted as a legitimate basis for the State's exercise of peremptory challenges.... [T]he use of such "proxies" by both the State and the defendant may be extremely useful in eliminating from the jury persons who might be biased in one way or another.[80]

The *Batson* majority opinion did not explain why the Court switched, in its earlier jurisprudence, from acknowledging the probative value of race to, in *Batson*, treating race as irrelevant. In *Powers v Ohio*, which held that white defendants have standing to object to strikes of African American jurors, the Court extended this analysis: "Race cannot be a proxy for determining juror bias or competence."[81] Similarly, in *Edmonson v Leesville Concrete Company, Inc.*, which extended *Batson* to civil cases, Justice Anthony Kennedy wrote:

> [I]f race stereotypes are the price for acceptance of a jury panel as fair, the price is too high to meet the standard of the Constitution. Other means exist for litigants to satisfy themselves of a jury's impartiality without using skin color as a test.[82]

I'll discuss the practical problems with this analysis in the next section. Here I simply want to note that this rhetoric of color-blindness is what conservative Justices have used to invalidate affirmative action programs, school desegregation plans, and voting rights measures.[83]

For example, in *Edmonson*, the Court stated, "If our society is to continue to progress as a multiracial democracy, it must recognize that the automatic invocation of race stereotypes retards that progress, and causes continued hurt and injury."[84] Kennedy's rhetoric, speaking about the jury system, is close to Justice Sandra Day O'Connor's, striking down a majority-minority voting district: "Classifications of citizens solely on the basis of race 'are by their very nature odious to a free people whose institutions are founded upon the doctrine of equality.' They threaten to stigmatize individuals by reason of their membership in a racial group and to incite racial hostility."[85]

---

[80] Id at 138–39.

[81] *Powers v Ohio*, 499 US 400, 499 (1991).

[82] *Edmonson v Leesville Concrete Co., Inc.*, 500 US 614 (1991).

[83] *Parents Involved*, 551 US.

[84] *Edmonson*, 500 US.

[85] *Shaw v Reno*, 509 US 630, 643 (1993) (citations omitted).

In an article called *Solving Batson*, Tania Tetlow suggested that *Batson* goes even further toward color-blindness than the rest of the Court's equal protection jurisprudence. Tetlow observed, "The *Batson* rule creates the strictest possible prohibition on the consideration of race, even when used to promote jury diversity. It proves far stricter than the cautious allowance of diversity in educational admissions, even though the harm to excluded students seems far greater than the harm to excluded jurors. It proves stricter even than the Court's requirement that legislatures not make it too obvious that they thought about race in legislative districting."[86]

Why did the liberal Justices sign on to Kavanaugh's opinion? Typically, they are critical of the doctrine of color-blindness in contexts outside of *Batson*. For example, Justice Ruth Ginsburg, dissenting in an affirmative action case, stated, "To say that two centuries of struggle for the most basic of civil rights has been mostly about freedom from racial categorization rather than freedom from racial oppression is to trivialize the lives and deaths of those who have suffered under racism."[87] Justice Sonia Sotomayor, dissenting in another affirmative action case, wrote, "The way to stop discrimination on the basis of race is to speak openly and candidly on the subject of race, and to apply the Constitution with eyes open to the unfortunate effects of centuries of racial discrimination. . . . Race also matters because of persistent racial inequality in society—inequality that cannot be ignored."[88]

It may be that the moderate Justices are focused on the equal protection rights of prospective jurors, and they see *Flowers* as a straightforward race discrimination case. The problem with that analysis is that, as discussed in Part III, Justice Clarence Thomas has put the Court on notice, since 1992, that race-consciousness in jury selection might benefit minority defendants, so the liberal Justices should at least be aware that the *Batson* line of cases are not as black and white as they might first seem.[89] Or it may be that the moderate Justices have a longer term goal in mind; perhaps they are trying to build a consensus toward abolishing peremptories, and it's helpful, as part

---

[86] Tetlow, 56 Wm & Mary L Rev at 1813 (cited in note 12).

[87] *Gratz v Bollinger*, 539 US 244, 301 (Ginsburg, J, dissenting).

[88] *Schuette v Coalition to Defend Affirmative Action*, 572 US 291, 380–81 (2014) (Sotomayor, J, dissenting).

[89] *Georgia v McCollum*, 505 US 42, 60 (1992) (Thomas, J, concurring).

of this project, to have conservative Justices acknowledge *Batson* violations.⁹⁰

The Supreme Court is expected to hear a case challenging affirmative action in college admissions in the near future.⁹¹ The *Batson/Flowers* rhetoric about the unconstitutionality of using race "as a proxy" is a core part of the challenge. We might expect *Flowers* to be cited as support for eliminating any form of race-consciousness. The Court's moderate and progressive Justices—all of whom voted in the majority in *Flowers*—will be portrayed as inconsistent or outcome determinative if they, as expected, support race-conscious remedies outside of the jury box.

The pre-*Batson* understanding that black jurors might evaluate evidence differently made it clear that excluding African American jurors could have a profound effect on the outcome of the trial. As the next section explains, for Mr. Flowers, African American jurors were literally the difference between life and death.

III. THE THOMAS DISSENT: KEEPING IT REAL

Justice Clarence Thomas dissented, joined in three of four parts by Justice Neil Gorsuch. Thomas wrote that the majority opinion "distorts the record of this case, eviscerates [their] standard of review, and vacates four murder convictions because the State struck a juror who would have been stricken by any competent attorney."⁹²

Thomas was also concerned that *Flowers* originated in a southern court. He stated that those courts have been "objects of the Court's scorn," particularly in cases involving race.⁹³ Thomas also suggests that certiorari may have been granted in *Flowers* due to the media attention the case had received, and warned that the Court was encouraging the "litigation and relitigation of criminal trials in the media, to the potential detriment of all parties."⁹⁴

---

⁹⁰ *Batson*, 476 US at 102–03 (Marshall, J, concurring). See Moriss B. Hoffman, *Peremptory Challenges Should Be Abolished: A Trial Judge's Perspective*, 64 U Chi L Rev 809 (1997); Harvard Law Review Association, *Judging the Prosecution: Why Abolishing Peremptory Challenges Limits the Dangers of Prosecutorial Discretion*, 119 Harv L Rev 2121 (2006).

⁹¹ *Students for Fair Admissions, Inc. v President & Fellows of Harvard Coll.*, 346 F Supp 3d 174 (D Mass 2018).

⁹² *Flowers v Mississippi*, No 17-9572, slip op at 3 (US June 21, 2019) (Thomas, J, dissenting).

⁹³ Id at 5 (quoting *United States v Windsor*, 570 US 744, 795 (2013) (Scalia, J, dissenting)).

⁹⁴ Id.

Most of Thomas's analysis focused on his contention that the state had race-neutral reasons for excluding African American jurors. His argument here is unpersuasive, mainly for the reasons stated in Kavanaugh's majority opinion. For example, as other commentators have observed, Thomas falsely claimed that in Flowers's first five trials, "49 out of the State's 50 peremptory strikes" were "race neutral."[95] Thomas appears to have made this up; there is nothing in the record to support it.[96]

At oral argument, Thomas asked about the race of the prospective jurors struck by Mr. Flowers's defense attorney.[97] This question was presumably meant to highlight that by striking eleven white prospective jurors, the defense itself recognized that race may affect the outcome of the case, and without peremptory challenges would not have been able to affect such strikes. The question also reflected Thomas's long-held contention that "black criminal defendants will rue the day that this Court ventured down this road that inexorably will lead to the elimination of peremptory strikes."[98] Thomas believes that African Americans benefit from race-based peremptory challenges because they can use them to strike white jurors who they suspect will be hostile, but cannot challenge for cause.

But, in the context of *Flowers*, as Justice Sotomayor pointed out during the oral argument, Flowers's attorney "didn't have any black jurors to exercise peremptories against."[99] Justice Kavanaugh's majority opinion made a broader related point:

> In the pre-*Batson* era . . . allowing each side in a case involving a black defendant to strike prospective jurors on the basis of race meant that a prosecutor could eliminate all of the black jurors, but a black defendant could not eliminate all of the white jurors. So in the real world of criminal trials against black defendants, both history and math tell us that a system of race-based peremptories does not treat black defendants and black prospective jurors equally with prosecutors and white prospective jurors.[100]

---

[95] *Flowers*, slip op at 3 (Thomas, J, dissenting).

[96] See Michael C. Dorf, *Wrap-Up of Three End-of-Last-Week's SCOTUS Cases and Anticipation of Today's Coming Decisions*, Dorf on Law (June 24, 2019), http://www.dorfonlaw.org/2019/06/wrap-up-of-three-end-of-last-weeks.html. See also Frampton, 72 Stan L Rev Online at 4 (cited in note 45).

[97] See Transcript of Oral Argument at 56–57, *Flowers*, slip op.

[98] *Flowers*, slip op at 42 (Thomas, J, dissenting).

[99] See Transcript of Oral Argument at 57, *Flowers*, slip op.

[100] *Flowers*, slip op at 15.

The final section of Thomas's dissent was not joined by Justice Gorsuch, but it is the most compelling. He writes, "*Batson*, requiring that a duly convicted criminal go free because a juror was arguably deprived of his right to serve on a jury, was suspect when it was announced and even more so today."[101]

Thomas's constitutional critique of *Batson* is that it emphasizes "the rights of excluded jurors at the expense of the traditional protections accorded criminal defendants of all races." He finds *Batson*'s focus on individual jurors' rights

> wholly contrary to the rationale underlying peremptory challenges. *Batson* claims to extend equal protection principles to individual peremptory strikes. However, the Court does not apply generally applicable equal protection principles to peremptory strikes. There is no strict scrutiny. . . . This is the Court's own jurisprudence recognizing that its equal protection principles do not naturally apply to individual, discretionary strikes.[102]

Thomas expresses important concerns about *Batson*'s focus on the rights of prospective jurors rather than defendants. In his view, *Batson* is more of a misguided project in "affirming the dignity of persons" than providing a fair jury.[103] Thomas contended that this focus on jurors "ignores the nature and basis of the peremptory strike and the realities of racial prejudice."[104] A peremptory strike, by nature, is not a judgment on a juror's competence, ability, or fitness, but "based on intuitions that a potential juror may be less sympathetic to a party's case."[105] This intuition should be allowed to include generalizations, "which may include their group affiliations, in the context of that case to be tried."[106]

Thomas argued for a return to a pre-*Batson* understanding of how litigants can deploy race in jury selection. According to Thomas, in this line of cases, the Court viewed peremptory strikes as "one of the most important 'of the rights secured to the accused.'"[107] He pointed out that peremptory strikes are, by their nature, arbitrary and

---

[101] Id at 33 (Thomas, J, dissenting).

[102] Id at 39–40.

[103] Id at 39 (quoting *Powers*, 499 US at 402).

[104] *Flowers*, slip op at 38.

[105] Id.

[106] Id at 39 (quoting *Swain*, 380 US at 221).

[107] Id at 37 (quoting *Swain*, 380 US at 219).

capricious, and must "be exercised with full freedom, or it fails of its full purpose."[108]

Thomas cited *Strauder v West Virginia* for the proposition that the Court recognized that the racial composition of a jury could affect the outcome of a criminal case.[109] He cited *Swain v Alabama* as an example of the Court affirming that the peremptory strike system "in and of itself, provides justification for striking any group of otherwise qualified jurors in any given case."[110]

It is tempting to dismiss Justice Thomas's dissent as just another example of his consistent hostility to civil rights claims brought by African Americans.[111] Indeed, his opinion has been widely criticized. *Slate* labeled it a "screed" and stated that "it's an encouraging sign that Kavanaugh just ignored Thomas' dissent, as it is really too wacky, too hostile, and aggrieved to merit a response."[112] Writing in the *New Yorker*, Jeffrey Toobin called Thomas's dissent "astonishing."[113] On the legal blog lawfare.com, Professor Bennett Gershman stated,

> Justice Thomas's dissenting opinion in *Flowers* was cruel and dishonest. He finds blameless a bad prosecutor, distorts the record, perverts the legal analysis, chastises the Court for taking the case, attacks the media for promoting the case, and advocates dismantling the landmark Supreme Court precedent *Batson v. Kentucky* that has stood for a generation as a powerful protection for black defendants from racist prosecutors like Evans. Whatever Justice Thomas's legacy, his opinion in *Flowers* should not be forgotten.[114]

To reiterate, I mainly agree with critiques that focus on Thomas's application of *Batson* to the facts of *Flowers*. As the headline of a

---

[108] *Flowers*, slip op at 40 (quoting *Lewis v United States*, 146 US 370, 378 (1892)).

[109] Id at 36–37 (citing *Strauder*, 100 US at 303).

[110] Id at 37 (quoting *Swain*, 380 US at 221).

[111] See Billy Corriher, *Clarence Thomas: The Anti-Thurgood Marshall*, Center for American Progress (July 9, 2013), https://www.americanprogress.org/issues/courts/news/2013/07/09/69044/clarence-thomas-the-anti-thurgood-marshall/; Benjamin L. Hooks, NAACP, and Julian Bond, *The NAACP Position on Clarence Thomas*, 22 The Black Scholar 144, 144–50 (1991).

[112] Stern, *Brett Kavanaugh's Latest Opinion* (cited in note 51).

[113] Jeffrey Toobin, *Clarence Thomas's Astonishing Opinion on a Racist Mississippi Prosecutor*, New Yorker (June 21, 2019), https://www.newyorker.com/news/daily-comment/clarence-thomass-astonishing-opinion-on-a-racist-mississippi-prosecutor.

[114] Bennett Gershman, *Clarence Thomas's "Cruel and Dishonest" Opinion Shouldn't Be Forgotten*, Law & Crime (July 1, 2019), https://lawandcrime.com/opinion/clarence-thomass-cruel-and-dishonest-opinion-shouldnt-be-forgotten/.

column in the *New York Times* by David Leonard stated, "Clarence Thomas v. the Evidence: This time, at least, the evidence won."

Yet the final section of Thomas's dissent should not be easily dismissed. In *Flowers*, Thomas, alone among the Justices, keeps it real about the role of race in the criminal legal process. He accurately stated that *Batson* "has blinded the Court to the reality that racial prejudice exists and can affect the fairness of trials."[115]

While Justice Thomas does not proclaim that he is "keeping it real," he does expressly claim that his opinion occupies the realm of "reality":

> The racial composition of a jury matters because racial biases, sympathies, and prejudices still exist. This is not a matter of "assumptions," as *Batson* said. It is a matter of reality. The Court knows these prejudices exist.... [W]hy else say here that "Flowers is black" and the "prosecutor is white"?[116]

It is true that Kavanaugh's opinion is replete with references to race, even as it made the case that race should not be a consideration in jury selection. Consider, for example, this passage in Kavanaugh's statement of facts:

> The total population of Winona is about 5,000. The town is about 53 percent black and about 46 percent white.... Three of the four victims were white; one was black. In 1997 the State charged Curtis Flowers with murder. Flowers is black.... The same state prosecutor tried Flowers each time. The prosecutor is white.[117]

I understand why Kavanaugh would focus on the race of jurors in a case about discrimination against prospective African American jurors. But Kavanaugh also refers to the race of the defendant, victims, and prosecutor. I agree with Thomas that Kavanaugh's statement of the facts implicitly acknowledges the significance of race at the same time that his legal analysis discounts it.

Justice Kavanaugh's majority opinion tried to use Justice Thurgood Marshall as a counterpoint to Thomas. Discussing Marshall's concurring opinion in *Batson*, Kavanaugh wrote:

> Justice Thurgood Marshall drove the point home: "Exclusion of blacks from a jury, solely because of race, can no more be justified by a belief that

---

[115] *Flowers*, slip op at 33 (Thomas, J, dissenting).

[116] Id at 41 (Thomas, J, dissenting).

[117] Id at 3.

blacks are less likely than whites to consider fairly or sympathetically the State's case against a black defendant than it can be justified by the notion that blacks lack the intelligence, experience, or moral integrity to be entrusted with that role."[118]

But Kavanaugh—and Marshall—are making a false equivalence. There is a categorical difference between not allowing African Americans to be considered for jury duty, as was the case in *Strauder*, and believing that African Americans, by virtue of their experience, might evaluate evidence in a criminal case differently than non-African Americans.

Many years ago, I served as a misdemeanor prosecutor in the District of Columbia. I had been hired by the United States Department of Justice to prosecute federal public corruption cases, but I didn't have any trial experience, so for a year I was detailed to the agency that prosecutes local crimes to learn how to try a case. We rookie prosecutors were trained to use group-based stereotypes when we exercised our peremptory challenges. Jurors to be avoided included scientists, because they might have too empirical a view of the requirement of "proof beyond a reasonable doubt," and people who were very religious, because they might have qualms about sitting in judgment of another person. To the best of my recollection, we were not given any formal instructions on gender, but we were informed of the prosecutor's lore that in cases involving sexual assaults of women, men were better jurors for the prosecution than women, because women would be more judgmental of other women.[119] Overall, Justice White's description, in *Swain*, of how lawyers use peremptories rings true: I, and I think most of the other prosecutors in my office, evaluated prospective jurors "in light of the limited knowledge counsel has of them, which may include their group affiliations, in the context of the case to be tried."[120]

We rookie prosecutors were also warned that there would be frequent nullification in drug possession cases with African American defendants because D.C. jurors would not want "to send another young black male to jail." In my recollection, the experienced prosecutors who described this phenomenon did not specifically mention

---

[118] Id at 14 (quotation marks and citations omitted).

[119] Note *JEB* had not been decided. *JEB v Alabama*, 511 US 127 (1994).

[120] *Swain*, 380 US at 221.

the race of the jurors, but they did not have to: at the time, "D.C. juror" was an adequate signifier of blackness. The vast majority of jurors in Washington, D.C., were African American. If we tried to strike every black juror, we would not have had enough people to form a jury.

In any event, *Batson* already had been decided. The law could not stop us from having thoughts about race, though, which we shared with our colleagues whom we trusted.

My sense is that many of my fellow prosecutors believed, as did I, that in certain cases, white jurors were better for the prosecution.[121] This included drug possession cases, because of concerns about nullification, and cases in which police were major witnesses, because African American jurors would be more skeptical of cops.[122]

A. SIXTY-ONE REASONS TO BELIEVE JUSTICE THOMAS

There is a crucial fact about race and the *Flowers* jurors that is not presented in any of the opinions, perhaps because it was not part of the record, or perhaps because the Court would have deemed it irrelevant. I think that this fact is evidence that enforcement of *Batson* is hopeless as a practical matter and supports eliminating peremptory challenges by prosecutors.

Here is the fact: In Curtis Flowers's six trials there were sixty-one white jurors, and every one of them voted to convict Mr. Flowers. Every single one. Of the eleven African American jurors, six voted for conviction and five voted to acquit.[123]

The lesson that I draw from these data, which are contained in an amicus brief filed by the Magnolia Bar Association, the Mississippi

---

[121] I should note that not all my colleagues shared this perspective; one thought that in cases with young black male defendants, which were most of the cases, a young black male was his ideal juror, because that juror would take pains to distinguish himself from the defendant.

[122] Indeed, there was a joke in the office regarding the standard jury instruction given when police officers are witnesses, which informs jurors they should not give police testimony more credibility just because the witness was a police officer. The joke was that in D.C., the instruction should be changed to police testimony should not have less credibility because the witness is a police officer.

[123] Brief of Amici Curiae the Magnolia Bar Association, Mississippi Center for Justice, and Innocence Project New Orleans, *Flowers*, slip op at 20–22 (US filed July 26, 2018). Those African American jurors are the only reason that Mr. Flowers's case ever got to the Supreme Court, and the only reason why a possibly innocent man who was on death row for twenty-one years might someday go free.

Center for Justice, and Innocence Project New Orleans, is that it would amount to something close to malpractice for a defense attorney in Mr. Flowers's case to ignore race.[124] Her case would depend on getting as many African Americans as possible seated on her jury, and therefore to strike nonblack jurors. And, likewise, it would be virtually impossible for a prosecutor to be indifferent between a white and black potential juror.

Although only the constitutionality of the sixth trial was before the Supreme Court in *Flowers*, it considered data regarding the prosecution's use of peremptory challenges in the preceding five trials as well. The data showed that in all of those trials, the prosecutor had used peremptory strikes against prospective black jurors in a vastly disproportionate manner compared to striking prospective white jurors. Justice Kavanaugh, writing for the majority, explained, "A court confronting that kind of pattern cannot ignore it."[125]

But looking at the data about how the jurors voted in the *Flowers* trials, it is obvious that race generally, and whiteness specifically, mattered enormously. One might paraphrase Justice Kavanaugh and say, "a lawyer confronting that kind of pattern cannot ignore it."

This phenomenon is not limited to Mississippi. Examining data regarding jury trials in Louisiana, which at the time did not require unanimous verdicts in criminal trials, Thomas Ward Frampton found, "In 199 serious felony 'guilty' verdicts reached by racially mixed, non-unanimous juries, black jurors were vastly overrepresented among those jurors holding out for an acquittal. This research confirms a large body of social science literature suggesting race matters in the jury box."[126]

Based on the empirical evidence and my experience as a prosecutor, I want to resist the widespread labeling of District Attorney Doug Evans as a "racist" simply because he struck African American prospective jurors. For example, an editorial in the *New York Times* stated, ". . . the real outrage of Mr. Flowers's many trials . . . is the clear

---

[124] Abbe Smith has argued that "it is unethical for a defense lawyer to ignore what is known about the influence of race and sex on juror attitudes in order to comply with *Batson v. Kentucky* and its progeny." Abbe Smith, *"Nice Work If You Can Get It": "Ethical" Jury Selection in Criminal Defense*, 67 Fordham L Rev 523, 531 (1998). Smith wrote that although *Batson* and *Georgia v McCollum* "has spawned an ethics of its own, this new ethics is at odds with other long-standing and controlling ethical obligations of criminal defense lawyers." Id.

[125] *Flowers*, slip op at 25.

[126] Frampton, 71 Vand L Rev at 1599 (cited in note 63).

racism that has visited the jury selection process from the start."[127] In the *New Yorker*, Jeffrey Toobin wrote, "A Mississippi prosecutor went on a racist crusade to have a black man executed."[128] Andrew Cohen, writing for the Brennan Center for Justice, observed, "In another jurisdiction, all of this misconduct, all of these racist tactics in jury selection, likely would have caught up to a prosecutor and he or she would be prosecutor no more."[129]

Evans might indeed be a racist. His prosecutorial misconduct and rush to judgment to convict and execute Curtis Flowers for the murders are extremely troubling in light of substantial evidence that Mr. Flowers is innocent.[130] The modest point I want to make is that we would need more information than his race-based use of peremptories to make that determination. By itself, all it demonstrates is that Evans is a lawyer, like I was, who wanted to win his case.

B. ALL BLACK EVERYTHING

Clarence Thomas is now the longest-serving Justice on the Supreme Court and, contrary to popular belief, probably the hardest working. He writes more opinions than any of the other Justices and his influence is increasingly acknowledged.[131] Angela Onwuachi-Willig observed, much earlier in his tenure, "Justice Thomas has expressed core principles of black conservative thought in his opinions.... Thomas is likely to continue to write and develop a 'raced' jurisprudence on certain issues."[132]

And so the Justice has. Several scholars, in addition to Onwuachi-Willig, have noted Thomas's steadfast attention to race, even in cases that do not seem to have obvious race nexuses. Mark Tushnet wrote

---

[127] Editorial Board, *Racism in Jury Selection Is Real. Can the Supreme Court Put an End to It?*, NY Times (Mar 21, 2019), https://www.nytimes.com/2019/03/21/opinion/curtis-flowers-supreme-court.html.

[128] Toobin, *Clarence Thomas's Astonishing Opinion* (cited in note 113).

[129] Andrew Cohen, *The Supreme Court Rights a Historic, Racist Wrong in Mississippi*, Brennan Center for Justice (June 24, 2019), https://www.brennancenter.org/our-work/analysis-opinion/supreme-court-rights-historic-racist-wrong-mississippi.

[130] *In the Dark: Season 2*, American Public Media (2018–19).

[131] Linda Greenhouse, *Is Clarence Thomas the Supreme Court's Future?*, NY Times (Aug 2, 2018), https://www.nytimes.com/2018/08/02/opinion/contributors/clarence-thomas-supreme-court-conservative.html.

[132] Angela Onwuachi-Willig, *Just Another Brother on the SCT? What Justice Clarence Thomas Teaches Us about the Influence of Racial Identity*, 90 Iowa L Rev 931, 1000 (2005).

that Thomas's opinions "contain a black nationalist strand."[133] Stephen F. Smith, who worked as a law clerk for Thomas, famously described him as "Clarence X—a jurist who is not only a constitutionalist, but a black nationalist as well."[134] In an essay contrasting the race performances of Thomas and Barack Obama, I wrote, "[Another] difference is their comfort level talking about race. Justice Thomas does it all the time; the president, since going into politics, does so rarely and reluctantly."[135] Corey Robin described Thomas as "a black jurist whose conservatism is defined by the interests of black people as he understands them."[136] Thomas Ward Frampton found "rumblings" of black nationalism in Thomas's jurisprudence.[137]

Of course not everyone who has examined Thomas's jurisprudence shares this understanding. Writing in *The Nation*, Randall Kennedy attacked Thomas for "deploy[ing] his blackness so effectively for such wrong-headed judgments and opinions, repeatedly invoking his racial minority status to reinforce his broadside attacks against affirmative action."[138] According to Kennedy, "a far better guide to Clarence Thomas's thinking than the Constitution or *The Autobiography of Malcolm X* are the platforms of the Republican Party and the talking points of Rush Limbaugh."[139]

Thomas has resisted the black nationalism characterization but acknowledged the centrality of race to his work.[140] In a speech to the National Bar Association, Thomas said, "It pains me deeply, or more deeply than any of you can imagine, to be perceived by so many members of my race as doing them harm. All the sacrifice, all the

---

[133] Mark Tushnet, *Clarence Thomas's Black Nationalism*, 47 Howard L J 323, 330 (2004).

[134] Stephen F. Smith, *Clarence X?: The Black Nationalist Behind Justice Thomas's Constitutionalism*, 4 NYU J L & Liberty 583, 586 (2009).

[135] Paul Butler, *The President and the Justice: Two Ways of Looking at a Postblack Man*, in Kenneth W. Mack and Guy-Uriel Charles, eds, *The New Black: What Has Changed—and What Has Not—with Race in America* 64, 68 (New Press, 2013).

[136] Corey Robin, *Clarence Thomas Is Not a "Sellout,"* NY Times (Sept 28, 2019), https://www.nytimes.com/2019/09/28/opinion/sunday/clarence-thomas-race.html.

[137] Frampton, 72 Stan L Rev Online at 6 (cited in note 45).

[138] Randall Kennedy, *Whose Side Is Clarence Thomas On?*, The Nation (Oct 29 2019), https://www.thenation.com/article/archive/enigma-clarence-thomas-book-review/.

[139] Id.

[140] Corey Robin, *The Enigma of Clarence Thomas* 32 (Metropolitan Books, 2019).

long hours of preparation were to help [the black community], not to hurt."[141]

Descriptions of Thomas's race jurisprudence highlight his "injection" of race in cases involving issues like campaign financing, gun control, and eminent domain; his profound distrust of white people; and his belief in black self-help. The latter two are an interesting lens through which to read the *Flowers* dissent.

Thomas thinks that white racism is an inevitable and irrevocable component of black existence. "There is nothing you can do to get past black skin," he told an interviewer.[142] In a commencement address at a historically black college, Thomas told the graduates, "[D]iscrimination, racism, and bigotry have gone no place and probably never will."[143] He commented about "young brothers dying in the street" and said that "if dogs were being struck down in the same way, there would be a society of blue-haired women to save our canine friends. But these are young black men bleeding in the gutter, and no one seems to give a damn."[144]

This skepticism about the good faith of white people is reflected in Thomas's concern in *Flowers* about all-white juries sitting in judgment of black defendants. Thomas views the ability to strike white jurors as a tool to arm them in the face of inevitable white racism. Peremptory strikes are best suited to address the racism that Thomas sees as most harmful, the "white liberal" brand that is more insidious, as opposed to "southerners," who "were upfront about their bigotry."[145] This also provides a context for the shade Thomas throws on the *Flowers* majority when he complains that southern courts had frequently been the objects of the Court's "scorn."

Thomas's opinions frequently laud black self-help and express suspicion of governmental or nonblack institutional efforts to help African Americans. He wrote, "If separation itself is a harm, and if

---

[141] Michael Fletcher, *Justice Thomas Faces Down Critics*, Wash Post (July 30, 1998), https://www.washingtonpost.com/wp-srv/national/longterm/supcourt/stories/wp073098.htm.

[142] Juan Williams, *A Question of Fairness* (The Atlantic, Feb 1, 1987), https://www.theatlantic.com/magazine/archive/1987/02/a-question-of-fairness/306370/.

[143] Robin, *The Enigma of Clarence Thomas* at 35 (cited in note 140) (quoting Justice Clarence Thomas, Commencement Speech at Savannah State College (June 9, 1985)).

[144] Jeffrey Rosen, *Moving On*, New Yorker: Annals of Law (April 22, 1996), https://www.newyorker.com/magazine/1996/04/29/moving-on.

[145] Robin, *The Enigma of Clarence Thomas* at 32 (cited in note 140) (citing Clarence Thomas, *My Grandfather's Son* 75–76 (Harper Collins, 2007)).

integration therefore is the only way that blacks can receive a proper education, then there must be something inferior about blacks."[146] One scholar described Thomas's hostility to affirmative action as a product of "his unshakeable confidence in the ability of blacks and black institutions to succeed on their own initiative, without what he regards as racial paternalism from whites."[147]

This confidence in the ability of African Americans—and suspicion of white racism—is reflected in Thomas's complaint in *Flowers* that "the Court continues to apply a line of cases that prevents, among other things, black defendants from striking potentially hostile white jurors."[148] Thomas "would return to our pre-*Batson* understanding— that race matters in the courtroom—and thereby return to litigants one of the most important tools to combat prejudice in their cases."[149]

Corey Robin has also observed the nexus between the *Flowers* dissent and black self-help. In an interview, Robin said,

> Notice that Thomas does not take the obvious liberal path of relying on the higher courts and the state to head off racial imbalances; instead, he wants to leave that task in the hands of African Americans through their power to strike potential jurors, again, merely because those jurors are white. Gorsuch joined him for part of the *Flowers* dissent—the part that had to do strictly with the facts of the case. But when Thomas then starts going off in the direction I just described, Gorsuch leaves, and Thomas is all by himself.[150]

In the end, Thomas's dissent is not, in Jeffrey Toobin's word, "astonishing." It is consistent with his worldview, and his writings in other *Batson*-derived cases. Thomas's dissent is inconsistent with his writing on equal protection in other areas, but, as discussed in Part II, he has this in common with the moderate Justices; when it comes to the jury box, Thomas and the Court's moderates are consistent in their inconsistency. It is certainly interesting that the only African American member of the Supreme Court diverges from seven of his colleagues to reject a claim of discrimination against an African

---

[146] *Missouri v Jenkins*, 515 US 70, 122 (1995) (Thomas, J, concurring).

[147] Smith, 4 NYU J L & Liberty at 615 (cited in note 134).

[148] Id at 42.

[149] *Flowers*, slip op at 36 (Thomas, J, dissenting).

[150] Joshua Cohen and Corey Robin, *The Conservative Black Nationalism of Clarence Thomas*, Boston Review (Sept 24, 2019), http://bostonreview.net/race/joshua-cohen-corey-robin-conservative-black-nationalism-clarence-thomas.

American, when there was overwhelming evidence of discrimination. Dismissing Thomas as a sell-out or a race traitor is, however, a reductive and incorrect way of understanding his motives.[151]

C. THAT ONE SENTENCE THOUGH

There is a line in Thomas's dissent that is chilling. To the extent that this essay argues that the final section of Thomas's *Flowers* dissent contains some important and persuasive ideas, I must distinguish this sentence. It is absolutely condemnable. Thomas wrote, "If [the Kavanaugh] opinion today has a redeeming quality, it is this: The State is perfectly free to convict Curtis Flowers again."[152]

Thomas wrote that after making a persuasive case that "racial prejudice exists and can affect the fairness of trials" and knowing that Mr. Flowers has never been convicted by a jury that had more than one African American.[153] Thomas was also aware that each of the overwhelmingly white juries sentenced Mr. Flowers to death. It is difficult to reconcile the race-consciousness that Thomas demonstrated in the final section of his dissent with his apparent glee in calling for Mr. Flowers's conviction "again." Here Thomas earned the title bestowed upon him, in 1992, in a *New York Times* editorial. Clarence Thomas is "the cruelest justice."[154]

IV. POST-RACE CHARADES

The year before *Batson* was decided, the *Michigan Law Review* published a seminal article on race and juries. In "Black Innocence and the White Jury," Professor Sheri Lynn Johnson offered social science evidence of a widespread tendency of white jurors to convict black defendants in instances where the same defendant would be acquitted if he or she were white.[155] Johnson thought that race mattered so much that she proposed that the Supreme Court recognize

---

[151] See Randall Kennedy, *The Case of Clarence Thomas*, in *Sellout: The Politics of Racial Betrayal* 87 (Vintage, Jan 8, 2008). But see Kennedy, *Whose Side Is Clarence Thomas On?* (cited in note 138).

[152] See note 52 above.

[153] *Flowers*, slip op at 33 (Thomas, J, dissenting).

[154] *The Youngest, Cruelest Justice*, NY Times A24 (Feb 27, 1992).

[155] Sheri Lynn Johnson, *Black Innocence and the White Jury*, 83 Mich L Rev 1611 (1985).

a defendant's right to have three jurors of their same race. Here lies another one of *Flowers*'s ironies. Mr. Flowers was represented, before the Supreme Court, by Professor Johnson. It was her argument that the jury selection was not color-blind that persuaded the Court.[156]

Batson and *Flowers* encourage ignorance, or at least the performance of an obstinate, counterfactual color-blindness by people who likely know better. Many years ago, I wrote a law review article in which I advised African American jurors to find black defendants accused of nonviolent offenses not guilty, even if the jurors believed that the defendant had committed the crime.[157] As a prosecutor, I observed jurors nullifying in this fashion; as an academic, I sought to lend scholarly weight to their project, and to help structure nullification to have the broadest political impact. My article was one of the first scholarly critiques of mass incarceration, which, in the mid-1990s, was a relatively novel phenomenon.

I began the essay with descriptions of defense attorneys who, it seemed to me and many others, including the judges they appeared before, had made racial appeals to D.C. jurors. One case involved the controversial prosecution of Marion Barry, the city's mayor, for cocaine possession and perjury. Barry had invited a few well-known African American activists, including Minister Louis Farrakhan, to attend the trial. The trial judge barred them from the courtroom, because he thought their attendance was designed to send a message of racial solidarity to the jury. The D.C. Court of Appeals rebuked the judge, as though it were silly to think a lawyer would try to do that, or that it would be an effective strategy if she did.[158]

In another case, a defense attorney who wore kente cloth—a fabric originating in West Africa popular among African Americans at the time—was admonished not to wear it in front of juries because, the

---

[156] In 2014, Professor Johnson wrote, "Nothing I have seen in the quarter of a century has dissuaded me from the view that a real commitment to racial equality in the administration of criminal justice would compel the inclusion of minority race jurors in minority race defendant cases." Sheri Lynn Johnson, *Batson from the Very Bottom of the Well: Critical Race Theory and the Supreme Court's Peremptory Challenge Jurisprudence*, 12 Ohio St J Crim L 71, 90 (2014). I should note that Professor Johnson is a first-rate lawyer for people, like Mr. Flowers, sentenced to death, and her argument in the case was not, in a formal sense, inconsistent with her scholarship. Her position in *Flowers* was simply that the prosecutor had violated *Batson*, which is undeniable.

[157] Paul Butler, *Racially Based Jury Nullification: Black Power in the Criminal Justice System*, 105 Yale L J 677 (1995).

[158] Id at 683–84.

judge said, he was trying to send a "secret message."[159] Many commentators contended that the judge's intuition was somehow unhinged, but I opined that was exactly the lawyer's aim. I concluded these stories by noting,

> I am fascinated by the refusal of these actors to take seriously the possibility and legal implications of black jurors' sympathy with black defendants. The criminal justice system would be better served if there were less reluctance to consider the significance of race in black jurors' adjudication of guilt or innocence.[160]

Flowers is an example of eight members of the Supreme Court still refusing to take this phenomenon seriously.[161] Ironically, the only member of the Court who entertained this possibility is Clarence Thomas, who is almost universally reviled by advocates for racial justice. I am not sure that Thomas draws the right conclusion from his accurate description of the significance of race, but he at least deserves credit for not playing along with the other Justices' game of post-race charades.[162]

It cannot actually surprise anyone—especially any lawyer—that race matters with regard to jury deliberation. But when people pretend that race is irrelevant, it makes honest conversations more difficult and encourages bad law and policy. An honest opinion in *Flowers* would have combined elements of the majority decision and the "keeping it real" part of the Thomas dissent. It would acknowledge the prosecutor's *Batson* error and then explain, as Thomas did, why the exclusion of black jurors matters to defendants. Given the current state of law, the majority opinion could not contain that analysis, because *Batson* is based on the legal fiction that race does not matter.

Further acknowledging the salience of race in jury deliberations could, in Justice Kavanaugh's phrase, "immediately revolutionize" the criminal trial process. Prosecutors might be prohibited from peremptory challenges because, experience has proven, it is exceedingly difficult for prosecutors to ignore race when selecting jurors. In cases with African American defendants, the result is that many prosecutors

---

[159] Id at 684–85.

[160] Id at 686.

[161] I include Justice Gorsuch in this group because he did not join the final section of the Thomas dissent. But see *Strieff*, 136 S Ct (Sotomayor, J, dissenting).

[162] See also Frampton, 72 Stan L Rev Online (cited in note 45).

try to stack the deck with white jurors, who are more likely to convict, even when they might not convict a white defendant based on the same set of facts.[163]

Defendants should still be allowed peremptory strikes to enhance their chances of striking, in Justice Thomas's words, "potentially hostile white jurors." If it seems unfair that prosecutors but not defense attorneys would be allowed peremptory strikes, recall that this was the law for the six years between *Batson* and *McCollum*.[164]

In addition, applying the same race-conscious analysis as in affirmative action and voting rights cases, minority defendants should have the right to a critical mass of people of their same race on their juries. Legal scholars have made persuasive arguments that the Sixth Amendment right to jury trial as well as the Equal Protection Clause would support this remedy to the persistent problem of white juror prejudice against minority defendants.[165]

I suffer no delusion that the Roberts Court is remotely close to supporting those kinds of interventions, which Dorothy Roberts might describe as "abolition constitutionalism."[166] But if *Flowers* is the best we can expect, it is cheap racial justice.

V. Conclusion

I anticipate that one response to my analysis in this essay will be that some black people are never satisfied. I would have been mad, the claim will go, if the Supreme Court had not found a *Batson* violation in *Flowers*, and now it seems like I am mad that it did.

I accept this critique. I think I would have been angrier if the Court had not found a *Batson* violation. *Flowers* presents a rare example of

---

[163] Johnson, 83 Mich L R (cited in note 155).

[164] In an amicus brief in *Georgia v McCollum*, the NAACP Legal Defense and Education Fund stated, "The ability to use peremptory challenges to exclude majority race jurors may be crucial to empaneling a fair jury. In many cases an African American, or other minority defendant, may be faced with a jury array in which his racial group is underrepresented to some degree, but not sufficiently to permit challenge under the Fourteenth Amendment. The only possible chance the defendant may have of having any minority jurors on the jury that actually tries him will be if he uses his peremptories to strike members of the majority race." *McCollum*, 505 US at 69 (O'Connor, J, dissenting) (citing Brief of Amici Curiae NAACP Legal Defense and Education Fund, Inc., *McCollum*, No 91-372, *9–10).

[165] See id; Nancy J. King, *Racial Jurymandering: Cancer or Cure? A Contemporary Review of Affirmative Action in Jury Selection*, 68 NYU L Rev 707 (1993); Tetlow, 56 Wm & Mary L Rev (cited in note 12); Paul Butler, *Affirmative Action and the Criminal Law*, 68 U Colo L Rev 841 (1997).

[166] Roberts, 133 Harv L Rev at 98 (cited in note 44).

the Roberts Court finding for a person of color, rather than a white person, in an Equal Protection Clause case. I say "think" rather than "know" because I am uncertain whether false hope is better than no hope at all.

When *Flowers* was announced, there was, in some progressive legal circles, a muted celebration. Maybe the Roberts Court, even with the recent additions of Justices Gorsuch and Kavanaugh cementing its right-wing majority, would not be as bad as we feared. One point of this essay is that, for the reasons I have stated, *Flowers* should not be celebrated. It is more consistent with the Supreme Court's work of maintaining racial subordination than eliminating it. We should not expect the Roberts Court to issue any consequential opinions that will undermine white supremacy. We should not be distracted from the vital political work that is unrelated to bringing court cases, and that is the only way that real racial justice will be achieved.[167]

---

[167] Paul Butler, *Chokehold: Policing Black Men* (New Press, 2017); Paul Butler, *The System Is Working the Way It's Supposed To: The Limits of Criminal Justice Reform*, 104 Georgetown L J 1419 (2016).

NICHOLAS O. STEPHANOPOULOS

THE ANTI-CAROLENE COURT

> [L]egislation which restricts those political processes which can ordinarily be expected to bring about repeal of undesirable legislation [should be] subjected to more exacting judicial scrutiny. . . .[1]

> [T]he fact that [partisan] gerrymandering is incompatible with democratic principles does not mean that the solution lies with the federal judiciary.[2]

Once upon a time, roughly in the middle of the twentieth century, *Carolene Products*'s famous footnote captured much of the Supreme Court's constitutional decision making.[3] *Carolene*[4] included three key prescriptions. First, the Court should *not* strike down ordinary social and economic legislation: the sorts of laws the Court had routinely nullified in the preceding *Lochner* era.[5] Second, the Court *should* block efforts by incumbent politicians to distort the political process in their favor. These efforts are a democratic malfunction—a breach of

---

Nicholas O. Stephanopoulos is Professor of Law, Harvard Law School.

AUTHOR'S NOTE: I'm grateful to Justin Driver and Rick Pildes for their invaluable comments. My thanks also to the workshop participants at Loyola University Chicago and the University of Chicago, where I presented earlier versions of the article.

[1] *United States v Carolene Products Co.*, 304 US 144, 152 n 4 (1938).

[2] *Rucho v Common Cause*, 139 S Ct 2484, 2506 (2019) (citations and quotation marks omitted).

[3] See *Carolene*, 304 US at 152 n 4; see also John Hart Ely, *Democracy and Distrust: A Theory of Judicial Review* (Harvard, 1980) (making this argument at length).

[4] I usually call the case *Carolene*, rather than *Carolene Products*, for the sake of brevity.

[5] See *Carolene*, 304 US at 152 ("[R]egulatory legislation affecting ordinary commercial transactions is [generally] not to be pronounced unconstitutional. . . .").

© 2020 by The University of Chicago. All rights reserved.
978-0-226-70856-0/2020/2019-0003$10.00

the majoritarian ideal—that the Court is well positioned to resolve.[6] And third, the Court should also intervene when a minority group is consistently the loser of political battles. There's no majoritarian problem in this scenario, but there *is* a violation of a different democratic value: pluralism, the idea that groups should endlessly make and break alliances as they compete over public policy, and no group should find itself perennially outside the winning coalition.[7]

It's evident that the contemporary Court no longer heeds *Carolene*'s first directive. A Court that prevents states from restricting the possession of firearms,[8] or that forbids Congress from mandating the purchase of health insurance under the Commerce Clause,[9] isn't a Court that's willing to defer to most social and economic legislation. It's equally plain that *Carolene*'s third pillar has crumbled. If it still stood, the Court would celebrate (or at least tolerate) laws that benefit politically weak minority groups, like affirmative action and school integration. But the Court subjects these policies to the strictest scrutiny and usually invalidates them,[10] even though it's implausible that America's white majority is the victim of a pluralist failure.

Some observers had thought, however, that the second leg of *Carolene*'s tripod was still sound: that the Court would still stop politicians from entrenching themselves in office through electoral machinations. Michael Klarman wrote in 1991 that the majoritarian "prong of political process theory has emerged relatively unscathed from the barbs of [its] critics."[11] A decade later, Michael Dorf and Samuel Issacharoff stated that "most have assumed that correcting [majoritarian] defects is a legitimate judicial function."[12] And at his

---

[6] See id at 152 n 4 (suggesting that "more exacting judicial scrutiny" might apply to "legislation which restricts those political processes which can ordinarily be expected to bring about repeal of undesirable legislation").

[7] See id (indicating that a "more searching judicial inquiry" might apply when "those political processes ordinarily to be relied upon to protect minorities" fail to function properly); see also Nicholas O. Stephanopoulos, *Political Powerlessness*, 90 NYU L Rev 1527 (2015) (discussing this *Carolene* prong in depth).

[8] See *McDonald v City of Chicago*, 561 US 742 (2010).

[9] See *NFIB v Sebelius*, 567 US 519 (2012).

[10] See, for example, *Fisher v Univ. of Texas*, 570 US 297 (2013); *Parents Involved v Seattle School Dist. No. 1*, 551 US 701 (2007).

[11] Michael J. Klarman, *The Puzzling Resistance to Political Process Theory*, 77 Va L Rev 747, 748 (1991).

[12] Michael C. Dorf and Samuel Issacharoff, *Can Process Theory Constrain Courts?*, 72 U Colo L Rev 923, 931 (2001).

2005 confirmation hearing, then-Judge John Roberts described the special judicial obligation to safeguard the electoral process: "Without access to the ballot box, people are not in the position to protect any other rights that are important to them."[13]

The Court's recent decision in *Rucho v Common Cause*[14] shows that the academic commentators were wrong. It also highlights the gulf between Roberts's 2005 words and his deeds as Chief Justice. The Court he now leads—and for which he wrote the majority opinion in *Rucho*—is comprehensively anti-*Carolene*, as hostile to its second directive as to its first and third. *Rucho* involved a partisan gerrymandering challenge to a North Carolina district plan. This plan had been drawn pursuant to an explicit "Partisan Advantage" criterion that required "[t]he partisan makeup of [the state's] congressional delegation" to be "10 Republicans and 3 Democrats."[15] Sure enough, Republican candidates won ten seats, and Democrats three, in both of the elections held under the plan, even though the state's voters barely preferred Republican candidates in the first election, and narrowly favored *Democrats* in the second.[16] The plan's 10–3 breakdown was also more pro-Republican than any of the thousands of maps randomly generated by an expert's computer algorithm.[17]

It's hard to imagine a stronger case for judicial intervention under *Carolene*'s second prong. North Carolina's gerrymander deliberately "restrict[ed] those political processes"—elections—"which can ordinarily be expected to bring about repeal of undesirable legislation"—by replacing one party's legislators with the other's.[18] But the Court declined to step in. And not only did it stay on the sidelines, it also barred any future Court from entering the field, by declaring partisan gerrymandering categorically nonjusticiable. And not only that, the Court also mocked the very idea of a judicial responsibility to

---

[13] Joan Biskupic, *The Chief: The Life and Turbulent Times of Chief Justice John Roberts* 163 (Basic Books, 2019).

[14] 139 S Ct 2484 (2019).

[15] Id at 2510 (Kagan, J, dissenting). A companion case to *Rucho* involved a Democratic gerrymander in Maryland.

[16] See Brief for Appellees League of Women Voters of North Carolina et al, *Rucho v Common Cause*, No 18-422, *15 (US filed Mar 31, 2019) ("LWV Brief"). Due to evidence of fraud, the Republican victory in one district in 2018 was never certified and a new election was called. See *Rucho*, 139 S Ct at 2492.

[17] See id at 2518 (Kagan, J, dissenting).

[18] *United States v Carolene Products Co.*, 304 US 144, 152 n 4 (1938).

guard the political process from the ploys of self-interested insiders. Yes, "gerrymandering is incompatible with democratic principles," the Court conceded.[19] But, contra *Carolene*, that "does not mean that the solution lies with the federal judiciary."[20]

I doubt anyone would seriously contest this claim: that *Rucho* is, at its core, an anti-*Carolene* decision. But I want to push the point further. Not only is *Rucho* an anti-*Carolene* decision, its *reasons* for defying *Carolene* are the same ones that judges and scholars have always given for resisting *Carolene*'s logic. *Rucho* is thus anti-*Carolene* in both result and analysis. Consider the Court's argument that, to strike down North Carolina's gerrymander, it would first need to determine what a "fair" district map is.[21] But "it is not even clear what fairness looks like in this context," and "[d]eciding among . . . different visions of fairness . . . poses basic questions that are political, not legal."[22]

The dissenters in the great one-person, one-vote cases of the 1960s objected to the Court's rulings in exactly these terms. In *Baker v Carr*, for example, the 1962 decision that authorized suits about unequal district population, Justice Felix Frankfurter wrote that malapportionment couldn't be condemned unless the Court could say how districts *should* be apportioned. "What is actually asked of the Court . . . is to choose among competing bases of representation—ultimately, really, among competing theories of political philosophy."[23] Similarly, when John Hart Ely published his seminal defense of *Carolene* in 1980,[24] the most common academic critique was that Ely, like *Carolene*, asked judges to make indeterminate, and inappropriate, decisions among dueling democratic theories. As Jane Schacter queried, "if political philosophers can agree on no singular formulation of democracy, how might we expect judges to do so?"[25]

Rucho, then, is an anti-*Carolene* decision from top to bottom. In some respects, though, it's only the tip of the Court's anti-*Carolene* spear, a portent of grimmer rulings, from a *Caroline* perspective, still

---

[19] *Rucho*, 139 S Ct at 2506 (quotation marks omitted).
[20] Id.
[21] See id at 2500.
[22] Id.
[23] 369 US 186, 300 (1962) (Frankfurter, J, dissenting).
[24] See Ely, *Democracy and Distrust* (cited in note 3).
[25] Jane S. Schacter, *Ely and the Idea of Democracy*, 57 Stan L Rev 737, 753 (2004).

to come. That's because *Rucho* only prevented the *federal courts* from hearing partisan gerrymandering claims. It didn't block *other* institutions, like Congress, state courts, and the people themselves via voter initiatives, from tackling gerrymandering. To the contrary, *Rucho* encouraged these other actors to intercede. "The States . . . are actively addressing the issue on a number of fronts," the Court remarked.[26] "Congress" also has "the power to do something about partisan gerrymandering [through] the Elections Clause."[27]

These invitations to other institutions ring hollow, however, given the Court's recent jurisprudence. In a 2015 dissent for four Justices (which would now probably command five votes), Chief Justice Roberts contended that the *only* state entity permitted to regulate redistricting is the *last* state entity that might wish to do so: the state legislature.[28] Taken to its logical endpoint, this position would preclude not just independent commissions adopted through voter initiatives (the subject of the 2015 case) but also state court suits and maybe even gubernatorial vetoes of gerrymandered maps. Chief Justice Roberts is the author, too, of *Shelby County v Holder*, the only Court decision in modern times to nullify a federal voting rights statute.[29] It's hardly a stretch that the *Shelby County* Court might look askance at congressional legislation, say, compelling states to use commissions to craft their district plans.[30]

Nor is this more aggressive form of opposition to *Carolene*—not just refusing to fix democratic malfunctions judicially, but also thwarting nonjudicial actors from dealing with them[31]—limited to the redistricting context. In a 2013 case, the Court warned that Congress may "regulate *how* federal elections are held, but not *who* may vote in them."[32] So "it would raise serious constitutional doubts" if Congress tried to stop vote-suppressing state policies like felon

---

[26] *Rucho*, 139 S Ct at 2507.

[27] Id at 2508.

[28] See *Ariz. State Leg. v Ariz. Independent Redistricting Comm'n*, 135 S Ct 2652, 2677–92 (2015) (Roberts, CJ, dissenting).

[29] 570 US 529 (2013).

[30] See, for example, HR 1, 116th Cong, 1st Sess, §§ 2400–35 (2019).

[31] I refer to decisions that prevent nonjudicial actors from correcting democratic failures as *perverse Carolene* decisions—in contrast to *reverse Carolene* decisions where the Court itself declines to intervene in the face of democratic malfunctions. See Part I.

[32] *Arizona v Inter Tribal Council of Ariz.*, 570 US 1, 16 (2013).

disenfranchisement laws or photo ID requirements for voting.[33] The Roberts Court has also been a relentless foe of campaign finance regulations, rejecting one such restriction after another.[34] But limits on electoral funding are usually passed after scandals by reformist coalitions—not by insiders guarding their privileged perches. Empirically, too, these measures boost competition (and challengers) because their bite is felt more acutely by incumbents.[35]

If the Roberts Court isn't a *Carolene* Court, though, what exactly *is* it? Judicial restraint—avoiding the "expansion of judicial authority" into "American political life," in *Rucho*'s words[36]—can't explain the Court's election law cases. *Rucho* might plausibly be seen as a restrained decision, but the Court's campaign finance rulings, systematically deregulating the funding of elections, can't possibly fit that mold. Nor is originalism a satisfying answer. Notably, North Carolina's sole *un*successful argument in *Rucho* was that "the Framers set aside electoral issues such as [partisan gerrymandering] as questions that only Congress can resolve."[37] Nor does concern for individual liberty weave together the various doctrinal strands. Free speech claims prevailed in the Court's campaign finance cases, of course. But they failed in *Rucho*, dismissed in a few cursory paragraphs.[38] And the franchise is a freedom, too, yet the Roberts Court has never found a violation of it.

This leaves more and less sympathetic accounts. More charitably, the Roberts Court might think that American democracy functions reasonably well, at present, except when the elected branches restrict the financing of campaigns. On this view, contemporary politicians pose no serious threat to the right to vote—certainly not compared to past abuses—but *do* often endanger the liberty of electoral donors and spenders. More cynically, the Roberts Court may be as aware as any other observer of the pathologies of modern American democracy: gerrymandering, voter suppression, the enormous influence of the wealthy, and so on. But a majority of the Justices may realize,

---

[33] Id at 17.

[34] See, for example, *Citizens United v FEC*, 558 US 310 (2010).

[35] See, for example, Thomas Stratmann, *How Close Is Fundraising in Contested Elections in States with Low Contribution Limits?* 9 (May 2009), archived at https://perma.cc/RC4Z-3Z7N.

[36] *Rucho v Common Cause*, 139 S Ct 2484, 2507 (2019).

[37] Id at 2495.

[38] See id at 2504–05.

consciously or not, that these pathologies redound largely to their ideological benefit. Flipping *Carolene* on its head, they may then intervene in the political process, or refrain from acting, in a pattern that perpetuates the pathologies.

The article proceeds as follows. In Part I, I identify the ways in which Court decisions may relate to *Carolene*. They may follow its logic correctly or mistakenly, or they may spurn its prescriptions for courts or for all institutions. Next, in Part II, I analyze *Rucho* through *Carolene*'s lens. *Rucho* is a classic anti-*Carolene* decision in both its holding and its reasoning. But its rationales are far from unassailable, as demonstrated by Justice Elena Kagan's dissent. In Part III, I then look beyond *Rucho* to other election law contexts. Throughout the field, the Court may soon converge on a maximally anti-*Carolene* stance: barring all institutions, not just federal courts, from correcting democratic failures. Lastly, in Part IV, I try to divine what's driving the Roberts Court in this area, since it's plainly not *Carolene*. The more benign possibilities seem inapt, raising the likelihood of more unsettling options.

I. Carolene Categories

It's hard to overstate the centrality of *Carolene* in modern constitutional law.[39] For decades, *Carolene*'s first directive—that "legislation affecting ordinary commercial transactions is [generally] not to be pronounced unconstitutional"—explained the Court's deference to the elected branches in most cases.[40] It also highlighted the cardinal sin of the earlier *Lochner* era: the Court's substitution of its own substantive values for those of the people's elected representatives. *Carolene*'s second insight, in turn, eventually launched the field of

---

[39] See, for example, *Schuette v Coalition to Defend Affirmative Action*, 572 US 291, 368 (2014) (Sotomayor, J, dissenting) ("The values identified in *Carolene Products* . . . are central tenets of our equal protection jurisprudence."); Lewis F. Powell, Jr., *Carolene Products Revisited*, 82 Colum L Rev 1087, 1088 (1982) (noting that *Carolene* "commenced a new era in constitutional law").

[40] *United States v Carolene Products Co.*, 304 US 144, 152 (1938). Note that I'm bracketing, for present purposes, the first paragraph of *Carolene*'s famous footnote calling for heightened judicial review "when legislation appears on its face to be within a specific prohibition of the Constitution." Id at 152 n 4. This is a textual rather than a democratic rationale for judicial intervention, and so represents "an idea quite foreign" to the rest of the footnote, in the words of the law clerk who originally drafted it. Louis Lusky, *Footnote Redux: A Carolene Products Reminiscence*, 82 Colum L Rev 1093, 1097 (1982).

election law.⁴¹ The discipline's foundational mission was identifying "legislation which restricts those political processes which can ordinarily be expected to bring about repeal of undesirable legislation": laws against which judicial intervention *is* arguably warranted.⁴² And *Carolene*'s third pillar justified the Court's vigilance, at least for a time, against measures targeting African Americans and other vulnerable groups. "[T]hose political processes ordinarily to be relied upon to protect minorities," *Carolene* recognized, don't always function properly without judicial oversight.⁴³

I only want to say a word here about *Carolene*'s first and third prongs, which is that the contemporary Court often honors them in the breach. The first prong holds that the Court should rarely invalidate acts of Congress, most of which are garden-variety social or economic legislation. But the Rehnquist Court struck down about two-fifths of the congressional statutes it considered, and the Roberts Court has nullified almost *three*-fifths. By comparison, the Vinson, Warren, and Burger Courts found unconstitutional only a quarter of the congressional laws they reviewed.⁴⁴ Likewise, *Carolene*'s third prong instructs the Court to be receptive to claims brought by politically weak minorities. But the Court has ruled in favor of just one African American plaintiff mounting an equal protection challenge in recent decades.⁴⁵ In contrast, myriad white litigants have prevailed in their equal protection suits—against affirmative action plans,⁴⁶

---

⁴¹ See generally Luke P. McLoughlin, *The Elysian Foundations of Election Law*, 82 Temple L Rev 89 (2009).

⁴² *Carolene*, 304 US at 152 n 4.

⁴³ Id; see also Stephanopoulos, 90 NYU L Rev 1527 (cited in note 7) (discussing in detail this *Carolene* prong).

⁴⁴ I calculated these fractions using Keith Whittington's illuminating dataset of Supreme Court cases involving constitutional challenges to acts of Congress. See Keith E. Whittington, *Judicial Review of Congress Database* (2019), archived at https://perma.cc/KF7P-J8NC; see also Michael J. Klarman, *Majoritarian Judicial Review: The Entrenchment Problem*, 85 Geo L J 491, 547 (1997) (concurring that the Court has "burst asunder the restrictions imposed on judicial review by political process theory").

⁴⁵ See *Johnson v California*, 543 US 499 (2005) (requiring strict scrutiny to be applied to an informal prison policy of racially segregating inmates during their initial evaluation). African American plaintiffs have also succeeded in recent racial gerrymandering cases, starting with *Alabama Legislative Black Caucus v Alabama*, 135 S Ct 1257 (2015), but the litigants' race was irrelevant to (and sometimes not even noted by) the Court's analysis.

⁴⁶ See, for example, *Fisher v Univ. of Texas*, 570 US 297 (2013). But see *Fisher v Univ. of Texas*, 136 S Ct 2198 (2016) (ultimately upholding the University of Texas's affirmative action program and thus demonstrating that affirmative action isn't (yet) categorically unconstitutional). Numerous successful challenges to affirmative-action plans also predate the

school integration programs,[47] districts electing minority candidates,[48] and the like. From a *Carolene* perspective, all these litigants should have lost, being members of a group that can hardly be said to be powerless.[49]

Turning to *Carolene*'s second prong—my focus in this article—its gist is reasonably clear. *Usually*, American democracy performs adequately. Usually, that is, "political processes" like free speech, free association, the franchise, and a properly structured electoral system "bring about [the] repeal of undesirable legislation" (or the enactment of desired policy).[50] Sometimes, though, self-interested politicians pass "legislation which restricts those political processes."[51] Sometimes, in Ely's indelible words, "the ins are choking off the channels of political change to ensure that they will stay in and the outs will stay out."[52] When this scenario arises, it's the Court's duty to intervene: to break up the blockage that's responsible for the democratic malfunction. Through its intercession, the Court doesn't frustrate but rather vindicates the popular sovereignty that's the core of the American constitutional order—by enabling the people (not the politicians) to *be* sovereign.

It's true that this account of *Carolene*'s second prong papers over some tricky conceptual issues. In particular, when do "political processes," in fact, "bring about [the] repeal of undesirable legislation"?[53] Just so long as everyone can freely speak, associate, and cast a ballot? Ely seemed to think so at times, labeling his elaboration of *Carolene* a "participation-oriented . . . approach to judicial review."[54] Or are "political processes" a synonym for majoritarian democracy—the idea that the will of a popular majority should generally control? This

---

Roberts Court, of course. See, for example, *City of Richmond v J. A. Croson Co.*, 488 US 469 (1989).

[47] See, for example, *Parents Involved v Seattle School Dist. No. 1*, 551 US 701 (2007).

[48] See, for example, *Shaw v Reno*, 509 US 630 (1993).

[49] See, for example, Reva B. Siegel, *Foreword: Equality Divided*, 127 Harv L Rev 1, 7 (2013) (agreeing that "courts enforcing equal protection claims have come to intervene in the decisions of representative government to protect members of majority groups in ways they scarcely ever intervene to protect members of minority groups," thus "turn[ing] the reasoning of *Carolene Products* on its head").

[50] *United States v Carolene Products Co.*, 304 US 144, 152 n 4 (1938).

[51] Id.

[52] Ely, *Democracy and Distrust* at 103 (cited in note 3).

[53] *Carolene*, 304 US at 152 n 4.

[54] Ely, *Democracy and Distrust* at 87 (cited in note 3).

is probably the most common view of *Carolene*,⁵⁵ and Ely expressed it, too, at other times.⁵⁶ Or is responsiveness to (rather than congruence with) public opinion the crux of *Carolene*'s "political processes"? This position, held by scholars like Samuel Issacharoff and Richard Pildes, stresses that as voters *change* their minds, public policy should *shift* accordingly.⁵⁷

I don't try to resolve this debate here. (I also don't think resolution is possible. *Carolene*'s second prong simply doesn't specify the precise form of democracy the Court had in mind.) But I do want to insist that *Carolene*'s "political processes" must encompass more than just unrestricted speaking, associating, and voting. This is because free participation, important as it is, doesn't necessarily "bring about [the] repeal of undesirable legislation." Say that citizens may participate as they please. But say that self-interested politicians get to choose how votes are *aggregated*: how votes, in other words, translate into legislative seats. Then there's no guarantee that unwanted policies will actually be reversed. It's perfectly possible that they'll remain in effect, shielded from the will of the electorate by a legislature that, thanks to the method of vote aggregation, fails to reflect public opinion.⁵⁸

To put the point another way, *Carolene*'s "repeal of undesirable legislation" is a reference to policy outcomes. A purely participational theory of democracy is silent about policy outcomes. It only stipulates that citizens should be able to speak, associate, and vote without restraint. It therefore can't be *Carolene*'s theory even if we remain unsure which democratic model that *does* incorporate the outputs of

---

⁵⁵ See, for example, Robert M. Cover, *The Origins of Judicial Activism in the Protection of Minorities*, 91 Yale L J 1287, 1293 (1982) ("[P]aragraph two of the footnote captures . . . the lesson of twentieth century perversions of the majoritarian forms of politics."); Owen M. Fiss, *Foreword: The Forms of Justice*, 93 Harv L Rev 1, 6 (1979) (noting *Carolene*'s "general presumption in favor of majoritarianism"). I'm also partial to a majoritarian theory of democracy, aiming above all for governmental outputs aligned with the preferences of the median voter. See generally Nicholas O. Stephanopoulos, *Elections and Alignment*, 114 Colum L Rev 283 (2014).

⁵⁶ See, for example, Ely, *Democracy and Distrust* at 7 (cited in note 3) ("[M]ajoritarian democracy is . . . the core of our entire system. . . .").

⁵⁷ See, for example, Samuel Issacharoff and Richard H. Pildes, *Politics as Markets: Partisan Lockups of the Democratic Process*, 50 Stan L Rev 643, 646 (1998) (asserting that "one of the central goals of democratic politics" is "that the policy outcomes of the political process be responsive to the interests and views of citizens").

⁵⁸ Election law has long recognized this point. See, for example, Pamela S. Karlan, *The Rights to Vote: Some Pessimism About Formalism*, 71 Tex L Rev 1705, 1707–08 (1993) (noting that voting implicates people's interests in participation, aggregation, and governance).

the political process—majoritarianism, responsiveness, or some other approach—is *Carolene*'s theory.

So understood, how may *Carolene*'s second prong relate to Court rulings? First, a *correct Carolene* decision accurately perceives a democratic defect: a practice that prevents certain people from engaging in politics or that distorts the translation of voter sentiment into representation. A correct *Carolene* decision also holds the practice unconstitutional, thereby furthering key democratic values.[59] In the Court's jurisprudence, the one-person, one-vote cases of the 1960s are probably the most famous examples of correct *Carolene* decisions.[60] Malapportionment on a massive scale had led to a "rural strangle hold" on the legislature in many states: a glaring democratic defect.[61] By requiring equally populated districts, the Court repaired the democratic damage, "releasing the strangle hold on the legislature" and ending the "frustration of the majority will."[62]

Second, a *mistaken Carolene* decision tries to heed *Carolene*'s logic but misdiagnoses the policy at issue. The Court may wrongly think the policy is benign—consistent with a properly functioning democracy—and so refrain from acting when it should have intervened. Or the Court may err by finding the policy democratically destructive, though in fact it's neutral or even helpful, and then invalidating a law it should have sustained.[63] I argue below that the Roberts Court's campaign finance cases are mistaken *Carolene* decisions. They assert that regulations of electoral funding are efforts by incumbents to squash competition. But these claims are incorrect; most campaign finance laws actually assist challengers. A *Carolene* Court should therefore have upheld these pro-competitive measures.[64]

---

[59] Alternatively, in the absence of a democratic defect, a correct *Carolene* decision refrains from intervention. This is the scenario covered by *Carolene*'s first prong.

[60] See, for example, Richard H. Pildes, *Foreword: The Constitutionalization of Democratic Politics*, 118 Harv L Rev 28, 44 (2004) ("Malapportionment . . . represents the paradigm instance of justified judicial oversight."); David A. Strauss, *Is Carolene Products Obsolete?*, 2010 U Ill L Rev 1251, 1259 ("Perhaps the most dramatic example[s] of a *Carolene Products* success story . . . [are] the so-called reapportionment decisions.").

[61] *Reynolds v Sims*, 377 US 533, 543 (1964).

[62] Id at 543, 576.

[63] Dorf and Issacharoff briefly note the possibility of mistaken *Carolene* decisions, "ask[ing] what happens if judges stray from the proper approach," and adding that "there [is] no guarantee that they would [apply *Carolene*] correctly." Dorf and Issacharoff, 72 U Colo L Rev at 941 (cited in note 12).

[64] See Part III.B.

Third, a *reverse Carolene* decision does the opposite of what *Carolene* instructs.[65] The Court acknowledges that a practice undermines democratic values by impeding political participation or skewing the conversion of voters' preferences into legislative influence. But the Court declines to step in because it rejects *Carolene*'s basic tenet. It disagrees that it should exercise its power of judicial review to break up blockages of the political process. The propriety of judicial intervention is untethered, in its view, from the operation of American democracy.[66] *Rucho*, I contend in the next Part, is a quintessential reverse *Carolene* decision. It freely concedes that partisan gerrymandering is undemocratic. But this admission is followed not by the gerrymander's dismantling—the next step under *Carolene*—but by its insulation from any further challenge in the federal courts.[67]

Lastly, a *perverse Carolene* decision heightens the Court's defiance of *Carolene* by another notch.[68] The Court sees other actors—Congress, state courts, ordinary people through voter initiatives—taking steps to fix democratic malfunctions. But the Court doesn't cheer these remedies as appealing alternatives to the judicial intervention it's unwilling to undertake. Instead, the Court stops the other actors' projects dead in their tracks, holding that they're barred by the federal Constitution. The Court thus prevents *any* entity from engaging in pro-democratic policymaking. It invokes its power of judicial review not to promote democracy but to ensure its continued subversion. Perverse *Carolene* decisions, I maintain below, have already begun to mar the Court's doctrine. And they may become even more common in the years ahead, particularly when the Court next considers the validity of redistricting commissions. These bodies are the primary nonjudicial response to gerrymandering. But the Court may well hold that they violate the Elections Clause or the First Amendment.[69]

---

[65] For another scholar using similar terminology in a helpful contribution, see Aaron Tang, *Reverse Political Process Theory*, 70 Vand L Rev 1427 (2017). Tang calls it reverse political process theory when the Court "afford[s] special protections . . . to politically powerful entities that are able to advance their interests full well in the democratic arena." Id at 1430–31. As the next paragraph explains, I refer to such rulings as *perverse Carolene* decisions, frustrating the efforts of nonjudicial actors to pursue democratic goals.

[66] Alternatively, a reverse *Carolene* decision *invalidates* a policy that's democratically *unproblematic*. But this scenario is better understood as a violation of *Carolene*'s first prong.

[67] See Part II.

[68] I previously discussed perverse *Carolene* decisions (without employing that nomenclature) in Nicholas O. Stephanopoulos, *Arizona and Anti-Reform*, 2015 U Chi Legal F 477, 487–91.

[69] See Part III.

Of course, this taxonomy of Court decisions is incomplete. It doesn't even try to incorporate most of the factors that drive judicial decision making: text, structure, history, precedent, and so on.[70] The taxonomy is thus best understood as the product of a thought experiment. If *Carolene*'s second prong—the proposition that judicial review should be pro-democratic—were its own modality of constitutional interpretation, then how could that modality be applied? How, that is, could the Court follow or flout *Carolene*'s command?

II. A Reverse Carolene Decision

One way the Court could flout the command is by issuing a ruling like *Rucho*. *Rucho*, I argue in this Part, is an archetypal reverse *Carolene* decision—a distillation of the genre to its purest form. The Court grants that partisan gerrymandering is undemocratic, yet bars federal courts from lifting a finger to stop it. I also situate *Rucho* within the corpus of anti-*Carolene* jurisprudence and scholarship. To an uncanny degree, the case echoes the positions of the one-person, one-vote dissenters of the 1960s and of the critics of Ely's political process theory. Those views, moreover, are far from irrebuttable. In her dissent in *Rucho*, in fact, Justice Kagan picks them apart, showing that while *Carolene* no longer animates a Court majority, its message still endures.

A. CAROLENE'S SPURNED LOGIC

The claim that partisan gerrymandering offends the democratic values that *Carolene* seeks to protect is uncontroversial. As I show below, even the *Rucho* Court agrees with that assessment (though not with what, under *Carolene*, courts should do about it). Nevertheless, it's useful to explain why, exactly, gerrymandering is undemocratic: both the North Carolina plan at issue in *Rucho* and the practice more generally. In a nutshell, gerrymandering awards the line-drawing party more seats than it would have earned under a neutral map. In a polarized era, these extra seats shift the ideological center of the legislature and, with it, the laws the legislature passes. Both legislative representation and enacted policy are thus skewed in the direction of the line-drawing party—and away from what voters actually want.[71]

---

[70] Cf. Philip Bobbitt, *Constitutional Fate: Theory of the Constitution* (Oxford, 1984).

[71] For a similar argument, see Stephanopoulos, 2015 U Chi Legal F at 489 (cited in note 68).

To phrase the point in terms of *Carolene*'s democratic values,[72] gerrymandering can lead to countermajoritarian outcomes. Sometimes the electorate prefers one party's candidates but, thanks to cleverly drawn districts, it gets a legislature run by the other party and advancing that party's agenda. Gerrymandering can also stifle electoral responsiveness. Modern map makers typically make their side's seats reasonably safe: closer to 60 percent of the vote (and a comfortable twenty-point margin) than 50 percent plus one.[73] Seats of this sort don't flip in all but the most extreme electoral environments, rendering futile even significant changes in voter sentiment. And gerrymandering can inhibit political participation, too. It doesn't *directly* prevent anyone from speaking, associating, or voting. But it *deters* some citizens from engaging in these activities since they realize, no matter how hard they try, their efforts will likely be in vain.

To make this discussion more concrete, consider the North Carolina plan in *Rucho*. Its architects weren't shy about their goal of guaranteeing ten seats for Republican candidates and three for Democrats—whether or not voters wanted so lopsided a congressional delegation. A legislative committee ratified a criterion explicitly labeled "Partisan Advantage," providing that "[t]he partisan makeup of the congressional plan" would be "10 Republicans and 3 Democrats."[74] The cochair of this committee added, in breathtakingly candid testimony, "I propose that we draw the maps to give a partisan advantage to 10 Republicans and 3 Democrats because I do not believe it's possible to draw a map with 11 Republicans and 2 Democrats."[75]

The plan's results realized its drafters' ambitions. In both of the elections in which it was used, ten Republican candidates and three

---

[72] Again, I don't try to choose among these values here, at least not beyond insisting that participation isn't the only relevant value.

[73] See, for example, *Common Cause v Rucho*, 279 F Supp 3d 587, 657–58 (MDNC 2018), rev'd, 139 S Ct 2484 (2019) (observing that "all ten Republican districts" in the North Carolina plan at issue in *Rucho* were "'safe,'" that is, "highly unlikely to change parties in subsequent elections").

[74] *Rucho*, 139 S Ct at 2510 (Kagan, J, dissenting).

[75] Id; see also id (quoting the cochair's comment that "I think electing Republicans is better than electing Democrats. So I drew this map to help foster what I think is better for the country."). In *Rucho*'s wake, such brazen partisan boasts are likely to become more common, as are even more aggressive gerrymandering techniques like drawing noncontiguous districts, redistricting more frequently than once per decade, and using computer algorithms to design more durably skewed maps. See Aaron Goldzimer and Nicholas Stephanopoulos, *Democrats Can't Be Afraid to Gerrymander Now*, Slate (July 3, 2019), archived at https://perma.cc/GQ96-2UVX.

Democrats won seats.[76] This breakdown held even though the second election—the Democratic wave of 2018—saw Democrats earn a majority of the statewide vote.[77] That election thus yielded both a countermajoritarian outcome and no responsiveness at all to the electorate's pro-Democratic swing. More sophisticated metrics tell the same story. According to one expert, the North Carolina plan was the single most biased congressional map of the last half-century.[78] That expert also found that it would take a pro-Democratic wave on par with the Watergate election of 1974 for the plan's bias to dissipate.[79] Another expert randomly generated thousands of North Carolina congressional maps based on all of the drafters' *non*partisan criteria. Not one of them was as tilted in Republicans' favor as the actual plan.[80]

But perhaps these statistics don't reveal a real democratic problem. Perhaps legislative representation and enacted policy still reflect voter opinion, when a map is gerrymandered, even if seat tallies are out of whack. Recent empirical research puts this rosy view to rest. When a state legislative[81] or congressional[82] plan is biased toward a party, the ideological midpoint of the chamber or delegation shifts significantly in that party's preferred direction. So, too, do the measures that become law. In fact, "a one standard deviation change in [a plan's bias] has a larger impact on state policy than a change in the party of the governor."[83] The effects of gerrymandering thus aren't limited to the seat and vote percentages that preoccupy election wonks. They extend, rather, to the ideological composition and policy output of the legislature—the very essence of democratic governance.

Indeed, they extend even further than that. Plaintiffs in several recent cases have testified that gerrymandering chills their political

---

[76] See *Rucho*, 139 S Ct at 2491–92; see also id (noting that one of the Republican victories in 2018 was tainted by fraud).

[77] See LWV Brief at *15 (cited in note 16).

[78] See id at *16–17; see also *Common Cause*, 279 F Supp 3d at 659–60.

[79] See *Common Cause*, 279 F Supp 3d at 660–61.

[80] See *Rucho*, 139 S Ct at 2518 (Kagan, J, dissenting).

[81] See Devin Caughey et al, *Partisan Gerrymandering and the Political Process: Effects on Roll-Call Voting and State Policies*, 16 Election L J 453, 462–64 (2017).

[82] See Nicholas O. Stephanopoulos, *The Causes and Consequences of Gerrymandering*, 59 Wm & Mary L Rev 2115, 2140–43 (2018).

[83] See Caughey et al, 16 Election L J at 464–66 (cited in note 81).

participation, discouraging them from speaking, associating, and voting in races whose results are foreordained. As one litigant in *Rucho* remarked, "I can't tell you how many people told me this election . . . 'This system is rigged. My vote doesn't count.' It was really hard to try to galvanize people to participate."[84] These anecdotes find support in new academic work. When a party is disadvantaged by a district plan, at either the state legislative or congressional level, its adherents suffer a host of participational harms. They become less likely to run for office; candidates who do choose to run have worse credentials; donors don't give as much money; and voters are less apt to turn out.[85] "Prevented [by gerrymandering] from attaining their electoral or policy objectives, elites and voters alike . . . perform their [various] functions with less enthusiasm."[86]

Unsurprisingly,[87] the *Rucho* Court didn't cite this (or any other) study. But it did repeatedly acknowledge that gerrymandering is undemocratic. (As Justice Kagan quipped in dissent, "really, how could it not?"[88]) "Excessive partisanship in districting," the Court observed, "leads to results that reasonably seem unjust."[89] "[G]errymandering is 'incompatible with democratic principles,'" the Court continued.[90] In fact, "partisan gerrymanders violate the core principle of [our] republican government . . . namely, that the voters should choose their representatives, not the other way around."[91] That's why the

---

[84] *Common Cause*, 279 F Supp 3d at 679; see also, for example, *Benisek v Lamone*, 348 F Supp 3d 493, 523 (D Md 2018), rev'd, 139 S Ct 2484 (2019) ("[T]estimony provided by several of the plaintiffs revealed a lack of enthusiasm, indifference to voting, a sense of disenfranchisement, a sense of disconnection, and confusion after the 2011 redistricting . . .").

[85] See Nicholas O. Stephanopoulos and Christopher Warshaw, *The Impact of Partisan Gerrymandering on Political Parties* 13–21 (Aug 21, 2019), archived at https://perma.cc/8KLL-S8XZ.

[86] Id at 4.

[87] Unsurprisingly, because Chief Justice Roberts, *Rucho*'s author, is a noted skeptic of empirical research. See, for example, Transcript of Oral Argument, *Gill v Whitford*, No 16-1161, *40 (Oct 3, 2017) (describing quantitative measures of partisan gerrymandering as "sociological gobbledygook").

[88] *Rucho v Common Cause*, 139 S Ct 2484, 2512 (2019) (Kagan, J, dissenting); see also id ("The majority disputes none of what I have said . . . about how gerrymanders undermine democracy.").

[89] Id at 2506.

[90] Id (quoting *Ariz. State Leg. v Ariz. Independent Redistricting Comm'n*, 135 S Ct 2652, 2658 (2015)).

[91] Id (quotation marks omitted).

Court "does not condone excessive partisan gerrymandering,"[92] but instead describes it, over and over, as a "problem."[93]

Under *Carolene*, the next step of the analysis is painfully obvious. Gerrymandering is "unjust," "incompatible with democratic principles," contrary to "the core principle of our republican government"—so therefore the Court should step in and halt the practice. In *Carolene*'s own words, gerrymandering "restricts those political processes" (legislative elections) "which can ordinarily be expected to bring about repeal of undesirable legislation" (by ousting unpopular legislators) and thus warrants "exacting judicial scrutiny."[94] Or as Jamal Greene recently put it, when a party "constructs district lines intentionally to maintain its own partisan advantage," "[i]ts behavior falls squarely, almost comically, into the second paragraph of *Carolene Products* footnote four."[95]

And yet the *Rucho* Court declined to invalidate the North Carolina plan, announcing instead that partisan gerrymandering claims are inherently nonjusticiable. In so ruling, the Court pointedly rejected *Carolene*'s central claim: that the state of American democracy and the need for judicial intervention should be linked. "Gerrymandering is incompatible with democratic principles"—but that "does not mean that the solution lies with the federal judiciary."[96] "Gerrymanders violate the core principle of our republican government"—but "[t]hat seems like an objection more properly grounded in the Guarantee Clause," which "does not provide the basis for a justiciable claim."[97] Some argue that "this Court *can* address the problem of partisan gerrymandering because it *must*"—but "[t]hat is not the test of our authority under the Constitution."[98]

---

[92] Id at 2507.

[93] Id at 2494, 2496, 2507.

[94] *United States v Carolene Products Co.*, 304 US 144, 152 n 4 (1938).

[95] Jamal Greene, *Foreword: Rights as Trumps?*, 132 Harv L Rev 28, 128 (2018); see also, for example, Pildes, 118 Harv L Rev at 55 (cited in note 60) ("Partisan gerrymandering is a paradigmatic instance of the structural pathology all democratic systems face."); Kathleen M. Sullivan and Pamela S. Karlan, *The Elysian Fields of the Law*, 57 Stan L Rev 695, 711 (2004) (Ely "would have been outraged by the Court's recent decision" refusing to rein in partisan gerrymandering).

[96] *Rucho*, 139 S Ct at 2506 (quotation marks omitted).

[97] Id (quotation marks and alterations omitted).

[98] Id at 2507 (quotation marks omitted). Or as Justice Kagan wrote in her dissent, "In the face of grievous harm to democratic governance," and "in the face of escalating partisan

These passages are some of the clearest repudiations of *Carolene* ever to appear in the United States Reports.[99] The Court almost seems to flaunt its view that minority rule, electoral nonresponsiveness, and chilled participation—all the democratic injuries caused by gerrymandering—are irrelevant to the Court's decision making. Democracy may be burning, but the Court flatly refuses any responsibility for extinguishing the flames. This position, of course, is the antithesis of *Carolene*, which holds that putting out the fire is the Court's most critical task. That's why I refer to *Rucho* as a paradigmatic reverse *Carolene* decision: as close to *Carolene*'s opposite as we're ever likely to see.

B. DOCTRINAL ECHOES

Rucho, however, does more than just abjure *Carolene*'s logic. It also gives *reasons* for its renunciation: *arguments* why judicial intervention should be unconnected to democratic malfunction. I now turn to these reasons, and contend that they strongly resemble the ones offered by the dissenters in the one-person, one-vote cases of the 1960s. Reading *Rucho*, in fact, any student of the Court's redistricting doctrine is likely to experience a powerful sense of déjà vu. It's as though the 1960s dissenters are speaking from the grave, only this time for a prevailing majority of the Court instead of a defeated minority.[100]

But why compare *Rucho* to the reapportionment cases of half a century ago? For one thing, those cases involved many of the same subjects as *Rucho*: redistricting, vote dilution, and the electoral influence of different groups. Those cases also *didn't* involve (at least not

---

manipulation whose compatibility with this Nation's values and law no one defends," "the majority declines to provide any remedy." Id at 2515 (Kagan, J, dissenting).

[99] As I discuss in the next section, the dissents in the one-person, one-vote cases of the 1960s are the other contenders to the anti-*Carolene* throne. See, for example, *Wesberry v Sanders*, 376 US 1, 48 (1964) (Harlan, J, dissenting) ("The Constitution does not confer on the Court blanket authority to step into every situation where the political branch may be thought to have fallen short."); *Baker v Carr*, 369 US 186, 270 (1962) (Frankfurter, J, dissenting) (asserting that "there is not under our Constitution a judicial remedy for every political mischief"). A striking earlier anti-*Carolene* decision was *Giles v Harris*, 189 US 475, 488 (1903), where the Court acquiesced in Alabama's refusal to register African American citizens on the ground that "relief from a great political wrong . . . must be given by [the state] or by the legislative and political department of the [federal] government."

[100] See, for example, Guy-Uriel Charles and Luis E. Fuentes-Rohwer, *Dirty Thinking About Law and Democracy in Rucho v. Common Cause*, 3 Am Const Soc'y Sup Ct Rev 293, 308 (2019) ("From an analytical perspective, there is nothing new in *Rucho*; Chief Justice Roberts basically sings from the standard hymnal.").

front and center[101]) the distinct issue of racial discrimination, the focus of *Carolene*'s third prong. Moreover, as noted earlier, those cases are widely regarded as the best historical examples of correct *Carolene* decisions.[102] According to Pamela Karlan, "[n]othing provides a better model of anti-entrenchment judicial review than the Warren Court's reapportionment cases," where "the Court confronted . . . textbook examples of the systematic restriction of the political process."[103] Lastly, those cases were hotly contested, featuring several Justices writing long, sophisticated dissents over a multiyear period. As a result, the rationales for pro-democratic judicial intervention were matched by rebuttals—thrust met by parry— in a vigorous debate unsurpassed before or since.

One of the *Rucho* Court's reasons for not tackling gerrymandering, then, was its view that neither the Constitution's text nor its history supports a judicial role in this area. Certain important modes of constitutional interpretation, in other words, don't corroborate *Carolene* and may even undercut it. Citing the Elections Clause, the Court observed that it "assign[ed] the issue [of redistricting] to the state legislatures, expressly checked and balanced by the Federal Congress."[104] "At no point was there a suggestion that the federal courts had a role to play" in curbing redistricting abuses.[105] The Court also commented that the constitutional provisions applicable to gerrymandering—the Elections Clause and the First and Fourteenth Amendments—are too abstract to be helpful. They "provide [ ] no basis whatever to guide the exercise of judicial discretion."[106] "But we have no commission to allocate political power and influence in the absence of a constitutional directive . . . to guide us in the exercise of such authority."[107]

---

[101] Several of the pivotal one-person, one-vote cases did arise in southern states (like Alabama, Georgia, and Tennessee) where racial discrimination was never far from the surface.

[102] See Part I.

[103] Pamela S. Karlan, *John Hart Ely and the Problem of Gerrymandering: The Lion in Winter*, 114 Yale L J 1329, 1333 (2005); see also, for example, Pildes, 118 Harv L Rev at 44 (cited in note 60); Strauss, 2010 U Ill L Rev at 1259 (cited in note 60).

[104] *Rucho*, 139 S Ct at 2496.

[105] Id; see also id ("Nor was there any indication that the Framers had ever heard of courts doing such a thing.").

[106] Id at 2506; see also id at 2505 (noting that justiciable claims "typically involve constitutional . . . provisions . . . confining and guiding the exercise of judicial discretion").

[107] Id at 2508; see also id at 2507 ("Federal judges have no license to reallocate political power between the two major political parties, with no plausible grant of authority in the Constitution. . . .").

This argument—call it the *conventional modalities* point—ran through the 1960s reapportionment dissents as well. Those opinions stressed that the Court's one-person, one-vote rule wasn't grounded in the Constitution's text, structure, or history. Justice John Marshall Harlan II thus wrote in *Wesberry v Sanders*, the 1964 case that applied the rule to congressional district plans, that "the language of [Article I], the surrounding text, and the relevant history are all in strong and consistent direct contradiction of the Court's holding.[108] In *Reynolds v Sims*, the case later in 1964 that extended the equal population principle to state legislative maps, Justice Harlan added that "the Equal Protection Clause was never intended to inhibit the States in choosing any democratic method they pleased for the apportionment of their legislatures."[109] "This is shown by the language of the Fourteenth Amendment taken as a whole, by the understanding of those who proposed and ratified it, and by the political practices of the States at the time the Amendment was adopted."[110] Justice Potter Stewart concurred in a companion case to *Reynolds*, opining that "[t]he Court's draconian pronouncement . . . finds no support in the words of the Constitution . . . or in the 175-year political history of our Federal Union."[111]

A second reason the *Rucho* Court gave for not intervening against gerrymandering was its uncertainty how to recognize a *non*-gerrymandered plan. "[I]t is not even clear what fairness looks like in this context," the Court remarked.[112] To some, a normatively attractive map "may mean a greater number of competitive districts."[113] To others, it may mean "ensur[ing] each party its 'appropriate' share of 'safe' seats."[114] Still others may think "fairness should be measured by adherence to 'traditional' districting criteria."[115] Faced with these competing districting goals, the Court threw up its hands. "Deciding

---

[108] 376 US 1, 41 (1964) (Harlan, J, dissenting).

[109] 377 US 533, 590–91 (1964) (Harlan, J, dissenting).

[110] Id at 591; see also, for example, id at 614–15 ("[T]oday's decisions are refuted by the language of the Amendment which they construe," as well as "by history and by consistent theory and practice . . .").

[111] *Lucas v Forty-Fourth Gen. Assembly of Colo.*, 377 US 713, 746 (1964) (Stewart, J, dissenting).

[112] *Rucho*, 139 S Ct at 2500.

[113] Id.

[114] Id.

[115] Id.

among just these different visions of fairness (you can imagine many others) poses basic questions that are political, not legal."[116] "There are no legal standards discernible in the Constitution for making such judgments. . . ."[117]

Justice Frankfurter made the same argument about the *lack of normative consensus* in *Baker v Carr*, the 1962 case holding that one-person, one-vote claims are justiciable.[118] "Apportionment, by its character, is a subject of extraordinary complexity," he wrote.[119] It raises "fundamental theoretical issues concerning what is to be represented in a representative legislature."[120] It also implicates more practical "considerations of geography, demography, electoral convenience, economic and social cohesions or divergences among particular local groups . . . and a host of others."[121] But "these are not factors that lend themselves to . . . judicial determinations."[122] To evaluate them, the Court would have to "choose among competing bases of representation—ultimately, really, among competing theories of political philosophy."[123] These aren't matters that "judges are equipped to adjudicate by legal training or experience or native wit."[124]

Third, the *Rucho* Court asserted that judges lack the empirical skills to assess district plans' electoral effects. The district court had included in its proposed test an element asking if a map's bias would likely persist in future elections.[125] In response, the Court described historical cases where "predictions of durability proved to be dramatically wrong" due to "flawed assumptions about voter preferences and behavior."[126] Generalizing its critique, the Court claimed

---

[116] Id.

[117] Id.

[118] 369 US 186 (1962).

[119] Id at 323 (Frankfurter, J, dissenting).

[120] Id.

[121] Id.

[122] Id at 324.

[123] Id at 300.

[124] Id at 324. In *Avery v Midland County*, 390 U.S. 474 (1968), similarly, Justice Harlan alleged that the Court had embraced "a particular political ideology" even though that view "has been the subject of wide debate and differences from the beginnings of our Nation." Id at 490 (Harlan, J, dissenting).

[125] See *Rucho v Common Cause*, 139 S Ct 2484, 2503 (2019).

[126] Id.

that voters' choices depend on a host of changeable conditions: "the quality of the candidates, the tone of the candidates' campaigns, the performance of an incumbent, national events or local issues that drive voter turnout," and so on.[127] Consequently, "asking judges to predict how a particular districting map will perform in future elections" would put them "on unstable ground outside judicial expertise."[128]

The 1960s dissenters also leveled this *judicial capacity* objection. Addressing the one-person, one-vote rule after it was floated by Justice William Douglas's concurrence in *Baker*,[129] Justice Frankfurter labeled it a "mathematical quagmire" of "judicially inappropriate and elusive determinants," from which there would be no "means of extrication."[130] "To charge courts with the task of [solving] these mathematical puzzles is to attribute . . . omnicompetence to judges."[131] Similarly, after *Reynolds* turned Justice Douglas's suggestion into the law of the land, Justice Harlan identified a series of empirical difficulties with the newly minted equal population principle. It couldn't "balance between keeping up with population shifts and having stable districts," nor could it say "how many legislative districts a State shall have," "what the shape of the districts shall be," or "where to draw a particular district line."[132] "In all these respects, courts will be called upon to make particular decisions" that "are not amenable to the development of judicial standards."[133]

Fourth, the *Rucho* Court worried about the unseemliness of involving the federal courts in partisan disputes over redistricting. Redistricting is "'a process that often produces ill will and distrust,'" the Court stated.[134] So it blanched at the idea that the "federal courts are to 'inject [themselves] into the most heated partisan issues' by

---

[127] Id.

[128] Id at 2504.

[129] See *Baker v Carr*, 369 US 186, 244 (1962) (Douglas, J, concurring) (suggesting that "a State [may not] weight the vote of one county or one district more heavily than it weights the vote in another").

[130] Id at 268 (Frankfurter, J, dissenting).

[131] Id.

[132] *Reynolds v Sims*, 377 US 533, 621 (1964) (Harlan, J, dissenting).

[133] Id; see also, for example, *Avery v Midland County*, 390 US 474, 487 (1968) (Harlan, J, dissenting) (criticizing "these adventures of the Court in the realm of political science").

[134] *Rucho v Common Cause*, 139 S Ct 2484, 2503 (2019) (quoting *Vieth v Jubelirer*, 541 US 267, 307 (2004) (opinion of Kennedy, J)).

adjudicating partisan gerrymandering claims."[135] This "expansion of judicial authority would not be into just any area of controversy, but into one of the most intensely partisan aspects of American political life."[136]

Again, Justice Frankfurter aired this *partisan entanglement* point first. In *Colegrove v Green,* the 1946 case that was overruled by *Baker,* he maintained that "the history of Congressional apportionment is its embroilment in politics, in the sense of party contests and party interests."[137] "From the determination of such issues this Court has traditionally held aloof," because "[i]t is hostile to a democratic system to involve the judiciary in the politics of the people."[138] Justice Frankfurter returned to this theme in his *Baker* dissent. "The Court's authority," he warned, would be undermined by "injecting itself into the clash of political forces in political settlements."[139] "It will add a virulent source of friction and tension . . . to embroil the federal judiciary" in "[a]pportionment battles" that are "overwhelmingly party or intraparty contests."[140]

And fifth, the *Rucho* Court thought it didn't have to grapple with gerrymandering because other actors could stop the practice instead. In some states, "[p]rovisions in state statutes and state constitutions . . . provide standards and guidance for state courts to apply."[141] "[O]ther States are restricting partisan considerations in districting through legislation," in particular by "placing power to draw electoral districts in the hands of independent commissions."[142] And Congress, too, has the "power to do something about partisan gerrymandering in the Elections Clause."[143] This authority underpins "[d]ozens of bills

---

[135] Id (quoting *Davis v Bandemer,* 478 US 109, 145 (1986) (opinion of O'Connor, J)).

[136] Id at 2507.

[137] 328 US 549, 555 (1946) (plurality), rev'd, *Baker v Carr,* 369 US 186 (1962); see also id at 553 ("[T]his controversy concerns matters that bring courts into immediate and active relations with party contests.").

[138] Id at 553–54.

[139] *Baker v Carr,* 369 US 186, 267 (1962) (Frankfurter, J, dissenting); see also id (asserting that the Court's legitimacy is "nourished by the Court's complete detachment . . . from political entanglements").

[140] Id at 324; see also id ("[I]n every strand of this complicated, intricate web of values meet the contending forces of partisan politics.").

[141] *Rucho,* 139 S Ct at 2507.

[142] Id.

[143] Id at 2508.

[that] have been introduced to limit reliance on political considerations in redistricting."[144] The Court's nonjusticiability holding thus didn't "condemn complaints about districting to echo into a void."[145]

Once more, the 1960s dissenters were the original exponents of this argument about *other actors*. In *Colegrove*, Justice Frankfurter noted that "[a]uthority for dealing with [malapportionment] resides elsewhere."[146] Congress has "authority to secure fair representation by the States in the popular House."[147] Another "remedy for unfairness in districting is to secure State legislatures that will apportion properly."[148] In *Baker*, Justice Frankfurter emphasized the power of public opinion. "[R]elief must come through an aroused popular conscience that sears the conscience of the people's representatives."[149] Justice Harlan also observed in *Baker* that state institutions may equalize districts' populations themselves. For the Court to intervene, then, would "turn our backs on the regard which this Court has always shown for the judgment of state legislatures and courts on matters of basically local concern."[150]

But so what if *Rucho* echoes the 1960s dissents? Why does it matter that *Rucho* gives the same reasons for not confronting gerrymandering that Justices Frankfurter, Harlan, and Stewart provided for allowing malapportionment to persist? It matters because it helps us to understand *Rucho*, to place it in doctrinal and historical perspective. *Rucho* plainly isn't a novel decision, devising creative arguments for holding gerrymandering nonjusticiable. Instead it's a deeply familiar decision, refusing to correct a democratic failure on the same grounds that anti-*Carolene* Justices have always invoked for their inaction. It's a decision that wouldn't have surprised had it been penned by the minority faction of the Warren Court rather than by the namesake of the Roberts Court.

---

[144] Id.

[145] Id at 2507.

[146] *Colegrove v Green*, 328 US 549, 554 (1946) (plurality), rev'd, *Baker v Carr*, 369 US 186 (1962).

[147] Id; see also id ("[T]he subject has been committed to the exclusive control of Congress.").

[148] Id at 556.

[149] *Baker v Carr*, 369 US 186, 270 (1962) (Frankfurter, J, dissenting); see also id ("Appeal must be to an informed, civically militant electorate.").

[150] Id at 332 (Harlan, J, dissenting).

The parallels between *Rucho* and the 1960s dissents also matter because the 1960s dissents were, well, dissents. Their objections to federal courts addressing unequally populated districts were *rejected*, not just once but over a series of major cases.[151] Yet those same objections carried the day in *Rucho*. Anti-*Carolene* rationales that had been thought discredited (or at least defunct) roared back to life, unabashedly espoused by a majority of the Justices. The point, of course, isn't that the Warren Court's reapportionment decisions required *Rucho* to come out the other way, let alone that *Rucho* overruled those decisions sub silentio. Stare decisis applies to the Court's holdings, not to its reasons. But the affinity between *Rucho* and the 1960s dissents does indicate that it's outside the central current of the Court's redistricting cases. If *Rucho* had followed from those cases, it would have carefully considered their logic and implications. It *wouldn't* have repeated, time and again, the arguments those cases rebuffed.[152]

C. ACADEMIC ECHOES

Just as *Rucho* should remind redistricting lawyers of the one-person, one-vote dissents, it should evoke for scholars a specific literature: the barrage of skeptical commentary that greeted the publication of John Hart Ely's landmark book, *Democracy and Distrust*, in 1980.[153] Ely's book was the academic analogue of the Warren Court's reapportionment decisions: a full-throated defense of *Carolene*'s thesis that democratic malfunction should prompt judicial intervention. Also like those decisions, *Democracy and Distrust* was criticized as soon as it appeared. Over the years, in fact, a whole cottage industry emerged to attack Ely's (and *Carolene*'s) idea of pro-democratic judicial review.

---

[151] See John Hart Ely, *Confounded by Cromartie: Are Racial Stereotypes Now Acceptable Across the Board or Only When Used in Support of Partisan Gerrymanders?*, 56 U Miami L Rev 489, 501 (2002) (describing these objections as "consigned to the dustbin of history").

[152] For a similar view of *Rucho*, see Joey Fishkin, *Rucho: A Sinkhole Dangerously Close to the House*, Election Law Blog (July 1, 2019), archived at https://perma.cc/2ZN8-8VUU. Also notably, *Rucho* didn't say a word about the Court's *racial* vote dilution precedents, even though they necessarily involve claims "for a fair share of political power and influence, with all the justiciability conundrums that entails." *Rucho v Common Cause*, 139 S Ct 2484, 2502 (2019). See Nicholas O. Stephanopoulos, *The Erasure of Racial Vote Dilution Doctrine*, Election Law Blog (June 28, 2019), archived at https://perma.cc/RH5W-JCHZ.

[153] Ely, *Democracy and Distrust* (cited in note 3). For another scholar noting the connection between partisan gerrymandering and Ely's political process theory, see Karlan, 114 Yale L J at 1349 (cited in note 103) ("[Ely] saw partisan line drawing . . . as a paradigmatic example of *Carolene Products* process failure.").

This cottage industry, I argue here, supplies *Rucho*'s intellectual scaffolding. *Rucho*'s reasons for holding gerrymandering nonjusticiable are also scholars' reasons for resisting Ely's political process theory. *Rucho* therefore shouldn't be seen exclusively in doctrinal terms, as an exemplary reverse *Carolene* decision. It also reflects (one side of) the academic debate over *Carolene*, copying that camp's claims with eerie precision.

Consider *Rucho*'s conventional modalities point: that the Constitution's text and history don't support a judicial role in the fight against gerrymandering.[154] Scholars on both the right and left criticized Ely (and *Carolene*) on just this basis—for urging the Court to vindicate democratic values even though standard legal sources don't authorize this course of judicial action. Prominent conservative scholar and judge Robert Bork thus wrote that Ely's "notion of representation-reinforcement finds no support as a constitutional value beyond those guarantees written into the [Constitution]."[155] Well-known originalist Larry Alexander also pointed out that "Ely cannot cite any provision in the Constitution" that endorses his "conception of broad participation in the processes of government."[156] Ely has no answer to "the troubling question of how [his] moral ideal relates to the actual Constitution and its text."[157]

Liberal academics who might not be expected to be as receptive to textual and historical claims joined in this line of attack as well. Discussing Ely's aspiration of majoritarian democracy, Lawrence Sager asserted that "the reach of that ideal is no more determinately fixed by the text or structure of the Constitution than is the reach of other rights-conferring principles."[158] Addressing an Ely-style proposal that courts decide election law cases based on the democratic value of

---

[154] See notes 104–07 and accompanying text.

[155] Robert H. Bork, *The Impossibility of Finding Welfare Rights in the Constitution*, 1979 Wash U L Q 695, 699.

[156] Larry A. Alexander, *Modern Equal Protection Theories: A Metatheoretical Taxonomy and Critique*, 42 Ohio St L J 3, 10 (1981) (italics, quotation marks, and alterations omitted).

[157] Larry Alexander, *Lost in the Political Thicket*, 41 Fla L Rev 563, 569 n 25 (1989) (discussing vote-dilution doctrine); see also, for example, Lawrence B. Solum, *The Constraint Principle: Original Meaning and Constitutional Practice* 121 (Apr 3, 2019), archived at https://perma.cc/Z75N-PLJF (commenting that, under Ely's theory, "it is not the original meaning of [constitutional] provisions that governs," but rather "the representation reinforcement principle").

[158] Lawrence G. Sager, *Rights Skepticism and Process-Based Responses*, 56 NYU L Rev 417, 423 (1981).

competitiveness, Nathaniel Persily objected that "it is completely disconnected from the text of the Constitution."[159] Even one of Ely's staunchest defenders in the academy, Michael Klarman, noted that "[o]ne might well question the *constitutional* basis for this anti-entrenchment theory of judicial review."[160] "Its grounding is not, in fact, the Constitution," he candidly added.[161]

Or take *Rucho*'s argument that there's no normative consensus what a nongerrymandered district plan looks like, meaning judges would have to resolve this value-laden issue themselves.[162] A close variant of this critique was the most famous riposte to Ely's political process theory. Ely had condemned all other approaches to constitutional interpretation on the ground that they allowed judges to impose their own substantive preferences.[163] A host of progressive scholars retorted that Ely's theory, too, despite the procedural name he assigned it, required all kinds of substantive choices. For instance, Laurence Tribe wrote that "[t]he process theme by itself determines almost nothing unless its presuppositions are specified, and its content supplemented, by a full theory of substantive rights and values—the very sort of theory the process-perfecters are at such pains to avoid."[164] Likewise, Mark Tushnet alleged that "[t]he fundamental difficulty with Ely's theory is that its basic premise, that obstacles to political participation should be removed, is hardly value-free."[165] And according to Paul Brest, "in his heroic attempt to establish a value-free mode of constitutional adjudication, John Hart Ely [came] as close as anyone could to proving that it can't be done."[166]

---

[159] Nathaniel Persily, *In Defense of Foxes Guarding Henhouses: The Case for Judicial Acquiescence to Incumbent-Protecting Gerrymanders*, 116 Harv L Rev 649, 652 (2002).

[160] Klarman, 85 Geo L J at 499 (cited in note 44).

[161] Id; see also, for example, Richard L. Hasen, *The Supreme Court and Election Law: Judging Equality from Baker v Carr to Bush v Gore* 153 (NYU, 2003) (noting the lack of "a 'textual hook' upon which to hang" an election-law approach focused on competitiveness).

[162] See notes 112–17 and accompanying text.

[163] See Ely, *Democracy and Distrust* at 1–72 (cited in note 3).

[164] Laurence H. Tribe, *The Puzzling Persistence of Process-Based Constitutional Theories*, 89 Yale L J 1063, 1064 (1980).

[165] Mark Tushnet, *Darkness on the Edge of Town: The Contributions of John Hart Ely to Constitutional Theory*, 89 Yale L J 1037, 1045 (1980).

[166] Paul Brest, *The Substance of Process*, 42 Ohio St L J 131, 142 (1981); see also, for example, Erwin Chemerinsky, *The Price of Asking the Wrong Question: An Essay on Constitutional Scholarship and Judicial Review*, 62 Tex L Rev 1207, 1223 (1984) ("[I]t is impossible for the Court to decide what is 'fair' or 'just' representation without making substantive value judgments.");

I just called this response to Ely a close variant of *Rucho*'s argument about the absence of normative consensus as to fair redistricting. The points aren't identical because the former targets the very need to make substantive (as opposed to procedural) choices while the latter frets about the intractability of a particular substantive decision: defining a nongerrymandered map. Other liberal academics, though, foreshadowed *Rucho*'s argument even more accurately. The problem with Ely's approach, they contended, wasn't that it asked judges to tackle substantive issues; it was that the specific substantive issue it forced them to confront—the right conception of democracy—is indeterminate and unsuited to judicial resolution. Jack Balkin thus observed that "at any point in time in American society there are competing visions of what democracy requires: some in ascendance, some in dissent, and some that are completely 'off the wall.'"[167] Jane Schacter also charged that "Ely's theory failed to treat democracy as the essentially contested concept that it is."[168] And Ronald Dworkin opined that Ely's approach "might be persuasive if democracy were a precise political concept," or "if the American experience uniquely defined some particular conception of democracy."[169] "But none of this is true."[170]

Turn next to *Rucho*'s claim that courts lack the capacity to evaluate district plans' electoral effects.[171] Progressive scholars expressed the same grievance with Ely (and *Carolene*): that they obliged judges to determine when democracy is, in fact, threatened by a given practice. Even if a single definition of democracy could be selected, these scholars maintained, judges don't have the ability to ascertain when the political process is operating smoothly and when it's misfiring. In David Strauss's words, "Ely's theory requires judges to be amateur political scientists: to determine when the channels of political change are blocked."[172] Or as Guy-Uriel Charles put it, Ely's

---

Daniel R. Ortiz, *Pursuing a Perfect Politics: The Allure and Failure of Process Theory*, 77 Va L Rev 721, 723 (1991) ("Ely's [theory] ultimately relies on substantive judgments, many of which are extremely controversial.").

[167] Jack M. Balkin, *The Roots of the Living Constitution*, 92 BU L Rev 1129, 1159 (2012).

[168] Schacter, 57 Stan L Rev at 738 (cited in note 25).

[169] Ronald Dworkin, *The Forum of Principle*, 56 NYU L Rev 469, 502 (1981).

[170] Id; see also, for example, Michael J. Perry, *Interpretivism, Freedom of Expression, and Equal Protection*, 42 Ohio St L J 261, 306 (1981) ("[C]onsensus as to a certain sort of democratic process . . . is nonexistent.").

[171] See notes 125–28 and accompanying text.

[172] David A. Strauss, *Modernization and Representation Reinforcement: An Essay in Memory of John Hart Ely*, 57 Stan L Rev 761, 777 (2004).

"inquiry presupposes that the Court is able to distinguish . . . a properly functioning democratic process from an improperly functioning one."[173] Or per Heather Gerken and Michael Kang, "[j]udges aren't particularly adept at adjudicating the inherently [empirical] claims at stake in election law cases."[174] "They don't possess the training to judge, let alone manage, politics."[175]

And last,[176] recall *Rucho*'s argument that courts would become entangled in raw partisan politics if they decided gerrymandering cases.[177] This, too, was a common academic critique of Ely (and *Carolene*). Many electoral laws are adopted for partisan purposes, ran the objection, so if courts strike down these measures because of their undemocratic implications, then courts will inevitably be drawn into heated partisan disputes. Following this logic, Peter Schuck called it "a chilling prospect" for a court following political process theory to, in effect, "prescrib[e] the partisan configuration of the legislature—the most political of tasks."[178] Gary Leedes also described "judicial involvement in [the] pursuit of political power" as "a form of entanglement so potentially divisive and disruptive that it should be avoided."[179] And Richard Hasen complained that "structural theories" like Ely's "require great intrusion by the judiciary into the political processes" and so "are misguided and dangerous."[180]

Again, my main goal here is to show the striking convergence between *Rucho*'s reasons for holding gerrymandering nonjusticiable and

---

[173] Guy-Uriel E. Charles, *Constitutional Pluralism and Democratic Politics: Reflections on the Interpretive Approach of Baker v. Carr*, 80 NC L Rev 1103, 1134 (2002).

[174] Heather K. Gerken and Michael S. Kang, *Déjà Vu All Over Again: Courts, Corporate Law, and Election Law*, 126 Harv L Rev F 86, 88 (2013).

[175] Id; see also, for example, Hasen, *The Supreme Court and Election Law* at 154 (cited in note 161) ("I have become skeptical that the judges [do] a good job examining the social science evidence regarding the effects of court-mandated regulation of the political process.").

[176] A careful reader may note that *Rucho* gave one more reason for holding gerrymandering nonjusticiable: that actors other than the federal courts may also take steps to stop gerrymandering. See notes 141–45 and accompanying text. This is *Rucho*'s sole justification that's rooted only in the 1960s reapportionment dissents and not also in the academic literature criticizing Ely.

[177] See notes 134–36 and accompanying text.

[178] Peter H. Schuck, *The Thickest Thicket: Partisan Gerrymandering and Judicial Regulation of Politics*, 87 Colum L Rev 1325, 1365 (1987) (discussing the regulation of partisan gerrymandering)

[179] Gary C. Leedes, *Supreme Court Mess*, 57 Tex L Rev 1361, 1424 (1979).

[180] Hasen, *The Supreme Court and Election Law* at 139 (cited in note 161) (discussing Issacharoff and Pildes's Ely-esque approach); see also, for example, Bruce E. Cain, *Garrett's Temptation*, 85 Va L Rev 1589, 1600 (1999) ("The structural approach leads inevitably to intrusive judicial involvement in states' political arrangements.").

the scholarly literature opposing Ely (and *Carolene*). *Rucho* doesn't cite this literature but it plainly echoes it—sings in its distinctive key. However, I also want to note the irony of the many liberal attacks on political process theory. Virtually every progressive scholar disagreed with the Court's decision in *Rucho*. By my count, almost a hundred professors signed amicus briefs backing the *Rucho* plaintiffs, while *not one* put her name on a brief for North Carolina.[181] Yet the *Rucho* Court channeled the progressive scholars' anti-Ely arguments, ticking through them point by point. Those arguments provided the intellectual backdrop that helped make the Court's ruling possible. Of course, the liberal critics mostly disparaged Ely from the left, urging *more* judicial intervention on grounds *beyond* democracy promotion. Nevertheless, it's remarkable how their own words came back to haunt them in *Rucho*. In a striking case of unintended consequences, work advocating a broader judicial role ended up enabling its contraction.

D. CAROLENE'S ENDURING APPEAL

The above discussion may suggest that *Rucho*'s reasons for holding gerrymandering nonjusticiable—which are also the 1960s dissenters' reasons for thinking malapportionment a political question and academics' reasons for objecting to political process theory—are highly persuasive. After all, I've now outlined those reasons several times, but I haven't yet identified any responses to them. I actually don't intend to rebut the arguments of the *Rucho* Court (and its kindred spirits) at length here. My aim in this article is to situate *Rucho* as a reverse *Carolene* decision, not to defend *Carolene*-style pro-democratic

---

[181] See, for example, Brief of 27 Election Law, Scientific Evidence, and Empirical Legal Scholars as Amici Curiae, *Rucho v Common Cause*, No 18-422 (US filed Mar 8, 2019); Brief of Amici Curiae First Amendment and Election Law Scholars, *Rucho v Common Cause*, No 18-422 (US filed Mar 8, 2019); Brief of Amici Curiae Historians, *Rucho v Common Cause*, No 18-422 (US filed Mar 8, 2019); Brief of Amici Curiae Political Science Professors, *Rucho v Common Cause*, No 18-422 (US filed Mar 8, 2019); Brief of Amici Curiae Professors Christopher Elmendorf et al, *Rucho v Common Cause*, No 18-422 (US filed Mar 8, 2019); Brief of Amici Curiae Professors Wesley Pegden et al, *Rucho v Common Cause*, No 18-422 (US filed Mar 8, 2019); Brief of Professor D. Theodore Rave as Amicus Curiae, *Rucho v Common Cause*, No 18-422 (US filed Mar 8, 2019).

Of course, there's no irony when liberal scholars criticize political process theory *and* oppose judicial intervention against partisan gerrymandering. That position is completely consistent. See, for example, Hasen, *The Supreme Court and Election Law* (cited in note 161); Daniel H. Lowenstein and Jonathan Steinberg, *The Quest for Legislative Districting in the Public Interest: Elusive or Illusory?*, 33 UCLA L Rev 1 (1985); Persily, 116 Harv L Rev at 649 (cited in note 159).

judicial review. As a backer of such review,[182] though, I also don't want to leave the impression that *Rucho*'s rationales are unassailable. Accordingly, I now explain how Justice Kagan, in her *Rucho* dissent, countered each of the majority's points. Her refutation shows that the debate over *Carolene* is just that: a genuine two-sided dialogue, not a rout in favor of the anti-*Carolene* camp. Justice Kagan's dissent also demonstrates that even as the Court's majority becomes increasingly anti-*Carolene*, a vocal minority remains committed to *Carolene*'s thesis.

Start with the *Rucho* majority's conventional modalities argument.[183] Justice Kagan pointed out that, even if the Constitution's text and history don't support a judicial role in the fight against gerrymandering, a third mode of interpretation, reasoning from precedent,[184] does. "The Fourteenth Amendment, we long ago recognized," forbids the practice of "vote dilution—the devaluation of one citizen's vote as compared to others."[185] This bar on dilutive policies is why "this Court in its one-person-one-vote decisions prohibited creating districts with significantly different populations."[186] It's also why the Court subsequently recognized a cause of action for racial vote dilution: the diminution of minority voters' electoral influence through at-large elections, carefully crafted districts, and other dilutive measures.[187] Returning to partisan gerrymandering, "[t]he constitutional injury . . . is much the same, except that the dilution is based on party affiliation."[188] "In such a case, too, the districters have set out to reduce the weight of certain citizens' votes, and thereby deprive them of their capacity to fully and effectively participate in the political process."[189]

---

[182] See, for example, Stephanopoulos, 114 Colum L Rev (cited in note 55); Nicholas O. Stephanopoulos and Eric M. McGhee, *Partisan Gerrymandering and the Efficiency Gap*, 82 U Chi L Rev 831 (2015).

[183] See notes 104–07 and accompanying text.

[184] See generally David A. Strauss, *Common Law Constitutional Interpretation*, 63 U Chi L Rev 877 (1996).

[185] *Rucho v Common Cause*, 139 S Ct 2484, 2514 (2019) (Kagan, J, dissenting); see also id at 2523 ("This Court has long understood that it has a special responsibility to remedy violations of constitutional rights resulting from politicians' districting decisions.").

[186] Id at 2514.

[187] See, for example, *White v Regester*, 412 US 755 (1973).

[188] *Rucho*, 139 S Ct at 2514 (Kagan, J, dissenting).

[189] Id (quotation marks and alterations omitted).

Justice Kagan also linked a different account of gerrymandering's constitutional harm to the Court's precedent. On this view, the problem with the practice isn't that it dilutes the votes of one party's adherents. The issue, instead, is that when the government gerrymanders, it injures voters because of their political beliefs and impedes their ability to associate with one another, in contravention of longstanding First Amendment principles. Justice Kagan thus cited cases holding that when the government "subject[s] certain voters to 'disfavored treatment' . . . because of 'their voting history and their expression of political views,'" it violates the First Amendment.[190] She referenced additional decisions establishing that when "the State frustrates [voters'] efforts to translate [their] affiliations into political effectiveness," the First Amendment is offended as well.[191] "In both of those ways, partisan gerrymanders . . . undermine the protections of 'democracy embodied in the First Amendment.'"[192]

The Court's precedent supplied Justice Kagan with one more response to the *Rucho* majority's argument about conventional modalities. If taken seriously, the Constitution's text and history indicate that courts shouldn't try to fix *any* democratic malfunctions: not partisan gerrymandering, and not malapportionment, racial vote dilution, or voter suppression either.[193] The Fourteenth Amendment, in particular, was originally intended to protect civil but not political rights,[194] and its language in no way distinguishes between gerrymandering and any other democratic failure. Yet as Justice Kagan remarked, "racial and residential gerrymanders were also once with us, but the Court has done something about that fact."[195] The Court, that is, has deemed those practices unconstitutional despite their validity under textual and historical modes of reasoning. The *Rucho* majority therefore can't "frame [its] point as an originalist constitutional argument."[196] Originalism would negate almost all of election

---

[190] Id (quoting *Vieth v Jubelirer*, 541 US 267, 314 (2004) (opinion of Kennedy, J)).

[191] Id (citing *Cal. Dem. Party v Jones*, 530 US 567, 574 (2000)); see also id ("[A]dded to that strictly personal harm is an associational one.").

[192] Id (quoting *Elrod v Burns*, 427 US 347, 357 (1976)).

[193] See notes 108–11 and accompanying text.

[194] See generally Travis Crum, *The Superfluous Fifteenth Amendment?*, 114 Nw U L Rev (forthcoming 2020).

[195] *Rucho*, 139 S Ct at 2512 (Kagan, J, dissenting).

[196] Id.

law, but the majority accepts "a role for the courts with respect to at least some [redistricting] issues."[197]

Consider, second, the *Rucho* majority's claim that no normative consensus exists as to what a nongerrymandered district plan looks like.[198] Relying on recent developments in the lower courts, Justice Kagan flatly denied this assertion. There now *is* consensus, she maintained, that a nongerrymandered plan is one that resembles maps that are randomly generated by a computer algorithm based only on a jurisdiction's lawful, nonpartisan criteria. A plan isn't a gerrymander, in other words, if it lies within the distribution of randomly created maps.[199] The *Rucho* majority thus "misses something under its nose: What it says can't be done *has* been done."[200] "Over the past several years, federal courts across the country ... have largely converged on a [single] standard."[201] This standard "takes as its baseline a State's *own* criteria of fairness, apart from partisan gain."[202] These criteria are used to produce "a large collection of districting plans that incorporate the State's physical and political geography."[203] Then "[w]e can line up those maps on a continuum" and "see where the State's actual plan falls on the spectrum."[204] "The further out on the tail, the more extreme the partisan distortion and the more significant the vote dilution."[205]

This approach, Justice Kagan continued, neatly sidesteps all of the *Rucho* majority's allegedly unanswerable questions. How competitive should a plan's districts be?[206] As vigorously contested as a state wants.

---

[197] Id at 2495–96. Justice Kagan added that "any originalist argument would have to deal with an inconvenient fact": that "[t]he Framers originally viewed political parties themselves (let alone their most partisan actions) with deep suspicion." Id at 2512 n 1 (Kagan, J, dissenting).

[198] See notes 112–17 and accompanying text.

[199] Of course, the fact that lower courts have arrived at a consensus doesn't mean it's shared by the rest of society. I, for one, have some discomfort with using randomly generated maps as a baseline when the maps happen to be skewed in a party's favor due to a state's political geography. In such cases, I would hesitate to deem a plan a gerrymander if it's *more* symmetric in its treatment of the major parties than most simulated maps.

[200] *Rucho*, 139 S Ct at 2516 (Kagan, J, dissenting).

[201] Id; see also, for example, id at 2509 ("The majority's abdication comes just when courts across the country ... have coalesced around manageable judicial standards to resolve partisan gerrymandering claims.").

[202] Id at 2516.

[203] Id at 2518.

[204] Id.

[205] Id.

[206] See note 113 and accompanying text.

How should parties' seats be related to their votes?[207] It depends on where voters happen to live and which nonpartisan districting principles a state employs. How much compliance with these principles is enough?[208] Again, it's up to each state. In Justice Kagan's words, "the comparator (or baseline or touchstone) is the result not of a judge's philosophizing but of the State's own characteristics and judgments."[209] These factors "create[] a neutral baseline from which to assess whether partisanship has run amok."[210] So the reference point is *not* (what the *Rucho* majority thought it had to be) "the maps a judge, with his own view of electoral fairness, could have dreamed up."[211]

Third, the *Rucho* majority contended that courts lack the capacity to assess district plans' electoral effects.[212] To the contrary, Justice Kagan responded, lower courts recently demonstrated their ability to do exactly that. In the years leading up to *Rucho*, five district courts (comprising fifteen federal judges) considered, and ruled in favor of, partisan gerrymandering claims in Maryland, Michigan, North Carolina, Ohio, and Wisconsin.[213] All of these cases involved voluminous empirical testimony. And in all of them, the courts' "findings about these gerrymanders' effects on voters . . . were evidence-based, data-based, statistics-based"—"[k]nowledge-based, one might say."[214] The courts "did not gaze into crystal balls, as the majority tries to suggest."[215] Instead "[t]hey evaluated with immense care the factual evidence . . . the parties presented."[216] "They looked hard at the facts, and they went where the facts led them."[217]

One conclusion to which the facts led them was that modern gerrymanders are quite durable. Recall that the *Rucho* majority

---

[207] See note 114 and accompanying text.

[208] See note 115 and accompanying text.

[209] *Rucho*, 139 S Ct at 2520 (Kagan, J, dissenting).

[210] Id.

[211] Id; see also id at 2518 n 3 ("[T]his distribution of outcomes provides what the majority says does not exist—a neutral comparator for the State's own plan.").

[212] See notes 125–28 and accompanying text.

[213] See *Rucho*, 139 S Ct at 2513, 2518 (Kagan, J, dissenting) (describing most of these suits).

[214] Id at 2519.

[215] Id.

[216] Id at 2525.

[217] Id at 2519.

stressed the volatility of voters, who supposedly change their minds from year to year, and split their tickets even in the same election, at a high rate.[218] The empirical evidence the lower courts heard contradicted these "unsupported and out-of-date musings about the unpredictability of the American voter."[219] In reality, today's voters tend to be strong partisans, meaning that party-switching over time and ticket-splitting in a single election are both infrequent.[220] As a result, "maps constructed with so much expertise and care to make electoral outcomes impervious to voting" don't often "come apart."[221] Most of the time, contemporary line-drawers "succeed[] in entrenching themselves in office" and thereby "beat[ing] democracy."[222]

Fourth, the *Rucho* majority objected to courts' entanglement in partisan politics, red in tooth and claw.[223] Justice Kagan replied that cases' partisan implications aren't a justification for judicial inaction. Yes, gerrymanders "have great political consequence."[224] But this impact is *harmful*: "a cascade of negative results" including "the death-knell of bipartisanship," "a legislative environment that is toxic and tribal," and "the polarized political system so many Americans loathe."[225] These adverse outcomes oblige the Court to intervene, not to stare impassively as democracy deteriorates. Gerrymanders "imperil our system of government," and "[p]art of the Court's role in that system is to defend its foundations."[226]

Justice Kagan also explained that courts' partisan entanglement wouldn't be as extensive as the *Rucho* majority feared. For one thing, her proposed standard (which mirrored that adopted by the lower courts) would reach only the "worst-of-the-worst cases of democratic subversion": the handful of district plans designed with partisan motives and yielding large, durable, and unjustified partisan effects.[227]

---

[218] See notes 126–28 and accompanying text.

[219] *Rucho*, 139 S Ct at 2519 (Kagan, J, dissenting).

[220] See LWV Brief at 25–26 (cited in note 16).

[221] *Rucho*, 139 S Ct at 2519 (Kagan, J, dissenting).

[222] Id; see also id at 2525 ("In North Carolina, however the political winds blow, there are 10 Republicans and 3 Democrats.").

[223] See notes 134–36 and accompanying text.

[224] *Rucho*, 139 S Ct at 2525 (Kagan, J, dissenting).

[225] Id (quotation marks omitted).

[226] Id at 2525.

[227] Id at 2509.

"[B]y requiring plaintiffs to make difficult showings relating to both purpose and effects, the standard [would] invalidate[] the most extreme, but only the most extreme, partisan gerrymanders."[228] For another, if the Court struck down a map or two, line-drawers would likely stop gerrymandering as much, and there would be less need for judicial involvement. "[S]moking guns" where politicians "openly proclaim their intent to entrench their party in office" would "all but disappear."[229] Fewer "officials [would] continue[] to try implementing extreme partisan gerrymanders."[230] After all, "[i]n districting cases no less than others, officials respond to what this Court determines the law to sanction."[231]

And fifth, the *Rucho* majority argued that it need not act thanks to the anti-gerrymandering efforts of other actors: legislators, voters via direct democracy, and state courts.[232] As to legislators, Justice Kagan accented the obvious; they're the people with the strongest incentive *to* gerrymander, so "[n]o one can look to them for effective relief" *from* the practice.[233] Yes, a few reformers occasionally introduce "bills limiting partisan gerrymanders."[234] But "what all these *bills* have in common is that they are not *laws*."[235] As to voter initiatives, Justice Kagan noted that they're frequently unavailable; "[f]ewer than half the States" permit them.[236] Even where voters can place measures directly on the ballot, redistricting initiatives tend to trigger furious opposition from the politicians whose mapmaking power is threatened. "[L]egislators often fight [those] efforts tooth and nail"—and often manage to defeat them.[237]

And as to state courts, Justice Kagan noted that they, too, are courts. How can gerrymandering not be justiciable for federal courts,

---

[228] Id at 2516; see also id at 2522 ("[T]he combined inquiry used in these cases set the bar high, so that courts could intervene in the worst partisan gerrymanders, but no others.").

[229] Id at 2522–23.

[230] Id at 2523; see also id at 2523 n 5 ("A decision of this Court invalidating the North Carolina and Maryland gerrymanders would of course have curbed much of that behavior.").

[231] Id at 2523 n 5.

[232] See notes 141–45 and accompanying text.

[233] *Rucho*, 139 S Ct at 2523 (Kagan, J, dissenting); see also id at 2524 ("The politicians who benefit from partisan gerrymandering are unlikely to change partisan gerrymandering.").

[234] Id at 2523.

[235] Id at 2524.

[236] Id.

[237] Id.

then, when it is for their state counterparts? "[W]hat do those courts know that this Court does not?"[238] "If they can develop and apply neutral and manageable standards to identify unconstitutional gerrymanders, why couldn't we?"[239] The answer isn't that state constitutions typically include more specific anti-gerrymandering provisions than the federal Constitution. For example, "[t]he Pennsylvania Supreme Court based its gerrymandering decision on a constitutional clause providing only that 'elections shall be free and equal.'"[240] Even more starkly, two months after *Rucho*, a court invalidated North Carolina's state legislative maps based on that state's analogues to the First and Fourteenth Amendments.[241] Those, of course, are the very provisions from which the *Rucho* majority supposedly *couldn't* derive a workable test.

As I mentioned above, I think the debate between the *Rucho* majority and Justice Kagan has a winner.[242] Point by point, I find her responses more persuasive than the majority's reasons for holding gerrymandering nonjusticiable. But even a reader inclined to agree with the majority must concede that its anti-*Carolene* position hasn't swept the field. Yes, that stance now commands the votes of five Justices. But that's all it commands. In the rest of the Court—and in the lower federal courts that ruled in favor of gerrymandering challenges prior to *Rucho*, and in the state courts that continue to uphold these claims, and in the academy that nearly unanimously backs judicial action against gerrymandering—*Caroline*'s message still appeals. David Strauss once provocatively titled an article, *Is Carolene Products Obsolete?*[243] Justice Kagan's dissent shows that it's not.

III. A Perverse Carolene Future?

More precisely, Justice Kagan's dissent shows that *Carolene* isn't *intellectually* obsolete. *Doctrinally*, though—as a matter of

---

[238] Id.

[239] Id.

[240] Id at 2424 n 6.

[241] See *Common Cause v Lewis*, No 18 CVS 014001, 2019 WL 4569584 (NC Super Ct Sept 3, 2019).

[242] See note 182 and accompanying text.

[243] See Strauss, 2010 U Ill L Rev at 1251 (cited in note 60). Strauss also answered his question in the negative. See id at 1269 ("If you have a better idea about what courts should be doing in difficult constitutional cases, let me know.").

constitutional law as fashioned by the current Court—*Carolene* is at grave risk of extinction. One threat to it comes from reverse *Carolene* decisions like *Rucho*. When the Court refuses to fix democratic malfunctions, it doesn't do the one thing that, *Carolene* holds, it should prioritize above all else. But I want to turn in this Part to a new and growing menace to *Carolene*: perverse (rather than reverse) *Carolene* decisions in which the Court prevents *other* actors from curbing democratic abuses and promoting democratic values.[244] Perverse decisions compound the damage of reverse decisions. They represent not judicial apathy in the face of democratic failure (bad enough, one might think) but rather affirmative judicial protection for the subversion of democracy.

Rucho's subject, partisan gerrymandering, is one area where perverse *Carolene* decisions are on the horizon (though not yet overhead). Nonjudicial actors often try to thwart gerrymandering by adopting independent redistricting commissions. But there may now be five votes on the Court (the same five votes that made up the *Rucho* majority) for the proposition that commissions with authority over congressional mapmaking unlawfully abridge state legislatures' right to draw the lines as they please. Other plausible challenges to commissions also wait in the wings. Outside the gerrymandering context, perverse *Carolene* decisions may greet any congressional attempts to defend the right to vote. The Roberts Court may view laws easing franchise access as violations of states' prerogatives to limit their electorates as they see fit. And in the campaign finance arena, perverse *Carolene* decisions already fill the case reporters. The Roberts Court has systematically blocked federal and state actors from countering the corrosive effects of massive electoral funding on American democracy.

A. PARTISAN GERRYMANDERING

1. *Elections Clause.* In one of *Rucho*'s most startling passages, Chief Justice Roberts framed redistricting commissions as a potential solution to the problem of gerrymandering. He observed that states are increasingly "placing power to draw electoral districts in the hands of independent commissions."[245] In the 2018 election, for instance,

---

[244] See notes 68–69 and accompanying text.
[245] *Rucho*, 139 S Ct at 2507.

"voters in Colorado and Michigan approved constitutional amendments creating multimember commissions that will be responsible . . . for creating and approving district maps for congressional and state legislative districts."[246] He also described "[t]he first bill introduced in the 116th Congress," which "would require States to create 15-member independent commissions to draw congressional districts."[247] This bill followed an earlier congressional proposal to "require every State to establish an independent commission to adopt redistricting plans."[248] By citing these efforts, the Court meant to show that it didn't "condone partisan gerrymandering" or "condemn complaints about districting to echo into a void."[249] Commissions, the Court suggested, could avert gerrymandering and address voters' complaints about the mapmaking process.

This passage isn't startling because of its prescription. Commissions are a common—and compelling—antidote to gerrymandering. Thirteen states currently use commissions to design their congressional districts, four of which switched to this line-drawing procedure in 2018 alone.[250] Abroad, every Western democracy whose legislators are elected from single-member districts entrusts redistricting to a commission.[251] And for good reason. The root cause of gerrymandering is legislators' self-interest: their desire to benefit their party and to shield themselves from meaningful competition. Commissions remove legislators' self-interest from the mapmaking equation. When properly structured, they're made up of members who *don't* have a personal stake in how the lines are drawn, and who set the boundaries based on criteria *other* than partisan advantage and incumbent protection.[252] As a result, commission-crafted plans are more compliant

---

[246] Id.

[247] Id at 2508.

[248] Id.

[249] Id at 2507.

[250] See Nat'l Conf. State Legislatures, *Redistricting Law 2010* at 197–99 (2009) (listing Arizona, Hawaii, Idaho, Montana, New Jersey, and Washington as states using congressional redistricting commissions as of 2009). I also count Iowa, where a state agency designs congressional districts, in this group. Since 2009, California (2010), New York (2014), Colorado (2018), Michigan (2018), Ohio (2018), and Utah (2018) have switched to congressional commissions as well. See also Justin Levitt, *Who Draws the Lines?*, All About Redistricting, archived at https://perma.cc/6E8W-X7BY.

[251] See Nicholas O. Stephanopoulos, *Our Electoral Exceptionalism*, 80 U Chi L Rev 769, 780–86 (2013).

[252] For a longer version of this argument, see Stephanopoulos, 2015 U Chi Legal F at 489–91 (cited in note 68).

with traditional districting principles,[253] more competitive,[254] and more balanced in their treatment of the major parties[255] than maps produced by politicians.

A majority of the Court was equally enthusiastic about commissions in the 2015 case *Arizona State Legislature v Arizona Independent Redistricting Commission*.[256] Commissions "address the problem of partisan gerrymandering—the drawing of legislative district lines to subordinate adherents of one political party and entrench a rival party in power," the Court gushed.[257] Commissions do so because they "check legislators' ability to choose the district lines they run in" and "impede legislators from choosing their voters."[258] Commissions thus "ensure that Members of Congress [will] have 'an habitual recollection of their dependence on the people.'"[259] They "restore the core principle of republican government, namely, that the voters should choose their representatives, not the other way around."[260]

The passage in *Rucho* is startling, then, because of its author rather than its argument. Chief Justice Roberts, who presented commissions as a solution to gerrymandering in *Rucho*, *dissented* in *Arizona State Legislature*, contending that Arizona's congressional redistricting commission is unconstitutional. His logic was as follows: The Elections Clause states that the "Times, Places and Manner" of congressional elections "shall be prescribed in each State *by the Legislature thereof*."[261]

---

[253] See, for example, Vladimir Kogan and Eric McGhee, *Redistricting California: An Evaluation of the Citizens Commission Final Plans*, 4 Cal J Pol & Pol'y 1, 11–16 (2012) (finding that when California switched to a commission, its districts split fewer political subdivisions and were more compact).

[254] See, for example, Jamie L. Carson and Michael H. Crespin, *The Effect of State Redistricting Methods on Electoral Competition in United States House of Representatives Races*, 4 St Pol & Pol'y Q 455, 461–62 (2004) (finding that commission usage increases the share of House districts won by fewer than twenty points).

[255] See, for example, Stephanopoulos, 2015 U Chi Legal F at 496–501 (cited in note 68) (finding that commission usage reduces the partisan bias of state legislative and congressional maps).

[256] 135 S Ct 2652 (2015).

[257] Id at 2658; see also id at 2677 (commissions "curb the practice of gerrymandering").

[258] Id at 2675–76.

[259] Id at 2677 (quoting Federalist 57 (Madison)); see also id at 2675 (commissions "advanc[e] the prospect that Members of Congress will in fact be 'chosen . . . by the People of the several States'" (quoting US Const, Art I, § 2)).

[260] Id at 2677 (quotation marks omitted).

[261] US Const, Art I, § 4 (emphasis added).

The "Legislature" is "the representative body which makes the laws of the people."[262] But in Arizona, "redistricting is *not* carried out by the legislature."[263] Instead, "an unelected body called the Independent Redistricting Commission draws the lines."[264] Aggravating the Elections Clause violation, the commission gained its mapmaking authority from not a legislative delegation but rather a voter initiative in which the legislature had no part.

Whatever the merits of this reasoning,[265] it plainly amounts to a perverse *Carolene* position. Partisan gerrymandering is undemocratic. Arizona voters found a way to prevent gerrymandering by adopting a commission. But the commission is unlawful because it offends the Elections Clause. Therefore the power to redistrict must return to the Arizona legislature, which will then be free to gerrymander to its heart's content. Or as Chief Justice Roberts put it, only slightly less starkly: "The people of Arizona have concerns about the process of congressional redistricting in their State," in that they don't want that process to yield an undemocratic gerrymander.[266] But alas, "the Elections Clause of the Constitution does not allow them to address those concerns by displacing their legislature."[267] So the legislature must remain responsible for redistricting, and the people's concerns about gerrymandering must stay unresolved.

Nor is the Arizona commission any more vulnerable to this attack than many other commissions. The Arizona commission's plans go directly into effect, without any need for legislative approval. So do the congressional maps drawn by the California, Colorado, Hawaii, Idaho, Michigan, Montana, New Jersey, and Washington commissions.[268] The Arizona commission was also created by a voter initiative that circumvented the legislature. So were the California and

---

[262] *Ariz. State Leg.*, 135 S Ct at 2679 (Roberts, CJ, dissenting).

[263] Id at 2678 (emphasis added).

[264] Id.

[265] The majority's main response is that "Legislature" actually means the "power that makes laws," and in Arizona, "initiatives adopted by the voters legislate for the State just as measures passed by the representative body do." Id at 2671 (quotation marks omitted).

[266] Id at 2692 (Roberts, CJ, dissenting).

[267] Id; see also, for example, id at 2678 ("No matter how concerned we may be about partisanship in redistricting, this Court has no power to gerrymander the Constitution."); id at 2690 ("[A] law's virtues as a policy innovation cannot redeem its inconsistency with the Constitution.").

[268] See Levitt, *Who Draws the Lines?* (cited in note 250).

Michigan congressional redistricting commissions.[269] Chief Justice Roberts's perverse *Carolene* position would thus nullify most American commissions. In fact, it would nullify the *best* American commissions: the ones that are most insulated from the individuals—self-interested legislators—who are most likely to gerrymander.[270]

Chief Justice Roberts's position could actually sweep even more broadly than that. Governors have the power to veto congressional district plans in forty-five states.[271] But governors are no more "the representative body which makes the laws" than are voters acting via direct democracy. Gubernatorial vetoes of congressional maps, then, might be unlawful under the Elections Clause.[272] Similarly, thirty state constitutions specify criteria like compactness and respect for political subdivisions for congressional districts.[273] But state *constitutions* aren't state *statutes*. They're not enacted by state legislatures pursuant to the bodies' ordinary lawmaking processes. So they may be invalid, too, to the extent that they regulate congressional redistricting. And courts play a ubiquitous role in disputes over congressional district plans. But the judiciary isn't "the Legislature" either, meaning this court function is suspect as well. In short, under Chief Justice Roberts's view, every nonlegislative actor might be constitutionally barred from participating in congressional redistricting. On this account, not only would the fox be *allowed* to guard the henhouse, the fox *alone* could do so.

It's true that Chief Justice Roberts's opinion in *Arizona State Legislature* was a dissent. But it was a dissent that three other Justices joined,[274] and one of the Justices in the majority, Justice Anthony

---

[269] See generally Nicholas Stephanopoulos, *Reforming Redistricting: Why Popular Initiatives to Establish Redistricting Commissions Succeed or Fail*, 23 J L & Pol 331 (2007) (discussing redistricting initiatives throughout American history).

[270] Chief Justice Roberts asserted that his view would "not affect most other redistricting commissions" because they generally "play an 'auxiliary role' in congressional redistricting." *Ariz. State Leg.*, 135 S Ct at 2691 (Roberts, CJ, dissenting). This is simply incorrect, at least with respect to the commissions cited here.

[271] See Levitt, *Who Draws the Lines?* (cited in note 250).

[272] Chief Justice Roberts's position might thus require the reversal of *Smiley v Holm*, 285 US 355 (1932), in which the Court approved a gubernatorial veto of a congressional map against an Elections Clause challenge.

[273] See Nat'l Conf. State Legislatures, *Redistricting Law 2010* at 125–27 (cited in note 250). Note that since this report's publication, California, Colorado, Florida, New York, and Ohio have adopted criteria for congressional districts.

[274] These were Justices Alito, Scalia, and Thomas. Justice Scalia's replacement on the Court, Justice Gorsuch, presumably shares his Elections Clause views.

Kennedy, has now been replaced by Justice Brett Kavanaugh. Unlike Justice Kennedy, Justice Kavanaugh believes that partisan gerrymandering is nonjusticiable; he was part of the *Rucho* majority.[275] It's at least plausible (and maybe even probable[276]) that Justice Kavanaugh would disagree with Justice Kennedy about the involvement of nonlegislative actors in congressional redistricting, too.

It's also the case that Chief Justice Roberts disclaimed the more radical implications of his Elections Clause stance, writing that "the state legislature need not be *exclusive* in congressional districting."[277] If this caveat were to hold, then gubernatorial vetoes, state constitutional criteria, and lawsuits would remain permissible with respect to congressional districts. Unlike the Arizona commission, these measures don't "*totally* displace[] the legislature from the redistricting process."[278] The caveat, however, is a classic ipse dixit. It's asserted without explanation after a long discussion of why "the Legislature" has to mean "the representative body which makes the laws."[279] The caveat also contradicts the preceding discussion. If that's the right definition of "the Legislature," then how can the term encompass actors who are indisputably nonlegislative? How are congressional district lines "prescribed in each State by the Legislature thereof" if they're shaped, in part, by the governor, the state constitution, or a court? For these reasons, the caveat seems unlikely to limit the scope of the perverse *Carolene* revolution that Chief Justice Roberts's dissent would augur, if it gained one more vote.

2. *Congressional authority.* Even at its most extensive, though, this revolution would affect only *state* regulations (by nonlegislative actors) of *congressional* redistricting. That was the sole topic addressed in *Arizona State Legislature* by the majority or the dissenters. But what if *Congress* tried to stop gerrymandering by requiring commissions to design states' congressional *and state legislative* maps? The first bill the House of Representatives passed in 2019, after switching from

---

[275] In contrast, Justice Kennedy pointedly refused to join the *Vieth* plurality's opinion deeming gerrymandering nonjusticiable.

[276] Maybe probable because, to date, Justice Kavanaugh's voting behavior on the Court has been nearly identical to Chief Justice Roberts's. See, for example, Adam Feldman, *So Happy Together*, SCOTUSblog (May 23, 2019), archived at https://perma.cc/UH56-V5QS.

[277] *Ariz. State Leg. v Ariz. Independent Redistricting Comm'n*, 135 S Ct 2652, 2687 (2015) (Roberts, CJ, dissenting) (emphasis added).

[278] Id at 2691 (emphasis added).

[279] See id at 2678–87.

Republican to Democratic control, would oblige states to create and use commissions for their congressional plans.[280] (This bill was the *Rucho* majority's lead example of how Congress could still curb redistricting abuses even after the Court withdrew from the field.[281]) Several commentators have also urged that the bill's coverage be broadened from congressional to state legislative maps, on the ground that the latter are just as susceptible to gerrymandering as the former.[282]

It's not alarmist to fear that this sort of legislation would receive a hostile reception from the Roberts Court. In the 1990s, an earlier conservative majority announced the so-called "anti-commandeering" doctrine, under which "the Federal Government may not compel the States to implement, by legislation or executive action, federal regulatory programs."[283] In a 2003 case, six Justices agreed (albeit in dicta) that the anti-commandeering doctrine applies to the Elections Clause: the most explicit grant of power to Congress to fight gerrymandering. Writing for a four-Justice plurality, Justice Antonin Scalia emphasized that his interpretation of a federal redistricting statute wouldn't "permit[] a commandeering of the machinery of state government."[284] Concurring for herself and Justice Clarence Thomas, Justice Sandra Day O'Connor rejected the view that "the anticommandeering jurisprudence is inapplicable to" the Elections Clause simply because that provision affirmatively contemplates congressional regulation of federal elections.[285]

---

[280] See HR 1, 116th Cong, 1st Sess, §§ 2400–35 (2019). This bill has gone nowhere in the Republican-controlled Senate.

[281] See *Rucho v Common Cause*, 139 S Ct 2484, 2508 (2019).

[282] I'm one of these commentators. See Nicholas Stephanopoulos, *H.R. 1 and Redistricting Commissions*, Election Law Blog (Jan 9, 2019), archived at https://perma.cc/C77S-P8HB; see also, for example, Ryan P. Bates, Note, *Congressional Authority to Require State Adoption of Independent Redistricting Commissions*, 55 Duke L J 333, 338 (2005) ("Congress would be both authorized and justified in requiring the states to adopt independent and nonpartisan commissions . . . both for congressional and state legislative districts.").

[283] *Printz v United States*, 521 US 898, 925 (1997); see also, for example, *New York v United States*, 505 US 144, 162 (1992) (Congress lacks "the ability to require the States to govern according to Congress' instructions").

[284] *Branch v Smith*, 538 US 254, 280 (2003) (plurality).

[285] Id at 301 (O'Connor, J, concurring in part and dissenting in part). But note that some lower courts, in cases prior to *Branch*, held that Congress *may* commandeer state governments when it legislates under the Elections Clause. See, for example, *Condon v Reno*, 913 F Supp 946, 965 (DSC 1995); *Wilson v United States*, 878 F Supp 1324, 1327–28 (ND Cal 1995).

If Congress can't commandeer state governments when it legislates under the Elections Clause, then it's easy to see why the House's recently passed bill might skate on thin constitutional ice. The bill states that "[e]ach State *shall* establish a nonpartisan agency in the legislative branch."[286] This agency "*shall* establish an independent redistricting commission" pursuant to a detailed appointment procedure.[287] And the commission, in turn, "*shall* establish single-member congressional districts" that comply with several specified criteria.[288] All these *shall*s are federal orders to the states: binding rules how (and by whom) their congressional districts must be drawn in subsequent cycles. That's why the House's bill, according to its conservative critics, "would likely run into the Supreme Court's doctrine against federal 'commandeering,'"[289] and "would surely invite legal challenge as a violation of the anti-commandeering doctrine."[290]

This objection would hold regardless of the electoral level. The allegation of commandeering, in other words, would apply whether Congress legislated about congressional or state legislative plans. If Congress required commissions to be used for state legislative maps, however, it would run into an additional obstacle. The Elections Clause only empowers Congress to regulate federal elections.[291] So to tackle gerrymandering at the state legislative level, Congress would have to find another source of regulatory authority. The Fourteenth Amendment's Enforcement Clause is the most likely candidate, given the Court's view (even in *Rucho*) that extreme gerrymandering violates the Equal Protection Clause.[292] But the Court has sharply restricted Congress's ability to legislate in furtherance of Fourteenth Amendment values. With respect to any enforcement statute, "[t]here must be a congruence and proportionality" between Congress's

---

[286] HR 1, 116th Cong, 1st Sess, §§ 2414(a)(1) (2019) (emphasis added).

[287] Id § 2411(a)(1) (emphasis added).

[288] Id § 2413(a)(1) (emphasis added).

[289] Walter Olson, *House Passes Political-Omnibus Bill H.R 1*, Cato at Liberty (Mar 11, 2019), archived at https://perma.cc/2RQM-TP2R.

[290] Ilya Shapiro and Nathan Harvey, *What Left-Wing Populism Looks Like*, National Review (Mar 7, 2019), archived at https://perma.cc/8T9U-JCCZ.

[291] See US Const, Art I, § 4 (referring to "Elections for Senators and Representatives").

[292] See, for example, *Rucho v Common Cause*, 139 S Ct 2484, 2504 (2019) (arguing that "separating constitutional from unconstitutional partisan gerrymandering" is impossible, but not disputing that unconstitutional gerrymandering exists).

means and the underlying constitutional "injury to be prevented or remedied."[293]

Rucho itself raises doubts whether the compulsory use of commissions is a congruent and proportional response to the problem of gerrymandering. To repeat, commissions are appealing because they're made up of members who have no incentive to benefit any candidate or party.[294] The *Rucho* majority, though, held that "securing partisan advantage" is "[a] *permissible* intent" that "does *not* indicate that the districting was improper."[295] In that case, commissions' removal of partisanship from the mapmaking process might be a non sequitur: a measure unrelated to the harm of gerrymandering, as understood by the *Rucho* majority. The House's bill also stipulates that districts must abide by traditional districting principles and must not, "when considered on a Statewide basis, unduly favor or disfavor any political party."[296] But the *Rucho* majority thought that "adherence to 'traditional' districting criteria" is just another contestable "vision[ ] of fairness."[297] It even more stridently criticized the idea that "a districting map is . . . unconstitutional because it makes it too difficult for one party to translate statewide support into seats in the legislature."[298] Again, then, core elements of the House's bill may have little to do with the *Rucho* majority's conception of gerrymandering.

There are good rejoinders, of course, to these arguments that Congress is powerless to force the use of redistricting commissions.[299] But whatever their flaws, the arguments are far from "off the wall,"[300]

---

[293] *City of Boerne v Flores*, 521 US 507, 520 (1997).

[294] See notes 250–60 and accompanying text.

[295] *Rucho*, 139 S Ct at 2503 (emphasis added).

[296] HR 1, 116th Cong, 1st Sess, §§ 2413(a)(1)–(2) (2019).

[297] *Rucho*, 139 S Ct at 2500.

[298] Id at 2499.

[299] To wit: The anti-commandeering doctrine has no textual basis and needlessly prevents Congress from relying on mandates to states in circumstances where they're the most effective tool. And the *Rucho* majority's view that gerrymandering is unrelated to partisan intent, noncompliance with traditional districting principles, and extreme partisan asymmetry is strange, to say the least. On an ordinary account of gerrymandering, commissions are certainly a congruent and proportional response to it, since they prevent it from occurring in the first place.

[300] See, for example, Jack M. Balkin, *Constitutional Redemption: Political Faith in an Unjust World* 177–83 (Harvard, 2011) (discussing how constitutional arguments can go from "off the wall" to "on the wall").

given the Roberts Court's prior record, as well as paradigmatic examples of perverse *Carolene* claims. No one (not even the *Rucho* majority) "disputes [that] gerrymanders undermine democracy."[301] Independent commissions are a common mechanism, in America and abroad, for preventing gerrymandering. But if Congress were to require commissions to redistrict, it's possible the Roberts Court would nullify its policy, thus allowing states to continue to gerrymander. This might be a correct decision, based on conventional modes of constitutional reasoning, or it might be a wrong one. From a *Carolene* perspective, though, it would certainly be a perverse one.

3. *First Amendment.* Opponents of independent redistricting commissions have one last arrow in their quiver. According to a recently filed complaint against Michigan's commission, the body's membership criteria violate the First Amendment.[302] These criteria exclude candidates for office, elected officials, party leaders, lobbyists, and the like from serving on the commission.[303] This exclusion, the complaint asserts, is unlawful discrimination in hiring based on prospective employees' political beliefs. "In excluding certain categories of citizens from eligibility based on their exercise of core First Amendment rights . . . the State has unconstitutionally conditioned eligibility for a valuable benefit on their willingness to limit their First Amendment right[s]."[304]

Like the other looming challenges to commissions, this First Amendment claim can't be ignored. It builds on the Roberts Court's campaign finance precedents: cases that, as I discuss below, take a very expansive view of political speech and association.[305] The claim is also supported by the Court's earlier decisions holding that the government can't hire or fire employees because of their partisan affiliations.[306] Generalizing from these decisions, the complaint plausibly states that "[c]onditions of employment that compel or restrain

---

[301] *Rucho*, 139 S Ct at 2512 (Kagan, J, dissenting).

[302] See Complaint, *Daunt v Benson*, No 1:19-cv-00614 (WD Mich filed July 30, 2019) ("*Daunt* Complaint").

[303] See id ¶ 1.

[304] Id ¶ 46.

[305] See id ¶ 53 (citing *Randall v Sorrell*, 548 US 230 (2006)).

[306] See, for example, *Rutan v Republican Party of Ill.*, 497 US 62 (1990); *Elrod v Burns*, 427 US 347 (1976).

belief and association . . . are inimical to the process which undergirds our system of government."[307]

The First Amendment theory would have more dramatic consequences, too, than the other objections to commissions. Chief Justice Roberts's dissent in *Arizona State Legislature* would only bar voters (and maybe other nonlegislative actors) from regulating congressional redistricting. The anti-commandeering and congruence-and-proportionality doctrines would only impede congressional attempts to compel the use of commissions. In contrast, the First Amendment theory would extend to *all* commissions, whether created by voter initiative, state legislation, or Congress, and whether responsible for congressional or state legislative redistricting. All commissions would be unconstitutional if they excluded certain citizens from membership, and all commissions would have to throw open their doors to all comers to remain in operation.

This would be another perverse *Carolene* outcome—indeed, a perverse *Carolene* outcome with a twist. If a commission were shuttered because of its exclusionary membership criteria (the fate the lawsuit says should befall Michigan's new body[308]), then the usual logic would apply. A court would have stopped a nonjudicial actor from addressing gerrymandering, ensuring that undemocratic redistricting practices would persist. On the other hand, if a commission dropped its membership criteria to avoid offending (this view of) the First Amendment,[309] then its capacity to draw fair lines would be compromised. Instead of being staffed by members with *no* reason

---

[307] *Daunt* Complaint ¶ 44 (cited in note 302). Again, that this argument is plausible under current law doesn't mean it's compelling. The Court's patronage cases allow the government to "choos[e] or dismiss[]" certain high-level employees on the basis of their political views." *Rutan*, 497 US at 74. Members of a redistricting commission are certainly "high-level employees." It's also more problematic for the government to hire or fire a *particular* party's adherents than for the government to exclude *all* highly partisan individuals from positions that are meant to be nonpartisan. Only the former is viewpoint discrimination. And even if the Michigan commission's membership criteria burden First Amendment rights and trigger heightened scrutiny, they should survive it. A commission staffed by partisans is unlikely to achieve its goal of preventing partisan gerrymandering. See Leah Litman, *Republicans Say the First Amendment Protects the Right to Gerrymander*, Slate (Aug 5, 2019), archived at https://perma.cc/5DVP-QAF5.

[308] See *Daunt* Complaint ¶¶ 48–56 (cited in note 302) (arguing that the Michigan commission's membership criteria can't be severed from the rest of the measure establishing the body).

[309] Of course, most commissions *can't* voluntarily drop their membership criteria because those criteria are prescribed by the legal instruments that created the bodies.

to seek partisan advantage or protect incumbents, the commission would have to welcome the individuals with the *strongest* incentive to pursue these goals. The commission could stay in business, but at the behest of the judiciary, it would have to let the fox back in the henhouse.

B. OTHER AREAS

1. *The right to vote.* All the perverse *Carolene* arguments, to this point, have been drawn from the partisan gerrymandering context. If accepted by the Roberts Court—a real possibility—they would invalidate redistricting commissions and thus thwart the main nonjudicial response to gerrymandering. Perverse *Carolene* claims, however, are hardly confined to the gerrymandering arena. They're increasingly being advanced in other election law fields, and the Roberts Court seems increasingly receptive to them. I now turn to these other fields, starting with the right to vote. I keep my discussion brief since the other fields aren't my focus in this article.

Access to the franchise, then, is often limited by state and local governments. Jurisdictions prohibit ex-felons from voting.[310] They require photo identification to vote and proof of citizenship to register to vote.[311] They close polling places and cut the period for early voting.[312] And they do so more and more; voting barriers have been erected over the last decade at the highest rate since the civil rights era.[313] These measures are obviously offensive from a *Carolene* perspective. They abridge a democratic value—political participation—that everyone agrees is protected by *Carolene*.[314] They *don't* need more sophisticated democratic theories of majoritarianism or responsiveness to be condemned.[315] And they burden a freedom, "the right to vote," that's *Carolene*'s lead example of "those political

---

[310] See *Felon Voting Rights*, Nat'l Conf. State Legislatures (Dec 21, 2018), archived at https://perma.cc/2CBK-ATEG.

[311] See *Voter Identification Requirements*, Nat'l Conf. State Legislatures (Jan 17, 2019), archived at https://perma.cc/B4XU-CZNC.

[312] See Christopher Ingraham, *Thousands of Polling Places Were Closed over the Past Decade. Here's Where*, Wash Post (Oct 26, 2018), archived at https://perma.cc/T7AB-MDLU.

[313] See *New Voting Restrictions in America*, Brennan Center for Justice (May 10, 2017), archived at https://perma.cc/B4XU-CZNC.

[314] See Part I.

[315] See id.

processes which can ordinarily be expected to bring about repeal of undesirable legislation."[316]

A correct *Carolene* decision would therefore strike down a voting restriction.[317] The Roberts Court has issued no such rulings; it has never nullified a law making it harder to vote.[318] A reverse *Carolene* decision, on the other hand, would uphold a voting restriction and so allow a jurisdiction to impede political participation. The Roberts Court has made several such rulings, sustaining, for instance, Indiana's photo ID requirement for voting[319] and Ohio's policy of purging nonvoters from the rolls.[320] And for a perverse *Carolene* decision to be possible, a nonjudicial actor would first have to facilitate access to the franchise. Most intuitively, Congress or a state government could enact a law permitting more people to vote or making voting easier for everybody.

The first bill the House of Representatives passed in 2019—the same bill that would mandate redistricting commissions—would do just that. Among other things, the bill would end the disenfranchisement of ex-felons, prohibit photo ID requirements for voting, ban purges of the voter rolls, and set a floor of fifteen days for early voting.[321] The bill, that is, would reverse most of the recent efforts by subfederal jurisdictions to inhibit voting. In addition, a number of states have liberalized their voting rules over the last few years. In particular, automatic voter registration—registering citizens when they interact with government agencies unless they affirmatively decline to be enrolled—has been adopted by sixteen states since 2015.[322]

---

[316] *United States v Carolene Products Co.*, 304 US 144, 152 n 4 (1938).

[317] I don't mean to suggest that *Carolene* requires all voting restrictions to be struck down. Some restrictions serve compelling governmental interests like an orderly electoral process and others are justified by normative judgments about who belongs to the political community. *Carolene* is thus better understood as a thumb on the scale for (not an absolute guarantee of) easier political participation by more people.

[318] Though on a few occasions, the Roberts Court has concluded it was too close to an election to disturb lower-court rulings striking down voting restrictions. See, for example, *Frank v Walker*, 135 S Ct 7 (2014) (vacating the Seventh Circuit's election-eve stay of a district court's injunction barring the use of Wisconsin's photo ID law). The Roberts Court also held in *Arizona v Inter Tribal Council of Ariz.*, 570 US 1, 16 (2013), that Arizona's proof-of-citizenship requirement for voter registration was preempted by the National Voter Registration Act. However, this was a statutory rather than a constitutional ruling.

[319] See *Crawford v Marion County Elections Bd.*, 553 US 181 (2008) (plurality).

[320] See *Husted v A. Philip Randolph Inst.*, 138 S Ct 1833 (2018).

[321] See HR 1, 116th Cong, 1st Sess, §§ 1401–08, 1201–02, 1611, 1903 (2019).

[322] See *Automatic Voter Registration*, Brennan Center for Justice (July 10, 2019), archived at https://perma.cc/JQ7C-8DBH.

If it became law, however, the House's bill would face a plausible constitutional challenge. Congress, again, is authorized by the Elections Clause to regulate the "Times, Places and Manner" of federal elections.[323] The Qualifications Clause, though, enables *states* to specify "the Qualifications requisite for [their] Electors" in state and federal elections.[324] Provisions like enfranchising ex-felons and allowing citizens to vote without photo IDs, the argument would thus run, exceed Congress's Elections Clause authority because they're not procedural regulations but rather attempts to choose states' voting qualifications for them. On this view, not having been convicted of a felony and possessing a valid ID are eligibility criteria that some states have adopted for voting, which Congress may not displace. As the Court put it in a 2013 case, "the Elections Clause empowers Congress to regulate *how* federal elections are held, but not *who* may vote in them."[325] "One cannot read the Elections Clause as treating implicitly what [the Qualifications Clause] regulate[s] explicitly."[326]

The Roberts Court might also be skeptical of automatic voter registration. In recent cases, the Court has deemed it unlawful "compelled speech" when public employees were required to pay dues to support unions' collective bargaining[327] and political[328] activities. Voter registration is arguably as communicative as union dues, indicating citizens' preferences to be included in the voter rolls and to participate in future elections.[329] Nor does it necessarily solve the coercion problem if citizens can decline to be registered, since in the Court's words, "[a]n opt-out system [still] creates a risk that [speech] will be used to further political and ideological ends with which [citizens] do not agree."[330] Parroting these points, the conservative

---

[323] See Part II.A.2.

[324] US Const, Art I, § 2 (House elections); see also US Const, Amend XVII (Senate elections).

[325] *Arizona v Inter Tribal Council of Ariz.*, 570 US 1, 16 (2013); see also id at 31 (Thomas, J, dissenting) ("The text of the Times, Places and Manner Clause . . . cannot be read to authorize Congress to dictate voter eligibility to the States."). One response to this argument is doctrinal. In *Oregon v Mitchell*, 400 US 112 (1970), the Court *upheld* a statutory provision lowering the voting age to eighteen in federal elections. The Court, in other words, *allowed* Congress to alter states' qualifications for voting.

[326] *Inter Tribal*, 570 US at 16.

[327] See *Janus v AFSCME*, 138 S Ct 2448 (2018).

[328] See *Knox v SEIU*, 567 US 298 (2012).

[329] Only arguably; one response is that voter registration expresses no political view at all and is better understood as bureaucratic record keeping.

[330] *Knox*, 567 US at 312.

chair of the Election Assistance Commission has called voter registration "the embodiment of political speech protected by the First Amendment."[331] Because "*not* registering to vote is a choice" just like registering is, "opt-out" allegedly isn't "adequate in the voter registration context."[332]

Right or wrong on non-*Carolene* grounds,[333] these are quintessential perverse *Carolene* claims. If the Qualifications Clause bars Congress from enfranchising ex-felons or allowing citizens to vote without photo IDs, then states will keep limiting their electorates in these ways. Thanks to the judiciary, political participation will continue to be curbed, despite a nonjudicial actor's attempt to expand it. Likewise, if the First Amendment forbids states (and Congress) from registering citizens automatically, then many citizens will remain unregistered. The voter pool won't be as deep as it could be, again because of the courts and against the wishes of the elected branches.

2. *Campaign finance.* Proceeding to campaign finance, it's the one area I examine where *private* activity—the funding of elections by wealthy individuals and organizations—constitutes the threat to democratic values. A large campaign contribution or expenditure may form half of a corrupt quid pro quo exchange, in which a candidate promises an official act in return for the money.[334] In this case, the act reflects the funder's rather than the electorate's priorities. Even when quids and quos aren't explicitly linked, politicians may be more responsive to those who give and spend on their behalf, and less attuned to their actual constituents. In this case, too, governmental policy may be more congruent with funders' than with voters' preferences. And because incumbent politicians may have stronger relationships with campaign donors and spenders (having already built those relationships to get elected), they may find it easier than challengers to raise funds. Challengers, then, may face the dual hurdles of opponents who are

---

[331] Christy McCormick, *Motor Voter Registration: Modernization and Challenges* 6, at https://electionlawblog.org/wp-content/uploads/Presentation_Christy_McCormick.pdf.

[332] Id; see also id at 5–6 (citing *Knox* and *Janus*).

[333] As noted above, I think these arguments are flawed on non-*Carolene* grounds too. See notes 325, 329.

[334] The Roberts Court has asserted that "independent expenditures . . . do not give rise to corruption or the appearance of corruption," *Citizens United v FEC*, 558 US 310, 357 (2010), but that's simply its ipse dixit, unsubstantiated by any evidence about the links between independent spending and corruption.

better known *and* better funded, yielding a lower level of electoral competition.[335]

Empirical evidence (which I recap here but have covered in more depth elsewhere[336]) confirms these effects. The ideological distributions of elected officials and of campaign donors are nearly identical: sharply bimodal patterns in which almost everyone is liberal or conservative and next to no one is politically moderate.[337] In contrast, the ideological distribution of the general public resembles a bell curve: fattest in the political center and thinning quickly to the left and right.[338] These findings suggest that campaign contributions lead politicians to mirror their donors' and discount their constituents' views. Why else would politicians risk ignoring the positions of the median voter?[339]

Similarly, when electoral funding is less regulated, incumbents massively outraise challengers and beat them by huge margins, on average.[340] But when electoral funding is restricted by contribution limits,[341] or subsidized by public financing,[342] incumbents' fiscal advantage shrinks significantly. Contribution limits have more bite for incumbents because they're able to solicit more and larger donations. Public financing is also more helpful for challengers because they're more cash strapped in the absence of governmental funds. And the result of greater resource parity is more electoral competition. When contribution limits and public financing are in place, incumbents tend

---

[335] I explore these threats to democratic values in more detail, while focusing on the possibility of campaign funding causing misalignment, in Nicholas O. Stephanopoulos, *Aligning Campaign Finance Law*, 101 Va L Rev 1425 (2015).

[336] See Nicholas O. Stephanopoulos, *Accountability Claims in Constitutional Law*, 112 Nw U L Rev 989, 1047–52 (2018); Stephanopoulos, 101 Va L Rev at 1474–79 (cited in note 335).

[337] See, for example, Joseph Bafumi and Michael C. Herron, *Leapfrog Representation and Extremism: A Study of American Voters and Their Members in Congress*, 104 Am Pol Sci Rev 519, 536–37 (2010); Michael J. Barber, *Representing the Preferences of Donors, Partisans, and Voters in the U.S. Senate*, 80 Pub Opinion Q 225, 236–37 (2016).

[338] See sources cited in note 337.

[339] There are actually several more reasons: politicians' own ideologies, pressure from party activists and leaders, strategies for professional advancement, and so on. Campaign finance is one, but not the only, explanation for misalignment between voters and their representatives.

[340] See, for example, Thomas Stratmann, *How Close Is Fundraising in Contested Elections in States with Low Contribution Limits?* 9 (May 2009), archived at https://perma.cc/XL2V-96WZ.

[341] See, for example, Thomas Stratmann and Francisco J. Aparicio-Castillo, *Competition Policy for Elections: Do Campaign Contribution Limits Matter?*, 127 Pub Choice 177, 198 (2006).

[342] See, for example, Andrew B. Hall, *How the Public Funding of Elections Increases Candidate Polarization* 11–12 (Jan 13, 2014), archived at https://perma.cc/43JP-SYAX.

to win by narrower margins and to be ousted more often by their opponents.[343]

Given this evidence, a correct *Carolene* decision would curb the private (or expand the public) funding of campaigns. It would thus reduce corruption, improve the ideological alignment of voters and politicians, and trigger more competitive elections, all in one stroke. Such a ruling, though, is hard to imagine in our constitutional order. In general, only state action can violate the Constitution, and private activity—even democratically destructive private activity—is constitutionally valid. By the same token, a reverse *Carolene* decision would be an odd concept. Technically, it would be a ruling declining to cut private (or boost public) campaign finance, thereby allowing the democratic harms of money in politics to persist. But again, it's awkward to criticize judicial passivity in this context since judicial *intervention*, here, is so foreign to the American legal framework.

On the other hand, a perverse *Carolene* decision is quite easy to conceptualize. It's simply a ruling blocking an attempt by a nonjudicial actor, like Congress or a state government, to regulate electoral funding and so to fight corruption, promote majoritarianism, and enhance competition. Perverse *Carolene* decisions aren't just readily imaginable; they're also doctrinally plentiful. In recent years, the Roberts Court has struck down regular contribution limits[344] as well as aggregate limits on how much donors can give to all recipients.[345] It has first narrowed[346] and then eliminated[347] the federal ban on corporate and union electoral spending. It has invalidated a law loosening contribution limits for candidates running against personally wealthy opponents.[348] And it has nullified a public financing scheme that tied the government's subsidies to the disbursements of privately funded candidates.[349] In all these cases, the Court's position was that the First Amendment protects the funding of elections and that the

---

[343] See, for example, Neil Malhotra, *The Impact of Public Financing on Electoral Competition: Evidence from Arizona and Maine*, 8 St Pol & Pol'y Q 263, 274, 276 (2008); Thomas Stratmann, *Do Low Contribution Limits Insulate Incumbents from Competition?*, 9 Election L J 125, 135 (2010).

[344] See *Randall v Sorrell*, 548 US 230 (2006) (plurality).

[345] See *McCutcheon v FEC*, 572 US 185 (2014) (plurality).

[346] See *FEC v Wisconsin Right to Life, Inc.*, 551 US 449 (2007) (plurality).

[347] See *Citizens United v FEC*, 558 US 310 (2010).

[348] See *Davis v FEC*, 554 US 724 (2008).

[349] See *Ariz. Free Enterprise Club's Freedom Club PAC v Bennett*, 564 US 721 (2011).

government's interests—even pro-democratic ones—can't justify the free speech burdens.

These cases' proponents, though, wouldn't concede that they're perverse *Carolene* decisions. Instead they would argue that they're *correct Carolene* decisions, intervening against laws that imperil democratic values. The proponents' reasoning is that most campaign finance regulations are enacted by self-interested incumbents. Surely these politicians wouldn't support measures that weaken their grip on their own offices. The proponents add that, to overcome voters' familiarity with incumbents, challengers typically need to raise and spend large sums of money. But campaign finance regulations impede this funding process, thereby lowering challengers' odds of success. As Justice Scalia wrote in a 2003 case, "[t]he first instinct of power is the retention of power," and "that is best achieved by the suppression of election-time speech."[350] *"[A]ny* restriction upon a type of campaign speech that is equally available to challengers and incumbents tends to favor incumbents."[351] Or as Chief Justice Roberts put it in 2014, "those who govern should be the *last* people to help decide who *should* govern."[352] When incumbents do limit electoral funding, they "compromis[e] the political responsiveness at the heart of the democratic process" by "favor[ing] some participants in that process" (themselves) "over others" (challengers).[353]

Scholars, even some progressives, have echoed this claim that the Roberts Court's campaign finance cases are correct *Carolene* decisions. "When incumbents limit the speech of their challengers . . . the Court's services as a referee are most urgently needed," Kathleen Sullivan and Pamela Karlan have asserted, in a piece trying to divine how Ely himself would have approached regulations of electoral funding.[354] Laurence Tribe has also explained how a "skeptical view"

---

[350] *McConnell v FEC*, 540 US 93, 263 (2003) (opinion of Scalia, J).

[351] Id at 249.

[352] *McCutcheon v FEC*, 572 US 185, 192 (2014) (plurality).

[353] Id at 227; see also, for example, *Citizens United v FEC*, 558 US 310, 354 (2010) (claiming that, by banning electoral spending by corporations, "the Government prevents their voices and viewpoints from reaching the public and advising voters on which persons or entities are hostile to their interest"); *Davis v FEC*, 554 US 724, 742 (2008) (maintaining that campaign finance regulations "arrogate the voters' authority to evaluate the strengths of candidates competing for office" and "use the election laws to influence the voters' choices").

[354] Sullivan and Karlan, 57 Stan L Rev at 702 (cited in note 95); see also Pamela S. Karlan, *Foreword: Democracy and Disdain*, 126 Harv L Rev 1, 30 (2012) ("It certainly is possible to defend the result in *Citizens United* as an application of process theory.").

of these laws, rooted in "a particular fear that legislatures will enact incumbent-protection provisions," "fits firmly into the political process tradition" and is "a descendant of the Warren Court's reapportionment cases."[355] And Jack Balkin has contended that "*Citizens United* offers the conservative version of Ely's *Democracy and Distrust*."[356] The decision "worries that because of defects in the political process, Congress is trying to snuff out political speech by defenseless corporations."[357]

As noted above,[358] both the Roberts Court and these academics have it wrong. In fact, most campaign finance regulations *disadvantage* incumbents and *increase* competition.[359] Most campaign finance laws were also passed by reformers in rare moments following corruption scandals—not by self-interested incumbents practicing politics as usual.[360] To the extent that *Citizens United* and its ilk are justified on *Carolene* grounds, then, the defense fails. These cases are *mistaken*, not correct, *Carolene* decisions that err in their arguments about how restrictions on electoral funding affect democratic values.

This error, though, is an interesting one. It highlights the hazards of commenting on policies' democratic implications in the absence of empirical evidence. Both the Roberts Court and the academics have reasonable intuitions about how campaign finance regulations shape the electoral landscape. But these intuitions are aired without facts to back them up—and it turns out the facts *don't* back them up. *Carolene*-style analysis thus shouldn't proceed on the basis of logic, precedent, or conventional wisdom. To be done right, it should focus relentlessly on how the data say that policies and democratic values are related. Sometimes the data correspond to observers'

---

[355] Laurence H. Tribe, *Dividing Citizens United: The Case v. the Controversy*, 30 Const Comm 463, 482 (2015).

[356] Balkin, 92 BU L Rev at 1160 (cited in note 167).

[357] Id; see also, for example, Daryl Levinson and Benjamin I. Sachs, *Political Entrenchment and Public Law*, 125 Yale L J 400, 461 (2015) ("Campaign finance regulations might well benefit incumbents at the expense of challengers. . . ."); Frederick Schauer, *Judicial Review of the Devices of Democracy*, 94 Colum L Rev 1326, 1339 (1994) ("[U]nder the line of argument in *Carolene Products* . . . campaign finance is subsumed under a larger topic in which constant judicial vigilance and consequent judicial jurisdiction are appropriate.").

[358] See notes 340–43 and accompanying text.

[359] See id.

[360] To take the two most prominent federal examples, the Federal Election Campaign Act was passed in 1974, in the wake of Watergate, and the Bipartisan Campaign Reform Act became law in 2002, after the Enron scandal.

expectations. But sometimes they don't, and in that scenario, heeding the empirics is the only way to avoid *Carolene* decisions that are simultaneously mistaken and perverse.

3. *Voting Rights Act.* Lastly, I want to say a word about the Voting Rights Act (VRA): a topic I have studiously avoided until now.[361] Most VRA litigation involves racial vote *dilution*: the reduction of minority voters' electoral influence through mechanisms like at-large elections and cleverly drawn districts.[362] Racial vote dilution is best understood as a ground for judicial intervention under *Carolene*'s third prong.[363] It's only possible when voting is racially polarized, that is, when minority and nonminority voters have different political preferences.[364] Racial polarization, in turn, is "a special condition, which tends seriously to curtail the operation of those political processes ordinarily to be relied upon to protect minorities."[365] Without racial polarization, in other words, minorities and nonminorities alike do well enough in the rough-and-tumble of pluralist politics, and *Carolene*'s third prong counsels judicial restraint.

Racial vote dilution, then, is beyond this article's scope because it involves *Carolene*'s third prong rather than its second. But the VRA also prohibits racial vote *denial*: measures making it more difficult for minority members to vote.[366] Unlike racial vote dilution, racial vote denial fits naturally under *Carolene*'s second prong. It hinders political participation: the least controversial democratic value underpinning

---

[361] I have also studiously avoided discussing the Court's racial gerrymandering precedents. These cases are based on the excessive consideration of race in the redistricting process: a factor unrelated to *Carolene*'s concerns about the abridgment of democratic values. In other words, the racial gerrymandering cases aren't an exercise of pro-democratic judicial review and so are unrelated to my project here.

[362] See, for example, Nicholas O. Stephanopoulos, *The South After Shelby County*, 2013 Supreme Court Review 55, 73–74 ("While the VRA prohibits both vote dilution and vote denial, the former has accounted for the vast majority of activity under both Section 2 and Section 5.").

[363] For another scholar agreeing with this framing, see Karlan, 114 Yale L J at 1336 (cited in note 103) ("[T]he analysis of racial vote dilution came essentially to unpack *Carolene Products*'s antidiscrimination rationale for judicial intervention . . .").

[364] See Nicholas O. Stephanopoulos, *Race, Place, and Power*, 68 Stan L Rev 1323, 1338 (2016) ("Conceptually, there can be vote dilution only if there is racial polarization in voting.").

[365] *United States v Carolene Products Co.*, 304 US 144, 152 n 4 (1938).

[366] For a full-length article on the VRA's treatment of racial vote denial, see Nicholas O. Stephanopoulos, *Disparate Impact, Unified Law*, 128 Yale L J 1566 (2019).

this part of *Carolene*.³⁶⁷ It can also lead to countermajoritarian outcomes if disenfranchised minority members would have changed election results had they been able to vote. Racial vote denial can undermine responsiveness, too, by allowing politicians to neglect the views of their minority constituents.³⁶⁸

I doubt I have to belabor how the categories of *Carolene* decisions would apply here. A correct *Carolene* decision would strike down a law making it harder for minority members to vote. A reverse *Carolene* decision would uphold it. And a perverse *Carolene* decision would prevent a nonjudicial actor—like Congress—from trying to stop racial vote denial—as through the VRA. Of course, the Roberts Court did exactly that in its 2013 ruling in *Shelby County v Holder*.³⁶⁹ For almost half a century, Section 5 of the VRA had barred certain jurisdictions, mostly in the South, from amending their election laws unless they first showed that their revisions wouldn't worsen the electoral position of minority voters.³⁷⁰ The *Shelby County* Court held that the formula for determining Section 5 coverage exceeded Congress's enforcement powers under the Reconstruction Amendments.³⁷¹ The Court thus nullified the most important provision ever passed to combat racial vote denial (and racial vote dilution).³⁷²

The Court's reasoning was as perverse, in *Carolene* terms, as its ruling. The Court conceded that racial discrimination in voting is undemocratic. It's "an insidious and pervasive evil" when "state and local governments work[] tirelessly to disenfranchise citizens on the basis of race."³⁷³ The Court also noted that Congress concluded that racial discrimination in voting continued to be common when it renewed Section 5. "Congress compiled thousands of pages of evidence before reauthorizing the Voting Rights Act," emphasizing, in

---

³⁶⁷ See Part I.

³⁶⁸ For another scholar concurring that racial vote denial offends *Carolene*'s second and third prongs, see Ortiz, 77 Va L Rev at 728 n 5 (cited in note 166) ("Paragraph two's and paragraph three's theories do overlap to some extent. Laws disenfranchising blacks, for example, both impose a formal blockage and reflect prejudice.").

³⁶⁹ 570 US 529 (2013).

³⁷⁰ See id at 537–39.

³⁷¹ See id at 542–57.

³⁷² See id at 562 (Ginsburg, J, dissenting) (describing Section 5 as "one of the most consequential, efficacious, and amply justified exercises of federal legislative power in our Nation's history").

³⁷³ Id at 535, 552 (quotation marks omitted).

particular, "'second-generation barriers,' which are . . . electoral arrangements that affect the weight of minority votes."[374]

But the Court then substituted its own judgment for Congress's. According to the Court, racial discrimination in voting is less widespread than in earlier eras, so Section 5 is an excessive response to a waning problem. "[T]hings have changed in the South," the Court opined.[375] "Blatantly discriminatory evasions of federal decrees are rare."[376] "Voter registration and turnout numbers in the covered States have risen dramatically."[377] "[H]istory did not end in 1965," with Section 5's original enactment, and "that [modern] history cannot be ignored."[378] Maybe the Court's view is correct or maybe it's mistaken.[379] What's undeniable, though, is that it's the *Court's* view of racial discrimination in voting, which diverges sharply from *Congress's* position on the subject. *Shelby County* thus introduced a novel rationale for a perverse *Carolene* decision. For the first time, the Roberts Court blocked a nonjudicial actor from curbing undemocratic practices based on the Court's unshared opinion that these practices no longer warranted legislative action.

IV. CAROLENE ALTERNATIVES

A. APOLITICAL ACCOUNTS

The Roberts Court, then, richly deserves its moniker as the anti-*Carolene* Court. Its decision in *Rucho* is the purest reverse *Carolene* ruling in memory, openly admitting that partisan gerrymandering is undemocratic but refusing to do anything about it. *Rucho* may soon be followed by perverse *Carolene* decisions invalidating redistricting commissions—the main nonjudicial option for thwarting gerrymandering—on any of several bases. And in other areas, perverse *Carolene* results have already arrived. The Roberts Court's campaign finance

---

[374] Id at 553; see also, for example, id at 559 (Ginsburg, J, dissenting) ("Congress determined, based on a voluminous record, that the scourge of discrimination was not yet extirpated.").

[375] Id at 540 (quotation marks omitted); see also id at 547 ("Nearly 50 years later, things have changed dramatically.").

[376] Id at 540 (quotation marks omitted).

[377] Id at 550.

[378] Id at 532.

[379] Justice Ginsburg's dissent makes a powerful case that it's mistaken. See id at 570–80 (summarizing the congressional record of continued racial discrimination in voting).

cases are classics of the genre, preventing federal and state authorities from addressing the harms of money in politics. *Shelby County* is another perverse *Carolene* masterpiece, announcing that Congress isn't free to check the undemocratic activity, racial discrimination in voting, that motivated both the Fifteenth Amendment and the VRA.

But the Roberts Court can't just *oppose Carolene*; it must also *favor* some other theory of judicial decision making.[380] What might this alternative theory be? If not the promotion of democracy, that is, what other approach might explain the Roberts Court's rulings in cases implicating *Carolene*'s second prong? One possibility, supported by language in *Rucho* itself, is a commitment to judicial restraint. Perhaps the Roberts Court seeks to avoid the "expansion of judicial power," especially into "intensely partisan aspects of American political life."[381] That way, perhaps the Court hopes to stop "the unelected and politically unaccountable branch of the Federal Government" from "assuming such an extraordinary and unprecedented role."[382]

Judicial restraint could indeed account for the Roberts Court's *reverse Carolene* decisions: rulings like *Rucho*, declining to strike down a partisan gerrymander, and *Crawford v Marion County Elections Board*, upholding a photo ID requirement for voting.[383] A *Carolene* Court would have intervened in these cases in order to vindicate democratic values. But a Court that prioritized the passive virtues could have justified its inaction on the ground that judges shouldn't nullify duly enacted laws in all but the most exceptional circumstances.[384]

Judicial restraint, however, can't possibly explain the Roberts Court's *perverse Carolene* decisions. In its campaign finance cases and in *Shelby County*, the Court didn't avoid the "expansion of judicial power" into "intensely partisan aspects of American political life."[385] The Court didn't practice the passive virtues. Instead it skeptically evaluated, and then invalidated, regulation after regulation of electoral funding as well as the crown jewel of the VRA. There's plainly

---

[380] I suppose it's possible, too, for the Court's rulings in this area to be ad hoc, unsystematic, and so irreconcilable by any single theory.

[381] *Rucho v Common Cause*, 139 S Ct 2484, 2507 (2019).

[382] Id.

[383] 553 US 181 (2008).

[384] See generally Alexander M. Bickel, *Foreword: The Passive Virtues*, 75 Harv L Rev 40 (1961).

[385] *Rucho*, 139 S Ct at 2507.

nothing restrained about these rulings. Nor would there be about the perverse *Carolene* decisions that may lie ahead: the elimination of redistricting commissions, the rejection of congressional efforts to facilitate access to the franchise, the conclusion that automatic voter registration violates the First Amendment, and so on. If they come about, these rulings would amount to unabashed judicial activism—"an extraordinary and unprecedented role" for "the unelected and politically unaccountable branch," in the *Rucho* majority's words.[386]

If not judicial restraint, then what about federalism? The claim that states should enjoy wide leeway in administering elections also appeared in *Rucho*. "The opportunity to control the drawing of electoral boundaries through the legislative process of apportionment," commented the majority, "is a critical and traditional part of politics in the United States."[387] Like judicial restraint, too, federalism may account for the Roberts Court's reverse *Carolene* decisions. When the Court sustains state laws like partisan gerrymanders or photo ID requirements for voting, it prevents state choices about electoral processes from being disrupted by a federal authority. And unlike judicial restraint, federalism may justify some of the Roberts Court's perverse *Carolene* rulings as well. A number of these cases have involved (or could soon involve) federal regulations of redistricting, the right to vote, campaign finance, and racial discrimination in voting. When the Court strikes down these regulations, it arguably creates space for states to manage their own elections, unimpeded by congressional mandates and proscriptions.[388]

Federalism, though, can't explain Chief Justice Roberts's *Arizona State Legislature* dissent. Arizona's own electorate (not any federal body) decided to establish an independent redistricting commission. Yet Chief Justice Roberts would have undone this state choice on the basis of federal constitutional law. Nor is federalism a theme of the Roberts Court's campaign finance cases. These cases have never distinguished between state and federal restrictions of electoral funding. In fact, several of the cases have nullified state policies like Vermont's

---

[386] Id.

[387] Id at 2498 (quotation marks omitted).

[388] Only arguably, because states may take advantage of this Court-created space to hinder participation, suppress competition, and otherwise undermine democratic values. The fear that states may act in these undemocratic ways, of course, is precisely why *Carolene* advocates judicial intervention and why Congress sometimes feels the need to constrain states' electoral decision making.

contribution limits³⁸⁹ and Arizona's system of public financing.³⁹⁰ And nor is federalism the impetus for the looming First Amendment attacks on redistricting commissions and automatic voter registration. These attacks pack exactly the same punch whether the measures are enacted by the federal government or by states.

The conventional modalities I alluded to earlier—in particular, the Constitution's text and history—are another possible driver of the Roberts Court's election law decisions.³⁹¹ Notably, the *Rucho* majority did analyze the language of the Elections Clause, the congressional regulations of redistricting passed pursuant to that provision, and the long and sordid history of gerrymandering.³⁹² But this analysis was just one of numerous reasons (I counted five in total³⁹³) that the *Rucho* majority gave for its ruling. The majority's other reasons had nothing to do with constitutional text or history. More importantly, the only argument of North Carolina's that *failed* to persuade the majority was the state's originalist claim. The state contended that, "through the Elections Clause, the Framers set aside electoral issues such as [partisan gerrymandering] as questions that only Congress can resolve."³⁹⁴ But the majority "d[id] not agree" because prior "cases have held that there is a role for the courts with respect to at least some issues that could arise from a State's drawing of congressional districts."³⁹⁵

The Constitution's text and history were also dogs that didn't bark in the Roberts Court's other key anti-*Carolene* decisions. In *Crawford*, the plurality neither quoted nor said anything about the ratification of the First and Fourteenth Amendments: the provisions that Indiana's photo ID requirement for voting was alleged to violate.³⁹⁶ In *Citizens United*, the majority was almost as taciturn, citing the First Amendment's text only in passing³⁹⁷ and responding in just one paragraph

---

³⁸⁹ See *Randall v Sorrell*, 548 US 230 (2006) (plurality).

³⁹⁰ See *Ariz. Free Enterprise Club's Freedom Club PAC v Bennett*, 564 US 721 (2011).

³⁹¹ See notes 104–07 and accompanying text.

³⁹² See id; see also *Rucho*, 139 S Ct at 2494–96.

³⁹³ See Part II.B.

³⁹⁴ *Rucho*, 139 S Ct at 2495.

³⁹⁵ Id at 2495–96.

³⁹⁶ See *Crawford v Marion County Elections Bd.*, 553 US 181, 185–204 (2008) (plurality).

³⁹⁷ See *Citizens United v FEC*, 558 US 310, 336 (2010).

(out of sixty-two pages in the United States Reports) to "the view that the First Amendment, as originally understood, would permit the suppression of [corporate] speech."[398] This view, in contrast, was developed in great detail by Justice John Paul Stevens's dissent.[399] And in *Shelby County*, it was again the dissent that was more rigorously originalist than the majority. The majority stressed a free-floating "principle of equal sovereignty"[400] as well as its idiosyncratic view that racial discrimination in voting is no longer a serious problem.[401] On the other hand, Justice Ruth Bader Ginsburg "firmly rooted" her dissent in the "constitutional text" and described the rationales of "the [Fifteenth] Amendment's framers" in "choosing this language."[402]

Of course, constitutional text and history aren't the only conventional modalities; reasoning based on the Court's precedents is another.[403] But respect for the Court's past rulings fares even worse as an explanation for the Roberts Court's election law oeuvre. *Rucho* itself reversed the Court's earlier holding, in the 1986 case of *Davis v Bandemer*,[404] that partisan gerrymandering claims are justiciable. In so doing, the *Rucho* majority liberally quoted Justice O'Connor's *Bandemer* dissent[405] while virtually ignoring the plurality opinion that controlled the case's outcome.[406] Elsewhere in the redistricting arena, Chief Justice Roberts's *Arizona State Legislature* dissent would have abrogated a series of early-twentieth-century cases. According to those cases, "the Legislature" empowered by the Elections Clause to regulate congressional elections includes not just "the representative body which makes the laws of the people"[407]—as Chief Justice

---

[398] Id at 353.

[399] See id at 425–32 (Stevens, J, dissenting).

[400] *Shelby County v Holder*, 570 US 529, 534, 540, 542, 544, 556 (2013).

[401] See Part III.B.3.

[402] *Shelby County*, 570 US at 567 (Ginsburg, J, dissenting).

[403] See generally Strauss, 63 U Chi L Rev at 877 (cited in note 184).

[404] 478 US 109 (1986); see also *League of United Latin Am. Citizens v Perry*, 548 US 399, 414 (2006) (noting that, while "[a] plurality of the Court in *Vieth* [*v Jubelirer*, 541 US 267 (2004)] would have held [partisan gerrymandering] challenges to be nonjusticiable political questions," "a majority declined to do so").

[405] See *Rucho v Common Cause*, 139 S Ct 2484, 2497, 2498, 2499, 2501, 2503 (2019).

[406] See id at 2497, 2500.

[407] *Ariz. State Leg. v Ariz. Independent Redistricting Comm'n*, 135 S Ct 2652, 2679 (2015) (Roberts, CJ, dissenting).

Roberts maintained—but also a popular referendum[408] and a gubernatorial veto.[409]

The Roberts Court has equally spurned stare decisis outside the redistricting context. In *Citizens United*, the Court reversed two prior decisions (one just seven years old at the time) that had upheld bans on corporate spending in elections.[410] In the 2014 case of *McCutcheon v FEC*, the Court abandoned its earlier position that aggregate contribution limits are constitutional.[411] And in *Shelby County*, the Court turned its back on *four* previous holdings that Section 5 of the VRA was a valid exercise of Congress's enforcement powers under the Reconstruction Amendments.[412] Until then, as Justice Ginsburg observed in her dissent, the Court had always "accorded Congress the full measure of respect its judgments in this domain should garner."[413]

A last account of the Roberts Court's election law jurisprudence might be libertarian. Maybe the Court strives to protect individual freedoms from governmental actions that threaten to abridge them. The Court's campaign finance cases certainly sound in this key. "[P]olitical speech must prevail against laws that would suppress it, whether by design or inadvertence," declared the majority in *Citizens United*.[414] "The First Amendment confirms the freedom to think for ourselves."[415] The other First Amendment claims discussed above—against redistricting commissions and automatic voter registration[416]—could also be justified on libertarian grounds. The claims' proponents would surely argue that they're defending people's rights to serve in government regardless of their political views and to choose for themselves whether to participate in the political process.

---

[408] See *Davis v Hildebrant*, 241 US 565 (1916).

[409] See *Smiley v Holm*, 285 US 355 (1932).

[410] These prior decisions were *Austin v Mich. Chamber of Commerce*, 494 US 652 (1990), and part of *McConnell v FEC*, 540 US 93 (2003).

[411] See 572 US 185, 200 (2014) (plurality) ("[W]e think [*Buckley v Valeo*'s] ultimate conclusion about the constitutionality of the aggregate limit in place under FECA does not control here.").

[412] These previous holdings were *South Carolina v Katzenbach*, 383 US 301 (1966), *Georgia v United States*, 411 US 526 (1973), *Rome v United States*, 446 US 156 (1980), and *Lopez v Monterey County*, 525 US 266 (1999).

[413] *Shelby County v Holder*, 570 US 529, 568 (2013) (Ginsburg, dissenting).

[414] *Citizens United v FEC*, 558 US 310, 340 (2010).

[415] Id at 356.

[416] See Parts III.A.3, III.B.1.

Rucho, however, involved a First Amendment challenge, too.[417] Witness testimony and academic evidence established that partisan gerrymanders deter voters from going to the polls, candidates from running for office, and donors from giving money.[418] These are burdens on speech and association at least as heavy as those imposed by campaign finance regulations, let alone redistricting commissions or automatic voter registration. Yet the majority thought the First Amendment couldn't supply "a serious standard for separating constitutional from unconstitutional partisan gerrymandering."[419] Speech and association also aren't the only rights protected by the Constitution. "The precious right to vote," as Justice Ginsburg called it at a recent oral argument, is jealously guarded as well.[420] Yet as noted earlier, the Roberts Court has never found that a law impermissibly interferes with citizens' exercise of the franchise.[421] For any libertarian theory of the Court's doctrine, this is embarrassing. A libertarian Court, after all, would champion *all* constitutional freedoms. It wouldn't pick and choose among them.

B. POLITICAL ACCOUNTS

None of the usual models of judicial decision making, then, can render coherent the Roberts Court's record in cases implicating *Carolene*'s second prong. Judicial restraint, federalism, constitutional text and history, precedent, and individual freedom—all these approaches have been the exception as often as the rule. But maybe we're looking in the wrong place for a unifying principle. The subject of *Carolene*'s second prong is the well-being of American democracy: the performance of "those political processes which can ordinarily be expected to bring about repeal of undesirable legislation."[422] So maybe we should be trying to come up with an explanation whose thrust is the Roberts Court's opinion of how American democracy is functioning.

---

[417] See *Rucho v Common Cause*, 139 S Ct 2484, 2504–05 (2019).

[418] See notes 84–86 and accompanying text.

[419] *Rucho*, 139 S Ct at 2504.

[420] Transcript of Oral Argument, *Gill v Whitford*, No 16-1161, *24 (Oct 3, 2017); see also, for example, *Reynolds v Sims*, 377 US 533, 562 (1964) ("[A]ny alleged infringement of the right of citizens to vote must be carefully and meticulously scrutinized.").

[421] See note 318 and accompanying text.

[422] *United States v Carolene Products Co.*, 304 US 144, 152 n 4 (1938).

Proceeding sympathetically, a perspective could be imagined that would unify the Roberts Court's election law decisions. On this view, American democracy generally works well enough when voters, campaign funders, and state electoral regulators are left to their own devices. At least in the modern era, state regulators rarely engage in the blatantly undemocratic activities—the suppression of large swaths of the electorate, particularly on racial grounds, and extreme malapportionment—that necessitated judicial intervention in earlier periods. But, this postulated view goes on, today's electoral regulators (especially at the federal level) still pose their own threats to a vibrant democratic order. The most common of these is the constriction of electoral funding, which benefits incumbents, stifles competition, and distorts the public debate. Another danger is heavy-handed legislation on behalf of minority groups, which balkanizes society on racial lines and isn't warranted by current conditions. Further, emerging concerns include independent redistricting commissions, the federalization of election administration, and automatic voter registration, all of which would upend a system that's far from broken. The Court must continue to protect American democracy from these pitfalls.[423]

While it's possible to articulate this view, though, it's not as easy to defend it. To begin with, if the Roberts Court thinks that partisan gerrymandering, voter suppression, and racial discrimination in voting no longer imperil American democracy, the Court is wrong. Gerrymandering has been more severe in the current cycle—giving rise to district maps more biased in the line-drawing party's favor—than at any point in at least half a century.[424] This decade has also seen the passage of more laws making it harder to vote than any period since the civil rights era.[425] And the phenomenon that makes racial vote denial and racial vote dilution appealing to certain politicians, racial polarization in voting, has rebounded in recent years to the highest levels in modern times.[426] The Roberts Court may well be unaware of these facts. But even if so, the Court's lack of information

---

[423] For a similar effort to understand the Roberts Court's jurisprudence, albeit in the equal protection rather than the electoral context, see Bertrall L. Ross II, *Democracy and Renewed Distrust: Equal Protection and the Evolving Judicial Conception of Politics*, 101 Cal L Rev 1565 (2013).

[424] See Stephanopoulos and McGhee, 82 U Chi L Rev at 871–73 (cited in note 182).

[425] See note 313 and accompanying text.

[426] See Stephanopoulos, 68 Stan L Rev at 1354–58 (cited in note 364).

doesn't justify its reverse *Carolene* decisions. It makes them a series of *Carolene* mistakes.

The Roberts Court's perverse *Carolene* decisions, to date, rest on similar empirical misconceptions. As pointed out above, it simply isn't the case that most campaign finance limits help incumbents and throttle competition.[427] To the contrary, they typically have the opposite effects because they erode the fundraising edge that officeholders enjoy in the absence of regulation. The democratic case for invalidating minority voting rights legislation like the VRA is doubly flawed, too. Not only does persistent racial polarization in voting indicate the continuing need for such laws.[428] The VRA's signature remedy—the creation of districts where minority voters are able to elect their preferred candidates—also doesn't influence minority or nonminority voters' racial attitudes.[429] These districts thus improve minority representation without fomenting racial strife.

And as for the perverse *Carolene* rulings just over the horizon, they're usually urged *despite* their democratic implications, not because of them. Consider Chief Justice Roberts's *Arizona State Legislature* dissent. He never argued that Arizona's political system would function better without an independent redistricting commission.[430] His position, instead, was that democratic impact is irrelevant. "For better or worse, the Elections Clause of the Constitution does not allow [Arizonans] to address those concerns [about gerrymandering] by displacing their legislature."[431] Likewise, the other claims against redistricting commissions, as well as the objections to federalizing election administration and automatically registering voters, have no democratic basis. Their common stance is that the Constitution requires certain outcomes—and that, if democracy suffers as a result, well, that's the price of following the law.

If a sympathetic account of the Roberts Court's beliefs about American politics is unpersuasive, would a more cynical explanation

---

[427] See notes 336–43 and accompanying text.

[428] See note 426 and accompanying text.

[429] See Stephen Ansolabehere and Nathaniel Persily, *Testing Shaw v. Reno: Do Majority-Minority Districts Cause Expressive Harms?*, 90 NYU L Rev 1041 (2015).

[430] Though he did complain about the commission's supposed partisanship. See *Ariz. State Leg. v Ariz. Independent Redistricting Comm'n*, 135 S Ct 2652, 2691–92 (2015) (Roberts, CJ, dissenting).

[431] Id at 2692.

gain more traction? This thesis would go roughly as follows: Running like a red thread through the Roberts Court's anti-*Carolene* decisions is perceived, and actual, partisan advantage. Both when the Court intervenes and when it stays on the sidelines, its actions are consistent with the recommendations of conservative elites. Both the Court's intrusions into, and its abstentions from, the political process also empirically benefit the Republican Party, whose presidents appointed a majority of the sitting Justices.[432]

The amicus lineup in *Rucho* supports this legal realist thesis. Here's a list of every organization that filed an amicus brief on behalf of North Carolina: the Republican National Committee, the National Republican Congressional Committee, the National Republican Redistricting Trust, North Carolina's Republican members of Congress, the Republican-run Wisconsin State Legislature, ten other states with unified Republican governments, the Allied Educational Foundation, the American Civil Rights Union, Judicial Watch, the Public Interest Legal Foundation, and the Southeastern Legal Foundation.[433] Each of these entities is either (1) a Republican Party committee; (2) a Republican-run legislature or state government; or (3) a right-wing think tank. And each of these entities—and *no* other entities—advocated the nonjusticiability of partisan gerrymandering claims.

The story was much the same in the Roberts Court's other major anti-*Carolene* cases. In *Crawford*, the Republican National Committee, Senator Mitch McConnell and other Republican members of Congress, nine Republican-run states, and an array of conservative foundations advised the Court to uphold Indiana's photo ID requirement for voting.[434] In *Citizens United*, the amici arguing that the federal ban on corporate and union spending in elections should be struck down included Senator McConnell, the Chamber of Commerce,

---

[432] For a similar view of the Roberts Court by a pair of activists writing about the Court's entire docket, see Aaron Belkin and Sean McElwee, *Don't Be Fooled. Chief Justice John Roberts Is as Partisan as They Come*, NY Times (Oct 7, 2019), archived at https://perma.cc/23GR-ZNLB. For a similar view by a pair of academics writing about the right to vote, see Lisa Marshall Manheim and Elizabeth G. Porter, *The Elephant in the Room: Intentional Voter Suppression*, 2019 Supreme Court Review 213.

[433] See Docket, *Rucho v Common Cause*, Supreme Court of the United States, https://www.supremecourt.gov/search.aspx?filename=/docket/docketfiles/html/public/18-422.html (last visited Oct 1, 2019).

[434] See Docket, *Crawford v Marion County Elections Bd.*, Supreme Court of the United States, https://www.supremecourt.gov/search.aspx?filename=/docket/docketfiles/07-21.htm (last visited Oct 1, 2019).

the National Rifle Association, and many right-wing think tanks.[435] And in *Shelby County*, seven Republican-run states (across three separate briefs), eight former Republican Department of Justice officials, and the usual constellation of conservative groups asked the Court to nullify Section 5 of the VRA.[436] In none of these cases could the Justices have had much doubt about the wishes of elite Republican and right-wing actors. Their views, expressed at length in their amicus briefs, were plain as day.

Nor were these actors mistaken about the partisan consequences of their positions. Academic evidence confirms that their stands electorally benefit Republicans. Gerrymandering, first, has no necessary partisan valence. Either party can craft an advantageous map when it has the opportunity to draw the lines. In the current cycle, though, Republicans had many more such chances than Democrats. The well-timed wave election of 2010 gave them unified control of most states (including almost all swing states) right before the country's districts were due to be reconfigured. As a result, eight of this decade's ten most biased congressional plans were skewed in a Republican direction.[437] So were nine of this decade's ten most tilted state house maps.[438] Across all district plans nationwide, the median map was more pro-Republican than at any earlier time.[439]

Second, the partisan effects of photo ID requirements for voting are often overstated, but the measures do seem to shift the vote by up to a percentage point in Republicans' favor.[440] Democratic-leaning constituencies like minorities and the poor are less likely to possess valid IDs than whiter, wealthier Republican voters. Third, unlimited electoral spending by outside actors usually boosts Republicans because pro-Republican expenditures tend to exceed those backing

---

[435] See Docket, *Citizens United v FEC*, Supreme Court of the United States, https://www.supremecourt.gov/search.aspx?filename=/docket/docketfiles/08-205.htm (last visited Oct 1, 2019).

[436] See Docket, *Shelby County v Holder*, Supreme Court of the United States, https://www.supremecourt.gov/search.aspx?filename=/docket/docketfiles/12-96.htm (last visited Oct 1, 2019).

[437] These data are on file with the author and cover the 2012, 2014, and 2016 elections.

[438] These data also are on file with the author and apply to the 2012–16 period.

[439] See Stephanopoulos and McGhee, 82 U Chi L Rev at 873 (cited in note 182) (analyzing elections up to 2012). Post-2012 data on file with the author confirm these trends.

[440] See, for example, Stephanopoulos, 114 Colum L Rev at 328 (cited in note 55) (surveying the relevant academic literature).

Democrats. So after *Citizens United* removed the shackles on electioneering by corporations, unions, and other outside groups, Republican seat and vote shares surged in state legislatures.[441] And fourth, Section 5 of the VRA used to block covered jurisdictions (mostly Republican-run in recent years) from making it harder for minority voters (a heavily Democratic group) to cast ballots and earn representation. But since *Shelby County*, these jurisdictions have adopted scores of new voting restrictions, and in the next redistricting cycle, they will probably dismantle many districts that previously elected minority Democrats to office.[442]

To be clear, I have no interest in psychoanalyzing the Justices.[443] I don't know (or think it's critical) what subjectively motivates their rulings. So my argument here isn't that Chief Justice Roberts, or the Justices who typically vote with him in election law cases, are *trying* to assist Republicans. Instead, my claims are that the Roberts Court consistently decides these cases in the ways preferred by conservative elites; and that its resulting decisions do, in fact, consistently aid Republicans. Moreover, partisan advantage is a *more* reliable explanation than any other factor. Whether or not it consciously drives any Justice's behavior, it better accounts for the Roberts Court's election law rulings than any alternative hypothesis.

If these claims are correct, they provide a coda for the Roberts Court's anti-*Carolene* record. The Court often issues reverse *Carolene* decisions, declining to intervene when American democracy is endangered. (*Rucho* is the most recent example.) The Court also commonly hands down perverse *Carolene* decisions, preventing nonjudicial actors from curbing democratic abuses. (*Citizens United* and *Shelby County* are the archetypes here.) And the most convincing *reason* for this anti-*Carolene* activity is perceived, and actual, partisan gain. By holding its fire when *Carolene* says to shoot, and by stepping

---

[441] See, for example, Nour Abdul-Razzak et al, *After Citizens United: How Outside Spending Shapes American Democracy* 24–25 (Mar 2019), archived at https://perma.cc/7LX9-ZNTE.

[442] See, for example, Stephanopoulos, 2013 Supreme Court Review at 102–06 (cited in note 362).

[443] My reservations about attributing motives to the Justices (or anybody else) are why I have relegated this section to the end of the article. The article's core claim is that the Roberts Court is the anti-*Carolene* Court—not that partisanship is an explanation for the Roberts Court's anti-*Carolene* record (though I think it is). Even here, as the prior sentence makes clear, I only argue that partisanship is *an* (not *the*) explanation for the Roberts Court's record. I'm sure the other aspects of judicial decision making I have discussed play some role, too.

in when *Carolene* advises stepping back, the Court improves Republican electoral prospects at every turn.

If the claims are correct, they corroborate the objection to political process theory recently leveled by Eric Posner and Adrian Vermeule, too.[444] Process theory, Posner and Vermeule point out, requires judges not to succumb to the partisan and political pressures that influence legislative and executive officials.[445] Only if judges are insensitive to these forces can they protect "those political processes which can ordinarily be expected to bring about repeal of undesirable legislation"[446] (*Carolene*'s formulation) or stop "the ins [from] choking off the channels of political change"[447] (Ely's). But, Posner and Vermeule continue, this requirement is frequently unrealistic. "Because the executive and legislative [branches] jointly control the process of judicial appointments," the same group that dominates those branches may "filter out judges who would challenge [its] prejudices and filter in judges who share them."[448] That group may thus "structure judicial behavior so as to perpetuate [its] own power."[449]

Posner and Vermeule's model of judges as "inside the system"—not platonically outside it—seems to fit the Roberts Court. The members of its conservative majority have the same educations, affiliations, and qualifications as nonjudicial right-wing elites in the executive and legislative branches. These members were also selected for their positions precisely because of these backgrounds. So they may have no incentive to fix malfunctions in *Carolene*'s "political processes" that accrue to their copartisans' benefit. Why would they want to correct such useful flaws? They may also be disinclined, in Ely's terms, to block "the ins" from rigging the electoral system against "the outs." Again, why should they, when they're as much the ins as the politicians doing the rigging? And they may be keen to obstruct efforts by nonjudicial actors that threaten to advantage the outs. Once more, avoiding that edge for the outs takes priority over ameliorating American democracy.

---

[444] See Eric A. Posner and Adrian Vermeule, *Inside or Outside the System?*, 80 U Chi L Rev 1743, 1763–66 (2013).

[445] See id.

[446] *United States v Carolene Products Co.*, 304 US 144, 152 n 4 (1938).

[447] Ely, *Democracy and Distrust* at 103 (cited in note 3).

[448] Posner and Vermeule, 80 U Chi L Rev at 1765 (cited in note 444).

[449] Id.

V. Conclusion

It's an irony of history that the same lawyer, Emmet Bondurant, argued both *Wesberry*, the 1964 case that announced the one-person, one-vote rule for congressional districts, and *Rucho*, which held that partisan gerrymandering claims are nonjusticiable.[450] Bondurant made essentially the same point on both occasions. Malapportionment, he told the *Wesberry* Court as a twenty-six-year-old attorney just out of law school, is undemocratic because it allows a minority to entrench itself in power by cramming opposing voters into overpopulated districts.[451] Gerrymandering, he similarly explained to the *Rucho* Court as an eighty-two-year-old law firm partner with decades of legal experience, undermines democratic values in several ways. It, too, enables a minority to seize undeserved power, by cracking and packing the other side's voters so their ballots translate into fewer seats. Gerrymandering further stifles competition, by making most districts safe, and chills participation, by rendering futile voters' electoral efforts.[452]

But while Bondurant advanced the same arguments in *Wesberry* and *Rucho*, the cases' outcomes, of course, diverged. In *Wesberry*, the Court turned the political world upside down, declaring a principle of population equality that doomed most of the country's congressional districts and ended one of the most undemocratic features of mid-century America. In *Rucho*, in contrast, the Court slammed the door on partisan gerrymandering claims and thus permitted one of the most invidious practices in modern American politics to persist and even intensify. Why the difference? In a word, *Carolene*. The *Wesberry* Court was a true *Carolene* Court, committed to exercising (and refraining from exercising) judicial authority to serve democratic ends. The Roberts Court, on the other hand, is the anti-*Carolene* Court. It has a near-perfect record of doing nothing when it should have done something, doing all too much when it should have sat still, and promoting the same party's interests through all its maneuvers. *Rucho* is just the latest, saddest entry in this ledger of democratic frustration.

---

[450] For a nice story on this historical twist, see Johnny Kauffman, *55 Years Later, Lawyer Will Again Argue Over Redistricting Before Supreme Court*, NPR (Mar 24, 2019), archived at https://perma.cc/SH7U-T4QD.

[451] See Transcript of Oral Argument, *Wesberry v Sanders*, No 22 (Nov 18, 1964).

[452] See Transcript of Oral Argument, *Rucho v Common Cause*, No 18-422 (Mar 26, 2019).

KENT GREENFIELD

TRADEMARKS, HATE SPEECH, AND
SOLVING A PUZZLE OF VIEWPOINT BIAS

In the hierarchy of constitutional offenses to free speech principles, content discrimination is near the very top. Since the early 1970s, the Court has identified laws that regulate speech on the basis of its content as presumptively unconstitutional.[1] Content discrimination is considered an indication that the government is tipping the scales in public debate, the central ill against which the Free Speech Clause protects.[2] Unless there is a narrow exception in play, content-based laws are subject to strict scrutiny, upheld only if the government can show that the regulation is narrowly tailored to satisfy a compelling interest.[3] Only a handful of laws have satisfied such an exacting test.[4] The commitment to content neutrality has become so central to free

---

Kent Greenfield is Professor of Law and Dean's Distinguished Scholar, Boston College.

AUTHOR'S NOTE: The author thanks Marissa Lafayette and Matthew Burton for excellent research assistance. Thanks also to William Marshall, Geoffrey Stone, David Olson, and students in the 2019 Supreme Court Experience seminar and 2019 Speech and Religion course at Boston College Law School for help in thinking through these issues.

[1] See Paul B. Stephan III, *The First Amendment and Content Discrimination*, 68 Va L Rev 203 (1982) (pointing to the Court's announcement in *Police Dept. v Mosley*, 408 US 92, 95 (1972), that "above all else, the First Amendment means that government has no power to restrict expression because of its message, its ideas, its subject matter, or its content.").

[2] See Geoffrey R. Stone, *Content Regulation and the First Amendment*, 25 Wm & Mary L Rev 189 (1983).

[3] *Reed v Town of Gilbert*, 135 S Ct 2218 (2015).

[4] See, for example, *Williams-Yulee v Florida Bar*, 575 US 433 (2015).

© 2020 by The University of Chicago. All rights reserved.
978-0-226-70856-0/2020/2019-0004$10.00

speech doctrine that the Court has brought it to bear to strike down laws that are far afield from those that appear to pose a risk that "official suppression of ideas is afoot."[5]

But at the apex of free speech affronts is not content discrimination but viewpoint discrimination. While content-based laws make regulatory choices on the basis of the topic or subject matter of the speech in question (e.g., "no speech about abortion in public parks"), viewpoint-based laws make regulatory choices on the basis of the point of view of the speaker within a content category of speech ("no anti-choice speech in public parks"). The constitutional harm of content bias is setting aside categories of speech for greater or lesser protection based on its subject matter; the constitutional harm of viewpoint bias is setting aside speech within categories for greater or lesser protection based on its political, cultural, social, or economic point of view. Content bias skews debate by limiting categories of speech; viewpoint bias skews debate by limiting points of view within categories.

Content-based laws require strict scrutiny, but the Court has made clear that viewpoint bias is even worse than content bias. Justice Samuel Alito has called laws that discriminate on the basis of viewpoint "poison to a free society," and there is little apparent disagreement on this point among his colleagues. While some members of the Court have argued that the doctrinal fixation on content bias has gone too far,[6] no current Justice has come close to suggesting that the Court's fixation on ferreting out viewpoint bias is inappropriate. The unanimity is striking. While there have been a handful of instances where there was disagreement as to whether a specific law was viewpoint based or not,[7] there has not been a single instance in the last

---

[5] See *Reed*, 135 S Ct at 2327–38 (Kagan, J, concurring in the judgment) (critiquing Court's decision as an overly aggressive application of its skepticism of content discrimination beyond "its intended function").

[6] See id at 2328 (Kagan, J, concurring in the judgment) (arguing that the Court's fixation on content neutrality has led it to overreach, and the Court should instead "administer our content-regulation doctrine with a dose of common sense"); *Iancu v Brunetti*, 139 S Ct 2294, 2304 (2019) (Breyer, J, concurring in part and dissenting in part) ("Unfortunately, the Court has sometimes applied these rules—especially the category of 'content discrimination'—too rigidly.").

[7] See, for example, *Brunetti*, 139 S Ct 2294; *Rosenberger v Rector and Visitors of Univ. of Va.*, 515 US 819 (1995).

fifty years of the Court characterizing a law as viewpoint based and nevertheless ruling that the law satisfied strict scrutiny.[8]

Notwithstanding the Court's uniform condemnation of viewpoint bias, it is rarely a doctrinal game changer. A law that makes distinctions according to viewpoint also, by definition, makes distinctions according to content. A ban on anti-choice speech, for example, is both viewpoint based and content based. And because content discrimination usually triggers strict scrutiny by itself, the added constitutional affront of viewpoint discrimination does not increase the level of judicial scrutiny in the run of cases.[9] Viewpoint bias is only material as a matter of doctrine in those cases in which the Court might otherwise be open to accepting some level of content basis in a legal framework—such as in cases pertaining to commercial speech,[10] limited public forums,[11] or "low-value" speech such as fighting words.[12] In those cases, if the Court sees viewpoint bias, it ratchets up the level of scrutiny. In some cases, the Court has made clear that the viewpoint bias of the law increased the level of scrutiny over what would have been applied otherwise, but was vague in articulating what the final level of scrutiny should be.[13] In others, the Court has applied

---

[8] In *R.A.V. v City of St. Paul*, 508 US 377, 395–96 (1992), the Court conceded that the "hate speech" ordinance at issue was based on a compelling interest, but held that the ordinance was not narrowly tailored to satisfy that interest. See text below at notes 63–64.

[9] As a theoretical matter, viewpoint bias could have doctrinal effects even in cases in which content bias already requires strict scrutiny in that viewpoint bias would make it even more difficult for the state to show that the biased law is narrowly tailored to serve a compelling interest. Not only would the state have to show a compelling interest to regulate specific content but to regulate content of a specific point of view. The tailoring analysis, too, would be doubly difficult. The Court implied something like this in *R.A.V.*, when it conceded that the St. Paul ordinance served a compelling interest but failed tailoring. See text below at notes 63–64. But the Court has never struck down a viewpoint-biased law as failing strict scrutiny that the Court said would have survived a content-based application of strict scrutiny. This difference is thus mostly theoretical only.

[10] *Central Hudson Gas & Elec. Corp. v Public Service Comm. of NY*, 447 US 557 (1980).

[11] See, for example, *Good News Club v Milford Central School*, 533 US 98, 107 (2001); *Rosenberger*, 515 US at 831; *Lamb's Chapel v Center Moriches Union Free School Dist.*, 508 US 384, 392–93 (1993). See also *Legal Services Corporation v Velazquez*, 531 US 533, 544 (2001). As Justice Alito says in *Tam*: "When government creates such a forum, in either a literal or 'metaphysical' sense . . . some content- and speaker-based restrictions may be allowed. . . . However, even in such cases, what we have termed 'viewpoint discrimination' is forbidden." *Matal v Tam*, 137 S Ct 1744, 1763 (2017) (quoting *Rosenberger*, 515 US at 830–31).

[12] See *R.A.V.*, 508 US 377.

[13] See, for example, *Tam*, 137 S Ct at 1764 (Court need not decide level of scrutiny because provision would fail even intermediate review) (plurality); *Sorrell v IMS Health*, 564 US 552, 571 (2011) (describing level of review for viewpoint-based regulation of commercial speech as "heightened").

strict scrutiny to speech restrictions that would, but for the viewpoint bias, otherwise receive only rational basis review.[14]

In any event, over the past few decades the viewpoint discrimination of a law has been dispositive in only a handful of Supreme Court cases. That means that the Court has had few opportunities to articulate the contours and limits of what amounts to viewpoint bias. The core of what constitutes viewpoint bias may be more or less clear—when the government regulates one point of view within a category of speech differently from others. But the edges of the doctrine are still being defined.

One enduring puzzle dates from the Court's most famous modern viewpoint discrimination case, *R.A.V. v St. Paul*, from 1992.[15] There, the city made it a misdemeanor to place "on public or private property a symbol . . . including, but not limited to, a burning cross or Nazi swastika, which . . . arouses anger, alarm, or resentment in others on the basis of race, color, creed, religion, or gender."[16] This ordinance was clearly content based—it made distinctions among symbols on the basis of the content of the communication. But the law's content basis was not enough to trigger strict scrutiny alone, because (according to the Minnesota Supreme Court, whose interpretation was controlling for purposes of the case) the ordinance only applied to "fighting words," a low-value category of speech that the Court had long considered "not within the area of constitutionally protected speech."[17] But the U.S. Supreme Court nevertheless applied strict scrutiny and struck down the ordinance as discriminating on the basis of viewpoint.

One aspect of *R.A.V.* has remained unclear since its announcement nearly thirty years ago. What exactly made the St. Paul ordinance viewpoint based?[18] The text of the ordinance appears to ban a specific mode or manner of speech—fighting words that also contained some

---

[14] See *R.A.V.*, 508 US 377 (applying strict scrutiny to a viewpoint-based regulation of fighting words).

[15] Id.

[16] Id at 380.

[17] Id at 383, citing *Chaplinsky v New Hampshire*, 315 US 568, 571–72 (1942).

[18] Cf. Cass R. Sunstein, *On Analogical Reasoning*, 106 Harv L Rev 741, 762–63 & n 78 (1993) (R.A.V. ordinance not viewpoint based in practice); Elena Kagan, *The Changing Faces of First Amendment Neutrality: R.A.V. v St. Paul, Rust v Sullivan, and the Problem of Content-Based Underinclusion*, 1992 Supreme Court Review 29, 69–71 (R.A.V. ordinance viewpoint based in practice).

kind of racial, sexual, or religious epithet. The city argued that the law only applied to "racial, religious, or gender-specific symbols" and the Court interpreted the ordinance to mean that the use of such epithets "would be prohibited to proponents of all views." In other words, the ordinance was arguably an even-handed limitation of a mode or manner of speech—the use of epithets. But the Court nevertheless held the ordinance to be viewpoint biased. One way to read *R.A.V.*, then, is that specific limits on the mode or manner of speech can trigger the Court's ire against viewpoint discrimination.

That was not the only way to read the ordinance, and it is not the only way to read the Court's opinion in *R.A.V.* Was the ordinance viewpoint biased because of the underlying message of the speech, the idea expressed? Or was it because of the mode or manner regulated? In *R.A.V.* itself, the action that triggered the arrest under the ordinance was the burning of a cross on the lawn of a black family. The mode—the burning of the cross—expressed the idea—racial hatred. Justice Antonin Scalia's opinion for the Court muddled the analysis and left unclear whether the constitutional infirmity of the ordinance was its selection of a specific viewpoint for greater punishment or its selection of a specific mode of communication for greater punishment.

The difference between these two possible readings matters for a range of possible applications. For example, if limits on specific modes or manners of speech are deemed to be viewpoint discrimination, then it may be "virtually impossible" to enact a speech code at a university that would not trigger strict scrutiny.[19] Or, limits on sexually explicit speech in the workplace could be seen as constitutionally problematic.[20]

Notwithstanding the lack of clarity in *R.A.V.* and the important implications of the definitional uncertainty, the Court has not taken the opportunity to clarify whether specific limits on the mode and

---

[19] David L. Hudson Jr. and Lata Nott, *Hate Speech and Campus Speech Codes*, Freedom Forum Institute, March 2017, https://www.freedomforuminstitute.org/first-amendment-center/topics/freedom-of-speech-2/free-speech-on-public-college-campuses-overview/hate-speech-campus-speech-codes/ ("while speech codes faced an uphill battle under the constitutional precedent in place before *R.A.V.*, this decision made it virtually impossible for a speech code to pass constitutional muster") (quoting S. Douglas Murray, *The Demise of Campus Speech Codes*, 24 Western St U L Rev 247, 264–65 (1997); see also Erwin Chemerinsky, *Constitutional Law: Principles and Policies* 1013–14 (3d ed, 2006) (*R.A.V.* "makes it difficult for hate speech codes to survive judicial analysis; if they prohibit only some forms of hate, they will be invalidated as impermissible content-based discrimination"); id at 1007 ("there is a strong presumption against content-based discrimination within categories of unprotected speech").

[20] See text below at note 45.

manner of communication can amount to viewpoint bias. What we have known for the last generation is that viewpoint bias is the worst kind of First Amendment harm—but that its contours remain unclear. In the words of Justice Sonia Sotomayor, "the line between viewpoint-based and viewpoint-neutral content discrimination can be 'slippery.'"[21]

But the Court has recently offered help. In two cases over the last three Terms, the Supreme Court struck down provisions of the Lanham Act, the federal law governing the registration of trademarks, on the grounds that the laws discriminated on the basis of viewpoint. In the first, the 2017 case of *Matal v Tam*,[22] the Court declared unconstitutional the provision of the act that required the trademark office to refuse registration to those marks that "disparaged" individuals or groups. In the second, in *Iancu v Brunetti* from 2019, the Court ruled against the provision that prohibited the registration of marks that were "immoral" or "scandalous."[23]

According to the Court, both were straightforward viewpoint cases. Disparaging marks could not be trademarked, yet nondisparaging marks could. Marks celebrating immorality and scandalousness could not be registered, yet marks celebrating civility and decency could. The provisions put the government's thumb on the scale in favor of racial harmony and morality by creating a regulatory framework that benefited speech consistent with those views and refused benefits to speech inconsistent with those views. The Court reaffirmed its longstanding view that viewpoint discrimination is an "egregious form of content discrimination" and a presumptive First Amendment violation.[24] It was in his *Brunetti* concurrence that Justice Alito made his statement, mentioned above, that "viewpoint discrimination is poison to a free society."[25]

---

[21] *Brunetti*, 139 S Ct at 2313 (Sotomayor, J, concurring in part and dissenting in part) (quoting Caroline Corbin, *Mixed Speech: When Speech Is Both Private and Governmental*, 83 NYU L Rev 605, 651 (2008)). See also *Brunetti*, 139 S Ct at 2306 (Breyer, J, concurring in part and dissenting in part) ("As for the concepts of 'viewpoint discrimination' and 'content discrimination,' I agree with Justice Sotomayor that the boundaries between them may be difficult to discern."); *Rosenberger*, 515 US at 831 ("[T]he distinction is not a precise one").

[22] 137 S Ct 1744 (2017).

[23] 139 S Ct 2294 (2019).

[24] See *Rosenberger*, 515 US at 829 (1995). See also *Brunetti*, 139 S Ct 2294 at 2299 (quoting *Rosenberger*); *Lamb's Chapel*, 508 US at 394 ("[T]he First Amendment forbids the government to regulate speech in ways that favor some viewpoints or ideas at the expense of others").

[25] 139 S Ct 2294 at 2302.

Tam was largely unhelpful as a matter of definition and doctrine, however, because the Court struck down the disparagement provision without a majority opinion. Justice Alito wrote for himself and three Justices; Justice Anthony Kennedy headed up another contingent of four.[26] Both opinions described the disparagement provision as a violation of the First Amendment's bar on viewpoint discrimination, but arrived at that destination by different routes. Doctrinal uncertainty remained.

But this past Term's decision in *Brunetti* helped matters considerably. The Court struck down the provisions of the Lanham Act prohibiting the registration of "immoral" and "scandalous" marks as viewpoint biased. The Court's opinion was written by Justice Elena Kagan, and the main oppositional opinion—one concurring in part and dissenting in part—was penned by Justice Sonia Sotomayor. The conflict between the two in fact illuminated what appears to be an important area of agreement that, in all likelihood, is sufficient to control a majority of the Court. That agreement is this: that worries about viewpoint bias do not ordinarily come into play when the government regulates the mode and manner of communication as opposed to the ideas conveyed.

Such a principle would have a number of implications. Perhaps the most important is that *R.A.V.* is less significant in First Amendment doctrine than it has seemed for thirty years. Also, some kinds of speech codes could survive First Amendment challenge, as long as they apply in certain forums and are aimed at the mode and manner of communication rather than the ideas expressed. Another implication would be that it would be possible for Congress to rewrite the now-defunct provisions of the Lanham Act to survive First Amendment challenge and also satisfy much of Congress's original goals.

This essay proceeds as follows. I first describe two kinds of viewpoint bias, the first of which is "traditional" bias and the second "manner" bias. Traditional bias is when the government puts its finger on the scale in a cultural, social, ideological, or political debate by enforcing some kind of speech restriction against one side and not against the other. Manner bias is when the government restricts a mode or manner of communication. Manner bias is indeed bias—it is the government enforcing a view that a certain type of communication

---

[26] Justice Gorsuch took no part in the case.

is to be regulated in a different way than other kinds of communication. But it is a bias of a different kind than traditional viewpoint discrimination.

In Part II, I describe the lack of clarity in *R.A.V.* and other cases as to whether manner bias is constitutionally problematic. In Part III, I set out why the best reading of *Brunetti* is to exclude manner bias from the category of viewpoint bias the Court recognizes as constitutional "poison." Finally, in Part IV, I describe what I believe to be the best understanding of the doctrine of viewpoint bias after *Brunetti* and explain some of the implications of this doctrinal understanding.

I. CONTENT BIAS AND TWO TYPES OF VIEWPOINT BIAS

Consider a series of hypothetical local sign ordinances. The first reads:

> *Signs on Private Property:* Signs on private property are prohibited without a permit. Exempt from this prohibition shall be political signs (which shall be no larger than 20 square feet in size), ideological signs (which shall be no larger than 16 square feet in size), and temporary signs indicating directions to an event (which shall be no larger than 6 square feet).

Ordinances such as this are ubiquitous in the United States.[27] Cities and towns regulate the location, size, and appearance of signs in order to guard against the visual clutter and distraction that the absence of such ordinances would engender. And one might think it is reasonable for cities and towns to make some distinctions among the kinds of signs when it creates such ordinances.

But this hypothetical ordinance is a simplified version of the ordinance the Court struck down in *Reed v Town of Gilbert*. The Court ruled that the ordinance created "content-based restrictions of speech that cannot survive strict scrutiny."[28] As the Court explained, the regulations applicable to a particular sign "depend entirely on the communicative content of the sign."[29] According to the Court, government

---

[27] See *Reed*, 135 S Ct at 2236 (Kagan, J, concurring in judgment) ("Countless cities and towns across America have adopted ordinances regulating the posting of signs, while exempting certain categories of signs based on their subject matter"). For a critique of *Reed*'s reasoning and a description of why it has potentially broad-ranging impacts, see Genevieve Lakier, *Reed v Town of Gilbert, Arizona, and the Rise of the Anticlassificatory First Amendment*, 2016 Supreme Court Review 233 (2016).

[28] *Reed*, 135 S Ct at 2224.

[29] Id at 2222.

regulations of speech that depend on the content of the speech raise the possibility that the government is placing its thumb on the scale of public debate. Content-based regulations are "presumptively unconstitutional and may be justified only if the government proves that they are narrowly tailored to serve compelling state interests."[30]

Is this first ordinance viewpoint based? In a way, yes. The ordinance makes judgments about the allowable size of signs based on the subject matter of the speech conveyed by the sign. Political signs can be one particular size, ideological signs must be smaller, and directional signs smaller still. This hierarchy implies that the town had a viewpoint about the importance of political speech and the lesser importance of other kinds of speech. Political speech was sufficiently crucial to the town that its regulation is less intrusive than other kinds of speech.

But this classification of speech, even if it is based on a view about the relative importance of various subject matters, is *not* what the Court considers viewpoint discrimination. Justice Clarence Thomas, writing for the Court, made clear that the ordinance in *Reed* was not to be considered viewpoint based even though it established such a hierarchy. The Ninth Circuit below had opined that the ordinance should survive because it was not viewpoint based. In response, Thomas emphasized that content-based discrimination was enough to raise the level of judicial scrutiny and the ordinance was not required to be viewpoint based to trigger strict scrutiny. The sign ordinance was a "paradigmatic example of content-based discrimination." This was true "even if it does not target viewpoints within that subject matter."[31]

The distinction between content-based and viewpoint-based laws, then, is the difference between creating categories of speech for special treatment and creating advantages or disadvantages *within* those categories based on points of view. This is true even if the creation of the categories is based, as it would have to be, on some government view about the merits, importance, or harms flowing from different categories of speech. For an ordinance to discriminate on the basis of viewpoint, the views differentiated have to be about something

---

[30] Id at 2226.

[31] Id at 2223. The definitive scholarly treatment of subject matter distinctions within free speech law remains Geoffrey R. Stone, *Restrictions of Speech Because of Its Content: The Peculiar Case of Subject Matter Restrictions*, 46 U Chi L Rev 81 (1978).

exogenous to the category rather than endogenous to it. The Court has sometimes referred to this distinction as the difference between "subject matter" and "particular views taken by speakers on a subject."[32]

This distinction between content and viewpoint, assumed by the Court in *Reed*, makes sense. If the categorization of speech was itself a viewpoint, then there would be no difference between a content-based statute and a viewpoint-based statute. If the creation of a category of speech is viewpoint discrimination—because it would imply a point of view about that category—then viewpoint bias would collapse into content bias.[33]

Now consider a second hypothetical ordinance. A city council adopts the following sign ordinance:

> *Signs on Private Property:* Signs on private property are prohibited without a permit. Exempt from this prohibition shall be political signs, which shall be no larger than 20 square feet in size. But in no case shall a property owner erect a sign advocating Communism.

Such an ordinance would discriminate on the basis of viewpoint. Within the category of political signs, one point of view—support of Communism—is more heavily regulated than competing points of view, such as the advocacy of capitalism or opposition to Communism. The government is putting its thumb on the scale of public debate in favor of one position and against another. This is a violation of a core principle of the First Amendment that the government may not regulate speech because of the ideas expressed. We do not see

---

[32] *Rosenberger*, 515 US at 829. See id at 895 (Souter, J, dissenting) ("It is precisely this element of taking sides in a public debate that identifies viewpoint discrimination and makes it the most pernicious of all distinctions based on content.").

[33] In *Rosenberger*, Justice Souter in dissent accused the Court of doing this very thing. The University of Virginia refused funds for a student-run religious newspaper on the basis of a guideline prohibiting the use of student activity fees for any "religious activity," defined as any activity that "primarily promotes or manifests a particular belie[f] in or about a deity or an ultimate reality." 515 US at 825. Justice Souter dissented in the case, saying that this provision did not embody viewpoint discrimination because it excluded an entire category of subject matter from funding, whether it was to promote a Christian, Muslim, Buddhist, or even atheistic point of view. To Souter, the rule "den[ied] funding for the entire subject matter of religious apologetics." Id at 896 (Souter, J, dissenting). But Justice Kennedy's opinion for the Court interpreted the guideline differently, saying the "University does not exclude religion as a subject matter but selects for disfavored treatment those student journalistic efforts with religious editorial viewpoints." Id at 831. The university had identified a "prohibited perspective, not the general subject matter" for disfavored treatment. Id. For a critique of the Court's understanding of viewpoint bias in *Rosenberger*, see Kent Greenawalt, *Viewpoints from Olympus*, 96 Colum L Rev 697 (1996).

many of these blatant facial classifications in modern cases.[34] They are so clearly problematic that they do not easily win adoption, either out of a shared commitment to First Amendment principles or out of fear of litigation that will result in a quick and embarrassing defeat.[35]

For the purpose of this article, I will call this kind of law as exhibiting "traditional" viewpoint bias. Traditional bias is the kind of bias that occurs when within a category of speech one viewpoint is regulated differently from others. The viewpoint that is regulated has to be exogenous to, or a subset within, the category. This will become clearer in comparison to a third hypothetical ordinance.

Consider a third ordinance that reads as follows:

> *Signs on Private Property: Signs on private property are prohibited without a permit or unless they fall into certain exempt categories (detailed elsewhere). But in no case shall signs contain profanity.*

Such an ordinance limiting profanity would not be like the first ordinance above. It regulates content, to be sure. One can only determine whether a sign contains profanity prohibited by the ordinance by looking at the content of the sign. But the ordinance focuses on the mode or manner of the communication rather than the subject matter or issue area of communication. The profanity ban does not "single[] out specific subject matter for differential treatment,"[36] delineating signs for different levels of regulation based on the subject matter of the informational content the sign contains.

---

[34] One example was the ordinance at issue in *American Booksellers Association v Hudnut*, 771 F2d 323 (7th Cir 1985) aff'd mem 475 US 1001 (1986). There, an Indianapolis ordinance prohibited "pornography" defined as "graphic sexually explicit subjugation of women" that also met several other criteria focused on the depiction's degradation of women. Depictions of the subjugation of people not presenting as women were not regulated, nor were the depictions of women in a position of equality, no matter how sexually explicit. The Court of Appeals for the Seventh Circuit correctly held that the statute was viewpoint based, and the Supreme Court summarily affirmed. For such a law to survive, it would have to satisfy strict scrutiny. See Geoffrey R. Stone, *Anti-Pornography Legislation as Viewpoint-Discrimination*, 9 Harv J L & Pub Pol 461 (1986).

[35] The viewpoint bias of a law need not appear on its face. A facially neutral law regulating speech that is motivated by a desire to benefit or hurt a specific viewpoint and implemented to do so will also be seen as discriminating on the basis of viewpoint. See *Ward v Rock Against Racism*, 491 US 781, 791 (1989) ("The government's purpose is the controlling consideration."). See also Geoffrey R. Stone, *Content Neutral Restrictions*, 54 U Chi L Rev 46, 56 (1987) ("A central task of first amendment jurisprudence is to ferret out improper motivations when they in fact exist."); Lawrence H. Tribe, *American Constitutional Law* 794 (Foundation, 2d ed 1988) (law should be deemed content based if it is discriminatory on its face or it was "motivated by (i.e., would not have occurred but for) an intent to single out constitutionally protected speech for control or penalty").

[36] *Reed*, 135 S Ct at 2223.

Nor is this ordinance based on viewpoint like the second hypothetical above. It does not make distinctions within a category of speech based on viewpoints exogenous to, or a subset within, that category. It does not, for example, punish profanity against incumbents but permit profanity against political challengers. It does not prohibit profanity aimed at women but allow profanity aimed at men. It does not allow profanity aimed at anti-abortion protesters but prohibit it when aimed at pro-choice protesters.

Nevertheless, the anti-profanity ordinance does contain a viewpoint and regulates speech on the basis of that viewpoint. The law is inherently based on the view that profanity is of lower value than nonprofanity. A regulator could have this view about profanity for a number of reasons. It could be that the law is based on the notion that profanity is uncivil discourse, or that it is likely to irritate or enrage passers-by, or that the appearance of profane signs will be harmful to property values, or that ubiquitous profanity decays the civility that some citizens want their neighborhoods to characterize. A ban on communication that is profane undoubtedly embeds within it a viewpoint about profanity.

This point can be generalized. Any content-based limit on the mode or manner of speech embeds within it a viewpoint about the propriety of that mode or manner. A ban on profane speech contains a viewpoint about profanity. A ban on sexually explicit speech embeds within it a viewpoint about sexual explicitness. A ban on deceptive speech embeds within it a viewpoint about deception. Other examples arise as well. A ban on racial epithets in schools embeds within it a view of the propriety of epithets as compared to other modes of speech. A requirement that signs be written in English embeds within it a view that English is superior for that purpose than other languages. For purposes of this essay, I will refer to the kind of bias contained in content-based restrictions on the mode or manner of speech as "manner" bias.[37]

---

[37] One clarification is necessary here. The examples in the text pertain to limits on the mode or manner of speech that are attentive to the content of the speech. A ban on sexually explicit speech, profanity, deception, or racial epithets are limits that can only be determined by looking at the substance of the speech in question. So the viewpoint embedded in the limit is a viewpoint about speech. And the question considered by this article is whether that kind of "manner" viewpoint bias is the kind of viewpoint discrimination that the Court considers presumptively unconstitutional.

Other regulations of mode or manner are content neutral. For example, if a sign ordinance banned signs written in crayon, that would be a limit on the mode or manner of speech, but the limit would not discriminate on the basis of content. Similarly, a ban on graffiti on public

One might think that manner bias does not present the kinds of concerns that the doctrinal fixation on viewpoint bias is meant to address. Limits on the mode and manner of communication are ubiquitous, which might suggest that few regulators, legislators, or judges believe that such limits "give rise to an inference of impermissible government motive"[38] or present the "realistic possibility that official suppression of ideas is afoot."[39] It would not be unreasonable to think of these restrictions on mode and manner as being neutral vis-à-vis free speech values and principles.

But the lack of neutrality of a limit on mode or manner becomes clearer when there is a salient cultural or political debate about the propriety of the mode or manner of communication. In other words, when there is a public debate about communication itself, limits on the mode and manner of communication will indeed skew that debate. When there is public debate about whether certain modes of communication are proper, a government regulation of those modes will act as viewpoint discrimination in that discourse.

Consider a leading case on profanity, *Federal Communications Commission v Pacifica Foundation*.[40] An FM radio station broadcast George Carlin's famous satiric monologue about the seven "filthy words" not allowed on public air waves. The Court upheld the FCC's efforts to impose sanctions on the station for violating regulations proscribing "indecent" language.

The Court did not consider the regulation of profanity as viewpoint biased, and it was correct that the regulation did not raise traditional viewpoint problems.[41] A restriction on profanity would apply

---

buildings or a limit on the volume of sound trucks are both limits on the mode or manner of speech but would not be content based. These examples also embed in them a view about the value of crayons, graffiti, or loud noises. Indeed, all laws embed within them a viewpoint about the activity that the law regulates. But those viewpoints do not even arguably raise issues of free speech, since the viewpoint at issue is not about speech but about something else. A murder statute may embed within it a viewpoint about the propriety of murder, but that does not make it problematic under the First Amendment. It is only even arguably problematic as a matter of free speech doctrine when the regulation of a mode or manner of speech is content attentive. That is the focus of this article.

[38] *Reed*, 135 S Ct at 2237 (Kagan, J, concurring).

[39] *Davenport v Washington Education Association*, 551 US 177, 189 (2007) (quoting *R.A.V.*, 505 US at 390).

[40] 438 US 726 (1978).

[41] See *Pacifica*, 438 US at 745–46 & n 22 ("The monologue does present a point of view; it attempts to show that the words it uses are 'harmless,' and that our attitudes toward them are 'essentially silly.' . . . The Commission objects not to this point of view, but to the way in which it is expressed. The belief that these words are harmless does not necessarily confer a

neutrally in all discussions or debates (or comedy routines) focused on exogenous issues. Both George Carlin—politically liberal—and Roseanne Barr—politically conservative—would be limited by such a regulation, and the ban on profanity would apply uniformly to discussions about taxes, race relations, gender roles, and climate change. In that respect, the ban on profanity is neutral. But in other respects a ban on profanity is not neutral at all in that it embeds within it a view about the propriety of profanity. Carlin's monologue is itself a good illustration of this. His monologue was, in part, a broad attack on social prudishness, especially as embodied by limits on what was deemed appropriate on the public airways. And the speech regulation was about that very issue. In a debate about social prudishness, a regulation requiring prudishness acts as a government thumb on the scale to benefit one side of that debate and limit another. The advocates of profanity are hamstrung by the inability to use profanity to shock, surprise, challenge, titillate, and enliven the discussion. To limit Carlin's use of profanity was to force him to adopt a schoolmarm's norms in a debate about those norms.[42]

Limits on sexually explicit speech raise analogous problems of bias. There is a salient debate on whether, and to what extent, sexually explicit speech should be regulated. While obscenity meeting the definition set out in *Miller v California* is considered low-value speech and its regulation is not typically subject to strict scrutiny,[43] nonobscene, sexually explicit speech remains protected by the First Amendment. Nevertheless, limits on such speech appear as a part of broadcast regulations and zoning laws.[44] They also appear as a matter of

---

First Amendment privilege to use them while proselytizing, just as the conviction that obscenity is harmless does not license one to communicate that conviction by the indiscriminate distribution of an obscene leaflet.").

[42] One can imagine situations in which the opponents of profanity (or, for example, sexually explicit speech or epithets) use profanity (or sexually explicit speech or epithets) in their efforts to illustrate how distasteful profanity (or sexually explicit speech or epithets) can be. In that way, a limit on the mode or manner of speech operates to limit both sides of the debate about that mode or manner. But it is quite likely that such a limit would burden one side of the debate more than the other. The greater the differential, the more the limit on mode or manner would operate to skew the debate about the propriety of the mode or manner.

[43] 413 US 15 (1973). I say "typically" because it is possible after *R.A.V.* that the regulation of a subset of obscenity could raise the same kind of concerns raised by the regulation of a subset of fighting words. For one possible example, consider 18 US Code § 48, which creates additional penalties for the subset of obscenity that features cruel depictions of animal mistreatment. See text below at notes 153–54.

[44] Federal law makes it a crime to utter "any obscene, indecent, or profane language by means of radio communication." 18 USC § 1464. See also *City of Renton v Playtime Theatres*, 475 US 41 (1986) (upholding zoning restriction on adult theaters).

application in anti-discrimination law. Under Title VII of the Civil Rights Act of 1964, sexually explicit speech in the workplace can provide evidence of, and indeed embody, a hostile work environment constituting sexual harassment.[45]

These restrictions on sexually explicit speech are not traditional viewpoint discrimination—they limit the use of sexually explicit speech for both those who believe a woman's place is in the home and for those who believe a woman's place is in the White House or C-suite. It does not restrict the expression of views on either side of that debate or any other exogenous debate.[46] But these regulations do operate as manner bias—they restrict the use of sexually explicit language but not the use of nonsexual language.

Such restrictions certainly discriminate against the view that sexually explicit language is appropriate on airwaves, in neighborhoods, and in the workplace. Those who believe such explicitness is inappropriate do not have their language restricted (because they would not use such language anyway), but those who believe such language belongs in the workplace cannot use the language that best illustrates and embodies their viewpoint. As in the Carlin example, the advocates for the controlled mode of speech cannot use that speech to puncture the conventional wisdom about the possible dangers or harms arising from that mode of speech. Limits on sexually explicit speech skew the debate about sexual explicitness.

Limits on fraud, deception, and misrepresentation are another common example of restrictions on the mode and manner of speech. Communication that is deceptive is frequently regulated or banned; laws governing securities, consumer goods, home sales, and other business interactions routinely punish deception, misrepresentation, and fraud. Those laws govern speech, and while the Court has sometimes expressed skepticism about whether courts should be policing

---

[45] See, for example, *Wolak v Spucci*, 217 F3d 157, 160–61 (2d Cir 2000) ("the mere presence of pornography in a workplace can alter 'status of women' therein"); *Petrosino v Bell Atlantic*, 385 F3d 210 (2d Cir 2004) (sexually explicit speech in workplace supports hostile work environment claim).

[46] If, for example, Title VII is used by regulators or courts to restrict the expression of anti-woman views, however voiced, while allowing the expression of anti-man views, however voiced, then that would be a traditional viewpoint bias problem, not a manner bias problem. In the text I am focusing on the kind of hostile work environment case in which the language at issue is actionable because of sexual explicitness, not its use in favor of or against an exogenous viewpoint. See Eugene Volokh, *Freedom of Speech and Workplace Harassment*, 39 UCLA L Rev 1791 (1992).

the line between truth and falsity broadly,[47] laws against fraud and misrepresentation have not been thought to raise serious First Amendment problems when it comes to commercial speech.[48]

The ban does not operate as traditional viewpoint discrimination—it is unlawful to lie about the benefits of smoking or quitting; unlawful to lie about equity investments or bonds; unlawful to lie about the gas mileage of Volkswagens or Toyotas. But laws against lying and misrepresentation pose manner bias problems in the same way as bans on profane speech do. The restriction on the mode or manner of false communication operates as a government endorsement of truth over falsehood. In a debate over whether market participants should be required by law to tell the truth, the advocates of lying cannot use misrepresentation in their arsenal.

But these limits on deception do not seem as skewing to public debate as limits on profanity or sexual explicitness. That is not because there is any real difference as a matter of logic between a ban on deceptive speech and a ban on profane or sexually explicit speech. Instead, the failure to recognize bans on fraud as viewpoint bias is based more on the fact that there is not a salient argument in politics and culture about the propriety of lying, as compared with the salience of a cultural debate about whether language should be indecent or profane. When there is no public debate about the propriety of a mode or manner of speech, a limit on that mode or manner will appear neutral.

II. Is MANNER BIAS UNCONSTITUTIONAL VIEWPOINT BIAS?

Traditional viewpoint bias is a clear constitutional problem. In the modern cases in which the Court has seen it, the Court has been firm and uniform in its condemnation of viewpoint discrimination as constitutional "poison." Manner bias, on the other hand, does not raise the same level of difficulty as traditional bias but does

---

[47] See *United States v Alvarez*, 567 US 709 (2012). The Court seemed to be on the verge of protecting a corporate right to lie or mislead in noncommercial situations in the case of *Nike v Kasky*, 539 US 654 (2003), but the Court did not reach the merits.

[48] See *Virginia State Pharmacy Bd v Virginia Citizens Consumer Council*, 425 US 748, 771 (1976) (extending free speech protections to commercial speech but "foresee[ing] no obstacle" to dealing with "provably false" or "deceptive or misleading" commercial speech); *Central Hudson*, 447 US at 563 ("The government may ban forms of communication more likely to deceive the public than to inform it"). I have argued elsewhere that corporate entities can be held to a blanket obligation to avoid fraud even outside the commercial speech context. See Kent Greenfield, *Corporations Are People Too (and They Should Act Like It)* 140–45 (2018).

skew debate when there is a salient public discussion about the mode or manner of speech being regulated. Is manner bias constitutionally problematic?

One might think that the answer to this question is an easy "no." The Court has said that regulations governing the time, place, and manner of speech, as long as they are not content based, do not raise sufficient worries about speech freedoms to trigger strict scrutiny.[49] A city ban on sound trucks after 10 p.m. or a decibel limit for concerts in city parks are not seen as raising constitutional problems. And at least with regard to profanity, *Pacifica* implies that it can be regulated in certain circumstances without triggering the strictest of judicial scrutiny. Moreover, the ubiquity of restrictions on the mode and manner of speech is evidence that few regulators and courts have come to believe that such limits raise the kind of serious free speech concerns meriting strict scrutiny.[50]

But the answer is more complicated, and the Court's view is less clear. Limits on the mode or manner of speech of the kind discussed in the previous Part—limits on profanity, sexual explicitness, or deception—are indeed content based, so they are not subject to the usual allowance for content-neutral time, place, and manner regulations. Moreover, the Court has emphasized the usual rule that speakers should be able to choose both the substance and the mode of their communication. In *Cohen v California*, for example, the Court struck down the application of a disturbance of the peace ordinance to punish a war protester in a municipal building wearing a jacket proclaiming "Fuck the Draft."[51] The Court decided that "the State has no right to cleanse public debate to the point where it is grammatically palatable to the most squeamish among us."[52] Even though the word at issue was considered as "more distasteful than most," Justice John Harlan explained that it is "often true that one man's vulgarity is another's

---

[49] Ward, 491 US at 781.

[50] Other areas of federal, state, and local laws place limits on profanity in various ways. For example, under Coast Guard regulations, to gain federal registration a vessel may not have a name that is, or is phonetically identical to, obscene, indecent, or profane language, or to racial or ethnic epithets. 46 CFR § 67.117(b)(3). See also, for example, *American Freedom Defense Initiative v Mass Bay Transp. Auth.*, 989 F Supp 2d 182, 183 (Mass 2013) (limits on profanity on city-owned buses and billboards); *Bethel School Dist. No. 403 v Fraser*, 478 US 675, 677–78, 685 (1986) (upholding discipline of high school student for profanity at school event).

[51] 403 US 15 (1971).

[52] Id at 25.

lyric."⁵³ The Court recognized that the mode or manner of speaking is an important aspect of communication: "expression . . . conveys not only ideas capable of relatively precise, detached explication, but otherwise inexpressible emotions as well . . . words are often chosen as much for their emotive as their cognitive force."⁵⁴

The Court said something similar in *Texas v Johnson*, as it struck down a state law punishing flag burning. The state argued the law did not burden speech because someone wishing to criticize the government could do so in a way other than burning a flag. But the Court answered that the "enduring lesson" of the First Amendment—the notion "that the government may not prohibit expression simply because it disagrees with its message"—does not depend "on the particular mode in which one chooses to express an idea."⁵⁵ Both *Cohen* and *Johnson* can be read to mean that the choice of mode or manner of speech—profanity in *Cohen* and flag burning in *Johnson*—is an important part of free speech freedoms.

Neither, however, said that a limit on mode or manner is *itself* viewpoint discrimination. *Cohen* was decided before the Court routinely articulated its holdings as a function of content or viewpoint discrimination, and the Court did not describe its decision using that more modern doctrinal terminology. But even so, the ordinance was applied to punish expressive content, and that was enough to trigger the First Amendment's protection.⁵⁶ Whether the ordinance was applied in a viewpoint neutral way was not a material question in the case. A factual question may have lurked as to whether Cohen would have been arrested if his jacket had read "Fuck the Draft Dodgers" rather than "Fuck the Draft." It is reasonable to believe, given the historical context, that he would not have been. If that is true, then his arrest would have been a product of traditional viewpoint bias, not "manner" bias. In any event, and notwithstanding *Cohen*'s important

---

⁵³ Id.

⁵⁴ Id at 26. See also *Sable Communications v FCC*, 492 US 115 (1989) (striking down statute limiting indecent sex conversations by way of telephone); *Reno v ACLU*, 521 US 844 (1997) (striking down statutes limiting indecent communication on the internet).

⁵⁵ *Texas v Johnson*, 491 US 397, 416 (1989).

⁵⁶ See *Cohen*, 403 US at 18 ("Cohen could not, consistently with the First and Fourteenth Amendments, be punished for asserting the evident position on the inutility or immorality of the draft his jacket reflected."). The Court did worry about the importance of viewpoint neutrality, but used the worry to buttress a protection of content neutrality. See id at 27 ("Indeed, governments might soon seize upon the censorship of particular words as a convenient guise for banning the expression of unpopular views.").

language reminding us that "one man's vulgarity is another's lyric," the case should not be read to decide the doctrinal issue analyzed here—whether limits on vulgarity or other modes and manner of speech amount to viewpoint bias as opposed to mere content bias.

Nor should *Johnson* be read to establish a doctrinal rule saying limits on the mode or manner of communication, with nothing more, amount to viewpoint discrimination under the First Amendment. There, too, the statute banning flag burning was a regulation of expressive content, applied to punish an individual who was engaging in core political speech. And even though the statute was written in facially neutral terms, the Court made clear it had been adopted and applied to pursue a specific point of view about the sanctity and value of our national banner.[57] Those who burned the flag to protest the nation were arrested; those who burned it in respect to dispose of it were exempted from the law. As the Court explained, "To conclude that the government may permit designated symbols to be used to communicate only a limited set of messages would be to enter territory having no discernible or defensible boundaries."[58] That is *traditional* viewpoint discrimination of the most obvious and pernicious kind. The case cannot be read to say that *manner* bias alone amounts to viewpoint bias.

A. R.A.V. AND MANNER BIAS

R.A.V. is the case in which the Court comes closest to holding that a limit on a mode or manner or speech is viewpoint bias. The ordinance at issue was St. Paul's version of a hate speech code. The law provided:

> Whoever places on public or private property a symbol, object, appellation, characterization or graffiti, including, but not limited to, a burning cross or Nazi swastika, which one knows or has reasonable grounds to know arouses anger, alarm or resentment in others on the basis of race, color,

---

[57] *Johnson*, 491 US at 416–17 ("If we were to hold that a State may forbid flag burning wherever it is likely to endanger the flag's symbolic role, but allow it wherever burning a flag promotes that role—as where, for example, a person ceremoniously burns a dirty flag—we would be saying that when it comes to impairing the flag's physical integrity, the flag itself may be used as a symbol . . . only in one direction. We would be permitting a State to 'prescribe what shall be orthodox' by saying that one may burn the flag to convey one's attitude toward it and its referents only if one does not endanger the flag's representation of nationhood and national unity.").

[58] Id at 417.

creed, religion or gender commits disorderly conduct and shall be guilty of a misdemeanor.[59]

The state supreme court had previously ruled that the statute only covered "fighting words" within the meaning of *Chaplinsky v New Hampshire*—that is, those words that "by their very utterance inflict injury or tend to incite an immediate breach of peace."[60] But the St. Paul ordinance did not regulate all fighting words; some words arousing "anger, alarm or resentment" went unregulated by the statute. The statute focused on a subset of fighting words that aroused such feelings "in others on the basis of race, color, creed, religion or gender."

The Court struck down the ordinance as both content based and viewpoint based. Even though the category of fighting words had been considered prior to the case as "not within the area of constitutionally protected speech,"[61] the Court saw the ordinance as constitutionally problematic because the city had chosen to regulate only a subset of fighting words. According to the Court, the ordinance was content based because it defined the subcategory according to "specified disfavored topics."[62] The ordinance also "in its practical operation . . . goes even beyond mere content discrimination, to actual viewpoint discrimination." The viewpoint bias of the ordinance meant that the ordinance would fail even though the Court conceded that the city had a compelling interest in "ensur[ing] the basic human rights of members of groups that have historically been subjected to discrimination."[63] The Court implied that a law that discriminated on

---

[59] St. Paul Bias-Motivated Crime Ordinance, St. Paul, Minn, Legis Code § 292.02 (1990), as quoted in *R.A.V.*, 505 US at 380.

[60] *Chaplinsky*, 315 US at 571–72. Because the state supreme court was interpreting a state statute, the Court considered the state's interpretation as controlling for purposes of the case. *R.A.V.*, 505 US at 381.

[61] *R.A.V.*, 505 US at 383 (quoting *Chaplinksy*, 315 US at 571–72, among other cases).

[62] Id at 391. It remains unclear whether the Court believed that the content basis of the statute was sufficient to raise the level of judicial inquiry to strict scrutiny. The ordinance was aimed at fighting words, which would normally receive only rational basis review. The selection of fighting words as a category is, by definition, a content-based selection. The ordinance was *of course* content based, as is any law aimed at obscenity, threats, libel, commercial fraud, and other areas of low-value speech. Moreover, the selection of a subset of category of speech within a low-value category is not itself problematic unless the subset reveals a viewpoint bias of the government. *R.A.V.*, 505 US at 388–90 (describing reasons why the selection of a subset might not raise concerns of viewpoint discrimination). It was thus the viewpoint bias of the ordinance that deserves attention as triggering strict scrutiny.

[63] Id at 395.

the basis of viewpoint could never be narrowly tailored—the only interest "distinctively served" by such a law would be the city's interest in "displaying [its] special hostility towards the particular biases singled out."[64]

Thus, we know that the Court in *R.A.V.* believed viewpoint bias to be a significant constitutional problem. The difficulty in interpreting the Court's opinion is that it was not clear what exactly made the St. Paul ordinance viewpoint biased. Was it a law that exhibited traditional bias, mandating that one side of a social, political, or cultural debate use a smaller set of communicative tools than another side of the same debate? Or did the Court read the St. Paul ordinance as exhibiting manner bias, limiting the mode or manner of communication for all participants in an exogenous debate, but nevertheless seeing that limit on the mode or manner of communication to be itself tainted by viewpoint bias? At best, the Court's analysis is muddled on this point.

The most straightforward reading of the ordinance was that it exhibited manner bias, limiting a mode or manner of communication. The manner of communication it targeted was epithets of some kind, whether racial, ethnic, or gender based. The ordinance referenced a "burning cross or Nazi swastika" as examples of the subset of fighting words it banned, but was also clear that the subset was "not limited to" those examples. There is nothing in the ordinance to suggest that it could not extend to, for example, Black Lives Matter protesters who cried out an anti-white slur, or to feminist counterprotesters crying out anti-male epithets during a men's rights march. There is also nothing in the text of the ordinance itself that would require it to be used to punish "generic" fighting words—those that did not explicitly use racial, ethnic, or gender-specific epithets or terms.

This narrow reading of the ordinance was exactly the interpretation that the city had urged upon the Court. According to the city's merits brief, the ordinance applied only to "racial, religious, or gender-specific symbols" such as "a burning cross, Nazi swastika or other instrumentality of like import."[65] The ordinance was thus a limit of a subset of mode or manner of speech within fighting words—limits that would be applicable to all people expressing all viewpoints. Under

---

[64] Id at 396.
[65] Id at 393.

the city's interpretation, the ordinance could not be seen as exhibiting traditional viewpoint bias—it was not in "practical operation" banning all fighting words used in service of racial (or gender or religious) hatred but allowing them in service of racial (or gender or religious) harmony. Under the city's interpretation the ordinance was at most exhibiting manner bias, banning a subset of fighting words not based on the ideas expressed but because of the use of "racial, religious, or gender-specific symbols."

In part of Justice Scalia's opinion, the Court acknowledged this reading by the city and even characterized it as a concession. "The city concedes in its brief that the ordinance applies only to 'racial, religious, or gender-specific symbols.'"[66] If the Court took that limitation seriously, it would be difficult to consider the ordinance as embodying traditional viewpoint bias. No one would be able to use such "racial, religious, or gender-specific" fighting words, whether they were advocates of hatred or harmony. For such a limited ordinance to be seen as containing viewpoint bias, it would have to be because manner bias amounts to unconstitutional viewpoint bias.

Thus one common way to read *R.A.V.* has been to see it as designating a ban on a mode or manner of speech as viewpoint biased. On this reading, *R.A.V.* holds that manner bias is the kind of bias that constitutes an "egregious" form of content discrimination and is presumptively unconstitutional.[67] Moreover, this reading of *R.A.V.* would make it virtually impossible to craft any regulation on fighting words (or, presumably of any other low-value speech such as threats) that explicitly limited its focus to racial, ethnic, or gender-based epithets.[68]

---

[66] Id.

[67] For examples of decisions of courts that interpreted *R.A.V.* this way, see *State v Vawter*, 136 NJ 56, 75 (NJ 1994) (striking down statute punishing a subset of threats, saying "our statutes proscribe threats 'on the basis of race, color, creed or religion.' Under the Supreme Court's ruling in *R.A.V.*, that limitation renders the statutes viewpoint-discriminatory and thus impermissible."); *Washington v Talley*, 122 Wn2d 192 (1993) (striking down portion of state's anti-harassment law on the basis of *R.A.V.*). See also *Court Overturns Stanford University Code Barring Bigoted Speech*, NY Times 28 (March 1, 1995) (Stanford speech code banning "gutter epithets" and other insults based on race and sex struck down under state law requiring private universities to offer speech protections of public universities); Murray, 24 Western St U L Rev at 267–70 (cited in note 19) (discussing Stanford case).

[68] Scholars have interpreted *R.A.V.* in this very way. See, for example, Nadine Strossen, *Hate: Why We Should Resist It with Free Speech, Not Censorship* 74 (Oxford, 2018) (describing *R.A.V.* as striking down the St. Paul ordinance "because it selectively outlawed only 'abusive invective' that was based on 'race, color, creed, religion or gender'"; a law that is "underinclusive" "embodies viewpoint discrimination"); Chemerinsky, *Constitutional Law* at 1013–14

But the Court's opinion in *R.A.V.* also lends itself to a different reading, one that is based on a broader interpretation of the St. Paul ordinance and that would lead to less dramatic doctrinal implications. Two pages before the Court discussed the city's asserted narrow reading of the statute, the Court agreed that the law's ban of "some words—odious racial epithets, for example" would apply to "proponents of all views."[69] To that extent, the Court seemed to adopt the city's reading. But the Court went further, saying that other fighting words that did not themselves "invoke race, color, creed, religion, or gender"—Justice Scalia suggested an example was "aspersions upon a person's mother"—could be used by advocates of harmony but not by advocates of hatred.[70] That is, "generic" fighting words could be used by those arguing in favor of "tolerance and equality" but not by those arguing on the other side.[71] According to the Court, the city "has no authority to license one side of a debate to fight freestyle, while requiring the other to follow Marquis of Queensberry rules."[72]

By this reading, the ordinance was not viewpoint based because it banned all fighting words that themselves invoked race, color, creed, sex, and the like. What made the ordinance viewpoint biased was that it would ban *generic* fighting words—something like "you're a piece of shit"—if used by one side of a public debate about race but not if used by the other. The ordinance did not "single[] out an especially offensive mode of expression." Instead, the ordinance "proscribed fighting words *of whatever manner* that communicate messages of racial, gender, or religious intolerance."[73] This imbalance made it clear to the Court that the ordinance was "directed at expression of group hatred"[74]—"a distinctive idea"[75]—and thus viewpoint biased.

(*R.A.V.* "makes it difficult for hate speech codes to survive judicial analysis; if they prohibit only some forms of hate, they will be invalidated as impermissible content-based discrimination") (cited in note 19); Murray, 24 Western St U L Rev at 264–65 ("while speech codes faced an uphill battle under the constitutional precedent in place before *R.A.V.*, this decision made it virtually impossible for a speech code to pass constitutional muster") (cited in note 19); Hudson and Nott, *Hate Speech and Campus Speech Codes* (same) (cited in note 19).

[69] *R.A.V.*, 505 US at 391.
[70] Id.
[71] Id.
[72] Id at 392.
[73] Id at 393–94 (emphasis added).
[74] Id at 392.
[75] Id at 393.

This broad reading of the ordinance makes the Court's opinion a commonplace and limited application of the long-standing skepticism of traditional viewpoint discrimination. A law cannot empower one side of a public debate to use certain words while the other side of a public debate cannot. That would be "proscribing speech . . . because of disapproval of the ideas expressed."[76]

If this is the correct reading of the ordinance, the law indeed looks like it was aimed at punishing underlying ideas rather than a mode or manner of communication. The law's defect was its traditional viewpoint bias, and the Court's ruling striking it down was straightforward and unsurprising. It also means that *R.A.V.* should *not* be read to hold that manner bias is constitutionally problematic.

R.A.V., then, can be seen as either a case that significantly broadened the definition of viewpoint bias to include laws that limit the mode and manner of communication (manner bias) or a case that merely applied a classic and well-understood understanding of traditional viewpoint bias to a statute that criminalized speech on the basis of "disapproval of the ideas expressed." The distinction matters. If *R.A.V.* is read narrowly, so that worries about viewpoint bias are triggered only when the government is picking sides in a cultural, social, or political debate, then *R.A.V.* is merely an iteration of the mainstream and conventional understanding of the importance of government not punishing citizens for their ideas. If, on the other hand, *R.A.V.* is read broadly to mean that worries about viewpoint bias kick in whenever the government punishes or regulates communication based on the mode or manner of that communication, then a host of regulations become subject to strict scrutiny. *R.A.V.* did not make clear which it was.

B. RECONCILING R.A.V. AND BLACK

The Court offered a clue eleven years later in *Virginia v Black*,[77] which considered a challenge to a Virginia state law that banned cross burning. The statute read:

> It shall be unlawful for any person or persons, with the intent of intimidating any person or group of persons, to burn, or cause to be burned, a cross on the property of another, a highway or other public place.

---

[76] Id at 382.
[77] 538 US 343 (2003).

This statute was different from the ordinance in *R.A.V.* in that it regulated speech that met the definition of threats rather than the definition of fighting words. Those are distinct categories—threats focus on the fear caused by a promise of violence against the hearer, while the category of fighting words focuses on words creating a likelihood of violence against the speaker caused by the hearer's anger or distress at the speaker's words. But both are categories of speech long thought to be low value, regulable without triggering strict scrutiny.[78]

The question, then, was whether the Virginia statute raised the same constitutional difficulties presented by the statute in *R.A.V.* Both statutes identified a subset of a less-protected category of speech for special regulation. In both cases, the subset of highly regulated speech was identified with regard to its tendency to intimidate or alarm on the basis of a characteristic that subjected people to discrimination and prejudice. The St. Paul ordinance made that connection explicit, identifying the traits ("race, color, creed, religion or gender") at which the fighting words had to be targeted to be actionable. The Virginia law did not make the link explicit, though the long history of using cross burnings as a way to threaten African Americans was clear and well understood.[79] The Virginia law was also narrower in that it was aimed only at cross burning, and the St. Paul ordinance allowed prosecutions for the use of symbols other than burning crosses, such as a "Nazi swastika or other instrumentality of like import."[80]

One might expect that given *R.A.V.*, the law in *Black* would be even more problematic as a matter of viewpoint bias. It was certainly content based, in that it regulated one kind of content (the burning of crosses to intimidate and threaten) more than other kinds of content (the use of curse words to intimidate and threaten, for example). And because the law was even more targeted than the one in St. Paul, it could be said to have been even more viewpoint based, in that it was based on a view that the kind of racial hatred embodied in cross burning was worse than other kinds of threats, even those based on

---

[78] See id at 359 ("The First Amendment permits 'restrictions upon the content of speech in a few limited areas, which are 'of such slight social value as a step to truth that any benefit that may be derived from them is clearly outweighed by the social interest in order and morality.'") (quoting *R.A.V.*, 505 US at 382–83, and *Chaplinsky*, 315 US at 572).

[79] Which the Court acknowledged. See, for example, 538 US at 352 ("Burning a cross in the United States is inextricably intertwined with the history of the Ku Klux Klan.").

[80] *R.A.V.*, 505 US at 393.

sex, religion, or creed. In fact, the Virginia Supreme Court had struck down the cross-burning statute as "analytically indistinguishable" from the St. Paul ordinance because it "selectively chooses only cross burning because of its distinctive message."[81]

But the U.S. Supreme Court upheld the part of the Virginia statute banning cross burning for the purpose of intimidation and threat.[82] The Court believed the law survived *R.A.V.* because the reason for focusing on the subset of cross-burning threats was the same reason that all threats are punishable.[83] In *R.A.V.*, the Court had said that an exception to its skepticism of creating subsets of speech categories might arise when the subcategory is identified and regulated for reasons that are identical to the reason the entire category receives lesser First Amendment protections. And the Court in *Black* said that "The First Amendment permits Virginia to outlaw cross burnings done with the intent to intimidate because burning a cross is a particularly virulent form of intimidation" with a "long and pernicious history as a signal of impending violence."[84]

The problem with this rationale is that if threats based on race are regulable because they are an especially dangerous subset of threats, the same should have been true in *R.A.V.* itself. The defendants in both cases had burned a cross on the yard of a black family.[85] For *Black* to be correct that the Virginia statute constitutionally punished cross burning and *R.A.V.* to be correct that the St. Paul ordinance *un*constitutionally punished cross burning, one would have to believe that a subset of threats based on race can be punished more than generic threats, but that a subset of fighting words based on "race, color, creed, religion or gender" cannot be punished more than generic fighting words. In both cases, the reason why threats and fighting words are regulable—that their propensity to induce fear and violence outweighs their value in the "exposition of ideas" (to quote *Chaplinsky*)[86]—is doubly true when those words are aimed at people

---

[81] *Black*, 538 US at 351.

[82] The Court struck down the part of the law that established a prima facie evidentiary presumption that the burning of a cross amounted to a threat. Id at 363–68 (O'Connor, J) (plurality).

[83] Id at 361–62.

[84] Id at 363.

[85] *R.A.V.*, 505 US at 379; *Black*, 538 US at 350.

[86] *Chaplinsky*, 315 US at 572.

because of some characteristic that has historically been the basis of social prejudice, bias, violence, and hatred. The Court recognized this truth in *Black* but not in *R.A.V.*[87]

Perhaps one could distinguish the cases by saying that Virginia punished the most dangerous kind of threat given its history, but that St. Paul punished more than the most dangerous fighting words. According to *Chaplinsky*, fighting words are those that are "likely to provoke the average person to retaliation,"[88] which will turn on a judgment of what the "average" person responds to with violence. Such a formulation has obvious gender and power discrepancies—those with less power will respond less often with violence than those with more prerogative. "You're an asshole" aimed at an "average" male may be more likely to provoke violence than "you're a whore" aimed at the "average" female, even though the latter would be fighting words based on "race, color, creed, religion or gender." That difference is an unfortunate outcome of a test for fighting words that bases its definition on the likelihood that the hearer will react violently.[89] But if taken seriously, that would ironically suggest that the St. Paul ordinance, which included gender as one of its identifiers,

---

[87] In fact, of the seven Justices who were on the Court for both cases, four of them believed the cases should come out identically. That is, two of the Justices (Stevens and O'Connor) believed that the St. Paul ordinance was viewpoint neutral and also believed the Virginia ordinance was constitutional (either because it was viewpoint neutral or fell into one of the *R.A.V.* exceptions). Another two (Kennedy and Souter) believed both statutes to be unconstitutionally viewpoint based. The difference in outcome in the two cases was driven by the three Justices (Rehnquist, Scalia, and Thomas) who switched from voting to strike down the St. Paul ordinance as viewpoint based to voting to uphold the Virginia law.

[88] *Chaplinsky*, 315 US at 574.

[89] See Melody L. Hurdle, *R.A.V. v. City of St. Paul: The Continuing Confusion of the Fighting Words Doctrine*, 47 Vand L Rev 1143 (1994) ("fighting words may cause certain persons to withdraw, not fight, because individuals subject to verbal abuse often internalize their harm rather than escalate to conflict"); Cynthia Grant Bowman, *Street Harassment and the Informal Ghettoization of Women*, 106 Harv L Rev 517, 560–61 (1993) ("Unfortunately, the fighting words standard, as it has been interpreted thus far, is based upon a male stereotype; it presupposes an encounter between two persons of relatively equal power who have been socialized to respond to insults with violence. Although men may react to abusive language by engaging in a physical fight, women are neither socialized to fight in general nor secure enough—for good reason—to do so in a street harassment situation. Far from fighting back, the average female target of street harassment is likely to react with fear, to freeze, and to pretend to ignore what is happening to her."); Kent Greenwalt, *Insults and Epithets: Are They Protected Speech?*, Rutgers L Rev 287, 296–97 (1990) ("The *Chaplinsky* language reflects the propensity of courts to imagine male actors for most legal problems."); Mari J. Matsuda, *Public Response to Racist Speech: Considering the Victim's Story*, 87 Mich L Rev 2320, 2355 (1989) ("insults of such dimension that they bring men—this is a male-centered standard—to blows are subject to a first amendment exception").

was further away from the core of fighting words than the Virginia law was from the core of threats.[90]

Another, less problematic way to distinguish the outcomes in *R.A.V.* and *Black* would be to focus on the difference between traditional viewpoint bias and manner bias. This differentiation would take seriously the Court's intimations in *R.A.V.* that the St. Paul ordinance was in fact a cloak for traditional viewpoint bias. In this reading of *R.A.V.*, the ordinance was best read broadly, to penalize not only fighting words using specific symbols but also generic fighting words that advocated racial, ethnic, and gender hatred. And because the ordinance ranged so broadly it was best seen as a law flawed by traditional viewpoint bias.

In *Black*, on the other hand, the law was a limitation on a specific mode or manner of speaking—a threat using a specific symbol—and would be applied to whomever used that specific mode or manner, regardless of the viewpoint of the speaker. The law banned a threatening use of a burning cross whether it was aimed at a black family or a white family, a cleric or an atheist, a fan of the Virginia Cavaliers or the Richmond Spiders. As the Court said in *Black*, "Unlike the statute at issue in *R.A.V.*, the Virginia statute does not single out for opprobrium only that speech directed toward 'one of the specified disfavored topics.'"[91] The Court emphasized that "as a factual matter it is not true that cross burners direct their intimidating conduct solely to racial or religious minorities" and the statute would apply to threatening cross burnings directed at people for other reasons, such as union membership.[92] In other words, the law was not viewpoint biased in a traditional way, even though it did create a very specific limit on the mode or manner of expressing a threat.

This reading of *R.A.V.* and *Black* would suggest that while traditional viewpoint bias remains especially "egregious" from a First Amendment perspective, manner bias does not raise particular constitutional difficulties. But neither Court described its holding in this way.

---

[90] This discussion assumes that the definition of fighting words is not expanded by the *Chaplinsky* phraseology that they include words that "by their very utterance inflict injury." Id at 771–72. If this adds to, rather than replicates, the attention the test pays to potential violence, then the St. Paul ordinance would be on stronger footing and the difference between the holdings in *R.A.V.* and *Black* less reconcilable.

[91] *Black*, 538 US at 362, quoting *R.A.V.*, 505 US at 391.

[92] Id.

III. THE TRADEMARK CASES AND MANNER BIAS

The two trademark cases decided by the Court over the past three Terms were both decided on the basis that the challenged language of the Lanham Act discriminated on the basis of viewpoint. In *Tam*, the Court struck down the law's ban on the registration of "disparaging" marks. In *Brunetti*, the Court struck down the law's ban on the registration of "immoral" or "scandalous" marks. While there was no majority opinion in *Tam*, Justice Elena Kagan penned a short, punchy opinion in *Brunetti* that garnered six votes. Implicit in the opinion is a distinction between traditional viewpoint bias and manner bias. This difference was made explicit in the separate concurrence of Justice Alito, and in the opinions concurring in part and dissenting in part by Chief Justice John Roberts and Justices Stephen Breyer and Sonia Sotomayor. *Brunetti* may thus be more than a straightforward trademark case. *Brunetti* may represent the clearest statement by the Court to date that manner bias does not constitute the kind of viewpoint bias the Court considers presumptively unconstitutional.

A. BRUNETTI'S NARROW VIEW OF VIEWPOINT BIAS

The language at issue in *Brunetti* was the Lanham Act's prohibition of the registration of "immoral" or "scandalous" trademarks. The U.S. Patent and Trademark Office (PTO) had denied the trademark application of Erik Brunetti, "an artist and entrepreneur who founded a clothing line that uses the trademark FUCT."[93] The Lanham Act created a federal registration system for trademarks, and a successful federal registration affords certain benefits to the trademark registrant. The act prohibits registrations of marks that would create confusion among consumers, are "merely descriptive" of the goods so marked, or are deceptive. There are a handful of other restrictions as well, including a prohibition on the registration of marks that use the flag of a state or a country, or that depict a living person or a (recently) dead President.[94]

Brunetti challenged the denial of his registration application, arguing that the ban on "immoral" and "scandalous" marks violated the

---

[93] *Brunetti*, 139 S Ct at 2294.

[94] The bar on using a likeness of a live person can be waived with the person's consent; the bar on the use of a presidential likeness ends at the death of the President's "widow." 15 USC § 1052(c). Presumably, "widow" will be read to mean "widower" or "spouse" going forward.

First Amendment. The law was clearly content based, since it required the PTO to make judgments about marks based on the content of those marks. This is true not only for the "immoral" and "scandalous" restrictions, but also for the other restrictions of marks based on their deceptiveness, their probability of causing confusion, and their use of flags or likenesses of dead Presidents. But the content basis of the law was not enough to require strict scrutiny alone. Though the Court did not explicitly explain, the reason was likely that trademark registration is best seen as the regulation of commercial speech and thus subject to intermediate scrutiny unless there is some reason—for example, viewpoint bias—to increase the level of scrutiny.[95] Another possible reason that attentiveness to content would not alone be sufficient to necessitate strict scrutiny is that the entire field of trademark law requires the regulation of content.[96] It would be nonsensical to allow the registration of trademarks only if such registration could be performed without attention to content. Registration is the protection of marks, based on their content. Such regulation, in the words of the Court in *R.A.V.*, presents "no realistic possibility that official suppression of ideas is afoot."[97]

For Brunetti to win, he had to show more than that the statute discriminated on the basis of content; he had to show it discriminated on the basis of viewpoint. That would raise the level of scrutiny from whatever it was—the Court never said for sure—to strict scrutiny. Because of *R.A.V.*, we know that viewpoint bias requires strict scrutiny even when it appears in a regulation otherwise receiving only rational basis review. Even if the Lanham Act would otherwise survive rational or intermediate scrutiny, it would require strict scrutiny as a matter of First Amendment law if the Court determined it discriminated on the basis of viewpoint.

Whether the act exhibited traditional viewpoint bias or manner bias turned on a question of statutory interpretation. Like the ordinance in *R.A.V.*, the speech restriction could be read either of two

---

[95] See *Central Hudson*, 447 US at 557.

[96] See *Brunetti*, 139 S Ct at 2306 (Breyer, J, concurring in part and dissenting in part) ("Moreover, while a restriction on the registration of highly vulgar words arguably places a content-based limit on trademark registration, it is hard to see why that label should be outcome-determinative here, for regulations governing trademark registration inevitably involve content discrimination.") (internal quotation omitted); Sonia K. Katyal, *Trademark Intersectionality*, 57 UCLA L Rev 1601, 1602 (2010) (trademark law is "indelibly rooted in content-based considerations").

[97] *R.A.V.*, 505 US at 390.

ways, one creating traditional viewpoint bias and the other only manner bias. One way to read the statute would be to have the words "immoral" and "scandalous" be a limitation on marks that promoted depravity and wickedness, while allowing marks that favored civility and decency. This would suggest a traditional viewpoint discrimination against the idea of immorality, conventionally described. The other way to read the statute was to see the words as imposing a mode or manner limitation, similar to a limit on profanity.

If the Court had ignored or muddled the statutory question, as it had done in *R.A.V.*, readers of the opinion might assume that the statutory question did not matter—that the difference between traditional bias and manner bias was not a constitutional difference. But the Court did focus on the statutory question, and the disagreement between the Court's opinion and the opinions of Chief Justice Roberts and Justices Breyer and Sotomayor turned on this very difference. Most of the Court read the statute as exhibiting traditional viewpoint discrimination—as restricting marks not on the basis of their mode or manner but because of their viewpoint in favor of civility, decency, and morality, and against depravity and scandal. A minority of the Court read the statute, at least in part, to impose a mode or manner limitation. And every Justice who interpreted a portion of the statute that way would have voted to uphold that portion.

1. *Sotomayor.* It is easiest to understand these alternate readings by studying Justice Sotomayor's separate opinion. Sotomayor believed the restriction on "immoral" marks should be read separately from the limitation on "scandalous" marks, and she believed the best reading of "immoral" was that it imposed a traditional viewpoint bias on trademark registrations. "[T]here is no tenable way" to read "immoral" other than to "connote[] a preference for 'rectitude and morality' over its opposite."[98] In this respect Sotomayor agreed with Justice Kagan's opinion for the Court. A limitation on "immoral" marks "infringes the First Amendment" because, as Justice Kagan said, it "disfavors certain ideas"[99]—namely, the idea of immorality. The provision was not neutral—it was a thumb on the scale of rectitude and uprightness as defined by conventional social and cultural mores. Marks consistent with morality could win registration under this

---

[98] *Brunetti*, 139 S Ct at 2309 (Sotomayor, J), quoting the Court's opinion, 139 S Ct at 2299.
[99] Id at 2297.

provision, and those that were not consistent with morality could not be registered.[100] This was traditional viewpoint bias, and the Court unanimously saw it as such.

But Sotomayor saw the limitation on "scandalous" marks differently. She conceded that the ban on scandalous marks could be seen as "something similar to 'immoral' and thus favor some viewpoints over others."[101] That is, it could be read to create a traditional viewpoint bias problem. But the better reading of the statute, she believed, was that it was a limitation on mode or manner. "To say that a word or image is 'scandalous' can instead mean that it is simply indecent, shocking, or generally offensive."[102] Sotomayor made the distinction explicit: "The word 'scandalous' . . . can be read broadly (to cover both offensive ideas and offensive manners of expressing ideas), or it can be read narrowly (to cover only offensive modes of expression)."[103] She distinguished between offensiveness resulting "from the views expressed" and offensiveness "result[ing] from the way in which those views are expressed."

Sotomayor made a strong statutory argument that "scandalous" should be read to focus on an offensive mode of communication while "immoral" is best read to cover ideas offensive on their own accord. But one need not take a position on the statutory question to recognize that the doctrinal implication of Justice Sotomayor's narrow reading is significant. Sotomayor argued that if focused only on the mode or manner of communication, the "scandalous" limitation of the Lanham Act would not constitute viewpoint bias, would not require strict scrutiny, and would survive. That is, Sotomayor says more clearly than in any other Supreme Court case that manner bias is not constitutionally problematic. "Properly narrowed, 'scandalous' is a viewpoint-neutral form of content discrimination that is permissible in the kind of discretionary program or limited forum typified by the trademark registration system."[104] She explains that "restrictions on particular modes of expression do not inherently qualify as viewpoint

---

[100] For example, the PTO denied registration to marks glamorizing drug use but granted them for marks urging sobriety. The PTO granted registration to pro-religious marks but denied marks that seemed to denigrate religion. See 139 S Ct at 2300–01.

[101] Id at 2309.

[102] Id.

[103] Id.

[104] Id at 2303.

discrimination" because they do not target "particular views taken by speakers on a subject."[105]

Sotomayor even describes a hypothetical about sexually explicit communication similar to the one spelled out above in Part I. "Some people," she says, "may have the viewpoint that society should be more sexually liberated and feel that they cannot express that view sufficiently without the use of pornographic words or images. That does not automatically make a restriction on pornography into viewpoint discrimination, despite the fact that such a restriction limits communicating one's views on sexual liberation in that way." In other words, limitations on the mode and manner of communication are not unconstitutionally viewpoint based even when there is a social and political debate about the appropriateness of that communication.

She suggests that under her reading of the statute and her reading of First Amendment requirements, a variety of speech limitations should survive, including limits on obscene words and "lewd or 'swear' words that cause a visceral reaction."[106] She also implies, by reference to a Coast Guard regulation of vessel names, that the use of "racial or ethnic epithets" could be limited. And she laments that the Court's ruling will compel the PTO to register "one particularly egregious racial epithet"[107]—presumably the n-word—though her reading of the statute would not.

Sotomayor's opinion is the clearest statement to date that laws containing what I have called manner bias—laws that restrict the mode or manner of speech—are not what the Court should consider as viewpoint based under the First Amendment. If her view controls a majority of the Court, it would provide important doctrinal clarity.

2. *The other Justices in Brunetti.* Clues as to whether Justice Sotomayor's narrow definition of viewpoint bias describes the doctrinal position of the entire Court can be gleaned from the votes and other opinions in *Brunetti*. Justice Breyer joined Sotomayor's opinion, so he can be safely counted as holding the same view. He wrote separately to set out his broader critique of the Court's free speech jurisprudence as too formalistic and categorically rigid.[108] But his judgment

---

[105] Id at 2313, quoting *Rosenberger*, 515 US at 829.

[106] Id at 2309.

[107] Id at 2313 & n 5.

[108] *Brunetti*, 139 S Ct at 2306 (Breyer, J, concurring in part and dissenting in part) ("I believe we should focus on the interests the First Amendment protects and ask a more basic

with regard to whether a restriction on the mode or manner of communication amounts to unconstitutional viewpoint bias can be counted with Sotomayor's.[109]

Chief Justice Roberts also wrote separately. He did not join Sotomayor's opinion, but he announced his agreement with her narrower statutory construction of "scandalous"—that it can be read to focus on mode or manner—and believed that it could survive First Amendment challenge on that reading. "[T]he term 'scandalous' need not be understood to reach marks that offend because of the ideas they convey; it can be read more narrowly to bar only marks that offend because of their mode of expression—marks that are obscene, vulgar, or profane."[110]

This correlates with a question the Chief Justice asked in oral argument. Counsel for Brunetti, John R. Sommer, was being pressed as to the meaning of viewpoint discrimination. He suggested that a limit on offensiveness was viewpoint bias because his client's "viewpoint is, as already pointed out, I can be offensive, I don't have to obey the authority. And that's viewpoint." In other words, counsel was arguing that manner bias was unconstitutional because those who disagreed with the limitation were silenced. The Chief responded by saying, "but that's completely circular. It's like saying my protest is that I want to use words . . . not given trademark protection, and because I have that viewpoint, you have to give them trademark protection . . . that's totally circular."[111] This makes clear that with Sotomayor and Breyer, the Chief would make three votes in favor of the notion that manner bias does not amount to unconstitutional viewpoint bias under the First Amendment.

The other separate opinion was penned by Justice Alito. He joined the Court's opinion, but he wrote a separate opinion of two paragraphs, each making a single clarifying point. First, he emphasized the importance of standing firm against viewpoint bias: "Viewpoint discrimination is poison to a free society."[112] He asserted that "free

---

proportionality question: Does the regulation at issue work harm to First Amendment interests that is disproportionate in light of the relevant regulatory objectives?") (internal quotation omitted).

[109] Id ("it is hard to see how a statute prohibiting the registration of only highly vulgar or obscene words discriminates based on 'viewpoint'").

[110] Id at 2304 (Roberts, CJ, concurring in part and dissenting in part).

[111] *Iancu v Brunetti*, Tr of Oral Arg at 38.

[112] *Brunetti*, 139 S Ct at 2303 (Alito, J, concurring).

speech is under attack" in the United States and abroad, and that it was "especially important for this Court to remain firm on the principle that the First Amendment does not tolerate viewpoint discrimination."[113]

Nevertheless, Alito posited that "our decision does not prevent Congress from adopting a more carefully focused statute" that limits trademarks containing "vulgar terms that play no real part in the expression of ideas." Such a redrafted statute would allow the PTO to refuse to register Brunetti's proposed mark, which is "not needed to express any idea . . . and generally signifies nothing except emotion and a severely limited vocabulary."[114] This passage makes clear that Alito voted to strike down the "scandalous" language not because he believed that regulations of mode or manner of speech are constitutionally problematic. Rather, he believed the statute was best read as embodying traditional viewpoint bias, and that "we are not legislators and cannot substitute a new statute for the one now in force."[115] That makes four votes.

Justice Kagan's short opinion for the Court falls short of explicitly declaring that manner bias does not constitute viewpoint discrimination. But the insinuations are there. Justice Kagan explained that the "immoral" and "scandalous" provisions were best read as a unitary provision even though they are separated by the adjective "deceptive" in the text of the act. On this interpretation, the two words read together "distinguishes between two opposed sets of ideas: those aligned with conventional moral standards and those hostile to them; those inducing societal nods of approval and those provoking offense and condemnation. The statute favors the former, and disfavors the latter."[116]

Kagan thus describes the statute as embodying traditional viewpoint bias. Under the PTO's application of the law, it had "refused to register marks communicating 'immoral' or 'scandalous' views about (among other things) drug use, religion, and terrorism. But all the while, it has approved registration of marks expressing more accepted views on the same topics."[117] The PTO was "disfavoring 'ideas that

---

[113] Id.
[114] Id.
[115] Id.
[116] Id at 2300.
[117] Id at 2300–01.

offend'" and thus "discriminat[ing] based on viewpoint, in violation of the First Amendment."[118]

The government had argued that the statute should survive under a reading that would limit its application to marks that were "offensive . . . because of their *mode* of expression, independent of the views that they may express."[119] The government argued that such a bar "would not turn on viewpoint" and could be upheld by the Court.[120] That is, the government argued that the Lanham Act embodied manner bias only, which did not amount to unconstitutional viewpoint discrimination.

In answering the government's contention, the Court did not say the distinction was immaterial. Kagan said instead that the statute could not bear the narrower reading that it contained manner bias but not traditional viewpoint bias. The statute did not, according to the Court, "refer only to marks whose 'mode of expression,' independent of viewpoint, is particularly offensive." Throughout this passage, Kagan continued the distinction between traditional bias and manner bias. She implied that a restriction on mode is not a restriction on viewpoint, because she juxtaposed the two: the statute "covers the universe of immoral or scandalous . . . whether the scandal or immorality comes from mode or *instead* from viewpoint."[121] In a footnote, she makes the point more strongly. In answering Sotomayor's statutory argument, Kagan counters that even if separated from the "immoral" term, "the category of scandalous marks thus includes *both* marks that offend by the ideas they convey *and* marks that offend by their mode of expression. And its coverage of the former means that it discriminates based on viewpoint."[122]

Kagan wrote in the same footnote that the Court "say[s] nothing at all about a statute that covers only . . . lewd, sexually explicit, and profane marks." One might read this as saying that the Court remained agnostic as to whether such a statute would survive First Amendment scrutiny, and as a matter of technical Court practice it is certainly the case that a future Court would not feel bound by

---

[118] Id at 2301.

[119] Id (emphasis in Court's opinion) (quoting Tr of Oral Arg at 11).

[120] Id.

[121] Id at 2301–02.

[122] Id at 2302 note *.

Brunetti to consider a statute containing manner bias as viewpoint neutral. But even this throw-away line by Kagan is probably best read not as an affirmative claim that manner bias embodies viewpoint discrimination. Instead it is best read to mean that there may be First Amendment challenges to such a statute other than on the basis that it is viewpoint biased.

All in all, as a matter of description and even prediction, *Brunetti* should stand for the proposition that regulations of mode and manner of communication will not be viewed by the Court as embodying viewpoint discrimination. Four Justices say so more or less explicitly. And the Court's opinion by Justice Kagan seems to make the same assumption.

B. REVISITING TAM AFTER BRUNETTI

One possible objection to reading *Brunetti* to limit the meaning of viewpoint bias is that *Tam* came out the other way. The Court decided *Tam* in 2017, two years before *Brunetti*, ruling that the so-called "disparagement clause" of the Lanham Act violated the First Amendment because of its viewpoint discrimination.[123] The provision prohibited the registration of a trademark "which may disparage . . . persons, living or dead, institutions, beliefs, or national symbols, or bring them into contempt, or disrepute."[124] The PTO had denied registration to a rock band's proposed mark, "The Slants." The band's lead singer, Simon Tam, chose the name for the band to reclaim what is typically a slur and epithet against Asian Americans.[125]

Justice Alito wrote the main opinion, but spoke for the Court only in the early, introductory portions. His reasoning for striking down the disparagement clause attracted only three other votes (the Chief Justice and Justices Thomas and Breyer). Meanwhile, Justice Kennedy wrote an opinion for himself and three other Justices (Ginsburg, Sotomayor, and Kagan) reaching the same outcome with slightly different reasoning. But all eight Justices agreed that the disparagement clause constituted viewpoint discrimination. (Justice Gorsuch took no part in the case.) In a portion of his opinion in which he spoke for the entire Court, Alito explained that the provision "offends a

---

[123] *Tam*, 137 S Ct 1744 (2017).
[124] 15 USC § 1052(a).
[125] See *Tam*, 137 S Ct at 1754.

bedrock First Amendment principle: Speech may not be banned on the ground that it expresses ideas that offend."[126]

Does *Tam* stand for the proposition that the regulation of mode or manner of communication embodies viewpoint discrimination? Or is the best reading of *Tam*'s two opinions consistent with the interpretation of *Brunetti* above? The answer to this depends on if one can glean from the opinions whether the Justices saw the disparagement clause as embodying traditional viewpoint bias or only manner bias. If manner bias only, and the Court nevertheless struck down the provision as discriminating on the basis of viewpoint, then the reading of *Brunetti* suggested above is less persuasive.

Alito's opinion is not absolutely clear on this point. One passage does appear, at first look, to suggest that he found the disparagement clause to be about mode or manner rather than ideas. In describing the operation of the provision, he said it operates "evenhandedly" by banning the "disparagement of all groups."[127] "It applies equally to marks that damn Democrats and Republicans, capitalists and socialists, and those arrayed on both sides of every possible issue."[128] The law required the PTO to refuse registration to any mark "that is offensive to a substantial percentage of the members of any group." He went on to say that "in the sense relevant here," such a limitation on registration is "viewpoint discrimination" because "giving offense is a viewpoint."[129]

That does sound as if Alito believed that a ban on offensive language constitutes viewpoint discrimination. The law would be viewpoint biased, "in the sense relevant here"—that is, under the First Amendment—because a law that limits offensiveness is discrimination against offensiveness. That seems to suggest he thinks the disparagement clause presents a problem of manner bias, which constitutes viewpoint discrimination under the First Amendment.

But the remainder of the opinion did not build on that contention. Instead, the opinion is best read as interpreting the disparagement clause as not limiting the mode or manner of offensive speech but limiting speech because of the disparaging ideas behind it. After the

---

[126] Id at 1749.
[127] Id at 1763.
[128] Id.
[129] Id.

passage in which he said that offensiveness "is a viewpoint," he explained that "the public expression of ideas may not be prohibited merely because the *ideas* are themselves offensive to some of their hearers."[130] He quoted the Court's opinion in *Texas v Johnson*, the flag-burning case, repeating, "If there is a bedrock principle underlying the First Amendment, it is that the government may not prohibit the expression of an *idea* simply because society finds the idea itself offensive or disagreeable."[131] Later in the opinion, Alito made clear that his reading of the statute requires the PTO to refuse marks that disparage on the basis of the idea conveyed in the mark rather than the mode or manner of the mark. He said the bans would apply "to trademarks like the following: 'Down with racists,' 'Down with sexists,' 'Down with homophobes.'"[132] That made clearer that Alito's disagreement with the disparagement clause was not that it regulated the mode or manner of speech but that it punished "ideas that offend."[133]

Kennedy's opinion, which spoke for four Justices, revealed a similar conviction that the disparagement clause punished ideas. He began his opinion by asserting the "fundamental principle of the First Amendment that the government may not punish or suppress speech based on disapproval of the ideas or perspectives the speech conveys."[134] The Lanham Act, according to Kennedy, acted as a requirement to be nice to people—"an applicant may register a positive or benign mark but not a derogatory one."[135] The law "mandat[ed] positivity." This might be seen as an indication that Kennedy saw the disparagement clause as a limitation on mode or manner. But given the opinion's emphasis on the argument that the statute discriminated on the basis of ideas, Kennedy likely interpreted the statute as a mandate that marks be supportive of the idea that people and groups are praiseworthy and not worthy of scorn. And that is traditional viewpoint bias, not manner bias.

---

[130] Id at 1763–64 (quoting *Street v New York*, 394 US 576, 592 (1969)) (emphasis mine).

[131] Id at 1764 (quoting *Texas v Johnson*, 491 US 397, 414 (1989)) (emphasis mine).

[132] Id at 1765.

[133] Id at 1751.

[134] *Tam*, 137 S Ct at 1765 (Kennedy, J, concurring in part and concurring in the judgment) (quoting *Rosenberger*, 515 US at 828–29).

[135] Id at 1750.

To be sure, it remains unclear whether Kennedy would have signed onto Sotomayor's opinion in *Brunetti* making a distinction between traditional viewpoint bias and manner bias for purposes of the First Amendment. In all likelihood, Kennedy did not consider the distinction in *Tam*, and he left the Court before *Brunetti*. But of course even if Kennedy did think that regulations of mode or manner embodied viewpoint bias, he never said so explicitly, and there is nothing in Kennedy's plurality opinion in *Tam* that would bar the Court's adoption of Sotomayor's *Brunetti* taxonomy going forward. Not only was his opinion in *Tam* not an opinion for the Court, Justice Sotomayor joined him. It would be unusual for Sotomayor to sign onto an opinion in *Tam* that she believed was inconsistent with her views in *Brunetti* two years later. *Brunetti*'s doctrinal analysis of viewpoint bias (springing both from Kagan's majority and Sotomayor's separate opinion) is more uniform, coherent, and sophisticated than anything in either opinion in *Tam*.

IV. Viewpoint Bias after Brunetti

It would be easy for *Brunetti* to be ignored by scholars as a small-bore decision in the narrow field of trademark law. What's more, one could see its outcome as unsurprising and even preordained given the outcome in *Tam* two years before. But *Brunetti* is more significant than that. Reading the various opinions together, *Brunetti* offers more clarity on what does and does not constitute viewpoint discrimination as a matter of First Amendment doctrine than in any case in decades. Remember that viewpoint bias is only doctrinally material in a small subset of First Amendment cases—that is, when content discrimination itself is insufficient to trigger strict scrutiny. That means that the Court has few opportunities to define the contours of viewpoint bias, which the Court readily admits is slippery and imprecise.[136] *Brunetti* should be taken seriously, therefore, as the most recent and most revealing statement by the Court to date about the limits of what constitutes viewpoint discrimination. This final Part will describe what is the best understanding of viewpoint discrimination

---

[136] See *Rosenberger*, 515 US at 831 ("[T]he distinction is not a precise one"); *Brunetti*, 139 S Ct at 2313 (Sotomayor, J, concurring in part and dissenting in part) (saying the definition of viewpoint bias is "slippery"); *Brunetti*, 139 S Ct at 2305–06 (Breyer, J, concurring in part and dissenting in part) ("As for the concepts of 'viewpoint discrimination' and 'content discrimination,' I agree with Justice Sotomayor that the boundaries between them may be difficult to discern.").

after *Brunetti* and then describe some of the implications of this new, clearer, and narrower understanding.

A. MANNER BIAS DOES NOT COUNT AS VIEWPOINT BIAS

Brunetti reaffirms that traditional viewpoint discrimination is an "egregious form of content discrimination"[137] that triggers strict scrutiny and is presumptively a violation of the First Amendment. That is, the government discriminates on the basis of viewpoint when it regulates private communication in such a way so as to support or hinder an idea, point of view, opinion, or perspective, as compared to competing ideas, points of view, opinions, or perspectives. Regulations of fighting words that punish those who use such words to call for racial conflict, but do not punish those who use such words to call for racial harmony, discriminate on the basis of viewpoint. Regulations that grant trademark protections to marks that urge morality and decency, but deny protections to marks urging depravity, discriminate on the basis of viewpoint.

But regulations of mode and manner of speech do not constitute viewpoint bias under the First Amendment and should not be seen as an "egregious form of content discrimination." That is, the government does not discriminate on the basis of viewpoint when the government regulates private speech in such a way as to discourage or punish a mode or manner of communication. This is true even when there is a salient public debate about whether such mode or manner should be regulated. A ban on profane trademarks, for example, does not discriminate on the basis of viewpoint. A ban on threats that contain racial epithets does not discriminate on the basis of viewpoint. A restriction on sexually explicit displays in workplaces does not discriminate on the basis of viewpoint.

To be clear, to say that these regulations of mode or manner of communication do not embody viewpoint bias is not to say that they should survive First Amendment challenge. Strict scrutiny might by triggered for other reasons. Courts may see regulations that are *viewpoint* neutral as nevertheless discriminating on the basis of *content*, subject to the long-standing rule that content discrimination

---

[137] See *Rosenberger*, 515 US at 829. See also *Brunetti*, 139 S Ct at 2299 (quoting *Rosenberger*); *Lamb's Chapel*, 508 US at 394 ("[T]he First Amendment forbids the government to regulate speech in ways that favor some viewpoints or ideas at the expense of others").

presumptively triggers strict scrutiny.[138] Or limits on mode or manner that are applied in a nonneutral way would be viewpoint biased in application even if not facially. For example, the outcome in *Cohen*, the "fuck the draft" case, does not need rethinking under this understanding of viewpoint bias. Limits on profanity in public places are regulations of content and presumptively subject to strict scrutiny even if applied evenhandedly to those protesting the draft and those protesting draft dodgers. And if a ban on profanity is selectively applied to draft protesters but not draft-dodging protesters, then the profanity ban is in application exhibiting traditional viewpoint bias rather than merely manner bias; it is no longer viewpoint neutral.

Consider again *R.A.V.* in this context. After *Brunetti*, the best reading of that case is that the Court thought of the city ordinance as imposing a limit on fighting words used to express the idea of racial disharmony, while not imposing a limit on fighting words used to express the idea of racial harmony. That is traditional viewpoint discrimination. If instead the Court had read the ordinance as banning all fighting words containing a racial epithet—but not banning "generic" fighting words even if they expressed the idea of racial disharmony—then the ordinance would have embodied only manner bias and would not have triggered strict scrutiny.

B. SOME IMPLICATIONS

Consider a few concrete implications of this more precise understanding of viewpoint discrimination. First, and most obviously, Congress could amend the Lanham Act as Chief Justice Roberts and Justices Alito, Breyer, and Sotomayor suggested in their separate writings. There is little doubt that the Court would uphold a new provision prohibiting the registration of marks containing words that are "obscene," "lewd," "profane," or "vulgar."[139]

Congress could also amend the Lanham Act—as Justice Sotomayor suggested in her concurrence—to bar the registration of marks containing "racial or ethnic epithets."[140] If properly applied by the

---

[138] See *Reed*, 133 S Ct 2218.

[139] *Brunetti*, 139 S Ct at 2304 (Roberts, CJ, concurring in part and dissenting in part) ("obscene, vulgar or profane"); id at 2304 (Breyer, J, concurring in part and dissenting in part) ("vulgar or obscene"); id at 2303 (Alito, J, concurring) ("vulgar"); id at 2311 (Sotomayor, J, concurring in part and dissenting in part) ("lewd or 'swear' words").

[140] Id at 2311.

PTO, such a limit should be seen as a limit on mode or manner of communication rather than a discrimination against racist viewpoints. A restriction of racist epithets is not the same as a restriction on the communication of racist ideas, and a framework of trademark registration that prohibited the registration of marks containing epithets would not be seen as discriminating on the basis of viewpoint. This is true even though the broader disparagement clause was struck down in *Tam*. That clause banned disparagement generally, regardless of the mode or manner in which it was communicated. A narrower ban on racial epithets should survive. This distinction is strengthened by reference to *Virginia v Black*, the case that upheld Virginia's ban on threats made by way of burning a cross. The ban on cross burning in that case was a limit on the mode or manner of expressing a threat, and the Court did not see it as discriminating on the basis of viewpoint.

These points can be generalized to other First Amendment contexts in which content discrimination alone does not trigger strict scrutiny. In a limited public forum, for example, limits on the mode or manner of communication should not trigger the exacting scrutiny that comes with viewpoint discrimination.[141] One application would be schools' or universities' limits on lewd language and epithets that reference racial, sexual, ethnic, or other characteristics. In light of *Brunetti*, such limits on the mode or manner of communication in educational settings should be upheld, as long as the forum in question is correctly seen as a limited public forum (as opposed to a public forum).[142]

One way to characterize this reading of *Brunetti* is as a caution to not over-read or over-emphasize *R.A.V.* Before *Brunetti*, it would be easy to interpret *R.A.V.* as creating a broad definition of viewpoint bias that would doom virtually any attempt to draft a so-called "hate speech code."[143] As explored in Part II above, it was possible before

---

[141] If, however, public officials were to apply such limits on mode or manner to benefit a point of view or the other, then the limits would of course violate the presumption against viewpoint bias. See *Ward*, 491 US at 791 ("The government's purpose is the controlling consideration.").

[142] See *Bethel School Dist. No. 403 v Fraser*, 478 US 675, 685 (1986) (treating punishment of "offensively lewd and indecent speech" as viewpoint neutral).

[143] See Murray, 24 Western St U L Rev at 264–65 ("while speech codes faced an uphill battle under the constitutional precedent in place before *R.A.V.*, this decision made it virtually

Brunetti to read *R.A.V.* to mean that a law discriminates on the basis of viewpoint if it identifies a subset of speech for extra penalties by reference to that subset's focus on racial, sexual, ethnic, or other such characteristics. This was not the only way to read Justice Scalia's opinion in *R.A.V.*, but it was a reasonable way to read it.[144] Now, however, such a broad reading of *R.A.V.* is less convincing. Instead, *R.A.V.* should be read as a straightforward application of the Court's long-standing rule against traditional viewpoint bias.[145] In other words, the ordinance in St. Paul should have survived if it were a law punishing racist epithets, assuming it was applied equally to speakers on all sides of the racial divides in the city.

Another possible application of this new narrower interpretation of viewpoint bias is to so-called "gruesome speech."[146] According to Eugene Volokh, "recent years have seen a striking" number of instances in which "courts have concluded that [content-based] restrictions on the public display of 'gruesome images,' usually of aborted fetuses, are permissible" under the First Amendment.[147] Some jurisdictions have sought limits or punishments for the display of graphic depictions of not only aborted fetuses, but also victims of murder, violence, or other abuse.[148] Perhaps also included in this speech category

---

impossible for a speech code to pass constitutional muster") (cited in note 19); Hudson and Nott, *Hate Speech and Campus Speech Codes* (same) (cited in note 19).

[144] See, for example, Strossen, *Hate* at 74 (describing *R.A.V.* as striking down the St. Paul ordinance "because it selectively outlawed only 'abusive invective' that was based on 'race, color, creed, religion or gender'"; a law that is "underinclusive" "embodies viewpoint discrimination") (cited in note 68); Chemerinsky, *Constitutional Law* at 1013–14 (*R.A.V.* "makes it difficult for hate speech codes to survive judicial analysis; if they prohibit only some forms of hate, they will be invalidated as impermissible content-based discrimination") (cited in note 19); id at 1007 ("there is a strong presumption against content-based discrimination within categories of unprotected speech").

[145] More precisely: The ordinance in St. Paul was not a ban on (a subset of) a subset of speech based on the mode or manner of that communication, but a ban on (a subset of) a subset of speech based on the point of view that speech conveyed. The ordinance only applied to a subset of a fighting words, itself a subset of speech.

[146] See Eugene Volokh, *Gruesome Speech*, 100 Cornell L Rev 901 (2015).

[147] Id at 902. Volokh cites the following cases as embodying this trend: *Frye v Kansas City Missouri Police Department*, 375 F3d 785, 790–91 (8th Cir 2004); *Tatton v City of Cuyahoga Falls*, 116 F Supp 2d 928, 931, 934 (ND Ohio 2000); *Saint John's Church in the Wilderness v Scott*, 296 P3d 273, 281–85 (Colo App 2012); Preliminary Injunction at 3–4, *Wilkerson v Scott*, No 728883, 1999 WL 34994617 (Cal Super Ct, June 11, 1999); see also *Olmer v City of Lincoln*, 192 F3d 1176, 1180 (8th Cir 1999) (stating that a restriction on gruesome images focused on shielding young children would be constitutional); *Operation Save America v City of Jackson*, 275 P3d 438, 460–61 (Wyo 2012) (similar).

[148] Volokh, 100 Cornell L Rev at 910–11 (cited in note 146).

could be so-called "crush videos"—depictions of the maiming or killing of animals, usually done for sexual pleasure.[149]

These limits on gruesome displays would certainly be content based, in that they create regulations that depend entirely on the content of the speech.[150] But they would not be viewpoint based, even though they embed within them a view that gruesomeness is a problematic subset of speech. Volokh agrees: "All these restrictions are viewpoint-neutral—they ban pictures of nudity, vulgarities, or violent images without regard to the viewpoint that the words or images are used to convey."[151] That would mean, for example, that limits on gruesome speech could very well survive in limited public forums, where content discrimination alone does not trigger strict scrutiny.[152]

Another implication would be that the current version of the federal law criminalizing animal "crush videos" is constitutional. In 2010, the Court struck down a previous version of the law as content based and overbroad.[153] Congress quickly amended and repassed the statute, but limited its scope to only those videos that depict defined animal cruelty and that are also obscene.[154] In other words, Congress identified a subset of obscenity—that which portrays cruelty to animals—as subject to heightened penalties. Because Congress is making content distinctions within the category of obscenity, a category of "low-value" speech the regulation of which does not ordinarily trigger strict scrutiny, the law should only require strict scrutiny if the law fails *R.A.V.*'s bar on the selection of subcategories for reasons of viewpoint bias. But we know after *Brunetti* that the selection of a subcategory by reason of a mode or manner such as gruesomeness is not discriminating on the basis of viewpoint.

---

[149] See *United States v Stevens*, 559 US 460 (2010) (striking down 18 USC § 48, a federal law criminalizing the commercialization of animal crush videos, as overbroad).

[150] See Volokh, 100 Cornell L Rev at 911 ("Under well-established First Amendment doctrine, such statutes are content-based because they ban depictions of particular acts or things.") (cited in note 146).

[151] Id at 912.

[152] Volokh makes this point as well. Id at 948 (if "the government is concerned simply that the gruesome image will disgust and alienate customers, quite apart from its political message . . . then the gruesome-image restriction is likely to be treated as facially viewpoint-neutral, even though it disproportionately affects some viewpoints. The restriction would still be content-based, but it would be viewpoint-neutral, and that is sufficient in nonpublic fora and limited public fora.").

[153] See *Stevens*, 559 US at 460.

[154] See 18 US Code § 48; Pub L No 111-294, § 2, Dec 9, 2010, 124 Stat 3177.

V. Conclusion

In a compact and efficient opinion for the Court in *Iancu v Brunetti*, Justice Elena Kagan reaffirmed "a core postulate" of the First Amendment: that "government may not discriminate against speech based on the ideas or opinions it conveys."[155] A law that "disfavors certain ideas"[156] is "presumptively unconstitutional"[157] and dooms the law in question.[158] While the Court occasionally allows content discrimination in certain settings and in certain categories of analysis, the Court is firm and consistent in its suspicion of viewpoint choices by the government. Once a law falls into the "discriminates on the basis of viewpoint" box, it is done for. In that respect, *Brunetti* is an unremarkable, straightforward application of long-standing free speech doctrine.[159]

But a significant contribution to that doctrine can be derived from the exchange between Kagan's opinion for the Court and the opinion concurring in part and dissenting in part by Justice Sonia Sotomayor. The disagreement between them was not a matter of free speech doctrine but a matter of statutory interpretation. Sotomayor read the ban on the registration of "scandalous" trademarks to be a manner restriction rather than a viewpoint restriction. As a restriction on manner or mode of communication, Sotomayor argued that the provision was viewpoint neutral and did not trigger strict scrutiny. At least three other Justices explicitly agreed with Sotomayor's description that a limit on mode or manner would not trigger the Court's ire against viewpoint bias. And nothing in Kagan's opinion is inconsistent with this understanding of viewpoint bias—the disagreement between her and Sotomayor was statutory, not doctrinal. Nor would anything in the two plurality opinions in *Tam* stand in the way of Sotomayor's narrow reading of viewpoint discrimination.

This is an important clarification of the Court's doctrine of viewpoint discrimination. It is now clear, for example, that *R.A.V.* is best

---

[155] *Brunetti*, 139 S Ct at 2299.

[156] Id at 2297.

[157] Id at 2299 (quoting *Rosenberger*, 515 US at 829–30).

[158] Id (discussing how viewpoint bias "doomed the disparagement bar" in *Tam*).

[159] The *Brunetti* opinion allowed Justice Kagan to reaffirm what she had said as a legal scholar more than twenty-five years earlier. See Elena Kagan, *Regulation of Hate Speech and Pornography after R.A.V.*, 60 U Chi L Rev 873, 877 (1993) ("What R.A.V. shows, then, is the depth, not the tenuousness, of the Court's commitment to a viewpoint neutrality principle.").

seen as a case about traditional viewpoint bias, rather than a case that stands for a notion that limits on the modes or manner of speech discriminate on the basis of viewpoint. Limits on mode or manner of communication—including the regulation of profanity, racial epithets, sexually explicit speech, or the like—will continue to be constitutionally problematic in settings in which content discrimination alone triggers strict scrutiny. But in contexts in which content discrimination is not itself sufficient to require strict scrutiny—in limited public forums, in commercial speech, or when regulating "low-value" speech such as threats and fighting words, for example—courts should not presume the unconstitutionality of limits on the mode or manner of communication fairly applied to all speakers.

This is true even when there is a debate about the mode or manner of communication itself. A ban on racial epithets applied to both anti-white and anti-black protesters, for example, is not constitutionally identical to a ban on racial epithets applied to only one side. Because of *Brunetti*, we now know that while the latter is correctly seen as discriminating on the basis of viewpoint, the former is not. While the exact contours of viewpoint bias main remain "slippery,"[160] they are clearer than ever before.

---

[160] *Brunetti*, 139 S Ct at 2313 (Sotomayor, J, concurring in part and dissenting in part) (quoting Corbin, 83 NYU L Rev at 651) (cited in note 21).

JENNIFER M. CHACÓN

THE INSIDE-OUT CONSTITUTION: DEPARTMENT OF COMMERCE v NEW YORK

On June 27, 2019, the U.S. Supreme Court issued its decision in *Department of Commerce v New York*.[1] The case involved a challenge to the Commerce Department's proposed addition of a citizenship question to the 2020 census. The matter drew significant public attention because it highlighted the potential power of executive branch officials to manipulate the census to enhance the electoral power of one racial group at the expense of others, and it raised the question of whether the Court was willing to stop this.[2] Many observers believed that the Court would not interfere.[3] In a move that surprised many,

---

Jennifer M. Chacón is Professor of Law at UCLA School of Law.

AUTHOR'S NOTE: I am grateful to Justin Driver for his insightful editorial comments, Eliana Navarro Gracian for her helpful research assistance, and Mary Ann Cancellare for her patience throughout the writing process.

[1] *Department of Commerce v New York*, 139 S Ct 2551 (2019) (hereafter "*Dep't of Commerce v New York*" or "the Census 2020 Case").

[2] See, for example, Michael Wines, *Lawsuit Says Citizenship Question on Census Targets Minorities for Political Gain*, NY Times (May 31, 2018), available at https://www.nytimes.com/2018/05/31/us/politics/2020-census-citizenship.html.

[3] See, for example, Linda Greenhouse, *The Supreme Court, the Census Case and the Truth*, NY Times (May 9, 2019), available at https://www.nytimes.com/2019/05/09/opinion/supreme-court-census-trump.html ("The smart money says the Trump administration is going to prevail at the Supreme Court in its effort to add a citizenship question to next year's census. Having read the transcript and listened to the audio file of the recent argument, I don't challenge that forecast.").

© 2020 by The University of Chicago. All rights reserved.
978-0-226-70856-0/2020/2019-0005$10.00

however, Chief Justice John Roberts voted with the Court's more liberal Justices in holding that the administration's stated reason for its decision to include the question was pretextual in violation of the Administrative Procedures Act.[4]

The plaintiffs' narrow victory in this case was hard fought and politically significant. Most notably, it kept the administration from adding the citizenship question to the upcoming census. The outcome might also be read to hint that there is at least some small possibility of success for litigants in *Department of Homeland Security v Regents of the University of California*,[5] the case challenging the Trump administration's rescission of the Deferred Action for Childhood Arrivals program (DACA). After all, the claims of the DACA plaintiffs rest, in part, on the same sort of argument about the administration's reliance on a pretextual rationale for its actions. More generally, the Census 2020 Case might be read to signal a hopeful break from a course of judicial deference to the Trump administration in its review of policies that discriminate against racial and religious minorities. A closer look at the Court's decision in the census case, however, suggests far less reason for optimism for those who look to the courts to protect historically marginalized groups from government oppression.

To best understand the full meaning and limitations of the Census 2020 Case, it is useful to think about it in the context of the Trump administration's policies affecting immigrant communities. The Census 2020 Case was not an immigration case. Strictly speaking, it does not involve questions of the rights of a noncitizen to enter or remain. It can be (and has been) fruitfully analyzed outside of the immigration context as a window on the Court's appetite for reviewing politically motivated agency actions.[6] But another way to understand the case is to consider it as one of several important cases involving immigrant communities. In this contextual frame, it follows the Muslim Exclusion Case, *Trump v Hawaii*,[7] decided in the 2018 Term, and precedes the DACA Case, *Department of Homeland Security v Regents of the University of California*, which will be decided in 2020.

---

[4] *Dep't of Commerce v New York*, 139 S Ct at 2575–76 (finding that the administration's proffered justification for the addition of the census question was pretextual).

[5] *Department of Homeland Security v Regents of the University of California*, 139 S Ct 2779 (2019) (hereafter *Dep't of Homeland Sec. v U.C. Regents* or "the DACA Case").

[6] See Comment, *Department of Commerce v New York*, 133 Harv L Rev 372 (2019).

[7] *Trump v Hawaii*, 138 S Ct 2392 (2019) (hereafter *Trump v Hawaii* or "the Muslim Exclusion Case").

All three of these cases involve challenges to executive branch policies that primarily target legal "outsiders." These outsiders have included noncitizens[8] seeking entry at the nation's borders, noncitizens counted (or not) by the census,[9] and noncitizens wishing to remain in the country in which they grew up.[10] In all of these cases, the policies aimed at legal outsiders would also circumscribe the political and social power of the racialized immigrant[11] communities to which these noncitizens belong. The policies tolerate, and indeed intentionally generate, limitations on the rights of legal "insiders"—U.S. citizens. In each of these cases, this administration has structured the challenged policies to signal to certain groups their outsider status or to reinforce that outsider status, and have done so in the service of what the Supreme Court once called "White Supremacy."[12] And in each of these cases, affected parties have asked the Supreme Court to intervene.

---

[8] I use the term "noncitizen" throughout this essay to refer to people who do not have U.S. citizenship. It applies regardless of an individual's formal immigration status. The terms "citizens" and "noncitizens" are reductively binary and worthy in themselves of critical interrogation. See, e.g., Nina Glick Schiller and Noel B. Salazar, *Regimes of Mobility across the Globe*, in Nina Glick Schiller and Noel B. Salazar, eds, *Regimes of Mobility: Imaginaries and Relationalities of Power* 183 (Routledge, 2014) (urging critical interrogation of "conceptual orientations built on binaries of difference that have impeded analyses of the interrelationship between mobility and stasis" and introducing a series of essays critical of facile binaries that plague migration studies and conceptions of immigration). Far from being fixed and certain, citizenship is a legal category plagued with ambiguity, governed by dynamic legal regimes, and subject to frequent misrecognitions. Jacqueline Stephens, *Introduction*, in Benjamin N. Lawrance and Jacqueline Stevens, eds, *Citizenship in Question: Evidentiary Birthright and Statelessness* 9 (Duke, 2017) (summarizing the collected essays as "revealing micro-level ... confusion about citizenship [and] challenge the assumption that citizenship is the sort of self-evident characteristic that one either has or lacks."). Readers should accordingly imagine quotation marks around the term "noncitizen" each time it is used. The significant legal distinctions that the law creates around the unstable legal category of citizenship can also facilitate the racialization of any outgroup regardless of legal citizenship status, blurring the distinctions between the categories. See discussion in Part III.

[9] *Dep't of Commerce v New York*, 139 S Ct 2551 (2019).

[10] *Dep't of Homeland Sec. v U.C. Regents*, 139 S Ct 2779 (2019).

[11] The term "immigrant" is used throughout this essay in the colloquial sense, meaning noncitizens who have migrated to the United States. It encompasses groups of people who are categorized as both "nonimmigrants" and "immigrants" under U.S. immigration law, and it encompasses authorized as well as unauthorized immigrants. I use the term "unauthorized immigrants" to refer to noncitizens who currently lack federal authorization to be in the United States.

[12] *Loving v Virginia*, 388 US 1, 12 (1967). As the Court made clear in *Loving*, the antimiscegenation law in question was a product of a commingled racist and nativist legislative movement aimed at preserving white racial purity and supremacy. Jennifer M. Chacón, *Loving Across Borders: Immigration Law and the Limits of Loving*, 2007 Wisc L Rev 343, 345 (2007).

For a complete discussion of President Trump's efforts to advance a white nationalist agenda through his immigration policies, see, e.g., Jayashri Srikantiah and Shirin Sinnar, *White Nationalism as Immigration Policy*, 71 Stan L Rev 197, 198–200 (2019) (citing examples of the

Far from protecting legal insiders, however, thus far the Court has largely treated the harms to them as irrelevant. In the Muslim Exclusion Case, the Supreme Court upheld the President's proclamation banning entry for many noncitizens seeking admission from five majority-Muslim countries, notwithstanding the clear discriminatory effects of the entry ban and the surrounding context of express anti-Muslim statements by the President. In that case, Muslim families in the United States alleged a direct harm from the administration's denial of entry to their family members. This harm was intertwined with a second harm: the social harm of officially sanctioned animus. The Court's decision focused narrowly and mechanically on the exclusion, and applied a test devised for universities whose speaker faced an entry bar to evaluate the rights of family members to reunify in the United States.[13] Both in its application of this test and in it broader reasoning, Chief Justice Roberts's opinion for the majority treated the harm of officially sanctioned religious animus as a symbolic irrelevance rather than a real and lasting constitutional harm. In the resulting decision, the Court not only affirmed the power of the President to exclude individuals from entry on the basis of their nationality, but also effectively announced the President's unlimited power to couple such

---

President's racist rhetoric both within and beyond the sphere of immigration policy). In these pages, Mark Tushnet characterized the President as a "virulent racist." Mark Tushnet, *Trump v Hawaii: "This President" and the National Security Constitution*, 2018 Supreme Court Review 1, 9 (2018). The plaintiffs in the 2020 Census litigation submitted evidence of the overtly and implicitly racist and nativist statements made by President Trump, former Attorney General Jefferson Beauregard Sessions, and former Kansas Secretary of State Kris Kobach, who advised Secretary Wilbur Ross on census matters during periods relevant to the litigation. See *New York v Department of Commerce*, Plaintiffs' Joint Proposed Findings of Fact ¶¶ 939–48, Nov 21, 2018.

A recently released trove of emails of top presidential advisor Stephen Miller reveals his deep ties to white nationalist websites and his reliance on grotesquely racist literature in his thinking about immigration policy. Katie Rogers and Jason DeParle, *The White Nationalist Websites Cited by Stephen Miller*, NY Times (Nov 18, 2019), available at https://www.nytimes.com/2019/11/18/us/politics/stephen-miller-white-nationalism.html. Rogers and DeParle note, among other things, Miller's citations to Jean Raspail's racist novel *The Camp of the Saints* in framing his thinking around immigration and refugee policy. "'The key themes [of that book] are actually white supremacy and the end of white civilization as the West knows it—infestation, invasion, hordes of nameless, faceless migrants who come to indeed invade the West and bring about its end,' says Chelsea Stieber, professor of French and Francophone studies at Catholic University of America." Lulu Garcia Navarro, *Stephen Miller and "The Camp of the Saints," a White Nationalist Reference*, National Public Radio (Nov 19, 2019), available at https://www.npr.org/2019/11/19/780552636/stephen-miller-and-the-camp-of-the-saints-a-white-nationalist-reference.

[13] This is not the first time that the Court has relied on the test devised in *Kleindeist v Mandel*, 408 US 753 (1972), requiring only a "bona fide and legitimate reason" for the exclusion of a family member. Justice Kennedy also did so in his concurring opinion necessary to the holding in *Kerry v Din*, 135 S Ct 2128, 2139–41 (2015).

exclusionary decisions with the overt denigration of religious communities in the United States. In Chief Justice Roberts's opinion, the right of legal insiders to be free from official religious discrimination was an unacknowledged casualty of the Court's belief in the President's broad constitutional and statutory authority to exclude legal outsiders.

The Census 2020 Case is also a case that involves the linked fate of legal insiders and legal outsiders. Like the Muslim Exclusion Case, it provides a useful lens through which to examine how this administration has sought to take advantage of the legal vulnerabilities of the classic legal outsiders—noncitizens, and particularly those lacking formal legal immigration status—to limit the political power and official protection of legal insiders. Notwithstanding the apparent difference in outcomes, the Court's ruling in *Department of Commerce v New York*, just like its ruling in the Muslim Exclusion Case, demonstrates that a majority of the Supreme Court's Justices are comfortable placing legal insiders outside of the scope of the Constitution's protections. Both decisions also illustrate how they can easily do so, as both a doctrinal and a discursive matter, because of the proximity of these legal insiders to legal outsiders.

Read together, the Court's decisions in both the Muslim Exclusion Case and the Census 2020 Case suggest an inside-out Constitution, with the Court treating the Constitution's insiders in ways typically reserved for those outside the scope of its protection. The Census 2020 Case, in particular, highlights two important ways that the Court has constructed this inside-out Constitution. First, as discussed in greater detail in Part II, the decision offers a clear picture of how the Court has created almost insurmountable barriers for plaintiffs seeking to challenge white supremacy through equal protection claims.[14] The fate of the equal protection claim in the Census 2020 Case is a logical sequel to the fate of the First Amendment discrimination claim in the Muslim Exclusion Case, *Trump v Hawaii*. Both cases illustrate the near impossibility of vindicating claims of racial or

---

[14] The racial discrimination claims in *Department of Commerce v New York* were brought under the Fifth Amendment Due Process Clause, which incorporates the Fourteenth Amendment's equal protection principle after *Bolling v Sharpe*, 347 US 497 (1954). In the discussion that follows, I am referring to the plaintiffs' claims as "equal protection claims" even though they are more precisely characterized (as they are in the litigation) as Fifth Amendment due process claims.

religious animus against historically disadvantaged groups under existing constitutional antidiscrimination jurisprudence.

The Census 2020 Case also illustrates how the substantive-rights claims advanced by parties seeking redress for invidious racial discrimination by the government are increasingly vindicated, if they are vindicated at all, through procedural channels. But even when plaintiffs prevail in their procedural claims, as in the Census 2020 Case, the resulting remedies are no match for the underlying equality harms generated by the challenged policies. Racial animus is whitewashed. The Court never grapples with the identity-based dignity and status harms suffered by nonwhite plaintiffs as the result of challenged policies. As a practical matter, the result of the Court's failure to grapple with the equality concerns at stake is procedural protections much narrower in scope than the underlying threats to equality require. The Census 2020 Case not only illustrates this point, but also provides a useful preview of how the Court will analyze the claims raised in *Department of Homeland Security v U.C. Regents*.

After a brief summary of the background of *Department of Commerce v New York*, I will elaborate upon each of these themes in turn.

I. The 2020 Census Litigation

The Constitution requires an "Enumeration" of the population every ten years, to be made "in such Manner" as Congress "shall by Law direct."[15] The Constitution specifies that this census count provides the basis for apportioning congressional representation.[16] As a practical matter, the count is also used to determine the appropriate distribution of "billions of dollars in federal, state and local funds."[17] And it provides useful demographic information about the U.S. population.[18]

With the passage of the Census Act, Congress delegated to the Secretary of the Department of Commerce the responsibility for administering the census.[19] Under that law, the Secretary is aided in this

---

[15] US Const, Art I, § 2, cl 3; US Const, Amend XIV, § 2.
[16] Id.
[17] *New York v United States Department of Commerce*, 351 F Supp 3d 502, 514–15 (2019).
[18] Id at 515.
[19] 13 USC § 141(a).

task by the Commerce Department's Census Bureau.[20] The Census Bureau is headed by a political appointee, the Director of the Census.[21]

On March 26, 2018, Secretary of Commerce Wilbur Ross released a memorandum stating that the 2020 census would include a question about whether each person in the household is a citizen of the United States.[22] A question about citizenship first appeared on the census in 1820, and was asked in some form or another until 1950,[23] though it has never asked for the citizenship status of each individual household member.[24] After 1950, the Commerce Department only included a citizenship question in the long-form version of the census, which is administered to about 2% of households; it has not appeared on the general household census since that time, and it did not appear on any census form in 2010.[25] Social scientists (and Republican election consultants[26]) agree that the likely effect of inserting the citizenship question to the census at this political moment will be to overcount "non-Hispanic whites," particularly by depressing response rates in immigrant communities—a dampening effect that will redound to the particular disadvantage of Latino[27] voters, since immigrants in the

---

[20] 1902 legislation created the Census Office. In 1954, Congress enacted legislation combining the existing laws governing the Census Bureau's statistical programs. An Act to Revise, Codify, and Enact into Law Title 13, USC (Aug 31, 1954) (PL No 83-740).

[21] 13 USC § 21(a)(1).

[22] Letter-Memorandum from Wilbur Ross, Secretary of Commerce, to Karen Dunn Kelley, Under Secretary for Economic Affairs, on Reinstatement of a Citizenship Question on the 2020 Decennial Census Questionnaire (March 26, 2018), available at https://www.commerce.gov/sites/default/files/2018-03-26_2.pdf.

[23] *Dep't of Commerce v New York*, 139 S Ct at 2561.

[24] Hansi Lo Wang and Renee Klahr, *See 200 Years of Twists and Turns of Census Citizenship Questions*, National Public Radio (April 23, 2019), available at https://www.npr.org/2019/04/23/630562915/see-200-years-of-twists-and-turns-of-census-citizenship-questions.

[25] *New York v U.S. Dep't of Commerce*, 351 F Supp 3d at 642 (2019) (relating these facts and noting that the Secretary's statutorily required report to Congress about these facts was misleading).

[26] Michael Wines, *Deceased G.O.P. Strategist's Hard Drives Reveal New Details on the Census Citizenship Question*, NY Times (May 30, 2019), available at https://www.nytimes.com/2019/05/30/us/census-citizenship-question-hofeller.html (discussing Republican election consultant Thomas Hofeller's understanding that the inclusion of the question would have a negative effect of the response rate of these populations).

[27] The U.S. Census Bureau defines "Hispanic" or "Latino" to refer to "a person of Cuban, Mexican, Puerto Rican, South or Central American, or other Spanish culture or origin regardless of race" and states that Hispanics or Latinos can be of any race, any ancestry, any ethnicity. Throughout this essay, I generally use the term "Hispanic" when I am referencing documents that use the term. At other times, I use the term "Latino" to refer to the same population.

The census treats the "Hispanic" or "Latino" group as transracial and transethnic, but Latinos are a racialized group in the United States, and the Court has treated discrimination against

"Hispanic" census category make up the largest immigrant group in the country, and Latinos in the United States have a higher percentage of immigrant family members—and unauthorized immigrant family members—than any other census group.[28]

In his memorandum explaining the addition of the citizenship question, Secretary Ross wrote that he was acting at the request of the Department of Justice, which was seeking more accurate citizenship data "for purposes of enforcing the Voting Rights Act [VRA]."[29] Secretary Ross's memo stated that he had considered several options for gathering the citizenship data purportedly necessary for enforcing the VRA, including developing improved modeling for providing census-block estimates drawing on the existing American Community Survey. Rejecting this option as unlikely to provide "a sufficient degree of accuracy," the Secretary also considered reinstating a citizenship question on the decennial census, using administrative records from other agencies, such as the Social Security Administration and U.S.

Latinos and Latino subgroups as racial discrimination. For example, in *Peña-Rodriguez v Colorado*, the Court wrote:

> Juror H. C.'s bias was based on petitioner's Hispanic identity, which the Court in prior cases has referred to as ethnicity, and that may be an instructive term here. *See, e.g., Hernandez v. New York*, 500 U.S. 352, 355 (1991) (plurality opinion). Yet we have also used the language of race when discussing the relevant constitutional principles in cases involving Hispanic persons. *See, e.g., ibid.; Fisher v. University of Tex. at Austin*, 570 U.S. ___ (2013); *Rosales-Lopez v. United States*, 451 U.S. 182, 189–190 (1981) (plurality opinion). Petitioner and respondent both refer to race, or to race and ethnicity, in this more expansive sense in their briefs to the Court. This opinion refers to the nature of the bias as racial in keeping with the primary terminology employed by the parties and used in our precedents.

137 S Ct 855, 863 (2015).

Similarly, for purposes of this essay, I will refer to Hispanics/Latinos as a racial group. In cases like *Dep't of Commerce v New York*, it is their social construction as a racial group that facilitates the discrimination against them, even as the discrimination against the group reifies the boundaries around it, hardening it into a racial category. See Michael Omi and Howard Winant, *Racial Formation in the United States from the 1960s to the 1990s* (Taylor & Francis, 1994) (propounding a theory of a social process of racial formation); Ian Haney-López, *White by Law: The Legal Construction of Race* (New York University, 1996) (explaining the role of law and legal decisions in defining racial boundaries and shaping racial hierarchies); Natalia Molina, *How Race Is Made in America: Immigration, Citizenship and the Historical Power of Racial Scripts* (University of California, 2014) (describing how racial groups were produced through definition in relation to one another through, among other things, immigration and naturalization law).

[28] For a more detailed discussion of the demographics of immigrant communities in the United States, see the discussion in Part III of this essay accompanying notes 124–34.

[29] *Dep't of Commerce v New York*, 139 S Ct at 2562.

Citizenship and Immigration Services, or combining those two methods in order to provide the Justice Department with the desired citizenship data.[30] The Secretary ultimately asked the Census Bureau to develop a combined option—the reinstatement of a citizenship question on the census questionnaire, along with enhancement of the bureau's administrative data and statistical models.[31] The Secretary's memorandum stated that he had "carefully considered" the possibility that reinstating a citizenship question would have an adverse effect on the response rate and decrease the accuracy of the census, but contended that the evidence about the adverse effect was insufficient and inconclusive.[32]

Upon the Secretary's announcement of his decision to include the question, two groups of plaintiffs filed lawsuits in federal district court in New York challenging the legality of the Secretary's decision. One group of plaintiffs included governmental entities: eighteen states, the District of Columbia, cities, counties, and the U.S. Conference of Mayors.[33] They challenged the Secretary's decision on the grounds that it violated the Enumeration Clause of the U.S. Constitution and that it violated the Administrative Procedures Act. The second group of plaintiffs were nongovernmental organizations that work with immigrant communities and communities of color.[34] They argued that the Secretary's decision also violated the Constitution's guarantee of equal protection, running afoul of the Fifth Amendment Due Process Clause.

Federal District Court Judge Jesse Furman granted the government's motion to dismiss the Enumeration Clause claim, but allowed the remaining claims to proceed to the discovery phase.[35] The materials

---

[30] Id at 2562–63.

[31] Id at 2563.

[32] Id.

[33] *New York v Department of Commerce*, 315 F Supp 3d 766, 773–74 (SDNY 2018).

[34] I use the term "communities of color" to signal predominantly nonwhite communities. I do not use the term "minority" because in many places, including in some of the jurisdictions involved in the litigation, non-Hispanic whites are a numerical minority. The plaintiffs in the litigation used the term "communities of color," and it appears in the opinions and orders of the district court. See, for example, *New York v Dep't of Commerce*, 315 F Supp 3d at 807. In the litigation, the plaintiffs specifically mentioned Latinos, Asian-Americans, and Arab-Americans but also included in the list of harmed groups other "immigrant communities of color." Id at 806.

[35] Id.

disclosed by the government during discovery demonstrated that Secretary Ross actually began to consider the addition of the citizenship question in early 2017 and then prodded the Department of Justice to request the addition of the citizenship question for purposes of VRA enforcement.[36] The request for data did not originate with the Justice Department, though the department obliged Secretary Ross and made the request that he had been seeking.

In light of this evidence confirming that the Secretary's origin story concerning the census question was false, the plaintiffs successfully petitioned Judge Furman to expand discovery beyond the administrative record. He granted their request for depositions of certain key Commerce and Justice Department officials.[37] The government appealed this decision and the Supreme Court stayed Judge Furman's order authorizing the deposition of Secretary Ross,[38] though the Court did permit the discovery of other extra-record evidence.[39] After an eight-day bench trial in November 2018, the District Court concluded that the plaintiffs had established that the Secretary's action was arbitrary and capricious in violation of the APA, that it also violated the APA because it was based on a pretextual rationale, and that it violated certain provisions of the Census Act.[40] The District Court denied the equal protection claim.[41]

The Supreme Court granted the government's petition to review the District Court's decision directly, bypassing the court of appeals, "because the case involved an issue of imperative public importance, and the census questionnaire needed to be finalized for printing by the end of June 2019."[42] The Court also requested that the parties address the question of whether the Enumeration Clause provided an alternative basis to affirm the lower court's decision.[43]

---

[36] *Dep't of Commerce v New York*, 139 S Ct at 2564 (2019).

[37] Id.

[38] *New York v Dep't of Commerce*, 351 F Supp 3d 502, 671 (2019).

[39] *Dep't of Commerce v New York*, 139 S Ct at 2564.

[40] Id; see also *New York v Dep't of Commerce*, 351 F Supp 3d at 635–64.

[41] *New York v Dep't of Commerce*, 351 F Supp 3d at 670–71. The reasoning behind the denial of this claim and the implications of the resolution of the plaintiffs' equal protection claim are discussed in Part II.

[42] *Dep't of Commerce v New York*, 139 S Ct at 2564.

[43] *Dep't of Commerce v New York*, 139 S Ct at 16 (2019).

On June 27, 2019, the Supreme Court issued its opinion in the case. Chief Justice Roberts summarized the background facts for a unanimous court in Part I of the opinion, including a discussion of the discovery process in the District Court and of the Supreme Court's decision to consider evidence beyond the scope of the submitted administrative record in reaching its factual and legal conclusions.[44] The Justices also unanimously joined Part II of Chief Justice Roberts's opinion concluding that the Court possessed jurisdiction and that "at least some of the respondents" had Article III standing to bring the case.[45]

But that is where the agreement ended. The Court's four other conservative Justices—Justice Thomas, Justice Alito, Justice Gorsuch, and Justice Kavanaugh—joined Part III of the Chief Justice's opinion, holding that the Enumeration Clause had not been violated, citing permissive past precedent that rejected "challenges to the conduct of the census" based upon the Enumeration Clause where the Secretary's decisions bore a "reasonable relationship to the accomplishment of an actual enumeration."[46] The five conservative Justices concluded that the clause "permits Congress, and by extension the Secretary, to inquire about citizenship on the census questionnaire."[47] The Court's four liberals—Justice Breyer, Justice Ginsberg, Justice Sotomayor, and Justice Kagan—declined to join that conclusion. Chief Justice Roberts was also joined by all but Justice Gorsuch and Justice Alito in Part IV.A. of the opinion, concluding that the Secretary's decision was reviewable under the Administrative Procedures Act.[48] Justice Alito's dissent maps out his extensive objection to the Court's review of what he views as a legitimate policy decision by the Secretary.[49]

Only the four conservative Justices joined with Chief Justice Roberts to conclude that the Secretary had not abused his discretion in violation of the APA.[50] The conservative majority found that the evidence before the Secretary could be read to suggest that each of

---

[44] *Dep't of Commerce v New York*, 139 S Ct at 2574.
[45] Id at 2565–66.
[46] Id at 2566.
[47] Id.
[48] Id at 2567–69.
[49] Id at 2597 (Alito, J, dissenting).
[50] Id at 2569–71.

the available alternatives for increasing access to citizenship data for purposes of VRA enforcement "entailed tradeoffs between accuracy and completeness."[51] The District Court judge had seen no such tradeoffs, and illustrated that the addition of the citizenship question would *always* generate worse results in terms of accuracy and completeness as compared to options that did not rely on such a question.[52] Justice Breyer's dissenting opinion reached the same conclusion.[53] He noted that the evidence before the Secretary conclusively and indisputably established that the addition of the citizenship question would suppress the response rates of immigrants and "Hispanics,"[54] and that all reasoning to the contrary was refuted by the record evidence.[55] The same was true of the negative impact of the addition of a citizenship question on census accuracy.[56]

The same alignment of Justices recurred in the next subsection of the opinion, concluding that the Secretary had not violated the Census Act. In the majority's view, Secretary Ross had not run afoul of the act's requirement that the Secretary acquire data, where possible, from other agencies and government entities rather than through direct inquiries[57] because he had concluded that direct inquiries would yield better data,[58] as noted in the analysis concluding that his actions were not "arbitrary and capricious" within the meaning of the APA. The dissenters disagreed, for the same reasons that they disagreed with the majority's arbitrary-and-capricious analysis. The conservative Justices also concluded that Secretary Ross had not violated the Census Act's requirements governing the Secretary's obligations to report the content of the upcoming decennial census to Congress.[59]

---

[51] Id at 2569.

[52] *New York v Dep't of Commerce*, 351 F Supp 3d at 649–51.

[53] *Dep't of Commerce v New York*, 139 S Ct at 2587–89 (2019) (Breyer, J, concurring in part and dissenting in part).

[54] Id at 2587.

[55] Id at 2589–90.

[56] Id at 2590–92.

[57] 13 USC § 6(c).

[58] *Dep't of Commerce v New York*, 139 S Ct at 2571–72.

[59] The statute provides in relevant part:

> With respect to each decennial ... census conducted under subsection (a) ... of this section, the Secretary shall submit to the committees of Congress having legislative jurisdiction over the census—

But just when it appeared as if the plaintiffs' lawsuits were going nowhere, Chief Justice Roberts reprised his pivotal role in *National Federation of Independent Business v Sebelius*,[60] joining the Court's four liberal Justices to reach a result at odds with the one desired by his conservative colleagues. Part V of the *Department of Commerce v New York* opinion contained this unexpected twist. Chief Justice Roberts reasons that:

> Altogether, the evidence tells a story that does not match the explanation the Secretary gave for his decision. In the Secretary's telling, Commerce was simply acting on a routine data request from another agency. Yet the materials before us indicate that Commerce went to great lengths to elicit the request from DOJ (or any other willing agency). And unlike a typical case in which an agency may have both stated and unstated reasons for a decision, here the VRA enforcement rationale—the sole stated reason— seems to have been contrived. We are presented, in other words, with an explanation for agency action that is incongruent with what the record reveals about the agency's priorities and decisionmaking process. It is rare to review a record as extensive as the one before us when evaluating informal agency action—and it should be. But having done so for the sufficient reasons we have explained, we cannot ignore the disconnect between

---

(1) not later than 3 years before the appropriate census date, a report containing the Secretary's determination of the subjects proposed to be included, and the types of information to be compiled, in such census;

(2) not later than 2 years before the appropriate census date, a report containing the Secretary's determination of the questions proposed to be included in such census; and

(3) after submission of a report under paragraph (1) or (2) of this subsection and before the appropriate census date, if the Secretary finds new circumstances exist which necessitate that the subjects, types of information, or questions contained in reports so submitted be modified, a report containing the Secretary's determination of the subjects, types of information, or questions as proposed to be modified.

13 USC § 141(f).

The five conservatives allowed that Secretary Ross's initial March 2017 report to Congress did not indicate that a citizenship question would appear on the census. But, they noted that "[t]he Secretary's March 2018 report," which was sent later and in compliance with other statutory provisions, did satisfy 13 USC § 141(f)(3). *Dep't of Commerce v New York*, 139 S Ct at 2572. "By informing Congress that he proposed to include a citizenship question," Chief Justice Roberts wrote, "the Secretary necessarily also informed Congress that he proposed to modify the original list of subjects that he submitted in the March 2017 report." Id.

[60] 567 US 519 (2012). Chief Justice Roberts sided with the other conservatives in finding that the Affordable Care Act's provision conditioning states' receipt of federal Medicaid dollars on their expansion of Medicaid violated the Tenth Amendment of the Constitution and that the mandate that residents purchase insurance coverage (the "individual mandate") exceeded Congress's Commerce Clause powers. But he joined the more liberal Justices to uphold the individual mandate as a constitutional exercise of Congress's power to tax and spend. Id at 558–74.

the decision made and the explanation given. Our review is deferential, but we are "not required to exhibit a naiveté from which ordinary citizens are free." United States v. Stanchich, 550 F.2d 1294, 1300 (CA2 1977) (Friendly, J.).[61]

So while Chief Justice Roberts concluded that the Secretary's decision to include a citizenship question was not "arbitrary and capricious" in light of the evidence before him, he also found that the Secretary's decision was not based on a valid reason, and that this was an independent violation of the APA. Chief Justice Roberts therefore affirmed the District Court's remand to the agency, concluding, "[w]e do not hold that the agency decision here was substantively invalid. But agencies must pursue their goals reasonably. Reasoned decision-making under the Administrative Procedure Act calls for an explanation for agency action. What was provided here was more of a distraction."[62] The Chief Justice, however, never explained or even acknowledged from what the Secretary might have been trying to distract the Court.

II. See No Evil

Two years ago, the Supreme Court decided *Trump v Hawaii*, affirming the constitutionality of President Trump's ban on entry for noncitizens seeking admission from six predominantly Muslim countries and two other countries added to the list on the third iteration of the ban.[63] In addition to statutory claims, the plaintiffs in that case also raised an Establishment Clause claim that was premised on the theory that the ban amounted to unconstitutional discrimination against Muslims on the basis of their religion.[64] Typically, a claim alleging a Free Exercise Clause deprivation would cause the Court to invoke strict scrutiny. As Justice Gorsuch explained in a case decided within days of *Trump v Hawaii*: "[W]hen the government fails to act neutrally toward the free exercise of religion, it tends to run into trouble. Then the government can prevail only if it satisfies strict scrutiny, showing that its restrictions on religion both serve a compelling interest and are narrowly tailored."[65] As with equal protection

---

[61] *Dep't of Commerce v New York*, 139 S Ct at 2575.

[62] Id at 2576.

[63] *Trump v Hawaii*, 138 S Ct at 2423.

[64] Id at 2415–16.

[65] *Masterpiece Cakeshop Ltd. v Colo. Civil Rights Comm'n*, 138 S Ct 1719, 1734 (2018) (Gorsuch, J, concurring) (citing *Church of Lukumi Babalu Aye, Inc. v Hialeah*, 508 US 520, 546 (1993)).

challenges based on claims of racial discrimination, evidence relevant to the assessment of governmental neutrality in religious discrimination claims includes "the historical background of the decision under challenge, the specific series of events leading to the enactment or official policy in question, and the legislative or administrative history, including contemporaneous statements made by members of the decisionmaking body."[66] Where, as in the Muslim Exclusion Case, there is massive evidence of discriminatory intent and a clear discriminatory impact, the Court generally applies strict scrutiny to the policy, even if it is facially neutral.[67]

But that did not happen in *Trump v Hawaii*. The Court applied only rational basis review to the ban, asking whether the ban was "plausibly related" to the government's stated objectives.[68] The Court justified this deferential review by referencing the national security concerns implicated by immigration admissions decisions.[69] But the Court's application of rational basis review was distinctly troubling in *Trump v Hawaii*. Unlike in prior cases, in its application of "rational basis review" here, the Court actually acknowledged and then proceeded to treat as irrelevant ample and express evidence of discriminatory intent.[70] The Court also willed away the law's discriminatory effects.[71]

---

[66] *Masterpiece Cakeshop*, 138 S Ct at 1722 (citing *Church of Lukumi Babalu Aye*, 508 US at 540 (1993)). The court relies on similar factors in race-based equal protection claims. See, for example, *Village of Arlington Heights v Metropolitan Housing Development Corp.*, 429 US 252, 268 (1977) ("The historical background of the decision is one evidentiary source, particularly if it reveals a series of official actions taken for invidious purposes.... The specific sequence of events leading up to the challenged decision also may shed some light on the decisionmaker's purposes.... Departures from the normal procedural sequence also might afford evidence that improper purposes are playing a role. Substantive departures too may be relevant, particularly if the factors usually considered important by the decisionmaker strongly favor a decision contrary to the one reached").

[67] See, for example, *Hunter v Underwood*, 471 US 222 (1985) (striking down Alabama's criminal disenfranchisement provision where the evidence demonstrated that the law would disproportionately harm African American voters and that this was the intent of the legislature).

[68] *Trump v Hawaii*, 138 S Ct at 2420.

[69] Id at 2423.

[70] Adam Cox, Ryan Goodman, and Cristina Rodríguez, *The Radical Supreme Court Travel Ban Opinion—But Why It Might Not Apply to Other Immigrants' Rights Cases*, Just Security (June 27, 2018), available at https://www.justsecurity.org/58510/radical-supreme-court-travel-ban-opinion-but-apply-immigrants-rights-cases/ (noting that the Court "admits that the policy could very well be based on unconstitutional grounds, but concludes that this fact is irrelevant so long as a separate and additional non-illicit reason for the policy is available.").

[71] It was clear from the outset that the Muslim ban would disproportionately impact Muslims, given the demographics of the profiled countries. And while Chief Justice Roberts's majority opinion banked on the waiver system to alleviate any unequal effects, nothing of the sort has happened. The effects of the policy are clear. For people born in Iran, only 537 immigrant visas were issued in 2018 for the twelve months after the travel ban went into

As Jayashri Srikantiah and Shirin Sinnar have noted, "the Court's full-throated invocation of deference—and its citation to classic cases upholding discriminatory immigration policies—does not bode well for equal protection claims" in immigration cases.[72] Indeed, in immigration law, there is now a straight line from the Chinese Exclusion Case[73] (decided in the era of *Plessy v Ferguson*'s embrace of "separate but equal"[74]) to the Muslim Exclusion Case. The line passes straight through the era of the civil rights revolution without evidence that any disruptive force has been exerted upon it.

The problems of an equal protection doctrine that does not protect is not limited to the immigration sphere. Outside of the immigration context, equal protection claims challenging existing racial hierarchy also fare poorly.[75] The Supreme Court has developed an equal protection analysis that applies strict scrutiny to government actions that

---

effect compared to 6,643 visas issued in the previous year—a 92% decrease in number of visas issued. Somalia experienced an 86% decrease in number of immigrant visas issued during the twelve months after the travel ban went into effect. Yemen's visas fell by 83%. Libya and Syria had the smallest change among the Muslim countries in the ban, decreasing by 80% and 77%, respectively. The number of visas issued to the two other countries included in the ban—Venezuela and North Korea—did not decline. In fact, North Korea experienced a 40% increase in visas granted. Vahid Niayesh, *Statistics Show Trump's Travel Ban Was Always a Muslim Ban*, Quartz (Oct 28, 2019), available at https://qz.com/1736809/statistics-show-that-trumps-travel-ban-was-always-a-muslim-ban/.

[72] Srikantiah and Sinnar, 71 Stan L Rev at 204 (cited in note 12); see also Aziz Huq, *The Future of Constitutional Discrimination Law After Hawai'i v Trump*, Take Care (June 26, 2018), available at https://takecareblog.com/blog/the-future-of-constitutional-discrimination-law-after-hawai-i-v-trump ("So long as the government asserts some kind of public security justification when it wishes to coerce or confine, a litigant alleging bias must lose.").

[73] *Chae Chan Ping v United States*, 130 US 581, 606 (1889) ("It matters not in what form ... aggression and encroachment come, whether from the foreign nation acting in its national character, or from vast hordes of its people crowding in upon us. If ... the government of the United States, through its legislative department, considers the presence of foreigners of a different race in this country, who will not assimilate with us, to be dangerous to its peace and security, their exclusion is not to be stayed because at the time there are no actual hostilities with the nation of which the foreigners are subjects. . . .").

[74] *Plessy v Ferguson*, 163 US 537, 544 (1896) ("Laws permitting, and even requiring, their separation in places where they are liable to be brought into contact do not necessarily imply the inferiority of either race to the other, and have been generally, if not universally, recognized as within the competency of the state legislatures in the exercise of their police power.").

[75] Kimberlé W. Crenshaw, *Demarginalizing the Intersection of Race and Sex: A Black Feminist Critique of Antidiscrimination Doctrine, Feminist Theory and Antiracist Politics*, U Chi L Forum 139, 149–50 (1989); Ian Haney-López, *Intentional Blindness*, 87 NYU L Rev 1779, 1784–88 (2012); Russell K. Robinson, *Unequal Protection*, 68 Stan L Rev 151, 172–73 (2016); Reva B. Siegel, *Why Equal Protection No Longer Protects: The Evolving Forms of Status-Enforcing State Action*, 49 Stan L Rev 1111, 1139–46 (1997).

are either expressly race-based,[76] or that evince both discriminatory impact and discriminatory intent.[77] In an era in which facially discriminatory laws are rare, the result is a jurisprudence that reflects robust judicial skepticism toward efforts to upend the existing racial hierarchy and an apparent judicial sympathy for white plaintiffs seeking the maintenance of that hierarchy.[78] In race-discrimination claims, the Court treats existing racial hierarchy and inequality as a neutral baseline. Rather than finding equal protection violations when governmental actions exacerbate or entrench those inequalities, for the past three decades the Court has focused the brunt of its judicial power on policies that expressly attempt to overcome past racial injustice.[79]

Like *Trump v Hawaii*, the case of *Department of Commerce v New York* again raised the question of the extent to which the Court was willing to ignore evidence of discriminatory purpose in order to allow the Trump administration to pursue discriminatory policies. As in *Trump v Hawaii*, the administration argued that it was acting lawfully, pursuant to a broad delegation of discretionary authority by Congress. But this time, the question arises in a context in which the government invoked no immigration or national security justifications. In this purely domestic, nonsecurity context, the Court did not invoke the deferential standard of review that it relied upon in *Hawaii*, but even as it was nominally applying a more stringent standard of

---

[76] See, for example, *Fisher v University of Texas at Austin*, 136 S Ct 2198 (2013).

[77] *Washington v Davis*, 426 US 229, 239 (1976) ("[O]ur cases have not embraced the proposition that a law ... without regard to whether it reflects a racially discriminatory purpose, is unconstitutional...."); see also Richard H. Fallon, Jr., *Implementing the Constitution* 90 (Harvard, 2001) (the Court has "expressly rejected arguments in favor of effects and balancing tests and made discriminatory purpose the touchstone of equal protection inquiries.").

[78] See, for example, *Ricci v DeStefano*, 557 US 557 (2009) (finding that a city's decision not to certify the results of a job-placement exam that would generate a discriminatory racial hiring effect as against African American job applicants was discriminatory as against the predominantly white plaintiffs); see also Cheryl I. Harris and Kimberly West-Faulcon, *Reading Ricci: Whitening Discrimination, Racing Test Fairness*, 58 UCLA L Rev 73, 82 (2010) ("Over the long colorblind march of the past two decades, the Court has embraced the view ... that racially attentive actions or public policy are inherently suspect, no matter the motive. This doctrinal move has effectively constrained the operation of anti-discrimination law and remedies—indeed turning the remedies into racial injuries and further legitimizing a narrative in which whites are (or are at risk of being) repeatedly victimized because of their race.... [T]he underlying racial frame is that present-day discrimination is largely a problem confronting whites.").

[79] See, for example, *Parents Involved in Community Schools v Seattle School District No. 1*, 551 US 701 (2007) (invalidating school districts' voluntarily adopted racial integration plan); *Gratz v Bollinger*, 539 US 244 (2003) (striking down the University of Michigan's affirmative action program for considering race too explicitly and quantifiably in admissions decisions).

review, a norm of deference exerted strong pull on the Court's reasoning. Ultimately, the Court remained unwilling to take seriously the equal protection claims that weighed against the implementation of the Trump administration's racially discriminatory policies.

The plaintiffs' equal protection claim was strong. Their evidence established that the addition of the citizenship question would have a discriminatory impact. Among other things, their empirical studies demonstrated that adding a citizenship question to the census would have a significant dampening effect on the response rate of Latinos, which would in turn result in an undercounting of Latinos regardless of immigration status.[80] As Federal District Court Judge Jesse Furman ably reasoned, under every possible permutation studied by Secretary Ross, the addition of the citizenship question would have this racially discriminatory effect.[81] The record evidence left little room for doubt about the discriminatory effect of the addition of the citizenship question.

The harder point for the plaintiffs to prove was that the Secretary acted with discriminatory purpose. Proof of such purpose is also required to establish an equal protection violation.[82] In this case, Secretary Ross wanted to add a citizenship question to dampen the census response rates in immigrant communities—which would certainly mean reducing the count of Latino residents in the United States and artificially inflating the political power of "non-Hispanic White" voters as against Latinos, as well as Asians and Asian Americans, Arab Americans, and other immigrant communities. This amounted to a desire to harm Latino communities in the form of undercounting the federal benefits and electoral power that would flow to Latino residents and citizens. But despite this discriminatory intent, *proving* that intent to a Court bent on ignoring discrimination against nonwhite groups[83] was not possible.

---

[80] See, for example, Expert Report of Matthew A. Barreto, September 7, 2018, available at http://mattbarreto.com/papers/Declaration%20of%20Matthew%20A.%20Barreto%20-%20NY.pdf ("The survey data shows clear and statistically significant evidence that the citizenship status question will result in high rates of non-response in 2020, and that immigrant and Latino communities will be disproportionately undercounted and disadvantaged.").

[81] *New York v Dep't of Commerce*, 315 F Supp 3d at 649–51.

[82] *Washington v Davis*, 426 US 229, 239 (1976).

[83] Melissa Murray, *Inverting Animus: Masterpiece Cakeshop and the New Minority*, 2018 Supreme Court Review 257, 284–85 (2018) (summarizing the "inversion of animus" in race and

The plaintiffs in this case pointed to sufficient facts in support of their claim of discriminatory intent to survive a motion to dismiss. Judge Furman found that "'departures from the normal procedural sequence,' dictated the denial of the Defendants' motion to dismiss the equal protection claim at the earliest stages of the litigation."[84] Among other procedural irregularities, he cited the department's failure "to test the citizenship question," its decision to "ignor[e] the Census Bureau advisory committee's recommendations," the "oddities in the 'specific sequence of events leading up to the challenged decision,' such as Secretary Ross's shifting and inconsistent explanations of his motivation for reinstating the citizenship question; and the seemingly transparent pretext of the VRA-enforcement rationale...."[85]

But the plaintiffs ultimately were not able to offer sufficient evidence to convince Judge Furman to grant summary judgment on the equal protection claim. Although Judge Furman found enough evidence at trial to support the conclusion that Secretary Ross's stated rationale for the addition of the citizenship question was pretextual, the plaintiffs were unable to prove "that it was a pretext *for discrimination* prohibited by the Due Process Clause."[86] He noted that the plaintiffs had provided evidence of animus on the part of many of the President's staff and advisors, including Steve Bannon, Kris Kobach, and Jeff Sessions, but did not establish that these advisors communicated their discriminatory purpose to Secretary Ross "as would be necessary to impute their discriminatory purpose to him."[87] He concluded that they had also failed to substantiate a nexus between the President's documented statements reflecting racial animus and Secretary Ross's decision.[88]

The absence of evidence in this case was, of course, a result of earlier Supreme Court intervention. Judge Furman had authorized the deposition of Secretary Ross, who would have been able to speak to the question of what motivated his addition of the citizenship

---

gender discrimination claims and arguing that *Masterpiece Cakeshop* makes a similar move in First Amendment religious discrimination claims).

[84] *New York v U.S. Dep't of Commerce*, 351 F Supp 3d at 669 (2019) (citing *New York v Dep't of Commerce*, 315 F Supp 3d at 808–10).

[85] Id.

[86] Id at 669–70 (emphasis in original).

[87] Id.

[88] Id at 670.

question. But the Supreme Court stayed Judge Furman's order authorizing that deposition, making it impossible for the plaintiffs to gather evidence concerning his motives.[89] Judge Furman concluded that, without that testimony, there was no way to conclude that the decision to add the citizenship question to the census was tainted by impermissible motives to unfairly advantage "non-Hispanic white" voters.[90]

A series of revelations since the trial have more fully illuminated the Trump administration's racial motivation for adding the citizenship question. In fact, some of this information came to light shortly before the Supreme Court issued its opinion in the case. On May 30, 2019, mere weeks before the issuance of the Supreme Court opinion, litigants seeking to block the addition of the citizenship question to the census made a highly unusual discovery. They filed a motion in federal court highlighting evidence located on computer hard drives belonging to long-time Republican operative Thomas B. Hofeller—files that were turned over to them by Hofeller's estranged daughter after his death.[91] These files included a study by Hofeller demonstrating that the addition of the census question would work to the electoral advantage of "Republicans and non-Hispanic Whites."[92] Although the study contained no evidence that the addition of the question would improve the administration of the Voting Rights Act, Hofeller proposed this fabricated justification for the addition of the citizenship question.[93] This explained where Secretary Ross's strange invocation of VRA enforcement as a justification for the question had originated.

These late-breaking revelations were not formally considered by the Court. But they may well have had an impact on Chief Justice Roberts. As previously noted, he declined to find an equal protection violation. But he did side with the Court's liberals to find that the stated reason for adding the question—to improve enforcement of the Voting Rights Act—was not the actual reason for the change. Indeed, he wrote that a decision to the contrary would require "naiveté."[94]

---

[89] Id at 671; *In re Dep't of Commerce*, 139 S Ct 16, 17 (2018).

[90] *New York v U.S. Dep't of Commerce*, 351 F Supp 3d at 671.

[91] Wines, *Deceased G.O.P. Strategist's Hard Drives Reveal New Details* (cited in note 26).

[92] Id.

[93] Id.

[94] See discussion above at note 61 (citing *Dep't of Commerce v New York*, 139 S Ct at 2575).

At one level, that decision not to be naive appeared sound in light of the May revelations and even sounder given what is now known about this history of the proposed citizenship question. In continuing litigation,[95] the Department of Justice has released emails that it should have released in response to earlier discovery requests. These emails reveal that a high-level employee in the Commerce Department, Christa Jones, who had previously communicated at length with Hofeller about the actual effects and the possible (unrelated) justifications for the addition of the citizenship question, played a role in revising Commerce Department documents to add the VRA justification.[96] Mark Neuman, an advisor to Secretary Ross who has testified in litigation subsequent to the Supreme Court decision that he had no communication with Hofeller, actually sent a draft VRA enforcement justification of the question directly to Hofeller, asking that he "please make sure the language is correct."[97] In short, evidence that should have been produced in discovery during the Census 2020 litigation reveals that high-level officials in the Commerce Department sought to add the citizenship question in an effort to advantage Republicans and "non-Hispanic whites," knowing that it would increase the political power of those "non-Hispanic whites" at the expense of other racial groups. They orchestrated a charade with officials in the Department of Justice to attach a phony rationale to its scheme to secure unfair political advantages for white voters. They then failed to produce related evidence relevant to the plaintiffs' discovery requests—evidence that would have helped to establish the equal protection claim. In retrospect, avoiding naiveté seems like a good call.

At a deeper level, however, the Chief's opinion and track record in this litigation, like his opinion in *Trump v Hawaii*, is shot through

---

[95] Litigation continues in *New York v Dep't of Commerce*, Case No 18-CV-2921 (JMF), SDNY, on the question of, among other things, whether to impose sanctions on the government for misrepresentations in the discovery process.

[96] Michael Wines, *A Census Whodunit: Why Was the Citizenship Question Added?*, NY Times (Nov 30, 2019), available at https://www.nytimes.com/2019/11/30/us/census-citizenship-question-hofeller.html ("The disclosures ... indicate that a senior Census Bureau official and friend of [Republican political strategist, Thomas B.] Hofeller, Christa Jones, helped draft an explanation of that rationale, apparently for publication had the question been approved.").

[97] Hansi Lo Wong, *Email Trail on Citizenship Question Is Longer Than Trump Officials Said*, National Public Radio (Nov 27, 2019), available at https://www.npr.org/2019/11/27/782922571/email-trail-on-citizenship-question-is-longer-than-trump-officials-said (discussing Neuman's communications).

with dangerous racial naiveté. We can start where Judge Furman's opinion closed: with a missing link between the evidence that the President and his advisors are racists and the Secretary's actions in this particular case. No administration in recent history has been as clear and transparent about its intent to increase white political power at the expense of communities of color.[98] In light of this fact, the decision to treat Secretary Ross's decision-making process as presumptively normal and to decline to allow for an exploration of his motives in this case evinces profound naiveté.

This is particularly true in light of the pervasive evidence before the court of the discriminatory effect of the addition of the citizenship question. Yet nowhere in his opinion does Chief Justice Roberts acknowledge the record evidence that substantiates the plaintiffs' claim that the Secretary's decision would have a disparate impact on certain racial groups. Among other things, the District Court opinion made clear that the plaintiffs had proven that Secretary Ross's decision would decrease the response rates among Latinos and immigrants, and that the dampening effect would have an impact on the governmental resources allocated to Latino communities and on the relative strength of political representation of their communities in the House of Representatives. Chief Justice Roberts's majority opinion manages never to mention Hispanics or Latinos at all.[99]

Justice Breyer's dissenting opinion, on the other hand, does grapple with this established racialized harm of the citizenship question:

> The record demonstrates that the question would likely cause a disproportionate number of noncitizens and Hispanics to go uncounted in the upcoming census. That, in turn, would create a risk that some States would wrongfully lose a congressional representative and funding for a host of federal programs. And, the Secretary was told, the adverse consequences would fall most heavily on communities of color. The Secretary decided to ask the question anyway, citing a need for more accurate citizenship data. But the evidence indicated that asking the question would produce citizenship data that is *less* accurate, not more. And the reason the Secretary gave for needing better citizenship data in the first place—to help enforce the Voting Rights Act of 1965—was not convincing.

---

[98] For a discussion of the role of thinly coded racial appeals by politicians both in the lead-up to elections and during the course of their administrations, see, for example, Ian Haney López, *Dog Whistle Politics: How Coded Racial Appeals Have Reinvented Racism and Wrecked the Middle Class* (Oxford, 2015).

[99] For additional discussion on this point, see Part III.

In short, the Secretary's decision to add a citizenship question created a severe risk of harmful consequences, yet he did not adequately consider whether the question was necessary or whether it was an appropriate means of achieving his stated goal.[100]

As Justice Breyer's opinion makes plain, Secretary Ross planned to secure partisan electoral gains through the inclusion of a citizenship question that would result in the undercounting of immigrant communities—disproportionately Latinx communities—in favor of "whites." The Voting Rights Act was a transparently farcical justification for adding the question.[101] Yet Chief Justice Roberts made no finding of discriminatory intent, and sided with other Justices to block the plaintiffs from questioning the Secretary's motives notwithstanding the clear evidence all around them that this administration is frequently implementing policy changes such as these not merely in spite of but *because of* their discriminatory intent.

In these pages last year, Mark Tushnet, in describing the opinion in *Trump v Hawaii*, noted that in that case, "facial neutrality operates as an absolute screen to shield badly motivated actions from anything but the most minimal scrutiny."[102] Notwithstanding the fact that the 2020 Census Case is not a national security case, that same sort of deferential treatment characterized the Court's approach to the challenged administrative action in that litigation, too. Given what we know and continue to learn about this administration, it should be clear by now that this kind of deference can be deadly.[103]

---

[100] *Dep't of Commerce v New York*, 139 S Ct at 2584 (Breyer, J, dissenting).

[101] It has inspired a running gag on Twitter. See, for example, Leah Litman, Twitter post, Dec 13, 2019, 12:39 a.m., https://twitter.com/leahlitman (joking that the administration's failure to produce relevant discovery in the litigation occurred because it was too busy enforcing the Voting Rights Act).

[102] Tushnet, 2018 Supreme Court Review at 2 (cited in note 12).

[103] People are quite literally dying as a direct and immediate result of this administration's racist policies. See, for example, J. Wetson Phippen, *Trapped in Juárez: Life in the Migrant Limbo*, The Atlantic (Sept 16, 2019), available at https://www.theatlantic.com/international/archive/2019/09/us-mexico-mpp-ciudad-juarez/597796/ (noting that four migrants have been killed in Ciudad Juárez where they and other non-Mexican migrants have been required to wait to have their U.S. asylum claims heard, pursuant to Trump's ironically named "Migrant Protection Protocol" (MPP)); Chantal Da Silva, *Father Killed in Mexico While Waiting for Asylum Under Trump Policy Had Warned DHS His Family Did Not Feel Safe*, Newsweek (Dec 12, 2019), available at https://www.newsweek.com/el-salvadoran-father-killed-tijuana-mexico-while-waiting-asylum-1476999 (reporting the death of a migrant awaiting his asylum hearing in Tijuana, as required under MPP); Nicole Acevedo, *Why Are Migrant Children Dying in U.S. Custody?*, NBC News (May 29, 2019), available at https://www.nbcnews.com/news/latino/why-are-migrant-children-dying-u-s-custody-n1010316 (reporting that "[a]t least seven children are known to have died in immigration custody since last year, after almost a decade in which

One need not desire or seek to reify racial categories—products as they are of historical contingency and sociolegal construction[104]—to acknowledge the blunt fact that racism exists in the world. Yet Chief Justice Roberts writes his entire opinion as if he is living in a parallel universe in which political operatives are not trying to game the system to take advantage of racism and the political divides that racism creates.[105] He writes as if "the way to stop discrimination on the basis of race"[106] is simply to ignore all the ways that powerful majoritarian forces seek to use racial constructs to enhance white supremacy. But this see-no-evil approach not only fails to stop racial discrimination, it facilitates racial discrimination.

The Supreme Court is currently evaluating another case that raises similar claims regarding this administration's anti-Latino animus:

---

no child reportedly died while in the custody of U.S. Customs and Border Protection."); Katie Shepherd, *Doctors Protested Border Patrol to Offer Flu Vaccines to Detained Migrants. They Left in Handcuffs and Without Answers*, Wash Post (Dec 12, 2019), available at https://www.washingtonpost.com/nation/2019/12/12/doctors-protest-border-patrol-allow-flu-vaccines-detained-migrants/ (reporting on the arrest of doctors seeking, unsuccessfully, to be admitted to migrant detention facilities to provide flu vaccines to children and noting the "growing tensions under the Trump administration between federal immigration officials and medical experts who believe migrants are being denied lifesaving preventive medicine while held in federal detention centers."); Sarah Stillman, *When Deportation Is a Death Sentence*, New Yorker (Jan 8, 2018), available at https://www.newyorker.com/magazine/2018/01/15/when-deportation-is-a-death-sentence (reporting on at least sixty people killed after deportation, and noting that Trump immigration policies will exacerbate this problem); Mariel Padilla, *Body of Michigan Man Deported to Iraq Is Returned to the U.S.*, NY Times (Sept 1, 2019), available at https://www.nytimes.com/2019/08/31/us/jimmy-aldaoud-iraq-deport.html (reporting on the death of a forty-one-year-old Iraqi who was deported to Iraq after living for thirty years as a lawful resident in the United States and was found dead in a Baghdad apartment "after days of vomiting blood and begging to return to the United States.").

[104] See the discussion in note 27.

[105] On the role of race in election law and the difficulties that conjoined race and party affiliation poses for securing appropriate antidiscrimination outcomes in election law cases, see, for example, Richard L. Hasen, *Race or Party, Race as Party, or Party All the Time: Three Uneasy Approaches to Conjoined Polarization in Redistricting and Voting Cases*, 59 Wm & Mary L Rev 1837 (2018) (discussing the phenomenon of "conjoined polarization," in which race and party interest are heavily conjoined, and analyzing the difficulties this presents for legal doctrines attempting to prohibit unconstitutional racial gerrymandering); Franita Tolson, *Election Law "Federalism" and the Limits of the Anti-Discrimination Framework*, 59 Wm & Mary L Rev 2211 (2018) (analyzing the difficulties and limitations inherent in an approach focused on discriminatory intent).

[106] In *Parents Involved in Community Schools*, Chief Justice Roberts famously chided that "[t]he way to stop discrimination on the basis of race is to stop discriminating on the basis of race." 551 US at 748. This "mantra" has a long pedigree in Federalist Society circles. Justin Driver, *The Schoolhouse Gate: Public Education and the Battle for the American Mind* 297 (Knopf Doubleday, 2018). The truism does not offer a particularly useful analytical tool for actually eliminating impermissible governmental racism, though it is a fine way to make sure that laws are facially neutral, regardless of their actual effects on racial hierarchy.

Department of Homeland Sec. v U.C. Regents. The case involves the Trump administration's decision to rescind the Obama-era DACA program. DACA was announced in June 15, 2012, by then-Secretary of Homeland Security Janet Napolitano.[107] The program placed on hold governmental efforts to remove[108] qualifying young immigrants. To qualify, the recipient had to have been under age thirty-one on the date of the announcement; continuously present in the country since June 15, 2007; under age sixteen at the time they entered the United States; in school or possessing the equivalent of a high school degree or having an honorable military discharge; and free of convictions for felonies or significant misdemeanors.[109] Their discretionary designation as recipients of "deferred action" triggered the statutory and regulatory authorization of work permits[110] and driver's licenses.[111] Over 800,000 people received deferred action under DACA.[112]

On September 17, 2017, acting Secretary of Homeland Security Elaine Dukes issued a memorandum announcing the administration's decision to rescind DACA.[113] The decision was challenged on several grounds, including that it violated the equal protection requirement of the Fifth Amendment because it discriminates on the basis of race.[114] Several district courts enjoined the rescission on

---

[107] Memorandum from Janet Napolitano, Secretary of Homeland Security, for David V. Aguilar et al, *Exercising Prosecutorial Discretion with Respect to Individuals Who Came to the United States as Children* (June 15, 2012), available at http://www.dhs.gov/xlibrary/assets/s1-exercising-prosecutorial-discretion-individuals-who-came-to-us-as-children.pdf.

[108] Removal is a legal term in immigration law that encompasses both deportation, which applies to individuals present after some form of governmentally authorized admission, and exclusion, which applies to individuals who have never been formally admitted, including those who are physically present in the United States. DACA recipients fall into both categories.

[109] Napolitano, *Exercising Prosecutorial Discretion* (cited in note 107).

[110] 8 USC § 1324a(h)(3) (2018); 8 CFR § 274a.12(c)(14) (2014).

[111] REAL ID Act of 2005, PL No 109-13, div B, title 2, § 202, 119 Stat 231, 312–13 (2005).

[112] Gustavo López and Jens Manuel Krogstad, *Key Facts about Unauthorized Immigrants Enrolled in DACA*, Pew Research Center FactTank (Sept 25, 2017), available at https://www.pewresearch.org/fact-tank/2017/09/25/key-facts-about-unauthorized-immigrants-enrolled-in-daca/ ("Approximately 800,000 young unauthorized immigrants have received work permits and protection from deportation through the Deferred Action for Childhood Arrivals program, or DACA, since its creation five years ago. And nearly 690,000 of these immigrants are currently enrolled in the program, according to new data from U.S. Citizenship and Immigration Services.").

[113] Elaine C. Dukes, Acting Secretary of Homeland Security for James W. McCamment et al, *Memorandum on Rescission of Deferred Action for Childhood Arrivals (DACA)* (Sept 5, 2017), available at https://www.dhs.gov/news/2017/09/05/memorandum-rescission-daca.

[114] *Regents of the University of California v U.S. Department of Homeland Security*, 908 F3d 476, 492 (9th Cir 2019), cert granted sub nom. *Department of Homeland Security v Regents of*

statutory and constitutional grounds.[115] The Ninth Circuit affirmed a federal district court's conclusion that the plaintiffs' claim that the Trump administration had violated the equal protection requirements of the Due Process Clause was likely to succeed, justifying a preliminary injunction of the DACA rescission.[116] The Ninth Circuit noted that "the rescission of DACA disproportionately impacts Latinos and individuals of Mexican heritage, who account for 93% of DACA recipients."[117] Like the district court, they noted President Trump's pre-presidential and post-presidential statements evincing animus against Latinos as well as his role in the decision to end DACA.[118] They also concluded that the district court "properly considered 'the unusual history behind the rescission,'"—a "strange about-face, done at lightning speed, suggest[ing] that the normal care and consideration within the agency was bypassed."[119]

The Ninth Circuit distinguished *Trump v Hawaii*, taking the position that even though the DACA Case involves policy concerning the removal of immigrants, it is not a national security policy and therefore not subject to the same deferential review. It remains to be seen whether the Supreme Court, which has invoked national security and foreign affairs–based deference in many immigration cases

---

the University of California, 139 S Ct 2779 (2019) ("The complaints included claims that the rescission was arbitrary and capricious under the Administrative Procedure Act (APA); that it was a substantive rule requiring notice-and-comment rulemaking under the APA; that it violated the due process and equal protection rights protected by the U.S. Constitution; and that DHS was equitably estopped from using the information provided on DACA applications for enforcement purposes.").

[115] *Batalla Vidal v Nielsen*, Case No 1:16-cv-04756 (NGG) (JO) (EDNY, Feb 13, 2018) (granting motion for preliminary injunction requiring U.S. Citizenship and Immigration Services to accept DACA applications from people who have had DACA previously); *Regents of the Univ. of Calif. v Dep't of Homeland Sec.* (lead case), Case No 17-cv-05211 (ND Cal, Jan 9, 2018) (granting the preliminary injunction requiring the federal government to accept applications for renewal of DACA); *CASA de Maryland v Trump*, Case No 17-cv-02942-RWT (D Md, March 5, 2018) (granting summary judgment to the plaintiffs on their information-sharing estoppel claim, prohibiting the government from using or sharing information provided through the DACA application process for enforcement or deportation purposes); *NAACP v Trump*, Case No 17-cv-01907 (DDC, April 24, 2018) (granting summary judgment to the plaintiffs on grounds that the DACA termination was arbitrary and capricious, but staying for ninety days its order requiring the continued acceptance of first-time applicants in order to give the government time to issue a new memo or better explain why it ended DACA).

[116] *Regents of the Univ of California v U.S. Department of Homeland Security*, 908 F3d at 519.

[117] Id.

[118] Id.

[119] Id.

that appear only tenuously related, if at all, to genuine security and foreign affairs concerns and policies,[120] will accept this distinction. But even if they do, the level of scrutiny they applied toward the discrimination claim in the 2020 Census Case bodes ill for the plaintiffs' equal protection claim in the DACA Case. The evidence the DACA plaintiffs have presented is the same sort of evidence that the Court found insufficient in the 2020 Census Case—ample evidence of explicitly racist statements by the President and relevant advisors against Latinos and clear evidence of a discriminatory impact on Latinos. The certain and severe harms of DACA rescission, which will fall, in a massively disproportionate way, on members of the very same communities that would have been adversely affected by the citizenship question on the census, seem unlikely to convince this Court of the need to intervene against the Trump administration's continued devaluation and disenfranchisement of Latinos in the United States.

Ultimately, of course, the failure of the equal protection claim in the census litigation was not dispositive of the legality of the citizenship question. In their fight against the addition of the question, the plaintiffs ultimately prevailed on statutory claims based on the Administrative Procedures Act. The success of the DACA plaintiffs is also likely to stand or fall on similar statutory claims. The nature of the plaintiffs' victory in the census litigation therefore sheds light on how the Court might evaluate the DACA claims. More importantly, it illuminates both the possibilities and the significant limitations of such procedural claims as vehicles for vindicating the Constitution's guarantee of equal protection.

III. HEAR NO EVIL

There is something very strange about reading the Supreme Court's opinion in the 2020 Census Case. The majority opinion omits discussion of what for many observers was the heart of the matter, making it feel as though it were issued directly from *The Twilight Zone*. Were it not for Justice Breyer's dissenting opinion, a reader would not be able to tell that the crux of this case—the central reason that states and community organizations sued the Secretary—was a

---

[120] See, for example, *Arizona v U.S.*, 567 US 387, 395–96 (2012) (using a foreign-policy rationale to justify robust federal preemption in a case involving state policing practices and criminal law).

concern that the Secretary's actions were intended to and would actually have an adverse impact on the Latino community and other communities of color.

In evaluating the plaintiffs' claims that the Secretary's actions were "arbitrary and capricious" in violation of the APA, the only harm that Chief Justice Roberts alludes to as a possible result of the addition of the citizenship question is a "depressed" response rate.[121] Chief Justice Roberts does not specify that the decline in response rates would not be uniform across racial groups, let alone identify the particular communities that would be harmed by the change. Despite evidence (including in the administrative record, however narrowly construed) and clear findings by the District Court that the change in the census would have a disparate impact on Latino communities and other communities of color, and despite evidence and findings that Secretary Ross was fully aware of and considered this disparate impact in making his decision, Chief Justice Roberts eschews discussing the known racial disparities that the addition of the citizenship question would generate.

In determining whether the Secretary's decision was "arbitrary and capricious," Roberts briefly mentions that there is some evidence that the question might depress responses in "noncitizen households" before asserting that reasonable minds could differ on this point.[122] He notes Justice Breyer's conflicting assessment, but concludes that "[b]y second-guessing the Secretary's weighing of risks and benefits and penalizing him for departing from the Bureau's inferences and assumptions, Justice Breyer—like the District Court—substitutes his judgment for that of the agency."[123]

A more realistic assessment of the disagreement is that District Court Judge Furman, Justice Breyer, and the other dissenting Justices acknowledged the real harm involved—the harm actually assessed by the Secretary—namely, increasing the already problematic undercount of communities of color by further depressing Latino and immigrant response rates. Having named the actual problem, those judges found that under every permutation designed by the Commerce Department to improve the accuracy of the bureau's citizenship data, the

---

[121] *Dep't of Commerce v New York*, 139 S Ct at 2563 ("The Secretary 'carefully considered' the possibility that reinstating a citizenship question would depress the response rate.").

[122] Id at 2570–71.

[123] Id at 2571.

Secretary's choice worsened that harm. By naming a distinct harm—undercounting generally, or perhaps depressing count in undefined, deracinated "noncitizen households"—the Chief Justice avoids having to acknowledge this reality.

With his reference to "noncitizen households," one can only assume Roberts means households in which one or more noncitizens reside. But this is not a term of art and the term is never actually defined in the opinion. This lack of specificity may help explain why his broader analysis of the risks involved does not line up with that of the district court judge.

In reality, noncitizens live in mixed-status households and mixed-status communities.[124] They live with and alongside citizens—both naturalized former immigrants and those who are citizens by virtue of their bloodline or their birthplace. Noncitizen immigrants are an internally mixed bunch, too, segmented by additional legal modifiers: lawful permanent resident (LPR), temporary worker, student visa holder, Temporary Protected Status (TPS) designees,[125] DACA recipient, unauthorized immigrants, and many others. In 2017, there were 44.4 million people living in the United States who were not born with U.S. citizenship, and they account for almost 14% of the U.S. population.[126] Seventy-seven percent of those individuals have a legally recognized status,[127] either because they are now naturalized citizens (about 45%), because they are lawful permanent residents (about 27%), or because they have some form of temporary legal protection like TPS or DACA (about 5%).[128]

The heterogeneity of immigration statuses within households explains why a question about the individualized citizenship status of

---

[124] Jeffrey S. Passel and Paul Taylor, *Household Structure, Mixed Families*, in *Unauthorized Immigrants and Their U.S.-Born Children* (Aug 11, 2010), available at https://www.pewresearch.org/hispanic/2010/08/11/iii-household-structure-mixed-families/ ("According to a 2009 Pew Hispanic Center report (which was based on 2008 census data), 37% of all adult unauthorized immigrants were parents of children who are U.S. citizens.").

[125] 8 USC § 1254a (empowering the Secretary of the Department of Homeland Security to grant temporary residence and work authorization to foreign nationals who are unable to return to their country due to armed conflicts, natural disasters, or other widespread and disruptive conditions).

[126] Jynnah Radford, *Key Findings about U.S. Immigrants* (June 17, 2019), available at https://www.pewresearch.org/fact-tank/2019/06/17/key-findings-about-u-s-immigrants/.

[127] Id.

[128] Id. The last category has been shrinking over the last two years as a result of Trump administration policy.

every household member is likely to deter even citizens from answering a survey that potentially exposes themselves or their vulnerable family members to governmental scrutiny. And individuals who might be understood within a household as vulnerable certainly would not be limited to unauthorized migrants. Given this administration's routine attacks on legal immigration,[129] its considerable expansion of denaturalization efforts,[130] its skepticism of the birthright citizenship claims of Latinos born in the Rio Grande Valley of Texas,[131] and the like, the list of vulnerable individuals within a household extends far beyond unauthorized immigrants. It might reasonably be understood to include any noncitizen, as well as those whose citizenship might be called into question.

The deterrent effect of the citizenship question is distinctly racialized. Immigrants in the United States are a heterogenous bunch in terms of national origin and racial identity, but immigrants from Mexico and Central America account for about 33% of all immigrants. Immigrants from South and East Asia account for another 27%.[132] Europeans and Canadians make up 13% of immigrants, those from the Caribbean account for 10%, and sub-Saharan Africa accounts for 4%.[133] When policies negatively impact the complex kinds of "noncitizen households" just described, they have a disproportionately negative impact on Latino communities and, to a slightly lesser but growing extent, on Asian American communities,[134] including large numbers of citizens in those communities. The administration's relentless, negative focus on immigrants from Mexico and Central

---

[129] Ming Hsu Chen and Zachary New, *Silence and the Second Wall*, 28 S Cal Interdiscip L J 549, 558–67 (2019) (discussing mounting barriers to legal immigration imposed under President Trump).

[130] See, for example, Ronald Brownstein, *Trump Is Walling Off the GOP*, The Atlantic (Feb 7, 2019), available at https://www.theatlantic.com/politics/archive/2019/02/trumps-alienating-immigration-agenda/582265/ (noting that "Trump has used ... almost every administrative tool at his disposal to create more hurdles for legal immigrants.").

[131] Rachel E. Rosenbloom, *From the Outside Looking In: U.S. Passports in the Borderlands*, in *Citizenship in Question: Evidentiary Birthright and Statelessness*, in Benjamin N. Lawrance and Jacqueline Stevens, eds, *Citizenship in Question: Evidentiary Birthright and Statelessness* (Duke, 2017).

[132] Radford, *Key Findings* (cited in note 126).

[133] Id.

[134] Because the makeup of incoming migrants includes more Asian immigrants than immigrants from Mexico and Central and South America, the Pew Research Center estimates that by 2055, among new immigrant arrivals, "Asians will make up some 38% of all immigrants; Hispanics, 31%; whites, 20%; and blacks, 9%." Id.

America might also understandably increase the reticence of members of these groups, in particular, to disclose citizenship status to the federal government at this time.

Chief Justice Roberts never mentions the disparate racial impacts of the Secretary's proposal. Indeed, his only passing mention of "minority groups" comes in his discussion of the (invented) Department of Justice Voting Rights Act enforcement rationale for the question, which purportedly justified the addition of the question based on the need to collect data that would allow "federal courts [to] determine whether a minority group could constitute a majority in a particular district by looking to the citizen voting-age population of the group."[135] It is difficult to understand how Chief Justice Roberts could meaningfully assess Secretary Ross's evaluation of the risk of harm when he does not name the actual harm at all.

The plaintiffs in the 2020 Census Case, unlike those in *Trump v Hawaii*, nevertheless were able to vindicate their claim by establishing that the Secretary's justification for the addition of the citizenship question was pretextual. One might therefore assume that Chief Justice Roberts's unwillingness to call out racial discrimination against nonwhite plaintiffs is not particularly important. The basic legal effect of this decision—preventing the addition of the citizenship question to the 2020 census—was no different than the effect of a win on the equal protection claim would have been.

But this misses three important points. First, the resulting opinion leaves the door wide open for future inclusion of a citizenship question on the census, even if there is evidence of discriminatory impact and strong implications of discriminatory intent that could reasonably be investigated through the discovery process.[136]

Second and relatedly, in this particular case, the President was able to continue to threaten to include a question after the case was decided.[137] This threat had the effect of prolonging the period of

---

[135] *Dep't of Commerce v New York*, 139 S Ct at 2562.

[136] Id at 2576 ("We do not hold that the agency decision here was substantively invalid.").

[137] Indeed, for a couple of weeks after the decision, President Trump suggested that he was still trying to get the citizenship question on the census. Tara Bahrampour et al, *Trump Administration Scrambles to Save Citizenship Question on Census*, Wash Post (July 5, 2019), available at https://www.washingtonpost.com/politics/trump-administration-scrambles-to-save-citizenship-question-on-census/2019/07/04/238fe3fa-9e85-11e9-9ed4-c9089972ad5a_story.html ("Spurred on by President Trump, government lawyers scrambled Thursday to find a legal path to add a controversial citizenship question to the 2020 Census, despite their

uncertainty around the citizenship question. Immigrant legal service providers and others working with organizations serving immigrant communities expressed views, based on their interaction with community members, that the uncertainty around the census combined with the administration's harsh anti-immigrant rhetoric would likely chill responses to the census in their communities.[138]

Third, in failing to acknowledge the existence and nature of the substantive rights claims at stake, this opinion joins a long line of opinions that have increased the precariousness of some of the nation's most marginalized residents by guaranteeing only procedural fairness in lieu of meaningful substantive rights.[139] This third point has special significance because it also signposts the direction in which the Court could head in *Department of Homeland Security v U.C. Regents*, which the Court is poised to decide in 2020. This distressing possibility merits some elaboration.

Thirty years ago, Professor Hiroshi Motomura argued that "phantom constitutional norms" exerted a "gravitational pull" on statutory interpretation in immigration law.[140] Motomura noted that the Court

---

conclusions in recent days that no such avenue exists."). Until July 10, 2019, he was promising to issue an executive order to add the question—a course of action he abandoned not long thereafter. Dan Mangan and Tucker Higgens, *Trump Abandons Fight to Put Citizenship Question on Census, Says He Can Get Data from Existing Records*, CNBC (July 11, 2019), available at https://www.cnbc.com/2019/07/11/trump-abandons-fight-to-put-citizenship-question-on-census.html ("President Donald Trump on Thursday dropped a fight to put a citizenship question on the upcoming 2020 census—but ordered federal agencies to give the Commerce Department all records they have that are related to how many citizens and non-citizens live in the United States.").

[138] See, for example, Esther Yoon-Ji Kang, *Local Groups: "Damage Has Already Been Done" by Census Citizenship Question*, National Public Radio (July 4, 2019), available at https://www.npr.org/local/309/2019/07/04/738660741/local-groups-damage-has-already-been-done-by-census-citizenship-question ("Amid the back-and-forth reports on whether or not the citizenship question will be added to the 2020 census, local groups said Wednesday that the Trump administration's intended effect—to discourage the participation of immigrant groups—has already been achieved."); José A. Del Real, *When It Comes to the Census, the Damage Among Immigrants Is Already Done*, NY Times (June 27, 2019), available at https://www.nytimes.com/2019/06/27/us/supreme-court-citizenship-census-immigrants.html ("Maricela Rodriguez, who works in the California governor's office on civic engagement issues, said the state was already feeling the effects. 'Really, the damage in terms of creating fear around the census has been done,' she said. 'Whether the citizenship question is included or not included, there is already a lot of fear instilled in the immigrant community.'").

[139] For a more expansive exploration of this phenomenon in immigrant communities and beyond, see generally Jennifer M. Chacón, *Producing Liminal Legality*, 92 Denver L Rev 709 (2015) (exploring the vulnerabilities of liminal legal subjects and noting their imperfect overlap with formal citizenship categories).

[140] Hiroshi Motomura, *Immigration Law After a Century of Plenary Power: Phantom Constitutional Norms and Statutory Interpretation*, 100 Yale L Rev 545, 564 (1990).

expressly adhered to a notion that the political branches have plenary power in the realm of immigration law, but that nevertheless the Court occasionally found procedural deficiencies relative to immigration statutes sufficient to invalidate the laws and actions of those branches. He attributes this result to the fact that the courts are being influenced by rights-protective constitutional norms that shaped the jurisprudence beyond the immigration context.

One of the "phantom constitutional norms" that Motomura assessed was the norm against racial discrimination. In Motomura's view, the "background constitutional norm of racial equality"[141] exerted sufficient pull on the Court that in "contexts involving [noncitizens] the Court has adopted approaches that, despite variations among them, consistently conflict with the begrudging attitude toward [noncitizens] reflected in the plenary power doctrine."[142] Therefore, "even if constitutional doubts about an agency decision are insufficient to justify finding it unconstitutional, courts still express those doubts at a subconstitutional level through an 'arbitrary and capricious' or 'abuse of discretion' finding."[143]

Motomura reflected upon a number of cases involving the rights of noncitizens in which the Court substantively reviewed noncitizens' claims and sometimes even reached protective results invalidating executive branch actions against noncitizens, contradicting without ever disavowing the notion of that branch's "plenary" immigration power. The Court's approach allowed noncitizens to challenge discriminatory governmental actions, but not in a way that actually resulted in express acknowledgment of the noncitizens' right to equal

---

[141] Id at 564.

[142] Id at 565. Of course, the notion of a "plenary powers doctrine" is itself contested. See, for example, Gabriel J. Chin, *Is There a Plenary Power Doctrine?: A Tentative Apology and Prediction for Our Strange but Unexceptional Constitutional Immigration Law*, 14 Georgetown Immig L J 257 (2000) (arguing that these decisions track the same tolerance for invidious discrimination evident in domestic law); Kevin R. Johnson, *Race and Immigration Law and Enforcement: A Response to "Is There a Plenary Power Doctrine?,"* 14 Georgetown Immig L J 289 (2000) (arguing that there are important divergences between immigration law and other areas of law, particularly in the form of de facto discrimination in enforcement); Stephen H. Legomsky, *Immigration Exceptionalism: Commentary on "Is There a Plenary Power Doctrine?,"* 14 Georgetown Immig L J 307, 311 (2000) ("Professor Chin is on to something, but [ ] his conclusions should be expressed in a somewhat more qualified form. My reading of the evidence is that the pattern is mixed. Some of the worst plenary power cases can be explained by more generic contemporary norms, but many others reflect genuine immigration exceptionalism.").

[143] Motomura, 100 Yale L Rev at 583 (cited in note 140).

protection in the immigration context. As Motomura noted, "the Court has never held an immigration classification unconstitutional on the ground that it discriminates on the basis of race or national origin."[144]

Although Motomura observed that the force of phantom constitutional norms sometimes generated subconstitutional results favorable to noncitizens, he also lamented the fact that "subconstitutional decisions can be a problematic way to express a constitutional norm, because statutes and other subconstitutional texts provide judges with limited interpretive possibilities."[145] His concern was that judicial failure to forthrightly assess constitutional claims—and address constitutional errors in nineteenth-century foundations of contemporary immigration law—impaired reasoned discourse about the appropriate role of judicial review and the scope of individual constitutional protections in immigration cases.

The Court's recent decisions suggest the emergence of another concern that arises out of the Court's lack of forthright evaluation of constitutional claim, namely, that the Court's previous failures to constitutionalize rights protections, including antidiscrimination protections, for noncitizens in these earlier cases have made it possible for the Court to reverse course without constraint in cases like *Trump v Hawaii*.[146] But the 2020 Census Case suggests that something even more troubling may be happening: the phantom constitutional norms that limit judicial review and substantive rights in the immigration sphere arguably exert their own gravitational pull in cases outside the immigration sphere. Generally applicable equal protection norms have eroded in cases shaped by a constitutional norm that affirmatively and openly tolerates discrimination on the basis of race and

---

[144] Id at 593.

[145] Id at 600.

[146] It is worth noting that the equal protection norm that exerted gravitational pull in the cases Motomura analyzed in 1990 is itself greatly diminished. This trend was already in clear evidence when Motomura wrote *Phantom Constitutional Norms*. In light of what has transpired over the past two decades, his treatment of *Washington v Davis* as "underenforcement" of a constitutional antidiscrimination norm, rather than as an articulation of a general tolerance for pervasive discrimination against historically disadvantaged minorities as a background constitutional norm, seems overly optimistic. Because constitutional conceptions of equal protection have ebbed far from their high-water mark and now tend to favor status quo hierarchies over racial equality and integration, it would also be possible to explain what has happened in cases like *Trump v Hawaii* as responsive to the general contraction of equal protection within the Phantom Constitutional Norm framework.

religion in the immigration sphere.[147] This erosion has been exacerbated by Fourth Amendment doctrine that naturalizes race discrimination in immigration enforcement.[148]

As previously noted, Chief Justice Roberts's opinion in *Department of Commerce v New York* deliberately recasts the concerns of immigrant communities as the concerns of "noncitizen households." Framing the problem this way, he evades the pull of antidiscrimination norms that Motomura's theory suggests might otherwise prompt a more searching inquiry, if not an entirely different result, in much of his analysis of whether the Secretary's decision was arbitrary and capricious within the meaning of the APA. To evade this pull, Roberts strips immigrants from their community context and ignores the racial dimensions of the "noncitizen household."

But it is not just that the APA claims receive no thumb on the scale to account, in a sub rosa way, for the problem of racism. It is also that by treating this as a concern of "noncitizens," the Court evokes a very different phantom constitutional norm—one that favors highly deferential review in evaluating the discrimination claims of noncitizens.[149] While the Court does not expressly invoke rational basis review in evaluating the equal protection claim, the problematic treatment of not only that claim but also the APA "arbitrary and capricious" claim can be better understood with reference to phantom constitutional norms of immigration cases.

Chief Justice Roberts's opinion upholding the injunction of the addition of the citizenship question on the grounds that the administration's reasons were "pretextual" is certainly some sort of a

---

[147] In addition to cases like *Trump v Hawaii*, this tolerance for discrimination is evident in *Reno v American-Arab Anti-Discrimination Committee*, 525 US 471 (1999), in which the Court vacated on jurisdictional grounds an injunction against the selective prosecution of several members of the Popular Front for the Liberation of Palestine (PFLP). The Court's decision in this case effectively permits the government to target racialized minority groups or groups with disfavored political opinions for deportation without the threat of Court review.

[148] Jennifer M. Chacón and Susan Bibler Coutin, *Racialization through Enforcement*, in Mary Bosworth, Alpa Parmar, and Yolanda Vázquez, eds, *Race, Criminal Justice, and Migration Control: Enforcing the Boundaries of Belonging* 161–63 (Oxford, 2018); see also Johnson, 14 Georgetown Immig L J (cited in note 142).

[149] See, for example, *Trump v Hawaii*, 138 S Ct 2392 (2018) (applying a watered down rational basis review to the religious discrimination claims of noncitizens); *Matthews v Diaz*, 426 US 67 (1976) (applying rational basis review to a federal welfare law that discriminated against lawful permanent residents). In *Plyler v Doe*, 457 US 202 (1982), the Court struck down a Texas statute that discriminated against unauthorized immigrant children for purposes of public education access, but established that laws discriminating against unauthorized immigrants receive only rational basis review.

warning to the Trump administration. But a look at the case as a whole reveals this warning to be quite limited. His decision, particularly when read alongside *Trump v Hawaii*, merely communicates to the Trump administration the need to provide the Court with a plausible alternative justification to racism when enacting discriminatory policies. The concerns behind Chief Justice Roberts's pivot away from approving Secretary Ross's decision in the Census 2020 Case are purely institutional. His decision to refrain from naive acceptance of the administration's stated justifications evinces a desire that the Court not be treated as a rubber stamp for sloppy decision making by the executive branch. Some legitimating work is required to cover discriminatory purpose. But his opinion in the Census 2020 Case is absolutely not articulating any sort of commitment to protecting historically disfavored groups from the actual effects of the Trump administration's harmful racial discrimination.

This understanding of the Court's analytical approach in the Census 2020 Case has implications for the DACA Case, *Department of Homeland Security v U.C. Regents*. The DACA Case was argued before the Supreme Court on November 12, 2019. It is quite easy to predict that the Court's treatment of the equal protection claim in the 2020 Census Case and of the religious discrimination claim in *Hawaii* auger the unwarranted failure of the plaintiffs' solid equal protection claim in the DACA Case, too.[150]

The harder question is what the Court will make of the procedural claims. As in the Census 2020 litigation, the DACA plaintiffs are also arguing that the Department of Homeland Security's decision to rescind DACA was "arbitrary and capricious" in violation of the APA. Applying Motomura's model concerning the application of phantom constitutional norms while acknowledging the Court's hostility to the equal protection claims of noncitizens, the best-case scenario for the plaintiffs would see the Court affirming the injunction of the administration's DACA rescission using the insufficiency of the government's reasons as an indirect means of vindicating equal protection concerns. Yet even in the plaintiffs' best-case scenario, the turn to administrative procedural fairness rather than equal protection would give rise to only the narrowest legal protection. Under the terms of the plaintiffs' own arguments, the administration could still

---

[150] I elaborated further on this point in Part II.

rescind DACA later if it offered any policy reason to do so.[151] And even if the program were not rescinded because the administration is unwilling to take the blame for it, DACA recipients' ability to continue to renew their status and to avoid removal would turn on continued administrative grace from an administration that has been notoriously short on grace when it comes to immigrants.[152]

The plaintiffs' unresolved legal precarity is only one aspect of the larger loss that arises out of reliance on statutorily-based procedural claims to vindicate what should rightly be claims of right for long-term residents subject to the jurisdiction of the United States. The turn to these statutory procedure claims also obviates the need for the Court to acknowledge the tremendous personal costs at stake. As Rachel Moran concludes in her own assessment of the *U.C. Regents* case:

---

[151] At oral argument, in an effort to avoid the conclusion that a rescission based on a flawed legal analysis would violate the APA, Solicitor General Francisco argued that the administration had advanced not only legal but also policy justifications for the DACA rescission. *Dep't of Homeland Sec. v U.C. Regents*, Oral Argument Transcript 6 (Nov 12, 2019), available at https://www.supremecourt.gov/oral_arguments/argument_transcripts/2019/18-587_886a.pdf ("[W]e've put forward both legal and policy reasons for the rescission, so this case is on all fours with [Heckler v] Chaney [470 US 821 (1985)], where the FDA likewise put forth legal and policy reasons").

This was not the case. The Trump administration only provided the reason of the program's unlawfulness when it rescinded the program. For evidence of the existence of policy reasons, Solicitor General Noel Francisco relied on a letter by then-acting Department of Homeland Security Secretary Kirsten Nielson. Her letter was not part of the original rescission decision, but was submitted to a Washington D.C. district court judge during litigation, after the judge gave the administration ninety days to provide additional reasons for the rescission. The administration, apparently hoping to continue to be able to blame the courts for the DACA rescission, put forth only one additional ground for rescission in the letter—that DACA would be a magnate for future migration. But there were no supporting administrative materials to support the new policy rationale, and the letter itself indicated that the department was relying on the reasoning behind the initial decision. Without any supporting evidence, the new policy rationale doesn't make any sense because it is not intuitively evident why a program that only applies to people who were already in the United States in 2007 will somehow draw in future migrants.

[152] See the discussion in note 103 regarding the administration's deadly policy changes and the discussion accompanying notes 129–31 regarding the Trump administration's increasing restrictions on immigration. Indeed, the Department of Homeland Security has already started targeting DACA recipients for removal. Bob Ortega, *ICE Reopening Long-Closed Deportation Cases against Dreamers*, CNN (Dec 21, 2019), available at https://www.cnn.com/2019/12/21/us/ice-reopening-dreamer-deportation-cases-invs/index.html. President Trump has also opened up erroneous public attacks against the character of DACA recipients generally. Adam Liptak, *Supreme Court Appears Ready to Let Trump End DACA Program*, NY Times (Nov 15, 2019), available at https://www.nytimes.com/2019/11/12/us/supreme-court-dreamers.html ("'Many of the people in DACA, no longer very young, are far from 'angels,' [President Trump] wrote on Twitter. 'Some are very tough, hardened criminals.'").

Decades ago, *Plyler [v Doe]* embraced an undocumented student's right to become a capable adult as a defining expression of our shared democratic values. Now, the Dreamers ask only that courts hold agencies accountable for the expectations that they have created. With *Plyler* a jurisprudential anomaly, the promise of personhood can be heard not in a constitutional roar but in a procedural whisper.[153]

Chief Justice Roberts has a way to avoid taking the fall for the DACA rescission by following the same path he took in the Census 2020 litigation. It is a path that neither bestows substantive constitutional rights on immigrants nor requires him to acknowledge the racism that is driving the administration.[154] He may take that path and generate a win for the plaintiffs; he may not. But the 2020 Census Case clearly illustrates how that proceduralist approach leaves governmental actors unaccountable for their expressed racism, and, in turn, leaves citizens and residents vulnerable to the harsh effects of this racism, just as they were before their legal victory.

IV. Speak No Evil: Conclusions

Chief Justice Roberts has argued that "[t]he way to stop discrimination on the basis of race is to stop discriminating on the basis of race."[155] But what happens when a presidential administration is determined to discriminate on the basis of race—either because of the personal racist inclinations of the President and other members of his staff or because these men desire the political support of constituents whose loyalty is most easily won by appealing to white racial resentment? If a majority of Justices on the Court are unwilling to speak forthrightly about the racial animus driving this administration's policies, there is no reason to assume that administration will stop discriminating on the basis of race. The Chief Justice's concerns over institutional legitimacy may occasionally compel him to impede such policies on the narrowest of grounds, but his track record suggests that

---

[153] Rachel Moran, *Dreamers Interrupted: The Case of the Rescission of the Program of Deferred Action for Childhood Arrivals*, 53 UC Davis L Rev (forthcoming 2020).

[154] Some might argue that it is really a rule-of-law concern about executive power, and not racist appeals to white nationalist interests, that is driving the Trump administration. This might be plausible if it were not in tension with the expansive vision of executive power over immigration that the administration maintains it has in many other immigration matters it has litigated, including *Trump v Hawaii* and, more recently, in litigation pertaining to the funding and construction of a wall on the southern border.

[155] *Parents Involved in Community Schools*, 551 US at 748.

this means the administration needs only to devise better cover stories for racist policies.

The reality is that, as a political matter, President Trump did not really need any of his racially targeted policies to go into effect. By enacting an ill-designed ban on travelers from a handful of countries, he was able to claim credit for attempting a "Muslim ban." By threatening a citizenship question and a DACA rescission, he was able to demonstrate his toughness toward "Mexicans" and toward all undocumented immigrants and the communities of which they are a part. Even without accompanying action, his rhetorical support for these policies guaranteed him the loyalty of those constituents who appreciate overt expressions of bigotry. All President Trump ever really needed was to be able to say that he hoped and tried to implement these blatantly discriminatory policies. Yet the Court has ceded him a power to *implement* these policies unprecedented in the post–civil rights era. It has either greenlighted the policies or, as in the 2020 Census Case, provided a road map for how to implement them legally in the near future. This is a tragic judicial failure.

MICAH SCHWARTZMAN
AND NELSON TEBBE

ESTABLISHMENT CLAUSE APPEASEMENT

I. Introduction

Constitutional politics, like ordinary politics, has become increasingly polarized. This climate of conflict affects the Supreme Court along with the other branches of government. And with recent changes in its composition, the Court is not only more divided but also more clearly controlled by a majority of conservative Justices.[1]

Faced with sharper divisions and likely defeats, the Court's more liberal Justices must make difficult choices.[2] One option is simply to

---

Micah Schwartzman is Hardy Cross Dillard Professor of Law and Martha Lubin Karsh and Bruce A. Karsh Bicentennial Professor of Law, University of Virginia School of Law. Nelson Tebbe is Professor of Law, Cornell Law School.

Authors' note: For helpful comments and suggestions, we thank Nicholas Almendares, Charles Barzun, David Fontana, Linda Greenhouse, Paul Horwitz, Ira Lupu, James Nelson, David Pozen, Fred Schauer, Richard Schragger, Elizabeth Sepper, Reva Siegel, and David Strauss.

[1] See generally Neal Devins and Laurence Baum, *The Company They Keep: How Partisan Divisions Came to the Supreme Court* (Oxford, 2019); Rick L. Hasen, *Polarization and the Judiciary*, 22 Annual Rev Pol Sci 261 (2019); David E. Pozen, Eric L. Talley, and Julian Nyarko, *A Computational Analysis of Constitutional Polarization*, Cornell L Rev (forthcoming 2020), Joseph Fishkin and David E. Pozen, *Asymmetric Constitutional Hardball*, 118 Colum L Rev 915 (2018); Brandon L. Bartels, *The Sources and Consequences of Polarization in the U.S. Supreme Court*, in James A. Thurber and Antoine Yoshinaka, eds, *American Gridlock: The Sources, Character and Impact of Political Polarization* 171 (Cambridge, 2015).

[2] We use the terms "liberal" and "conservative" advisedly. These are general and imperfect labels, but they nevertheless track significant ideological differences among Supreme Court Justices. See Joshua B. Fischman and David S. Law, *What Is Judicial Ideology, and How Should We Measure It?*, 29 J L & Pol 133, 150–51 (2009) (noting that "[i]t is common to characterize judges and their votes as 'conservative' or 'liberal,' in much the same manner as we might describe the

© 2020 by The University of Chicago. All rights reserved.
978-0-226-70856-0/2020/2019-0006$10.00

follow their considered interpretations of the Constitution. They can act on what they believe is the most justified conception of the law without regard to whether it exacerbates conflict. Another option is to behave strategically. Especially in cases where considerations of principle or precedent could support a range of outcomes, the Justices in the minority might take instrumental considerations into account. They could compromise, offering concessions in exchange for incremental progress. Or they could work to co-opt Justices who they believe may be willing to vote with them in future cases, offering them cooperation today in the hope of an alliance tomorrow. These strategies are fairly familiar.

Yet the liberal Justices might follow another approach—they could engage in appeasement. In Part II, we define appeasement as a sustained strategy of offering unilateral concessions for the purpose of avoiding further conflict, but with the self-defeating effect of emboldening the other party to take more assertive actions. We recognize that any claim of appeasement carries powerful negative connotations due to the historical significance of the term. We disclaim any direct analogies to historical examples, but we retain the concept of appeasement because it is analytically distinctive and, for that reason, descriptively useful. No other concept identifies exactly the same strategy.

In Part III, we ask whether liberal Justices have adopted an appeasement strategy in cases involving religious freedom, especially under the Establishment Clause.[3] A pattern has emerged, in which Justices Breyer and Kagan either join conservative majorities or concur separately, while Justices Ginsburg and Sotomayor dissent. *American Legion v American Humanist Association*, a case last Term in which the Court rejected an Establishment Clause challenge to the Bladensburg Cross, is the most recent decision to display this vote distribution.[4] We

---

attitudes of any ordinary person or political actor"); Gregory S. Sisk and Michael Heise, *Ideology "All the Way Down"? An Empirical Study of Establishment Clause Decisions in the Federal Courts*, 110 Mich L Rev 1201, 1222 (2012) (using Common Place Scores to put judges on a "liberal-conservative continuum" for purposes of tracking judicial ideology in Establishment Clause cases); see also Adam Feldman, *Empirical SCOTUS: Changes Are Afoot—5–4 Decisions During October Term 2018*, SCOTUSblog (July 8, 2019), https://www.scotusblog.com/2019/07/empirical-scotus-changes-are-afoot-5-4-decisions-during-october-term-2018/ (coding Chief Justice Roberts and Justices Thomas, Alito, Gorsuch, and Kavanaugh as "conservative" and Justices Breyer, Ginsburg, Sotomayor, and Kagan as "liberal").

[3] Our focus is limited to cases involving religious freedom, including matters of disestablishment and free exercise. Although the Justices may be making similar strategic decisions in other areas of the law—or across other areas—we leave those matters aside here.

[4] *American Legion v American Humanist Association*, 139 S Ct 2067, 2074 (2019).

compare *American Legion* to cases that extend the pattern beyond state-sponsored religious symbols to government funding of religious organizations and to religious exemptions from general laws. Our claim is that these decisions provide some evidence that the Justices may be engaged in judicial appeasement.

In Part IV, we argue that appeasement carries particular risks in judicial decision making. It can affect outcomes, either by failing to placate others or by encouraging them to take more aggressive positions. But even apart from outcomes, appeasement can influence constitutional legitimacy. When liberal Justices support a conservative majority, they may lend credence to its decision and thereby weaken dissenting views. Appeasement may also impact the range of constitutional interpretations that are taken seriously at a given time. Arguments that might have been considered extreme or "off the wall" may gain plausibility when Justices from across the political spectrum endorse them. By contrast, *refusing* to concur—writing or joining a powerful dissent—can provide a counterweight to efforts by a majority to alter the boundaries of accepted constitutional argument.

If the liberal Justices are engaged in appeasement, it is important to appreciate the risks. But it is possible that the Justices are following other strategies. We consider two related possibilities: first, they may be pursuing praiseworthy compromise, not problematic appeasement; and, second, they may be working to co-opt Justices on the right, building trust in an effort to form a lasting coalition on questions of religious freedom. These possibilities have some plausibility. In any particular case, it may be difficult to determine whether a Justice has followed an appeasement strategy rather than one of compromise or co-optation. But we argue that across a number of landmark religious freedom cases, there is a discernible pattern of decision making in which some liberal Justices seem to have made significant concessions to conservative majorities and thereby risked conferring legitimacy on sweeping changes to the doctrine.

II. The Concept of Appeasement

Appeasement is obviously a freighted concept, often used as a political pejorative.[5] The term implicates conventional meanings and

---

[5] See, for example, Paul Kennedy, *A Time to Appease*, 108 Natl Interest 7, 13 (2010) ("Since [Munich], the various occasions on which the words Appeaser and Appeasement have been used are as countless as the stars in the sky; this poisonous term can be thrown about from town-hall meetings, to union wages negotiations, to handling IMF conditionality offers, at all levels.").

historical associations that not only are provocative but also risk being more distracting than illuminating.⁶ As much as possible, however, we want to guard against that risk by offering a clear definition of the concept and by indicating how our understanding of it departs from historical examples.

Some elements of appeasement are common in ordinary usage. Appeasement is a strategy for responding to an aggressive adversary.⁷ The idea is to placate or mollify the other party by addressing its grievances and removing its motivation for aggression, thereby avoiding further conflict.⁸ Appeasement is also asymmetric, in the sense that it entails concessions by one party that are not reciprocated by the other.⁹ The strategy is sustained, rather than isolated in time. And, lastly, a policy of concessions counts as appeasement when it leads (or is likely to lead) an adversary to respond by adopting an even more aggressive position, contrary to the intent of the appeaser. Bringing together these aspects of the concept, we can define appeasement as a strategy of asymmetric concessions made by one party for the purpose of avoiding conflict but with the self-defeating effect of emboldening the opposing party to take more assertive actions.

A few points about our definition of appeasement are worth noting. First, although we recognize that appeasement is tainted in our political culture because of its association with the Munich agreement of September 30, 1938, we otherwise disclaim any comparison to that moment in history.¹⁰ Our concerns about judicial appeasement in the

---

⁶ This risk has led some to suggest that use of the term should be abandoned. See, for example, John H. Herz, *The Relevance and Irrelevancy of Appeasement*, 31 Soc Research 296, 320 (1964).

⁷ The *Oxford English Dictionary* (online edition) gives one definition of appeasement, in part, as "any policy of pacification by concession to an enemy."

⁸ See Norrin M. Ripsman and Jack S. Levy, *Correspondence: Debating British Decision-Making toward Nazi Germany in the 1930s*, 34 Intl Security 173, 189 (2009) ("Conventional definitions of appeasement generally emphasize the use of concessions to satisfy an adversary's grievances, reduce tensions, and avoid war for the foreseeable future."); Stephen R. Rock, *Appeasement in International Politics* 12 (Kentucky, 2000) (defining appeasement as "*the policy of reducing tensions with one's adversary by removing the causes of conflict and disagreement*") (original emphasis).

⁹ See Norrin M. Ripsman and Jack S. Levy, *Wishful Thinking or Buying Time? The Logic of British Appeasement in the 1930s*, 33 Intl Security 148, 154 (2008) (defining appeasement as "a strategy of sustained, asymmetric concessions in response to a threat, with the aim of avoiding war, at least in the short term").

¹⁰ At Munich, Neville Chamberlain, who was the British prime minister, agreed to allow Adolf Hitler to occupy the Sudetenland, then part of Czechoslovakia. According to conventional

present context do not rely on and should not be construed as drawing analogies with Munich or any other historical episode.

Second, while the concept of appeasement can be specified in various ways,[11] we adopt a conception that incorporates a critical or negative judgment about the effects of granting asymmetric concessions, namely, that doing so fails (or will likely fail) to mollify an opposing party and instead incentivizes aggression.[12] Here we follow conventional understandings of the concept, according to which appeasement is futile or counterproductive. We do this both to avoid confusion and because ineffectiveness and self-defeat are part of what distinguishes appeasement from otherwise similar decision-making strategies. Negative consequences are especially likely where the appeaser lacks power relative to the appeased.[13]

---

accounts, Chamberlain believed that this concession would mollify Hitler, who would then have had no cause for grievance and no further reason to acquire territory. Upon returning to England, Chamberlain hailed the agreement as having secured "peace for our time." See Tim Bouverie, *Appeasement: Chamberlain, Hitler, Churchill and the Road to War* 287–88 (Tim Duggan Books, 2019) (recounting the circumstances of Chamberlain's infamous declaration). Winston Churchill, by contrast, denounced the Munich deal as delusional, a judgment that was confirmed on March 15, 1939, when Hitler seized the rest of Czechoslovakia, igniting World War II. See Avishai Margalit, *On Compromise and Rotten Compromises* 20 (Princeton, 2010).

There is a vast literature assessing the British policy of appeasement at Munich. For some recent accounts, see Ripsman and Levy, 33 Intl Security at 150–51 (cited in note 9); Stacie E. Goddard, *The Rhetoric of Appeasement: Hitler's Legitimation and British Foreign Policy, 1938–39*, 24 Security Studies 95 (2015); Sidney Aster, *Appeasement: Before and After Revisionism*, 19 Diplomacy & Statecraft 443 (2008); J. L. Richardson, *New Perspectives on Appeasement: Some Implications for International Relations*, 40 World Politics 289, 308–09 (1988).

[11] From the general concept of appeasement, it is possible to identify numerous conceptions. But to our knowledge, and perhaps surprisingly, there has been no sustained conceptual or philosophical analysis of the concept of appeasement. For the distinction between concept and conceptions, see John Rawls, *A Theory of Justice* 5 (Harvard, 1971); H. L. A. Hart, *The Concept of Law* 155–59 (Oxford, 1961).

[12] While appeasement commonly carries this negative connotation in modern usage, it does not always have that meaning. Some authors prefer to define the concept in neutral terms by leaving open whether a strategy of granting concessions can be rational or justified. See Ripsman and Levy, 33 Intl Security at 149 (cited in note 9) ("The effectiveness of appeasement is an empirical question and should not be incorporated into the definition.... Appeasement in itself may be good or bad according to the circumstances."); Daniel Treisman, *Rational Appeasement*, 58 Intl Org 345 (2004); Jack Hirschleifer, *Appeasement: Can It Work?*, 91 Am Econ Rev 342, 346 (2001) (defining appeasement as "the policy of making unilateral concessions to a challenger or potential challenger in the hope of avoiding or delaying conflict" and arguing that "unilateral concessions ... are sometimes a rational and effective survival strategy"); Rock, *Appeasement in International Politics* at 12 (cited in note 8) (adopting a "definition of appeasement that says nothing about the morality or immorality of the policy, nor about its ultimate success or failure").

[13] Cf. Treisman, 58 Intl Org at 358–60 (cited in note 12).

Third, and finally, our conception of appeasement makes relevant an actor's intentions, purposes, or motivations.[14] If, for example, we make an agreement *solely* because we believe it is the right thing to do, it is difficult to say we have engaged in appeasement. We are simply doing what we believe morality demands. Our moral judgment may be mistaken, but that alone does not make us appeasers. But if our aims are strategic, even if only in part, then we become more susceptible to standard charges of appeasement. Of course, no rational actor adopts a strategy that is intentionally self-defeating. But if we offer asymmetric concessions with the intention or purpose of avoiding conflict, and if doing so emboldens (or risks emboldening) our adversaries, then our strategy falls within the definition of appeasement.[15]

III. Appeasement under the Religion Clauses

Having sketched a conception of appeasement, we now ask whether liberal Justices have made concessions to conservative majorities with the aim of avoiding further conflicts in the context of decisions about religious freedom. In three areas of doctrine—involving government religious speech, state funding of religious activities, and religious exemptions from government regulation—the Court is moving toward inversions of the preexisting doctrine. In the context of government religious expression, the Court has shifted from a principle prohibiting government speech that has a primary effect of promoting (or inhibiting) religion, or that expresses government endorsement (or disparagement) of religion, to a principle that permits state support for sectarian religious symbols and speech.[16] In government funding, the Court has all but rejected the *Lemon* framework, which prohibited the state from subsidizing the religious activities of religious organizations, in favor of a "neutrality" model,

---

[14] See Ripsman and Levy, 34 Intl Security at 190 (cited in note 8) (defending a definition of appeasement that is sensitive to intentions, while recognizing that intentions are often difficult to ascertain). On the relevance of intentions in moral and political decisions, see Micah Schwartzman, *Official Intentions and Political Legitimacy: The Case of the Travel Ban*, in Jack Knight and Melissa Schwartzberg, eds, *NOMOS LXI: Political Legitimacy* 201 (NYU, 2019).

[15] To know whether a strategy counts as appeasement may require allowing enough time to pass to evaluate its effects. See Kennedy, 108 Natl Interest at 13 (cited in note 5) ("Certainty about such matters only comes, I suspect, with hindsight; and there we are wise, because we know what happened.").

[16] See Part III.A.

which not only allows but sometimes requires state funding of religion.[17] And with respect to exemptions, whereas the Burger and Rehnquist Courts were generally skeptical of religious accommodations, the Roberts Court has been solicitous of claims for legal exemptions, expanding them to include for-profit corporations and requiring them even when they result in significant harms to third parties.[18] When drawn together, these lines of doctrine result in a proposed church-state settlement that invites government religious speech, requires state funding of religious institutions, and mandates extensive religious exemptions, including those from civil rights laws. A majority of the Court has interpreted the Religion Clauses to facilitate a regime of religious preferentialism—not only state favoritism of religion over nonreligion, but favoritism of the majority religion, Christianity, over minority faiths.[19]

Here we focus on how the Court's liberal Justices have responded to these doctrinal inversions and to an emerging preferentialist regime. As the principle of religious neutrality has been enervated, even while conservative Justices sometimes claim to respect it,[20] liberal Justices have wavered in their responses. In some cases, they appear to be making strategic concessions, perhaps aiming to contain the reach of majority opinions. Whether for principled reasons or pragmatic ones, they have chosen not to protest or dissent from significant violations of core principles of religious freedom. But their tactics are proving to be powerless against a broader conservative strategy that seeks to dismantle restrictions on government support for religion.

A. EXPRESSION

To see the logic of appeasement at work in the context of government religious expression, we can start with the Court's decision in

---

[17] See Part III.B.

[18] See Part III.C.

[19] See Richard Schragger and Micah Schwartzman, *Establishment Clause Inversion and the Bladensburg Cross Case*, in Steven D. Schwinn, ed, *American Constitution Society Supreme Court Review 2018–19* 21, 57 (2019); see also Caroline Corbin, *The Supreme Court's Facilitation of White Christian Nationalism*, Ala L Rev (forthcoming) ("The Supreme Court's evisceration of the Establishment Clause has made possible the Christian nationalism vision of a pro-Christian state. Thus, the current Court is moving in the wrong direction, with its new doctrine facilitating Christian nationalism more than ever."); Mark Tushnet, *Religion and the Roberts Court: The Limits of Religious Pluralism in Constitutional Law*, in Micah Schwartzman et al, eds, *The Rise of Corporate Religious Liberty* 465, 466 (Oxford, 2016) (observing that under the "Roberts Court's approach to the Religion Clauses: Christianity is the unmarked religion").

[20] See Schragger and Schwartzman, *Establishment Clause Inversion* at 56 (cited in note 19).

American Legion v American Humanist Association.[21] The case involved a constitutional challenge to the Bladensburg Peace Cross, a forty-foot-tall Latin cross[22] owned by the government and maintained on public land as a World War I memorial. The outcome of this case was never in serious question. Although a lower court had held that state sponsorship of the Cross amounted to an endorsement of Christianity in violation of the Establishment Clause,[23] most observers of the litigation expected the Supreme Court to reverse that decision.[24]

The case nevertheless raised important questions about how the Court would justify state support for the preeminent symbol of Christianity. Would the Court take the opportunity to initiate sweeping changes to Establishment Clause jurisprudence? Would it finally jettison the much-criticized *Lemon* test?[25] Would it adopt a coercion theory, according to which the Establishment Clause is violated only if the state has coerced religious observance?[26] Or would the Court hold that the American Humanist Association lacked standing to challenge the constitutionality of the Cross, on the ground that observers of state-sponsored religious symbols suffer no cognizable injury?[27]

American Legion had the potential to be a transformative case. The Court was sent multiple invitations to reject decades of Establishment Clause precedent that limited government religious expression.[28] The

---

[21] 139 S Ct 2067, 2074 (2019).

[22] We follow the Court's practice of referring to a "cross" generally and to the Bladensburg Cross as "the Cross." See id at 2074.

[23] *American Humanist Association v Maryland-National Capital Park & Planning Comm.*, 891 F3d 117 (4th Cir 2017).

[24] See, for example, Adam Liptak, *Supreme Court Seems Ready to Allow Cross Honoring War Dead*, NY Times (Feb 27, 2019), https://www.nytimes.com/2019/02/27/us/politics/bladensburg-cross-supreme-court.html; Robert Barnes, *Supreme Court Seems to Seek Narrow Way to Uphold Cross that Memorializes War Dead*, Wash Post (Feb 27, 2019), https://www.washingtonpost.com/politics/courts_law/supreme-court-balances-history-and-religion-in-deciding-monuments-fate/2019/02/26/24688222-3a0e-11e9-a2cd-307b06d0257b_story.html.

[25] Under the *Lemon* test, to avoid violating the Establishment Clause, "[f]irst, the statute must have a secular legislative purpose; second, its principal or primary effect must be one that neither advances nor inhibits religion; finally, the statute must not foster an excessive government entanglement with religion." *Lemon v Kurtzman*, 403 US 602, 612–13 (1971) (quotation marks and citations omitted).

[26] See, for example, *County of Allegheny v ACLU*, 492 US 573, 661–63 (1989) (Kennedy, J, dissenting) (defending a coercion theory of the Establishment Clause).

[27] See *Hein v Freedom from Religion Foundation*, 551 US 587, 633–34 (2007) (Scalia, J, concurring in the judgment) (criticizing "Psychic Injury" as the basis for standing to raise challenges under the Establishment Clause).

[28] See Brief for the American Legion Petitioners, *American Legion v American Humanist Association*, No 17-1717, *16–47 (US filed Dec 17, 2018) (inviting the Court to reject the

significance of the case turned on whether the Court would accept those invitations to reshape constitutional doctrine governing nothing less than the relationship between church and state.

In presenting the Court with this opportunity, *American Legion* posed a challenge to the more liberal Justices. How should they approach the question of the Cross's constitutionality? Should they vote to uphold it, while trying to narrow the grounds for the decision in an effort to limit changes to Establishment Clause doctrine? Amici offered various "ways out" for the liberal Justices. One option was to say that the Cross had stood for nearly ninety years without controversy and could be grandfathered.[29] Another was to emphasize the uniqueness of the Cross as a World War I memorial.[30] A further suggestion was that the Cross could be interpreted as a gravestone for the particular veterans honored by it, all of whom were Christians.[31] But the liberal Justices also had the opportunity to reject those options. Instead of finding creative ways to join the majority, they could declare that state ownership and display of the Cross was unconstitutional. They thus faced a difficult choice between joining the majority in affirming the constitutionality of the Cross or protesting both the state's endorsement of Christianity and the Court's dismantling of decades of Establishment Clause doctrine designed to protect against government-sponsored religious favoritism. Perhaps not wanting to make either choice, some of the Justices looked for another way forward.

1. *American Legion's opinions.* Although the outcome was as expected, the decision in *American Legion* turned out to be highly

---

endorsement test and adopt a coercion theory of the Establishment Clause); Brief for the United States as Amicus Curiae Supporting Petitioners, No 17-1717, *13–21 (US filed Dec 26, 2018) (arguing that the Court should adopt a historical approach to the Establishment Clause that forbids coercion but permits government religious expression); Brief Amicus Curiae of the Becket Fund for Religious Liberty in Support of Petitioners, No 17-1717, *7–8, *29 (US filed Dec 24, 2018) (arguing that the Court should reject the *Lemon* test with a historical approach and that it should reject "offended-observer standing").

[29] See Brief of Baptist Joint Committee for Religious Liberty, et al, as Amici Curiae in Support of Respondents, *American Legion v American Humanist Association*, No 17-1717, *32 (US filed Jan 30, 2019) ("If the Court is unwilling to order the Bladensburg cross removed, it should turn to the bottom line of Justice Breyer's opinion in *Van Orden*. If the Bladensburg cross can remain in place, it is only because, like the Texas Ten Commandments monument, it has been there for many decades.").

[30] Brief of the Military Order of the Purple Heart as Amicus Curiae in Support of Petitioners, *American Legion v American Humanist Association*, No 17-1717, *7 (US filed Dec 26, 2018); Brief of Amici Curiae Retired Generals and Flag Officers Supporting Petitioners, *American Legion v American Humanist Association*, No 17-1717, *6–11 (US filed Dec 21, 2018).

[31] See Brief of Amici Curiae Professors Walter Dellinger and Martin S. Lederman in Support of Neither Petitioners Nor Respondents, *American Legion v American Humanist Association*, No 17-1717, *27–36 (US filed Dec 20, 2018).

fractured.[32] The majority of the Court adopted the narrowest grounds for affirming the Cross's constitutionality. Writing for five Justices, Justice Alito did not apply the *Lemon* or endorsement tests that the Court had previously used in cases involving government religious expression. Under the *Lemon* test, a law violates the Establishment Clause if it lacks a secular purpose, has a primary effect of advancing (or inhibiting) religion, or creates excessive entanglement with religion.[33] In a gloss on that test provided initially by Justice O'Connor[34] and later adopted by the Court,[35] the government is forbidden from conveying an endorsement of religion, which "sends a message to nonadherents that they are outsiders, not full members of the political community, and an accompanying message to adherents that they are insiders, favored members of the political community."[36] Over the span of two decades, the Court applied this nonendorsement interpretation of *Lemon* on multiple occasions to invalidate various forms of government religious expression.[37]

In *American Legion*, however, the Court avoided these tests and instead announced a "strong presumption of constitutionality" for "established, religiously expressive monuments, symbols, and practices."[38] The majority justified this presumption on four main grounds: First, it can be difficult to know the intent or purpose of government expression adopted many years ago.[39] Second, even if the original purpose was religious, that purpose can be obscured over time and new

---

[32] All told, the Justices delivered eight opinions, representing sharp disagreements about how to interpret and apply the Establishment Clause. The majority was composed of Chief Justice Roberts and Justices Alito, Breyer, Kagan, and Kavanaugh. Justice Alito wrote for the majority, but parts of his opinion were joined only by a plurality of four Justices, those in the majority minus Justice Kagan. So we count Justice Alito as having written, in effect, two opinions—one for the majority and one for a plurality. There were six additional opinions, with separate concurrences from Justices Breyer (joined by Justice Kagan), Kagan, Kavanaugh, Thomas, and Gorsuch (joined by Justice Thomas), and a single dissenting opinion from Justice Ginsburg (joined by Justice Sotomayor). *American Legion*, 139 S Ct at 2067.

[33] *Lemon v Kurtzman*, 403 US 602, 612–13 (1971).

[34] See *Lynch v Donnelly*, 465 US 668, 688 (1984) (O'Connor, J, concurring).

[35] See *County of Allegheny v ACLU*, 492 US 573, 593–94 (1989).

[36] *Lynch*, 465 US at 688 (O'Connor, J, concurring).

[37] See *McCreary County v ACLU of Ky*, 545 US 844, 862, 866 (2005) (using an objective observer approach to hold that Ten Commandments display on public property violated the secular purpose requirement under *Lemon*); *Santa Fe Independent School District v Doe*, 530 US 290, 309–10 (2000) (invalidating prayer in public school); *County of Allegheny*, 492 US at 579 (holding that crèche display in county courthouse was unconstitutional).

[38] *American Legion*, 139 S Ct at 2085.

[39] Id at 2082.

secular purposes ascribed to the government's expression.[40] Third, the messages associated with state-sponsored monuments, symbols, and practices can change over time, especially when they take on importance for a political community's identity.[41] Fourth, removing long-established forms of government expression may "no longer appear neutral" and "will strike many as aggressively hostile to religion,"[42] raising concerns about "religiously based divisiveness that the Establishment Clause seeks to avoid."[43] The Court then applied these general considerations and found them all to be reasons for upholding the Bladensburg Cross.[44]

Although the Court was careful not to jettison the *Lemon* and endorsement tests explicitly, it is clear that a majority of the Justices now reject them. In his opinion for the plurality, Justice Alito collected criticisms of those tests and noted that the Court had often declined to apply them.[45] Instead of attempting to bring together various strands of Establishment Clause jurisprudence under a unified test or standard, he proposed what he described as a "more modest approach that focuses on the particular issue at hand and looks to history for guidance."[46] In support of this approach, Justice Alito relied on the Court's legislative prayer decisions in *Marsh v Chambers* and *Town of Greece v Galloway*.[47] In those cases, the Court refused to apply *Lemon* and held that a tradition of legislative prayer going back to the Founding era was evidence that the practice was consistent with the meaning of the Establishment Clause.[48] Noting that there had been disagreement in *Town of Greece* about whether the town's prayer practice was sufficiently inclusive—a nod to the dissents in that case by Justices Kagan and Breyer—the plurality, now including Justice Breyer, nevertheless concluded that "what mattered was that the town's practice 'fi[t] within the tradition long followed in Congress and the state legislatures.'"[49]

---

[40] Id at 2082–83.
[41] Id at 2084.
[42] Id at 2084–85.
[43] Id at 2085 (quoting *Van Orden v Perry*, 545 US 677, 704 (2005)).
[44] Id at 2089–90.
[45] Id at 2080.
[46] Id at 2087.
[47] *Marsh v Chambers*, 463 US 783 (1983); *Town of Greece v Galloway*, 572 US 565 (2014).
[48] *American Legion*, 139 S Ct at 2087–88.
[49] Id at 2088–89 (quoting *Town of Greece*, 572 US at 577).

In separate concurring opinions, a number of the conservative Justices made clear that they would have gone further than the plurality in rejecting existing approaches to the Establishment Clause. For his part, Justice Kavanaugh declared that "the *Lemon* test is not good law."[50] Ignoring the plurality's admonition about "ambitious attempt[s] to find a grand unified theory of the Establishment Clause,"[51] he would replace the *Lemon* test with the following "overarching set of principles":[52]

> If the challenged government practice is not coercive *and* if it (i) is rooted in history and tradition; or (ii) treats religious people, organizations, speech, or activity equally to comparable secular people, organizations, speech, or activity; or (iii) represents a permissible legislative accommodation or exemption from a generally applicable law, then there ordinarily is no Establishment Clause violation.[53]

Under this test, Justice Kavanaugh explained that he would authorize not only long-standing monuments, like the Bladensburg Cross, but also "the practice of displaying religious memorials,"[54] which apparently would extend to the erection of new monuments as well.

For Justices Thomas and Gorsuch, all of this was more complicated than necessary. As in prior cases,[55] Justice Thomas wrote separately to say that the Establishment Clause should not be incorporated through the Fourteenth Amendment and applied to the states,[56] and that even if it were incorporated, it should only prevent states from engaging in coercion of religious practice—a limitation that would not reach government religious expression.[57] Justice Thomas would, of course, "overrule the *Lemon* test in all contexts."[58] The same went for Justice Gorsuch, who described *Lemon* as an indefensible "misadventure."[59] He wrote separately, joined by Justice Thomas, to indicate that he

---

[50] Id at 2093 (Kavanaugh, J, concurring).

[51] Id at 2087 (Alito, J) (plurality).

[52] Id at 2093 (Kavanaugh, J, concurring).

[53] Id.

[54] Id.

[55] See, for example, *Town of Greece*, 572 US at 604–07; *Van Orden*, 545 US at 692–93; *Elk Grove Unified School District v Newdow*, 542 US 1, 49–51 (2004).

[56] *American Legion*, 139 S Ct at 2095 (Thomas, J, concurring in the judgment).

[57] Id at 2096–97.

[58] Id at 2097.

[59] Id at 2101 ("*Lemon* was a misadventure.") (Gorsuch, J, concurring in the judgment).

would also deny standing to "offended observers" who objected to government religious expression, preventing federal courts from hearing their claims under the Establishment Clause.[60]

The only members of the Court who were willing to apply *Lemon* or the endorsement test were Justices Ginsburg and Sotomayor in dissent. They argued, correctly in our view,[61] that state ownership and support of the Bladensburg Cross violated a core principle of religious disestablishment, namely, that the government must be neutral among religions and between religion and irreligion.[62] The Court has often paid lip service to this principle, most recently in *Trump v Hawaii*, which rejected overwhelming evidence of religious hostility toward Muslims in the context of President Trump's travel ban,[63] even while repeating that "[t]he clearest command of the Establishment Clause is that one religious denomination cannot be officially preferred over another."[64] In *American Legion*, Justice Ginsburg applied that command to the Bladensburg Cross. She wrote that "when a cross is displayed on public property, the government may be presumed to endorse its religious content."[65] In some cases, that presumption could be overcome, but the history of this monument demonstrated that the Cross was exclusively sectarian, both at its inception and in its continued meaning over time.[66] Given its religious significance, the Cross could not represent non-Christian soldiers who fought and died for their country—a conclusion that had long been understood, including by those commemorating veterans in the immediate aftermath of World War I.[67] A government committed to a principle of religious neutrality, and to the value of equal citizenship that it protects, could

---

[60] Id at 2098–2100.

[61] See Nelson Tebbe, Richard Schragger, and Micah Schwartzman, *The Bladensburg Peace Cross Sends the Message That Some Citizens Are Valued Less Than Others*, Wash Post (Feb 26, 2019), https://www.washingtonpost.com/outlook/2019/02/26/bladensburg-peace-cross-sends-message-that-some-citizens-are-less-valued-than-others/.

[62] *American Legion*, 139 S Ct at 2105 ("[T]he government may not favor one religion over another, or religion over irreligion.") (quoting *McCreary County*, 545 US at 875) (Ginsburg, J, dissenting).

[63] See Leslie Kendrick and Micah Schwartzman, *The Etiquette of Animus*, 132 Harv L Rev 133, 168–69 (2018); Katherine Shaw, *Speech, Intent, and the President*, 104 Cornell L Rev 1337, 1392–95 (2019).

[64] 138 S Ct 2392, 2417 (2018) (quoting *Larson v Valente*, 456 US 228, 244 (1982)).

[65] *American Legion*, 139 S Ct at 2105 (Ginsburg, J, dissenting).

[66] Id at 2108–09.

[67] Id at 2109 ("The cross was never perceived as an appropriate headstone or memorial for Jewish soldiers and others who did not adhere to Christianity.").

not endorse "the principal symbol of Christianity ... suggesting official recognition of that religion's paramountcy."[68]

2. *Appeasement and the Cross.* The liberal Justices were divided in *American Legion*, producing a seven-to-two vote rejecting the challenge to the Cross. The question, for our purposes, is whether Justices Breyer and Kagan abandoned the dissenters and followed a policy of appeasement. There are several reasons for analyzing their decisions this way.

First, in his concurring opinion, Justice Breyer, joined by Justice Kagan, made significant concessions to the conservatives on the Court. In stating that the Cross "cannot reasonably be understood as a 'government effort to favor a particular religious sect' or 'to promote religion over nonreligion,'"[69] he gave away the core of the Establishment Clause challenge, which was that by endorsing the Cross, the state violated the principle of religious neutrality. To defend that judgment, Justice Breyer argued that the organizers of the Cross had a secular motive for creating it and that there was no evidence that they excluded other religious groups. But those claims were implausible. That the organizers chose a cross—the central symbol of Christianity—to commemorate veterans rather than numerous available secular symbols, which were commonly, and indeed predominantly, used for World War I memorials,[70] was more than sufficient evidence to conclude, reasonably, that state support of the Cross amounted to favoritism of Christianity over other religions.[71]

Given the weakness of Justice Breyer's argument about the religious neutrality of the Cross, a second reason provided in his concurring opinion reinforces our concern. Justice Breyer noted that the Bladensburg Cross had stood for more than ninety years without generating controversy, and he claimed that ordering its removal would

---

[68] Id at 2107.

[69] *American Legion*, 139 S Ct at 2091 (quoting *Van Orden*, 545 US at 702 (Breyer, J, concurring in the judgment)) (Breyer, J, concurring).

[70] See id at 2111–12 (Ginsburg, J, dissenting).

[71] For further argument on this point, see Schragger and Schwartzman, *Establishment Clause Inversion* at 57–58 (cited in note 19); Caroline Corbin, *The Christian Privilege of the Bladensburg Cross Decision*, Berkley Forum (Aug 23, 2019), https://berkleycenter.georgetown.edu/responses/the-christian-privilege-of-the-bladensburg-cross-decision; Ira C. Lupu and Robert W. Tuttle, *Symposium: A Splintered Court Leaves the Bladensburg Cross Intact*, SCOTUSblog (June 21, 2019), https://www.scotusblog.com/2019/06/symposium-a-splintered-court-leaves-the-bladensburg-cross-intact/.

show hostility toward religion, in violation of the Establishment Clause.[72] Justice Breyer had made a similar argument in an earlier case, *Van Orden v Perry*, in which he cast a decisive vote to uphold a Ten Commandments monument on the grounds of the Texas State Capitol. There, he also claimed that the monument did not favor one religion over another and that it had a "predominantly secular message"[73]—claims that were, as with the Cross in *American Legion*, unpersuasive when directed at a symbol with obvious religious significance. Perhaps recognizing as much, he then argued that "to reach a contrary conclusion here, based on the religious nature of the tablets' text would, I fear, lead the law to exhibit a hostility toward religion. ... And it could thereby create the very kind of religiously based divisiveness that the Establishment Clause seeks to avoid."[74] Despite claiming to recognize "the danger of the slippery slope"[75] that accompanies this argument, Justice Breyer extended it in *American Legion*. A decision against the Cross would invite charges of hostility to religion and generate social conflict over the Court's judgment.[76]

This divisiveness argument, and the desire to avoid further conflict, suggests that Justice Breyer may have made a political calculation about the effects of invalidating long-standing religious symbols. Even if those symbols show religious favoritism, one could justify allowing them to stand by giving priority to conflict avoidance over compliance with a principle of religious neutrality.[77] And that does seem to be a plausible explanation for Justice Breyer's decisions in both *Van Orden* and *American Legion*: he has conceded the constitutionality of religious symbols in an effort to avert a political backlash.[78] Now, he may have been seeking to avoid conflict *in the populace*, as opposed to with his

---

[72] *American Legion*, 139 S Ct at 2091 (Breyer, J, concurring).

[73] *Van Orden*, 545 US at 702 (Breyer, J, concurring in the judgment).

[74] Id at 704.

[75] Id.

[76] See *American Legion*, 139 S Ct at 2085 (Alito, J) (plurality) (claiming that "scrubbing away any reference to the divine will strike many as aggressively hostile to religion. ... [T]he image of monuments being taken down will be evocative, disturbing, and divisive," and comparing Breyer's argument about divisiveness in *Van Orden*).

[77] Id at 620 ("This result would be justified by a norm of nonestablishment that privileges the value of political nondivisiveness and understands the Court to be a central contributor to that state of affairs.").

[78] See Richard Schragger, *The Relative Irrelevance of the Establishment Clause*, 89 Tex L Rev 583, 618–19 (2011) ("This statement [in *Van Orden*] comes fairly close to an acknowledgment that a fear of political backlash animates Justice Breyer's decision.").

own colleagues.[79] Or he may have considered this mandate to be a matter of constitutional principle under the Establishment Clause.[80] Either way, however, Justice Breyer's principle—at least his claims about avoiding hostility to religion or the perception of such hostility—threatens to collapse into a policy of granting asymmetric concessions to those who otherwise reject a principle of religious neutrality. And to the extent that his reasoning supports such concessions, it is difficult to distinguish his view from appeasement.

A third consideration is Justice Breyer's emphasis on the distinction between old and new monuments. In his view, the removal or disturbance of old religious monuments would provoke conflict, and the same is true for constructing new ones—which is a reason generally to permit the former and not the latter.[81] This old/new distinction can be understood as an attempt to alleviate the concerns of religious traditionalists and others who support public sponsorship of religious—and, for the most part, Christian—symbols. But there is little reason to think that this distinction is responsive to their concerns. For those who believe that the state should be permitted to endorse religious symbols, the old/new distinction is not going to matter. They will point to the religious content of old symbols and argue that these are evidence of an ongoing tradition of allowing the state to favor one religion over another.[82] Indeed, no conservative Justice has ever embraced the old/new distinction, and a number of Justices have implicitly rejected it by adopting a coercion standard or a historical approach that would permit sectarian displays.[83] In *American Legion*, Justice Gorsuch made

---

[79] If so, Justice Breyer's view might be considered within the tradition of courts exercising the "passive virtues" of using various legal "techniques and allied devices" to avoid adjudicating highly controversial issues. See Alexander M. Bickel, *Foreword: The Passive Virtues*, 75 Harv L Rev 40, 51 (1968). But a strategy of avoiding backlash is not necessarily passive in Bickel's sense, because it might involve courts adjudicating on the merits. If Justice Breyer is engaged in appeasement, his strategy is, at least in part, active rather than passive. For further discussion of the passive virtues and avoidance of political backlash in the context of Establishment Clause decisions, see Schragger, 89 Tex L Rev at 600, 635–40 (cited in note 78).

[80] We are not denying that conflict avoidance is an important aim of the Establishment Clause. Our point is rather that granting asymmetric concessions in pursuit of that aim begins to look like an appeasement strategy.

[81] See *American Legion*, 139 S Ct at 2091 (Breyer, J, concurring).

[82] Justice Scalia made a version of this argument, claiming that religious neutrality could not be required by the Establishment Clause because past practice was filled with examples of government religious expression committed to monotheism within the "Judeo-Christian" tradition. See *McCreary County*, 545 US at 893–94 (Scalia, J, dissenting).

[83] See, for example, *County of Allegheny*, 492 US at 660–63 (Kennedy, J, dissenting) (defending a coercion standard); *McCreary County*, 545 US at 889 (Scalia, J, dissenting) (interpreting the

this point explicitly and, in effect, suggested there was an attempt at appeasement by his colleagues:

> Though the plurality does not say so in as many words, the message for our lower court colleagues seems unmistakable: Whether a monument, symbol, or practice is old or new, apply *Town of Greece*, not *Lemon*. Indeed, some of our colleagues recognize this implication and blanch at its prospect. See ... (Breyer, J., concurring); ... (Kagan, J., concurring in part).... But if that's the real message of the plurality's opinion, it seems to me exactly right—because what matters when it comes to a monument, symbol, or practice isn't its age but its compliance with ageless principles.[84]

As a strategy for containing further intrusions on the principle of religious neutrality and on the Establishment Clause more generally, the old/new distinction is unlikely to survive this guidance from Justice Gorsuch. The votes of Justices Breyer and Kagan are unnecessary to form a majority that would support new state-sponsored religious monuments, symbols, and practices. Concessions in *American Legion* would be futile or, worse, counterproductive, because they obscure the clear command of religious neutrality in cases of government religious expression.

A final and related concern focuses on doctrinal drift in the context of government religious expression. Justice Kagan wrote a brief concurrence in *American Legion* to indicate that, unlike Justice Breyer and others in the plurality, she is not prepared to abandon the secular purpose and effects inquiries under *Lemon*.[85] She also distanced herself from the plurality's reliance on *Marsh v Chambers* as the basis for a general historical approach to interpreting the Establishment Clause.[86] Justice Kagan had accepted *Marsh* as correctly decided in her powerful dissent in *Town of Greece*.[87] In *Marsh*, the Court had upheld the constitutionality of official prayer in a state legislature.[88] At the time, liberal Justices disagreed with that decision.[89] Yet a generation later in *Town of Greece*, no liberal Justice objected to it. And now *Marsh*,

---

Establishment Clause according to "history and traditions"); *American Legion*, 139 S Ct at 2092–93 (Kavanaugh, J, concurring) (same).

[84] *American Legion*, 139 S Ct at 2102 (Gorsuch, J, concurring in the judgment).

[85] Id at 2094 (Kagan, J, concurring in part).

[86] See id at 2087–88.

[87] *Town of Greece*, 572 US at 616 (Kagan, J, dissenting).

[88] *Marsh*, 463 US at 786.

[89] See id at 795 (Brennan, J, dissenting); id at 822 (Stevens, J, dissenting).

apparently agreed upon unanimously, serves as the precedential basis for an approach that "looks to history for guidance"[90] in order to authorize government sponsorship of religious expression. In her *American Legion* concurrence, Justice Kagan wrote that "out of perhaps an excess of caution" she would not "sign on to any broader statements about history's role in Establishment Clause analysis."[91] But by conceding the validity of *Marsh*, and now by approving its extension to state support for the preeminent symbol of Christianity, the liberal Justices have made it increasingly difficult to articulate and defend a coherent principle of religious neutrality.[92]

B. FUNDING

At the same time that the Court is in the process of shifting its doctrine on religious expression by the government, it is transforming its jurisprudence on religious funding. Whereas the Court once *prohibited* many forms of government aid for religion,[93] it increasingly *permits* material support for religious organizations.[94] Sometimes, it even *requires* that assistance. It is this last development that we are interested in here, not only because it is the most recent shift but also because it has been supported by liberals in a manner that ought to be surprising.

---

[90] *American Legion*, 139 S Ct at 2087 (Alito, J) (plurality).

[91] Id at 2094 (Kagan, J, concurring in part).

[92] An objection here might be that Justice Kagan, and perhaps other liberal Justices, believe that they have an obligation to follow *Marsh* as constitutional precedent. Although we agree that there may be principled reasons for deference to precedent, and that following precedent for those reasons does not implicate appeasement, no liberal Justice has offered such a reason for relying on *Marsh*. For her part, as noted above, Justice Kagan has indicated that *Marsh* was correctly decided because "legislative prayer has a distinctive constitutional warrant by virtue of tradition." *Town of Greece*, 572 US at 616 (Kagan, J, dissenting). But even if liberal Justices were inclined to follow *Marsh* as precedent, they might nevertheless be concerned that conservative Justices have paid little heed to precedent and issued numerous perpetual dissents in the Establishment Clause context. See, for example, Allison Orr Larsen, *Perpetual Dissents*, 15 Geo Mason U L Rev 447, 455 (2008) (noting Justice Thomas's call to "'rethink' the modern interpretation of the Establishment Clause"). Perhaps, at some point, asymmetric deference to precedent might be viewed as a form of unilateral concession, but we cannot pursue that argument here.

[93] We are thinking of the line of cases represented best by *Lemon v Kurtzman*, 403 US 602 (1971) (striking down programs that reimbursed private schools for certain teacher salaries).

[94] See *Zelman v Simmons-Harris*, 536 US 639 (2002) (upholding a school voucher program that channeled tax dollars to religious schools against an Establishment Clause challenge); *Mitchell v Helms*, 530 US 793 (2000) (upholding a federal program that supported the lending of educational materials to public and private schools, including religious schools).

While the early decisions limited public aid to religion under the Establishment Clause, these recent decisions rely on the Free Exercise Clause.[95] The most consequential recent case is *Trinity Lutheran v Comer*.[96] There, the Court held that Missouri could not exclude churches from its Scrap Tire Program, which provided reimbursement grants to qualifying nonprofits that installed playground surfaces made from recycled tires. Trinity Lutheran, a church with a preschool and daycare center, had applied for a grant and was otherwise qualified. But a provision of the Missouri constitution required a particularly strict separation of church and state. In part, it provided that "no money shall ever be taken from the public treasury, directly or indirectly, in aid of any church."[97] Observing that prohibition, Missouri denied the playground resurfacing grant to the church.[98] The Court held that Missouri's denial violated the Free Exercise Clause.

Writing for the majority, Chief Justice Roberts reasoned that the Missouri policy expressly discriminated against religious groups in the provision of a public benefit and therefore was presumptively unconstitutional.[99] Missouri put Trinity Lutheran to a choice: either continue as a religious institution or receive a government benefit. That kind of burden could survive only if it were narrowly tailored to a compelling government interest, and it was not. Missouri's interest was to zealously vindicate nonestablishment values. Chief Justice Roberts responded that "[i]n the face of the clear infringement on free exercise before us, that interest cannot qualify as compelling."[100] Because the question the Court was trying to answer was precisely whether the state policy violated free exercise, that reasoning was circular. The Court seemed to be driven by a raw intuition that Missouri's vision of nonestablishment simply "goes too far."[101]

---

[95] A parallel line of cases requires equal support to religious speakers under the Free Speech Clause. See *Lamb's Chapel v Center Moriches Union Free School District*, 508 US 384 (1993); *Rosenberger v Rector and Visitors of the University of Virginia*, 515 US 819 (1995); *Good News Club v Milford Central School*, 533 US 98 (2001).

[96] *Trinity Lutheran Church of Columbia, Inc. v Comer*, 137 S Ct 2012 (2017).

[97] Mo Const, Art I, § 7.

[98] Trinity Lutheran ranked fifth out of forty-four applicants to the program. Fourteen grants were awarded. In the letter to Trinity Lutheran rejecting its application, the program director explained that it could not provide financial support directly to a church under Art I, § 7. *Trinity Lutheran*, 137 S Ct at 2018.

[99] Id at 2021.

[100] Id at 2024.

[101] Id.

Chief Justice Roberts's opinion drew six votes with one notable exception: footnote 3 attracted only a plurality of four votes because it was opposed by Justices Gorsuch and Thomas. Footnote 3 was carefully worded:

> This case involves express discrimination based on religious identity with respect to playground resurfacing. We do not address religious uses of funding or other forms of discrimination.[102]

This language bracketed, among other things, the issue of school vouchers and other school choice programs. Ever since the Court upheld a school voucher program against a nonestablishment challenge,[103] there has been a question of whether jurisdictions can voluntarily exclude religious schools from voucher programs that are otherwise open to private schools.[104] Footnote 3 in *Trinity Lutheran* seemed designed to leave open the constitutionality of such programs, and it was perceived that way at the time.[105] Because religious schools frequently integrate core religious practices into their students' daily experience—for example, through chapel worship, theological instruction, or opening classes with prayers—state policies that exclude religious *uses* would present a different issue from state policies that exclude all religious institutions, regardless of their practices. Or so footnote 3 seemed to suggest.

Reinforcing that reading, Justice Gorsuch, joined by Justice Thomas, wrote separately to express doubt that a distinction between religious use and religious status could be maintained.[106] He also questioned whether such a distinction could matter under the Free Exercise Clause.[107] A person may be forced to choose between their right to free exercise and a public benefit regardless of whether that benefit excludes religious status or only religious uses. So Justice Gorsuch

---

[102] Id at 2024 n 3.

[103] *Zelman*, 536 US at 653.

[104] See *Eulitt v Maine Department of Education*, 386 F3d 344, 356 (1st Cir 2004) (upholding a Maine school choice program that excluded "sectarian" schools).

[105] See, for example, Frank Ravitch, *Symposium: Trinity Lutheran and Zelman—Saved by Footnote 3 or a Dream Come True for Voucher Advocates?*, SCOTUSblog (June 26, 2017), https://www.scotusblog.com/2017/06/symposium-trinity-lutheran-church-v-comer-zelman-v-simmons-harris-saved-footnote-3-dream-come-true-voucher-advocates/ ("On its face, footnote 3, combined with some other statements in the majority opinion, seems to limit the ruling to programs that have no direct religious content.").

[106] *Trinity Lutheran*, 137 S Ct at 2025 (Gorsuch, J, concurring in part).

[107] Id at 2026.

declined to join any reasoning in the majority opinion that relied on the distinction, including footnote 3. Though Justice Gorsuch did not mention school choice programs, he appeared to be suggesting that the logic of *Trinity Lutheran* would extend to them.

Justice Breyer concurred in the judgment, providing the seventh vote for the outcome. In a two-paragraph opinion, he explained that Missouri's program provided a "public benefit" that could not be prohibited to church schools without violating free exercise. Just as ordinary police and fire protection can be extended to churches, so too can playground resurfacing, which is designed solely to "improve the health and safety of children."[108] Justice Breyer concluded by noting that "[p]ublic benefits come in many shapes and sizes," and he favored leaving the application of free exercise to other benefits "for another day."[109]

Finally, Justice Sotomayor, joined by Justice Ginsburg, filed a lengthy, ringing dissent. She protested that the majority had "profoundly change[d]" the relationship between "church and state" by "holding, for the first time, that the Constitution requires the government to provide public funds directly to a church."[110] Her fundamental point was not just that the Free Exercise Clause does not require that result.[111] Rather, the Court was focusing on the wrong constitutional provision. The Establishment Clause prohibits cash aid that flows directly to a house of worship, according to a long line of precedents.[112]

Why did Justices Breyer and Kagan decline to dissent in *Trinity Lutheran*? Were they engaged in strategic behavior, at least in part? And if so, what sort of strategy were they pursuing?

It is possible that Justice Kagan extracted footnote 3 in exchange for her vote.[113] If so, her move might well have counted as appeasement.

---

[108] Id at 2027 (Breyer, J, concurring in the judgment).

[109] Id.

[110] *Trinity Lutheran*, 137 S Ct at 2027 (Sotomayor, J, dissenting).

[111] See id at 2031–41 (arguing that, even if the Establishment Clause does not prohibit Missouri from including religious organizations in its funding program, the Free Exercise Clause does not require it).

[112] Id at 2028–31. See also Ira C. Lupu and Robert W. Tuttle, *Trinity Lutheran Church v. Comer: Paradigm Lost?*, in Steven D. Schwinn, ed, *American Constitution Society Supreme Court Review 2016–2017* 131, 133 (2017) ("[T]he Supreme Court's decision in *Trinity Lutheran* ... represents a stunning and thoroughly unacknowledged move from the religion-distinctive principle of 'no funding' to one of nondiscrimination.").

[113] Alternatively, or additionally, Justice Kennedy may have played a role. It is unlikely that Chief Justice Roberts or Justice Alito initiated the footnote.

Her calculation could have been that she could offer to join the majority opinion while ensuring—or doing everything she could to ensure—that the Court would go no further. Footnote 3 does not commit the Court to stopping at cases where religious institutions are barred from government funding for secular uses. But at least it heads off a reading that would commit the Court to such a rule in this particular case. Understood this way, Justice Kagan's move could be seen as classic appeasement—an attempt to arrest the majority's march away from separationism in government funding, particularly in the context of schooling.

Although we do not yet have a full picture of Justice Kagan's views on nonestablishment with respect to government funding, we have seen some indications that she would have opposed *Trinity Lutheran* on principle. For instance, Justice Kagan dissented in *Arizona Christian School Tuition Organization v Winn*, which turned away a constitutional challenge to a school choice program.[114] Although Justice Kagan addressed only standing (because that was the basis for the majority's holding), she also gave some sense of her views on the merits. In particular, she described the "injury" as structural, rather that personal: "state sponsorship of religion" can harm individuals "in their capacity as contributing members of our national community."[115] Justice Kagan pointed out that James Madison opposed Virginia's plan to support religious groups with tax dollars even though the plan would have allowed objecting taxpayers to opt out.[116] As the Court had put it in an earlier decision, "[O]ne of the specific evils feared by those who drafted the Establishment Clause and fought for its adoption was that the taxing and spending power would be used to favor one religion over another or to support religion in general."[117] For Justice Kagan, the Establishment Clause cognizes harm that is structural in this way. If she does indeed hold such a view, then she would have had reason to oppose the holding of *Trinity Lutheran*, which contemplated the direct flow of tax money to a church.

---

[114] *Arizona Christian School Tuition Organization v Winn*, 563 US 125, 142–43 (2011) (holding that taxpayers lacked standing under the Establishment Clause to challenge a school choice program financed by tax credits rather than government expenditures).

[115] Id at 169 (Kagan, J, dissenting).

[116] Id at 166–67.

[117] Id at 163 (quoting *Flast v Cohen*, 392 US 83, 103 (1968)) (quotation marks and alterations omitted).

Any strategic calculation that footnote 3 would limit or delay the Court's march toward a ban on state separationism appears to have been misconceived. At the time of our writing, the Court has agreed to hear *Espinoza v Montana Department of Revenue*, which is a challenge to a Montana school choice program.[118] Montana's program allowed a taxpayer to receive a dollar-for-dollar tax credit of up to $150 per year for contributions made to a Student Scholarship Organization (SSO). The SSO would then make a contribution to a Qualified Education Provider (QEP), typically a private school.[119]

Although the state legislation setting up the program did not explicitly exclude religious schools, it directed the tax department to implement the program consistent with the Montana Constitution. And that law contained a provision, similar to Missouri's, that prohibited any "direct or indirect" government financial support for religious schools.[120] Accordingly, the tax department promulgated Rule 1, which excluded religious schools from qualifying as QEPs that are eligible to receive grants from SSOs.[121] The Montana Supreme Court agreed that the program violated the Montana constitution's prohibition on aid to religious schools but, in a twist, it also held that Rule 1 was outside the tax department's statutory authority.[122] Consequently, the state supreme court invalidated the entire school choice program. The Supreme Court granted certiorari.[123]

Although it is possible that the Supreme Court will dismiss *Espinoza* as improvidently granted or otherwise dispose of the case without reaching the main issue, many commentators expect the Court to hold that Montana contravened the federal Free Exercise Clause when its high court invalidated the school choice program because it included

---

[118] *Espinoza v Montana Department of Revenue*, 393 Mont 446 (2018), cert granted 2019 WL 1207018 (US 2019) (Mem).

[119] The Montana program was established in 2015, four years after *Winn*. See *Espinoza*, 393 Mont at 454. Presumably the state structured the program as a tax exemption, rather than as a voucher, to defeat taxpayer standing to challenge the program under the Establishment Clause.

[120] Mont Const, Art X, § 6 (1972) ("The legislature, counties, cities, towns, school districts, and public corporations shall not make any direct or indirect appropriation or payment from any public fund or monies, or any grant of lands or other property for any sectarian purpose or to aid any church, school, academy, seminary, college, university, or other literary or scientific institution, controlled in whole or in part by any church, sect, or denomination.").

[121] Mont Admin R 42.4.802.

[122] *Espinoza*, 393 Mont at 468–69.

[123] *Espinoza v Montana Department of Revenue*, 2019 WL 1207018 (US 2019) (Mem).

religious schools in violation of the state constitution.[124] Moreover, it seems likely that the Court will take this action on the strength of *Trinity Lutheran*. If that prediction proves to be correct, then any effort to demand footnote 3 in order to avoid or substantially delay the extension of *Trinity Lutheran* to school choice programs will have been futile. And, further, it probably was futile whatever happens in *Espinoza*. The Roberts Court is engaged in a program to slowly but significantly rework Establishment Clause doctrine surrounding government funding. Ever since Justice O'Connor was replaced by Justice Alito, that program has been predictable. Although it is true that *Trinity Lutheran* was decided while Justice Kennedy was still on the Court, his presence did not make the trend much less clear. After all, Justice Kennedy joined the majority in *Trinity Lutheran* and he wrote the majority opinion in *Winn*, to the degree that a standing case is relevant. Justice Kagan's decision to join the majority in *Trinity Lutheran* could do little to alter that trajectory, even if she did so in a successful effort to include footnote 3.

Not only was the effort futile, moreover, but it conceivably was counterproductive. Her decision, along with Justice Breyer's, made the vote on the outcome in *Trinity Lutheran* seven to two. And that lopsided vote added legitimacy to the Court's program to invalidate government decisions to exclude religious actors from funding programs.[125] Until *Trinity Lutheran*, after all, the Court had never required equal access for religious actors under the Free Exercise Clause—in fact, it had *upheld* one such exclusion.[126] So Chief Justice Roberts

---

[124] See Frank Ravitch, *Symposium: Espinoza v. Montana Department of Revenue: The Battle Between May Fund and Must Fund*, SCOTUSblog (Sept 18, 2019), https://www.scotusblog.com/2019/09/symposium-espinoza-v-montana-department-of-revenue-the-battle-between-may-fund-and-must-fund/ ("Although the Montana Supreme Court's ruling is consistent with Supreme Court precedent, including *Trinity Lutheran*, the Supreme Court is likely to overturn it."); Richard Garnett, *Symposium: Principles or Improvisations? Why (and How) the Justices Should Reject Anti-Religious Discrimination*, SCOTUSblog (Sept 18, 2019), https://www.scotusblog.com/2019/09/symposium-principles-or-improvisations-why-and-how-the-justices-should-reject-anti-religious-discrimination/ ("[T]he *Trinity Lutheran* footnote made it inevitable, given the policies and politics of education reform, that a school-aid case like *Espinoza* would come along, and it seems very likely that the other no-discrimination shoe will now, as it should, drop.").

[125] See, for example, Garnett, *Principles or Improvisations?* (cited in note 124) ("In *Trinity Lutheran*, the Supreme Court by a 7–2 vote rejected the argument that Missouri's similar no-aid rule justified banning a Lutheran preschool from a program that distributes playground-surfacing material made from recycled tires.").

[126] *Locke v Davey*, 540 US 712 (2004). As we have already noted, the Court had required equal access to funding programs under the Free Speech Clause. See note 95 (collecting cases).

significantly advanced that trendline by delivering a decision in *Trinity Lutheran* with only two Justices in dissent.

Justice Breyer, for his part, concurred only in the judgment, as we have noted. He too may have been acting strategically, at least in part. After all, Justice Breyer wrote a strong dissent in *Zelman*, the school voucher case.[127] There, he emphasized "the risk that publicly financed voucher programs pose in terms of religiously based social conflict," a risk that must be just as great in programs structured as tax credits rather than vouchers. The danger, of course, is that sectarian groups will vie with one another, and with secular groups, for control of public aid.[128] Now Justice Breyer did say in *Trinity Lutheran* that he viewed playground resurfacing as equivalent to police and fire protection, social services that do not cause social conflict because they are distributed evenhandedly and universally. So perhaps Justice Breyer had a purely principled reason for his vote—and his refusal to join the majority opinion lends some support to that theory. If so, it was not appeasement.

But then Justice Breyer must regret the unintended consequence, which is that the lopsided vote on the outcome in *Trinity Lutheran* makes it more likely that the Court will require the school choice program in *Espinoza* to include religious schools. And we know from Justice Breyer's opinion in *Zelman* that he opposes that outcome for deep reasons of constitutional theory. Any thought by Justice Breyer that concurring only in the judgment would hamper that development will probably turn out to have been too optimistic.

In sum, the Court's funding cases provide possible examples of futility and perhaps even counterproductivity in liberal strategy. At a time when the Roberts Court is engaged in a systematic program to rework the Establishment Clause rules concerning government financial support to religion, any efforts by liberals to soften or slow that program have been unsuccessful and maybe self-defeating.

C. EXEMPTIONS

Concerns about appeasement also apply in the context of religious exemptions. Historically, the Court was generally skeptical of

---

[127] *Zelman*, 536 US at 717 (2002) (Breyer, J, dissenting). He also joined Justice Souter's dissent for four Justices.

[128] Id at 718.

exemptions,[129] especially when they implicated the Establishment Clause by imposing significant burdens on others.[130] But here, too, there have been significant changes in recent years, suggesting an inversion of the doctrine. Where the Court had previously denied exemptions and limited those that harmed third parties, it has now become more solicitous of religious accommodations.[131] For example, in *Burwell v Hobby Lobby*, the Court applied the Religious Freedom Restoration Act (RFRA) to issue an exemption for a large for-profit corporation that objected to regulations mandating insurance coverage for contraception under the Affordable Care Act.[132] The Court has also extended constitutional protections in cases involving conflicts between religious liberty and civil rights laws.[133] To date, the most prominent case is *Masterpiece Cakeshop v Colorado Civil Rights Commission*, in which the Court was asked to decide whether wedding vendors who object on religious grounds to complying with state public accommodations laws are entitled to exemptions under the First Amendment.[134] The *Masterpiece* Court avoided answering that question and instead held that state officials had acted with religious hostility.[135] In reaching that conclusion, however, the Justices displayed a pattern of decision making similar to the cases discussed above, which gives us further reason to be concerned about appeasement.

---

[129] See Ira C. Lupu, *Hobby Lobby and the Dubious Enterprise of Religious Exemptions*, 38 Harv J L & Gender 35, 48–56 (2014) (surveying the history of religious exemptions and showing that the Court had granted few exemptions before *Smith*); James E. Ryan, *Smith and the Religious Freedom Restoration Act: An Iconoclastic Assessment*, 78 Va L Rev 1407, 1413–16 (1992) (same).

[130] See generally Micah Schwartzman, Nelson Tebbe, and Richard Schragger, *The Costs of Conscience*, 106 Ky L J 881, 888–94 (2018) (discussing Establishment Clause limits on exemptions that impose harms on others); Nelson Tebbe, *Religious Freedom in an Egalitarian Age* 49–70 (Harvard, 2017); Frederick Mark Gedicks and Rebecca G. Van Tassell, *RFRA Exemptions from the Contraception Mandate: An Unconstitutional Accommodation of Religion*, 49 Harv CR-CL Rev 343 (2014).

[131] See Schragger and Schwartzman, *Establishment Clause Inversion* at 27–28 (cited in note 19).

[132] *Burwell v Hobby Lobby*, 573 US 682 (2014).

[133] See, for example, *Hosanna-Tabor v Evangelical Lutheran Church and School v EEOC*, 565 US 171 (2012) (recognizing the "ministerial exception" as constitutionally grounded in both Religion Clauses). In our view, there are reasons to be concerned about appeasement in *Hosanna-Tabor* as well. See Micah Schwartzman and Nelson Tebbe, *Against Establishment Clause Concession*, Take Care Blog (Feb 2, 2019), https://takecareblog.com/blog/against-establishment-clause-appeasement. But see Ira C. Lupu and Robert W. Tuttle, *The Mystery of Unanimity in Hosanna-Tabor Evangelical Lutheran Church & School v EEOC*, 20 Lewis & Clark L Rev 1265, 1267 (2017) (arguing that the Court's unanimity in *Hosanna-Tabor* is explained and justified by the principle that courts may not decide "purely ecclesiastical questions").

[134] *Masterpiece Cakeshop v Colorado Civil Rights Commission*, 138 S Ct 1719 (2018).

[135] See Kendrick and Schwartzman, 132 Harv L Rev at 134 (cited in note 63).

In *Masterpiece Cakeshop*, the Court held that state officials had violated the religious liberty of a Christian baker, Jack Phillips, who had refused to serve a gay couple celebrating their wedding.[136] The couple claimed that the baker had discriminated against them in violation of Colorado's public accommodation law, which prohibits discrimination on the basis of sexual orientation and gender identity.[137] Phillips responded, in part, by claiming that he was entitled to a free exercise exemption under the First Amendment.[138] The Colorado Civil Rights Commission rejected Phillips's claim, and the Colorado Court of Appeals affirmed that decision.[139] But the Supreme Court reversed, with the majority holding that both the Commission and the Court of Appeals had shown hostility toward Phillips's religious views and denied him the "neutral and respectful consideration" to which he was entitled under the Free Exercise Clause of the First Amendment.[140] This ruling did not grant Phillips a religious exemption from a neutral law, because the Court found that Colorado had not acted neutrally. In fact, the Court signaled that public accommodations laws would not ordinarily admit religious exemptions.[141] But the outcome nevertheless favored Phillips.

As in *American Legion* and *Trinity Lutheran*, Justices Kagan and Breyer joined the conservative majority in *Masterpiece Cakeshop*, leading to a seven-to-two victory for the baker. Only Justices Ginsburg and Sotomayor dissented.[142] The question, again, is whether this division among the liberal Justices can be understood as appeasement.

Although Justice Kagan (joined by Justice Breyer) claimed in her concurring opinion that she joined the majority in full because the Colorado Civil Rights Commission failed to treat Phillips's claim with respect, it is difficult to accept that explanation as her entire rationale. To do so, one would have to imagine that she would have voted the same way even if the Court had a working majority that would have

---

[136] *Masterpiece Cakeshop*, 138 S Ct at 1722.

[137] Id at 1725.

[138] Id at 1726.

[139] Id at 1726–27.

[140] Id at 1729.

[141] Id at 1727 ("[I]t is a general rule that [religious and philosophical] objections do not allow business owners and other actors in the economy and in society to deny protected persons equal access to goods and services under a neutral and generally applicable public accommodations law.").

[142] Id at 1748 (Ginsburg, J, dissenting).

affirmed the civil rights of the gay couple over the baker's claim for a religious exemption. Suppose that Justice Merrick Garland had been seated on the Court instead of Justice Gorsuch, and that he would have voted with Justices Ginsburg and Sotomayor. Under those circumstances, would Justices Kagan and Breyer have cast decisive votes in favor of the baker and against the state's application of its civil rights law?

There are several reasons to doubt the plausibility of such a vote. First, the evidence of animus in *Masterpiece Cakeshop* was thin to nonexistent. Justice Kennedy offered two grounds for his finding of hostility toward religion. First, he cited statements made by members of the Colorado Civil Rights Commission, but his interpretation of those statements disregarded their context, imputed ambiguity where there was none, and, ironically, ignored the role of his own prior attributions of animus in cases involving discrimination on the basis of sexual orientation, which might well have informed the statements of the Colorado officials in question.[143] Next, Justice Kennedy imputed hostility to the Colorado Court of Appeals on the basis of its disparate treatment of Jack Phillips, who was required to bake a cake for a same-sex couple, and several other bakers, who were not required to bake cakes for William Jack, a Christian evangelical who had requested cakes with messages opposed to same-sex marriage. Justice Kennedy held that the Court of Appeals offered no "proper rationale" for denying Phillips an exemption while allowing the others to refuse to provide cakes with messages to which they objected.[144] But this argument also lacked merit. The Colorado Court of Appeals did not, as Justice Kennedy claimed, find that cakes disfavoring gay marriage were

---

[143] For a more extensive discussion of these claims, see Kendrick and Schwartzman, 132 Harv L Rev at 138–43 (cited in note 63). See also Ira C. Lupu and Robert W. Tuttle, *Masterpiece Cakeshop—A Troublesome Application of Free Exercise Principles By a Court Determined to Avoid Hard Questions*, Take Care Blog (June 7, 2018), https://takecareblog.com/blog/masterpiece-cakeshop-a-troublesome-application-of-free-exercise-principles-by-a-court-determined-to-avoid-hard-questions; Michael Dorf, *Masterpiece Cakeshop Should (But Probably Won't) Doom the Travel Ban*, Dorf on Law (June 4, 2018), http://www.dorfonlaw.org/2018/06/masterpiece-cakeshop-ruling-should-but.html; Marty Lederman, *State "Hostility" to Religion Without Religious Discrimination?: The Unexpected Free Exercise Issue Lurking in Masterpiece Cakeshop*, Balkanization (Dec 19, 2017), https://balkin.blogspot.com/2017/12/state-hostility-to-religion-without.html; Bernard Bell, *A Lemon Cake: Ascribing Religious Motivations in Administrative Adjudications—A Comment on Masterpiece Cakeshop (Part II)*, Yale J on Reg: Notice & Comment (June 20, 2018), http://yalejreg.com/nc/a-lemon-cake-ascribing-religious-motivation-in-administrative-adjudications-a-comment-on-masterpiece-cakeshop-part-ii.

[144] *Masterpiece Cakeshop*, 138 S Ct at 1730–31.

offensive, which would have amounted to impermissible viewpoint discrimination. Instead, the state court merely reported that the bakers who refused to provide such cakes did so because they found them to be offensive and not because of hostility toward the religion of the person who requested them.[145] In short, there were perfectly plausible readings of the facts that did not require a finding of hostility, or even the appearance of hostility, in the adjudication of Jack Phillips's free exercise claim.

Second, even if one accepted that state officials displayed hostility in *Masterpiece Cakeshop*, the Court's application of animus doctrine was dubious. The Court's main precedent for its inquiry into religious hostility was *Church of Lukumi Babalu Aye v Hialeah*, in which Justice Kennedy also wrote for the Court.[146] In that case, after finding that state officials had purposely discriminated against a religious minority, the Court applied strict scrutiny[147] and held that the state lacked both a compelling interest and the least restrictive means of achieving its purported interests.[148] By contrast, in *Masterpiece Cakeshop*, the Court ignored the compelling-interest analysis without explanation. It was the state's action of rejecting Phillips's claim that needed justification, not its officials' statements. Had the Court performed a full analysis, it would have had to confront the central question raised in the case, namely, whether the state could, in fact, have required compliance with its civil rights law, despite the baker's religious objection. Under strict scrutiny, the state would have had an opportunity to argue that it had an interest other than animus for applying its civil rights law to Phillips—just as the government did in *Lukumi*.[149] In that case, the government fell short of justifying its action. But in *Masterpiece Cakeshop*, Colorado could have argued that its enforcement of a core civil rights guarantee was narrowly tailored to achieve a compelling interest. Although the Court studiously avoided addressing that argument, it was the subject of dueling concurring opinions, with Justice Gorsuch claiming that the state lacked such an interest[150] and with

---

[145] See Kendrick and Schwartzman, 132 Harv L Rev at 144 (cited in note 63).

[146] *Church of Lukumi Babalu Aye v Hialeah*, 508 US 520 (1993).

[147] Id at 546 ("A law burdening religious practice that is not neutral or not of general application must undergo the most rigorous of scrutiny.").

[148] Id at 546–57.

[149] Id at 543–44.

[150] *Masterpiece Cakeshop*, 138 S Ct at 1734–40 (Gorsuch, J, concurring).

Justice Kagan arguing that it had a proper basis for enforcing its law.[151] Had there been five votes on the Court for the latter view, it seems unlikely that Justice Kagan would have voted to avoid reaching the issue. Animus doctrine did not require that result.[152]

Third, even supposing there was religious hostility and that the Court acted appropriately in refraining from conducting a compelling-interest analysis, the proper remedy in *Masterpiece* would have been to remand the case for impartial adjudication.[153] The Court provided no explanation for why it reversed without remanding for that purpose. Interestingly, in the same Term during which *Masterpiece Cakeshop* was decided, Justice Kagan wrote for a majority in *Lucia v SEC*, which held that the proper remedy for an adjudication tainted by a constitutional violation (in that case, a violation of the Appointments Clause) was to remand for a new adjudication by a properly appointed official.[154] The same logic would seem to hold for state officials involved in adjudicating civil rights claims. Thus, even given a finding of animus, had there been a possible fifth vote in favor of upholding application of Colorado's public accommodations law, it is hard to see why Justice Kagan (with Justice Breyer) would not have a joined a majority in favor of remanding for further proceedings.

Appeasement is a more plausible interpretation of the votes of Justices Kagan and Breyer in *Masterpiece Cakeshop*. Although the conservative Justices had a majority without their votes, perhaps these liberal Justices made concessions to alleviate Justice Kennedy's concerns about animus in the case. Or perhaps they voted with the majority for the purpose of living to fight another day. Justice Kagan's concurring opinion, which offered a principled basis for applying civil rights law in

---

[151] Id at 1732–34 (Kagan, J, concurring).

[152] Alternatively, the Court could have applied a mixed-motive inquiry following its precedent under the Equal Protection Clause. See *Village of Arlington Heights v Metropolitan Housing Development Corp.*, 429 US 252, 270 n 21 (1977) ("Proof that the [government's] decision ... was motivated in part by a racially discriminatory purpose would not necessarily have required invalidation of the challenged decision. Such proof would, however, have shifted ... the burden of establishing that the same decision would have resulted even had the impermissible purpose not been considered."); *Mt. Healthy City School District Board of Education v Doyle*, 429 US 274, 287 (1977) (requiring application of burden shifting analysis for possible mixed motives). But that inquiry would also have required the Court to address the state's argument that it had a valid justification for applying its public accommodations law. For further discussion, see Kendrick and Schwartzman, 132 Harv L Rev at 152–53 (cited in note 63).

[153] See Kendrick and Schwartzman, 132 Harv L Rev at 150 n 109 (cited in note 63).

[154] *Lucia v SEC*, 138 S Ct 2044, 2055 (2018).

the wedding vendor context, certainly suggests this possibility.[155] But that motivation does not rescue their votes. Attempting to delay a conflict—for example, over whether religious exemptions to public accommodations are required, or over whether the Establishment Clause sets limits on exemptions that burden others, including exclusion from public accommodations[156]—is a paradigmatic basis for appeasement.

IV. WHAT IS WRONG WITH APPEASEMENT?

So far, we have specified what we mean by appeasement, and we have presented some evidence that liberal Justices have engaged in this practice in a range of cases involving matters of religious freedom. We also have suggested that judicial appeasement presents significant risks. But which ones exactly?

In this part, we offer a more specific account of the normative difficulties with appeasement. We then consider the objection that liberal Justices are engaged in worthwhile compromise, not problematic appeasement. And we address the related possibility that they have undertaken a long-term campaign to win over centrist Justices. Here, as throughout, we are primarily interested in decisions by liberal Justices and other liberal constitutional actors to pursue nonideal or second-best outcomes in contexts where conservatives have the power to implement their legal views.[157]

A. OUTCOMES, LEGITIMACY, AND FEASIBILITY

Appeasement may have an impact on *outcomes*, in at least two ways. First, asymmetric concessions may be *futile* because they fail to mollify an adversary. Appeasers make a kind of mistake. They offer concessions with the aim of removing an adversary's source of grievance, but they actually fail to address the real motivation of that adversary, which is insensitive to their concessions.

---

[155] Cf. Lupu and Tuttle, *Masterpiece Cakeshop—A Troublesome Application of Free Exercise Principles by a Court Determined to Avoid Hard Questions* (cited in note 143) ("Why Justice Kagan or Justice Breyer felt pressure to conform to the majority's mischaracterization [of underlying agency opinions] in *Masterpiece* nevertheless remains a mystery. A 7-2 result (as compared to a 5-4) will not reduce national conflict over these issues, nor will these Justices' influence be any greater if and when these issues return.").

[156] See Kendrick and Schwartzman, 132 Harv L Rev at 157–58 (cited in note 63).

[157] For discussion of the distinctions between ideal and nonideal constitutional theories, and the idea of a constitutional second best, see Lawrence B. Solum, *Constitutional Possibilities*, 83 Ind L J 307, 309–12 (2008).

Second, appeasement may not only be ineffective, but it may also be self-defeating or counterproductive. An actor's appeasement strategy backfires when its concessions work to incentivize an adversary's aggressiveness. The actor is mistaken here, too. It not only fails to contain the damage, but it drives outcomes even further away from what it considers to be ideal. If, for example, an adversary has a grander ambition than the actor realizes, then the actor's concessions may encourage that adversary to continue or intensify its campaign.

Beyond outcomes, appeasement can also affect *legitimacy*. An actor that appeases can confer legitimacy on its adversary's assertive position. When, for instance, a liberal Justice signs onto a conservative majority, that gives credence to the decision, possibly even if the liberal Justice does so only in order to limit the reach of the opinion. A conservative member of the majority can then point to the vote of the liberal as evidence that the outcome is driven by more than just ideology.[158]

Similarly, that decision by a liberal Justice can diminish the force of the views offered by any remaining dissenters. Conservative members of the majority can then point to the dissent's reduced number of votes—three, two, or only one—to weaken its impact. By acquiescing, the appeaser helps to cast the dissent as unreasonable, extreme, or marginal. Here, appeasement does not only forfeit an opportunity to issue a protest that might be vindicated in the future,[159] but it sends a message that the dissent lacks authority. And that message can influence how seriously the dissent is taken, not only by the Justices themselves in future cases, but also by constitutional actors outside the Court and by the public.[160]

Related to legitimacy is the way appeasement affects the *range of constitutional positions that are viewed as reasonable* at any given moment in history. This range is sometimes called the "Overton Window," a

---

[158] Cf. Margaret Talbot, *Is the Supreme Court's Fate in Elena Kagan's Hands?*, New Yorker (Nov 18, 2019) ("David Fontana, a law professor at George Washington University, told me ... the compromises that Kagan has sanctioned not only fail to achieve 'justice from the progressive perspective'; they 'legitimate a conservative perspective'.... conservatives 'can respond to criticisms by saying their perspectives are so persuasive' that even a liberal Justice agrees with them.").

[159] See William J. Brennan Jr., *In Defense of Dissents*, 37 Hastings L J 427, 430–31 (1986).

[160] Cf. Jon D. Michaels, *Advancing a Left-Liberal Jurisprudence*, Take Care Blog (Oct 16, 2018), https://takecareblog.com/blog/advancing-a-left-liberal-jurisprudence ("When, as has often been the case, moderate (center-left) judges keep [advocates who propound left-liberal constitutional theories] at some distance, it becomes easier to readily and credibly dismiss those groups as outside of the jurisprudential mainstream—radicals shouting into the wind.").

term that describes the set of policy options that are feasible in the sense that those options have sufficient public support that political (or legal) actors will consider implementing them.[161] It can vary both in size—how wide or narrow the spectrum of acceptable views is—and also in political location—where the range is located on the so-called political spectrum. Note that whether an argument is within the window determines whether it is worth taking seriously, not whether it is correct. Reasonable disagreement will persist for many questions that arise under the Religion Clauses.

A decision by a constitutional actor to concede a position can affect the range of arguments taken seriously on a particular matter of First Amendment law. But a forceful objection that an argument is outside the realm of reasonable disagreement, and that it ought to remain there, can provide a counterweight to an assertive effort to widen or shift the range itself. And a failure to join a dissent of that kind can bolster the perception that in fact it is the dissent whose arguments should no longer be seen to carry weight.

In Part III, we identified places where decisions by liberal Justices carried all of these risks. If we are correct that the Roberts Court is shifting long-standing doctrine concerning government religious expression, for instance, then joining its decisions can work to assimilate positions that previously were out of bounds. Or consider liberal support for, or at least acquiescence in, the Court's decision to require cash aid to flow directly to a religious organization in *Trinity Lutheran*—an outcome that would have been remarkable in an earlier era.[162] And even on questions that are difficult and unsettled, such as conflicts between LGBT rights and religious liberty, it may be a mistake to legitimate shifts in the doctrine for the purpose of avoiding more immediate confrontations. Each particular decision could be defended as an effort

---

[161] *The Overton Window: A Model of Policy Change*, Mackinac Center for Public Policy, www.mackinac.org/OvertonWindow. The idea of the Overton Window is similar to the distinction between ideas that are "off the wall," meaning that they are thought to be out-of-bounds, crazy, or clearly mistaken, and those that are "on the wall," or deemed to be acceptable or at least plausible within a political or legal culture. See Jack Balkin, *From Off the Wall to On the Wall: How the Mandate Went Mainstream*, Atlantic (June 4, 2012), https://www.theatlantic.com/national/archive/2012/06/from-off-the-wall-to-on-the-wall-how-the-mandate-challenge-went-mainstream/258040/; see also Solum, 83 Ind L J at 314 (cited in note 157) (analyzing the notion of a "feasible choice set").

[162] Cf. *Mitchell v Helms*, 530 US 793, 839 (2000) (O'Connor, J, concurring in the judgment) ("We have never held that a government-aid program passes constitutional muster *solely* because of the neutral criteria it employs as a basis for distributing aid.").

to contain results that otherwise would have been mandated by the conservative majority. But if the Court is engaged in a sweeping effort to transform jurisprudence concerning the Religion Clauses, then incrementalism will fail to contain that effort and will even work to legitimate it.

B. THE VIRTUES OF COMPROMISE

An objection may be that liberal Justices are engaged not in appeasement, but rather in compromise. The two concepts can be distinguished in several ways. While appeasement is asymmetric, compromise is mutual: each side agrees to a position that is nonideal from its perspective.[163] And the parties' objective is not to avoid conflict as such, but instead to achieve some progress through agreement rather than remain locked in a stalemate. Unlike appeasement, moreover, compromise is rarely seen to be inherently problematic. If anything, there is a tendency to assume the opposite, namely, that compromise is usually worthwhile because both sides cooperate toward resolving their disagreements.[164]

According to this objection, Justices Breyer and Kagan were engaging in reasonable compromise in at least some of the cases that we have discussed. If they agreed to join the majority in *Bladensburg* or *Trinity Lutheran* or *Masterpiece Cakeshop* in order to contain the reach of those opinions, they gave up something valuable and received something valuable in return.[165] They may not have preferred those outcomes in an ideal world, but they acted shrewdly by accepting them in return for moderation by the majority.[166]

---

[163] We say mutual rather than symmetric because the parties may not concede equally or proportionately.

[164] See, for example, Amy Gutmann and Dennis Thompson, *The Mindsets of Political Compromise*, 8 Perspectives on Polit 1125, 1125 (2010) ("The resistance to democratic compromise is a problem for any democracy because it stands in the way of change that nearly everyone agrees is necessary. . . .").

[165] Cf. Talbot, *Is the Supreme Court's Fate* (cited in note 158) ("Erwin Chemerinsky . . . told me, 'Kagan will try whenever she can to forge a majority either by winning a conservative Justice over to the progressive side or on as narrow as possible grounds on the conservative side. She can count to five as well as you or I can, and the conservative majority will be there for a long time. She'll play a role to achieve as much as she can, given that, and when she can't she'll write the strongest dissent she can.'").

[166] They may have participated in what Stephen Choi and Mitu Gulati describe as "covering," which involves judges moderating their votes in exchange for obtaining reasoning that more closely aligns with their legal views. See Stephen J. Choi and G. Mitu Gulati, *Trading Votes for Reasoning: Covering in Judicial Opinions*, 81 S Cal L Rev 735 (2008). Choi and Gulati

Admiration for judicial compromise is part of a more general cultural phenomenon. Many claim that compromise is exactly what is needed at this moment of bitter political division. Adhering to principle is narrow-minded and unreasonable, for them, whereas compromising is practical and sensible.[167] Dissent is thought to worsen political division by communicating disrespect for those who disagree. Standing on principle and refusing to compromise is equated with promoting tribalism, which leads to permanent and intractable forms of hostility.[168] None of these ideas—dissent, principle, and tribalism—has a clear causal relationship to any other, but instead each is loosely tied to the others, according to this line of criticism.

Is this view correct, either generally or with respect to liberal Justices on questions of religious freedom? Certainly, dissent does reflect stubbornness in many situations, and compromise is often more productive than stalemate. But is dissent usually, let alone necessarily, unreasonable, and is compromise always, or almost always, laudable?

We can begin to answer these sorts of questions by defining compromise as mutual agreement to a position that each party believes to be nonideal but that is accepted given the fact of disagreement.[169] Agreeing to a second-best outcome allows each party to achieve something rather than nothing. And, classically, the other side views it that way as well. No one gets everything they want, but everyone gets

---

focus mainly on cases in which judges in the majority offer to moderate their votes in exchange for better reasoning and the avoidance of dissent. Id at 741. In the situations we describe, however, the dissenters are moderating their votes (by joining the majority), possibly for better reasoning or perhaps to avoid worse outcomes.

[167] See, for example, Andrew Koppelman, *Gay Rights vs. Religious Liberty? The Unnecessary Conflict* 1, 4 (Oxford, forthcoming 2020) ("Principles are a distraction, which make each side's claims seem more uncompromisable than they are. . . . Sometimes, the right thing to do is not to follow a principle, but to accurately discern the interests at stake and cobble together an approach that gives some weight to each of those interests."); Robert Tsai, *Practical Equality: Forging Justice in a Divided Nation* 6 (Norton, 2019) (describing a "tussle between principle and realism"); Gutmann and Thompson, 8 Perspectives on Polit at 1125 (cited in note 164) ("The resistance to democratic compromise is anchored in what we call an uncompromising mindset, a cluster of attitudes and arguments that encourage standing on principle and mistrusting opponents.").

[168] See Margalit, *On Compromise and Rotten Compromises* at 121 (cited in note 10) (defining tribalism as "a permanent state of hostility" to those outside one's own circle).

[169] Cf. Simon Căbulea May, *Principled Compromise and the Abortion Controversy*, 33 Phil & Pub Affairs 317, 318 (2005) ("Political compromise occurs when a political agent invokes the fact of disagreement as a reason to accept an alternative that she perceives to be worse on its own merits than her initial position.").

something. Being willing to engage in this kind of give and take is important for the success of democratic politics.[170]

Some hold that compromise can only ever be justified by pragmatic reasons,[171] while others believe that it can be justified by other types of reasons: to show respect for others, to observe reciprocity, to manage moral complexity, or to accommodate those with whom we disagree.[172] But under either of these views, compromise happens when parties respond to disagreement by accepting a result that they see as inferior to what they would otherwise regard as the best outcome.[173]

Although compromise is *often* justified, it is not *always* justified. There are times when declining to agree is not tribalistic or unnecessarily divisive. When the principled and pragmatic reasons for accepting a second-best outcome are insufficient to overcome the principled and pragmatic reasons for the first-best outcome, compromise is properly rejected in favor of continued disagreement or dissent. In those situations, a refusal to compromise is reasonable.

For example, dissent can be justified when the majority is arguing aggressively for outcomes that push beyond existing moral or political norms because that majority is engaged in an effort to widen or shift the range of acceptable or authoritative outcomes away from those that are ideal. Compromising in these circumstances may assist in the majority's efforts to manipulate the Overton Window. By contrast, protest raises an alarm—it warns that manipulation is afoot.

Here we follow Avishai Margalit in distinguishing between *effective politics*, which is designed to alter outcomes, and *expressive politics*, which does "not affect the outcome in the foreseeable future but merely express[es] an attitude toward the outcome, be it a negative

---

[170] See Max Weber, *Politics as a Vocation*, in H. H. Gerth and C. Wright Mills, trans and eds, *From Max Weber: Essays in Sociology* (Oxford, 1946) (arguing that politicians cannot adhere solely to an "ethic of ultimate ends" but must also act according to an "ethic of responsibility"); Amy Gutmann and Dennis Thompson, *Valuing Compromise for the Common Good*, 142 Daedalus 185, 187 (2013) ("Classic compromises serve the common good not only by improving on the status quo from the agreeing parties' particular perspectives, but also by contributing to a robust democratic process.").

[171] See May, 33 Phil & Pub Affairs at 347 (cited in note 169).

[172] See id at 338–46 (discussing but ultimately rejecting all these considerations as principled grounds for moral compromise). But see Daniel Weinstock, *On the Possibility of Principled Moral Compromise*, 16 Critical Rev Intl Soc & Pol Phil 537, 538 (defending principled compromise in response to May's criticisms).

[173] Compare Weinstock, 16 Critical Rev Intl Soc & Polit Phil at 539 (cited in note 172), with Simon Căbulea May, *Moral Compromise, Civic Friendship, and Political Reconciliation*, 14 Critical Rev Intl Soc & Polit Phil 581, 582–84 (2011).

attitude of protest or a positive attitude of support."[174] Whereas effective politics is an exercise of hard power, often to achieve immediate outcomes, expressive politics is an exercise of soft power that is designed to affect the range of accepted policy options in the long term.[175] Expression in politics is "a bet on the future," in Margalit's phrase.[176] Accordingly, refusing to compromise can communicate protest against an assertive effort to manipulate norms—a protest that might not be immediately effective but that may exert influence over time and into the distant future.

Expression matters here because compromise ordinarily confers legitimacy.[177] In fact, this feature makes it attractive, particularly in times of intense partisanship. Compromise lowers the temperature of conflict precisely because it involves an exchange of recognition. But it can become unattractive when there is a power disparity. When a party in power asks for a compromise, its goal may be public recognition by the weaker party.[178] And then a refusal by the weaker party can communicate a critique of the stronger party's claim to legitimacy.

Recall the argument that in the current climate of political polarization, principled decision making is the enemy of peace and therefore unreasonable. This pragmatic criticism captures something important about the zeitgeist, but it can be overstated. Principled reasoning need not demand absolutes, but instead it may interpret abstract values and apply them to specific situations.[179] The criticism also fails to acknowledge that phenomena like appeasement and compromise are second-best strategies that must be evaluated using a mix of practical and principled considerations.

In considering liberal Justices' decisions in religious freedom cases, it may be right to say that they are engaged in praiseworthy compromise in any given case, and perhaps even overall. But if the Roberts

---

[174] Margalit, *On Compromise and Rotten Compromises* at 110–11 (cited in note 10).

[175] Id at 112.

[176] Id.

[177] See id at 41. Margalit distinguishes between "sanguine compromise," which confers recognition and "legitimacy on the point of view of the other side," with "anemic compromise," a game theoretic conception that refers to any agreement within each party's bargaining range. He argues that sanguine compromise fits better with the "phenomenology of political compromise," by which he means "the central features of compromises, implicit in our practices, even before we are aware of any theory about it." Id at 42.

[178] Id at 112.

[179] See Nelson Tebbe, *Should the Left Dissent?*, 34 Const Comm 463 (2019).

Court is engaged in a broader and longer-term effort to remake its disestablishment and free exercise jurisprudence, pushing that law further away from what the liberal Justices take to be ideal, then cutting deals in particular cases may look less like compromise and more like appeasement. That is, it may be not bilateral but unilateral: these Justices are giving up something immensely valuable—their defense of ideal outcomes—in exchange for insignificant moderations that do little to stop or slow the doctrinal inversions that we are witnessing under the Religion Clauses.

C. CO-OPTATION

Another objection to our argument might be that Justices who lean left are engaged in a long-term effort to build good will with Justices on the right, in the hope that they can be persuaded to vote for progressive outcomes in future cases. That is, liberal Justices may be acting strategically, but their aim is to earn the trust of persuadable colleagues on the conservative side and to move them slowly in a liberal direction—if not overall, then in particular areas of law or at least in individual cases. We can call this a co-optation strategy.

Those who believe that co-optation can work may point to the examples of Justices O'Connor, Kennedy, and Souter, who were appointed by Republican presidents and who formed majorities with their liberal colleagues on a range of salient issues, including abortion, affirmative action, and LGBT rights.[180] According to this objection, the relative moderation of these Justices was due in part to cultivation by liberal Justices who were willing to reach across the aisle, so to speak, and build trust over a long duration.[181] Today, similarly, one might argue that liberal Justices are engaged not in appeasement but rather in an effort to form alliances with the more moderate members of the Roberts Court.

---

[180] For discussion of these Justices' jurisprudence during their years on the Rehnquist Court, see generally Mark Tushnet, *A Court Divided: The Rehnquist Court and the Future of Constitutional Law* (Norton, 2005); Tinsley E. Yarbrough, *The Rehnquist Court and the Constitution* (Oxford, 2000).

[181] See Linda Greenhouse, *Justice John Paul Stevens as Abortion-Rights Strategist*, 43 U C Davis L Rev 749, 777–82 (2010) (discussing Justice Stevens's efforts to build and mediate relationships with Justices O'Connor, Kennedy, and Souter in cases involving abortion rights); Charles F. Jacobs and Christopher E. Smith, *The Influence of Justice John Paul Stevens: Opinion Assignments by the Senior Associate Justice*, 51 Santa Clara L Rev 743, 752–62 (2011) (discussing efforts by Justice Stevens to win over or shore up Justice Kennedy's vote).

For example, Justice Kagan may be seeking to build up capital with conservatives. In a recent profile, Margaret Talbot wrote that "when Kagan votes with the conservatives on religious questions, as she did in the cross case, she may earn some long-term good will ... reminding them that she does not take the hard line that Ginsburg and Sotomayor do."[182] Talbot also quoted an unnamed lawyer involved in *Masterpiece Cakeshop*, who expressed disappointment in Justice Kagan's vote but also explained that "Kagan has to live with these five conservative Justices forever. She's playing the long game, saying, 'Look how reasonable I am.'"[183] And Talbot has observed that Justice Kagan is making arguments about the Court's legitimacy that are designed to appeal to Chief Justice Roberts, if not to some of those on his right.[184] So maybe her votes in support of conservative majorities, and those of Justice Breyer, are examples of co-optation rather than appeasement.

We take this objection seriously, but we believe it is open to doubt, at least in cases concerning disestablishment and free exercise. For our purposes, co-optation occurs when a party offers concessions in order to build an alliance with decision makers, in the hope that those decision makers will then support the party's preferred outcomes in the future. Like appeasement, co-optation is asymmetric in the sense that concessions are made with no (or only minimal) reciprocity in the immediate case. A strategy of co-optation is also sustained over a period of time. The co-opting party's goal is not merely conflict avoidance or containment, but instead to create a lasting coalition that can lead to more ideal outcomes in the long term.

Co-optation can shade into appeasement, however, when there is inattention to its possibility of success. If the targets of co-optation are not amenable—if instead they have the ambition and the political

---

[182] Talbot, *Is the Supreme Court's Fate* (cited in note 158).

[183] Id.

[184] Talbot notes that Justices Breyer and Kagan have emphasized the importance of precedent for the Court's legitimacy. She writes, "At Georgetown Law, in July, [Justice Kagan] said, 'Maybe the worst thing people could think about our legal system is that, you know, it's just like one person retires or dies, and another person gets on the Court, and everything is up for grabs.' That's the kind of appeal to the Court's long-term reputation and legitimacy that could continue to work on Roberts. It's not likely to persuade, say, Alito or Thomas. Samuel Bagenstos, a constitutional-law scholar at the University of Michigan, told me, 'Kagan's tactical approach can be helpful in cases where Justices do not feel a very deep ideological affinity—but a tactical approach is not going to overcome a real ideological push.'" Id.

power to move constitutional discourse in their preferred direction—then offering concessions may only lend legitimacy to their projects.

It is unclear whether the center-left Justices can succeed in winning over their center-right colleagues in religious freedom cases. However much credibility or personal and political capital they may have established—and they may have established a considerable amount—they are facing a conservative effort that is succeeding in revolutionizing constitutional law concerning both disestablishment and free exercise. That effort has deep roots and widespread support in conservative legal movements.[185]

Although we cannot pursue the point here, we also suspect that constitutional politics are different today from when Justices O'Connor, Kennedy, and Souter shifted to the left on various issues. Most obviously, political polarization on the Court and in the country has intensified significantly.[186] To take only one simplistic measure, Senate confirmation votes on those Justices were almost unanimous,[187] whereas the votes on Chief Justice Roberts and Justice Kavanaugh—the only realistic targets of a co-optation strategy—were not.[188] Those differences reflect changes in Senate culture, of course, but they also reflect changes in wider politics, which have in turn shaped the individual Justices, however indeterminately. Differences like those are going to make it more difficult for a co-optation strategy to succeed.

When a conservative majority has coalesced around a given issue—here, religious freedom—liberals and progressives face difficult strategic choices, some of which carry the dangers we have identified. How can they assess the likelihood that seeking to make common ground with the least conservative members of such a majority will not simply embolden a program of shifting constitutional norms away from protecting free and equal citizenship? There are no easy solutions, but recognizing the trajectory of religious freedom doctrine and appreciating

---

[185] See Schragger and Schwartzman, *Establishment Clause Inversion* at 51–56 (cited in note 19); Corbin, Ala L Rev (cited in note 19); Elizabeth Sepper, *Free Exercise Lochnerism*, 115 Colum L Rev 1457, 1507–18 (2015); Douglas NeJaime and Reva B. Siegel, *Conscience Wars: Complicity-Based Conscience Claims in Religion and Politics*, 124 Yale L J 2516, 2544–52 (2015).

[186] See sources cited in note 1.

[187] Justice Souter was confirmed in 1990 by a vote of 90 to 9. Justice Kennedy and Justice O'Connor were confirmed by unanimous votes in 1988 and 1981, respectively. United States Senate, Supreme Court Nominations *(Present–1789)*, https://www.senate.gov/legislative/nominations/SupremeCourtNominations1789present.htm.

[188] Chief Justice Roberts was confirmed in 2005 by a vote of 78 to 22, while Justice Kavanaugh was confirmed in 2018 by a vote of 50 to 48. Id.

the way political polarization has affected the distribution of constitutional perspectives can provide some guidance. Though polarization in party politics has influenced constitutional politics indirectly and incompletely, it has also done so unmistakably. And that makes a co-optation strategy riskier and more likely to collapse into appeasement.

V. Conclusion

The Court's decision in *American Legion* is part of a generational transformation taking place within Establishment Clause doctrine and within the law of religious freedom more generally. The Court continues to dismantle decades of separationist doctrine, replacing it with a regime that is far more solicitous of government favoritism toward the views of religious majorities. Although the outcome in *American Legion* was no surprise, and while the Court remains highly fractured in how to approach the proper interpretation of the Establishment Clause, the case is significant for what it says about the Court's future trajectory and about the willingness of liberal Justices to engage in protest and dissent. In our view, the lopsidedness of the vote in *American Legion*, a pattern also reflected in leading cases governing state funding and religious exemptions, raises concerns about appeasement.

We recognize that claims of appeasement are never welcome in our political culture. Despite widespread usage, the concept has retained its powerful negative historical association. There is, however, no adequate substitute for the concept, and clarity about its meanings should facilitate our understanding of political and legal decision making. Appeasement can be distinguished from other strategies, including compromise and co-optation, and it should be possible to ask probing questions about whether judges have adopted any of these strategies and what the normative implications might be. We have offered one set of arguments in the context of the Court's recent Establishment Clause jurisprudence and asked whether appeasement is at work and, if so, what risks that might entail as the Court reshapes its understanding of religious freedom.

WILLIAM BAUDE

PRECEDENT AND DISCRETION

Supreme Court precedent is a topic of perennial prominence. The Court overruled or severely limited multiple precedents last year, just as it did the year before that. Because of our widely repeated norm of stare decisis, every overruling is criticized. Scholars have then debated whether the Court needs a stronger norm of stare decisis, so that it overrules fewer cases.[1]

This focus is misguided. Rather than worrying about which cases will be cast aside, we should pay more attention to those precedents that are left standing in place. Many of the Court's questionable precedents nonetheless go unquestioned. The real problem is not that the Court overrules too much, but that it overrules without a theory that explains why it overrules so little.

At last, it seems such theories may be coming. Last Term, Justice Thomas (in *Gamble v United States*)[2] and Justice Alito (in *Gundy v United States*)[3] each attempted to explain some of their decisions to

---

William Baude is Professor of Law and Aaron Director Research Scholar, University of Chicago Law School.

AUTHOR'S NOTE: Thanks to Sean Frazzette and Kurtis Michael for their research assistance and to the students in my 2019 Precedent seminar for their valuable feedback on the topic. Further thanks to Tom Adams, Sam Bray, Justin Driver, Chad Flanders, Jeff Hetzel, Richard Re, Stephen Sachs, and my colleagues at the University of Chicago Faculty Workshop for their comments on an initial draft.

[1] Compare Randy J. Kozel, *Settled Versus Right* (Cambridge, 2017), with Frederick Schauer, *Stare Decisis—Rhetoric and Reality in the Supreme Court*, 2018 Supreme Court Review 121, 141–43 (2019).

[2] 139 S Ct 1960 (2019).

[3] 139 S Ct 2116 (2019).

© 2020 by The University of Chicago. All rights reserved.
978-0-226-70856-0/2020/2019-0007$10.00

reject and adhere to precedent. These explanations deserve serious scholarly scrutiny, which they have not yet received.

Unfortunately, these interventions do not solve, and indeed they exacerbate, the problem. What they propose is neither a regime of adherence to precedent, nor a regime without precedent, but rather a regime in which individual Justices have substantial discretion whether to adhere to precedent or not. This turns precedent from a tool to constrain discretion into a tool to expand discretion, and ultimately into a tool to evade more fundamental legal principles.

Part I describes the state of stare decisis in the Court today. Part II discusses Justice Thomas's theory that precedent must be overruled when it is "demonstrably erroneous." Part III describes Justice Alito's theory that precedents ought not be overruled on the basis of "halfway originalism." Part IV explains why discretionary precedent—of which these theories are examples—is worse than no precedent at all.

I. Precedent in the New Roberts Court

The Supreme Court's commitment to precedent has become a central topic of both legal theory and legal politics. This development is predictable when the working majority of the Court changes, because of the mismatch between the cases that have been decided in the past and the way the same Justices would decide them today.

During the last two Supreme Court nomination hearings, precedent was cast in a starring role. Now-Justice Gorsuch repeatedly answered questions about past cases by promising to analyze them under the "law of precedent"[4] and reminded the Senators that he had coauthored an "excellent doorstop"[5] of a book on that topic. Now-Justice Kavanaugh (also a coauthor of that doorstop) went further, arguing to the Senators that "the system of precedent comes from Article III itself."[6]

Last Term put those commitments to the test. The Court had four cases that directly confronted the question of whether to overrule

---

[4] Confirmation Hearing on the Nomination of Hon. Neil M. Gorsuch to be an Associate Justice of the Supreme Court of the United States, 115th Cong, 1st Sess 74–76, 135 (2017).

[5] Id at 74. See also id at 135 ("great doorstop"). See generally Bryan A. Garner, ed, *The Law of Judicial Precedent* (West, 2016).

[6] Confirmation Hearing on the Nomination of Hon. Brett M. Kavanaugh to be an Associate Justice of the Supreme Court of the United States, 115th Cong, 2nd Sess 226 (2018) (Kavanaugh Confirmation Hearing). See also id at 149, 157, 503–04.

past Supreme Court cases, as well as two more in which the Court was asked to formally limit or narrow[7] a precedent:

In *Knick v Township of Scott*,[8] the Court overruled *Williamson County Regional Planning Commission v Hamilton Bank*,[9] making it easier to bring federal takings claims. And in *Franchise Tax Board of California v Hyatt*,[10] the Court overruled *Nevada v Hall*,[11] making it possible for states to demand sovereign immunity in other states' courts.

Meanwhile, in *Gamble v United States*,[12] the Court declined to overrule three cases establishing a "dual sovereignty exception" to the principle of double jeopardy.[13] And in *Kisor v Wilkie*,[14] the Court declined to overrule two cases requiring deference to agency interpretations of ambiguous regulations,[15] albeit with some warnings about the narrow scope of those cases.

Additionally, in *American Legion v American Humanist Association*,[16] the Court expressly disavowed the applicability of a prior Establishment Clause precedent—*Lemon v Kurtzman*[17]—to "longstanding monuments, symbols, and practices."[18] And in *Herrera v Wyoming*,[19] the Court wrote of its precedent in *Ward v Race Horse*[20] that while the case had not been "expressly overruled" it was nonetheless "repudiated" in its reasoning.[21]

---

[7] See generally Richard M. Re, *Narrowing Precedent in the Supreme Court*, 114 Colum L Rev 1861 (2015).

[8] 139 S Ct 2162 (2019).

[9] 473 US 172 (1985).

[10] 139 S Ct 1485 (2019).

[11] 440 US 410 (1979).

[12] 139 S Ct 1960 (2019).

[13] See, for example, *United States v Lanza*, 260 US 377 (1922); *Abbate v United States*, 359 US 187 (1959); *Bartkus v Illinois*, 359 US 121 (1959).

[14] 139 S Ct 2400 (2019).

[15] See *Auer v Robbins*, 519 US 452 (1997); *Bowles v Seminole Rock & Sand Co.*, 325 US 410 (1945).

[16] 139 S Ct 2067 (2019).

[17] 403 US 602 (1971).

[18] *American Legion*, 139 S Ct at 2081–82 (plurality). Justice Thomas voiced his express agreement with this part of the plurality opinion and noted that he would "take the logical next step and overrule the *Lemon* test in all contexts." Id at 2097 (Thomas, J, concurring in the judgment).

[19] 139 S Ct 1686 (2019).

[20] 163 US 504 (1896).

[21] *Herrera*, 139 S Ct at 1697.

The obvious accusation is that the Roberts Court is poised to cut a swath through any precedent that a five-Justice majority believes to be incorrect—a warning sounded in dissents by both Justice Breyer and Justice Kagan,[22] in cynical echo of Justice Brennan's saying that "with five votes, you could accomplish anything."[23] This complaint has been echoed in much commentary about the Court as well.[24]

But things are not so simple. Nobody on the Court believes in absolute stare decisis.[25] Nobody thinks it was wrong for the Court to overturn, say, *Plessy v Ferguson*[26] during the 1950s. Moreover, the most systematic reviews of Supreme Court overruling suggest that there is no increasing trend: the Roberts Court overrules precedent less often than the Rehnquist, Burger, or Warren Courts.[27]

This leads us to the more important concern. Compared to the small number of Supreme Court decisions that have been overruled, what about the many precedents that the same Justices have *not* overruled, and often refused to even consider whether to overrule? The Court's decisions to stand by precedent are far more common, and often less justified, than its decisions to overrule. For instance:

In 2018 the Supreme Court decided *Janus v AFSCME*,[28] overturning part of its prior decision in *Abood v Detroit Board of Education*,[29]

---

[22] *Knick*, 139 S Ct at 2190 (Kagan, J, dissenting); *Franchise Tax Board*, 139 S Ct at 1506 (Breyer, J, dissenting).

[23] Seth Stern and Stephen Wermiel, *Justice Brennan: Liberal Champion* 196 (Houghton Mifflin, 2010). But for an ambiguity here, see Mark Tushnet, *Themes in Warren Court Biographies*, 70 NYU L Rev 748, 763 (1995) ("Some clerks understood Brennan to mean that it takes five votes to do anything, others that with five votes you could do anything").

[24] See, for example, Charles Fried, *Not Conservative*, Harv L Rev Blog (July 3, 2018), archived at https://perma.cc/G568-Y5LU; *The Activist Roberts Court, 10 Years In*, New York Times (July 4, 2015), archived at https://perma.cc/M64X-YZ86; Erwin Chemerinsky, *Does Precedent Matter to Conservative Justices on the Roberts Court?*, ABA J (June 27, 2019), archived at https://perma.cc/F3TM-7F9X.

[25] Justice Kagan, who voted to uphold precedent in five of the six cases, still voted to repudiate *Race Horse* in *Herrera*. At the other extreme, Justice Gorsuch voted against precedent in all six cases.

[26] 163 US 537 (1896), overruled at least as to education by *Brown v Board of Education*, 347 US 483, 494–95 (1954), and then rejected as to transportation in *Gayle v Browder*, 352 US 903 (1956).

[27] See *Supreme Court Decisions Overruled by Subsequent Decision* (Government Printing Office, 2017), archived at https://perma.cc/V6YJ-TEP5; Jonathan Adler, *The Stare Decisis Court*, Reason: The Volokh Conspiracy (July 18, 2018), archived at https://perma.cc/3A2P-D437; Brandon J. Murrill, *The Supreme Court's Overruling of Constitutional Precedent*, Congressional Research Service (Sept 24, 2018), archived at https://perma.cc/TM8N-YFYV.

[28] 138 S Ct 2448 (2018).

[29] 431 US 209 (1977).

and rendering mandatory contributions to public sector unions unconstitutional. But the Court did not seriously question the other half of its decision in *Abood*—the half that was actually wrong—which had subjected such contributions to First Amendment scrutiny in the first place.[30]

In its 2019 decision in *Franchise Tax Board*, the Supreme Court overturned its precedent in *Nevada v Hall*, despite plausible arguments for retaining the decision. But the Court did not revisit several jurisdictional precedents that were far more clearly erroneous.[31] Indeed, the Court didn't even mention the problem, even though those issues were jurisdictional.

In case after case, the Court has applied the doctrine of qualified immunity to protect officers from liability for their unconstitutional actions. It has done so despite a civil rights statute that explicitly creates official liability, and despite the lack of a valid legal source for the judge-crafted doctrine.[32] Even as various Justices have expressed misgivings about the doctrine,[33] all of them have continued to apply it and the Court has declined to revisit it.

And of course similar examples abound. Adherence to precedent is still the rule, not the exception, in nearly every case before the Court.

The real problem with the Supreme Court's decisions to overrule precedent is not *how much*, but *when*. The Court does not consistently adhere to its precedents, but it does not consistently revisit them either.

The Court's own cases do invoke reasons when they decide whether prior cases should be overruled. But there are competing sets of reasons, laid down in highly controversial cases,[34] and they leave plenty of discretion in the hands of the Court, as evidenced from its recent disagreements. That 800-page doorstop coauthored by Justices Gorsuch and Kavanaugh contains little guidance on the seemingly

---

[30] See William Baude and Eugene Volokh, *Compelled Subsidies and the First Amendment*, 132 Harv L Rev 171, 180–89 (2018).

[31] See William Baude and Stephen E. Sachs, *The Misunderstood Eleventh Amendment* (October 8, 2019) 14–15, 17–20, 40–46, online at https://ssrn.com/abstract=3466298.

[32] See William Baude, *Is Qualified Immunity Unlawful?*, 106 Cal L Rev 45, 77 (2018).

[33] See *Ziglar v Abbasi*, 137 S Ct 1843, 1871 (2017) (Thomas, J, concurring in part and concurring in the judgment); *Kisela v Hughes*, 138 S Ct 1148, 1161 (2018) (Sotomayor, J, dissenting, joined by Ginsburg, J).

[34] Compare *Payne v Tennessee*, 501 US 808, 828–30 (1991), with *Planned Parenthood of Southeast Pennsylvania v Casey*, 505 US 833, 854–61 (1992), and *Citizens United v Federal Election Commission*, 558 US 310, 362–65 (2010).

central question of when the Supreme Court should overturn its own case law.[35] In the last volume of this review, Professor Frederick Schauer concluded that stare decisis doctrine is so "tissue-thin" that it has little or no constraining effect on the Court.[36]

In principle, the Court could perhaps transcend this disagreement if there were at least agreement on a valid *legal source* of precedent, sufficiently determinate that it could derive rules to govern the Court's practice. But that determinate source has not materialized either. So it appears that the Justices do not in fact acknowledge a law of precedent, and maybe not even a "semblance of law" to use in law's stead.[37]

This lack of doctrine was on display last Term. No Justice was in the majority in all six of the Court's confrontations with precedent. All of the Justices, for instance, who were in the majority in *Knick* and *Franchise Tax Board* refused to join *Herrera* or *Kisor* or both. This is partly a consequence of a multimember Court; even if the Justices are individually consistent, the institution as a whole inevitably will not be.[38] It also suggests the lack of any *shared* account of stare decisis.[39]

Even if the Court as an institution is inconsistent, we might still hope for individual Justices to be consistent.[40] What made last Term somewhat hopeful was that oral arguments revealed that some of the Justices finally seemed to recognize the need for a transsubstantive, content-independent account of stare decisis. Schauer pointed out that a doctrine of stare decisis is only rhetoric unless it operates to protect some decisions that you dislike;[41] Justice Kagan started invoking the doctrine in criminal procedure cases where we might at least imagine she disagrees with the precedents.[42] Across multiple

---

[35] Garner, *Judicial Precedent* at 396–409 (cited in note 5) (describing competing "Reasons For Overruling" and "Reasons Against Overruling").

[36] Schauer, *Stare Decisis*, 2018 Supreme Court Rev at 132, 135, 137–30 (cited in note 1). See also Jeffrey A. Segal and Harold J. Spaeth, *The Influence of Stare Decisis on the Votes of U.S. Supreme Court Justices*, 40 Am J Pol Sci 971 (1996).

[37] See generally Stephen E. Sachs, *Precedent and the Semblance of Law*, 33 Const Comm 417 (2018).

[38] Frank H. Easterbrook, *Ways of Criticizing the Court*, 95 Harv L Rev 802, 812 (1982).

[39] See id at 818 n 39 ("Stare decisis is applied so loosely that it seems fair to say that it does not exist as a doctrine").

[40] Id at 832 ("There is no reason why we cannot ask each Justice to develop a principled jurisprudence and to adhere to it consistently").

[41] Schauer, 2018 Supreme Court Review at 128 (cited in note 1).

[42] See Oral Argument, *Gamble v United States*, No 17-647, *20, 38–40 (Dec 6, 2018); Oral Argument, *Ramos v Louisiana*, No 18-5924, *21–22, 29–30, 37–39, 49–50 (Oct 7, 2019).

cases Justice Kavanaugh began to float a theory that stare decisis was binding unless a prior decision was either "grievously" or "egregiously" wrong, plus several other factors.[43] But in the end, neither of these Justices provided a theory of precedent in writing.

Two other Justices, however, did provide an account of how they would confront precedent. Justice Thomas did so in an extended concurrence in *Gamble v United States*, maintaining that he was forbidden to follow precedent in any case where it was "demonstrably erroneous."[44] Justice Alito did so in a much shorter concurrence in *Gundy v United States*,[45] which seemed to echo a passage in his previous opinion in *Janus* decrying "halfway originalism."[46]

These accounts deserve further scrutiny. They confront serious problems about the role of precedent in the Supreme Court. Indeed, they deserve plaudits for addressing overarching theories of precedent at all. And they each provide accounts that may initially seem startling, but are plausible upon closer inspection.

Nonetheless, despite the credit they deserve, both of these accounts of precedent ultimately share a disconcerting feature: they end up giving the Justices an important degree of discretion in deciding whether to adhere to an erroneous precedent. That discretion, as I will eventually explain, mutates precedent into the opposite of what it should be.

II. Justice Thomas and the Demonstrable Error

Justice Thomas's separate opinion on precedent arrived as a concurrence to the Court's decision in *Gamble*, which decided to retain the "dual sovereignty exception" to the doctrine of double jeopardy. The merits of the case are of only tangential relevance here. The dual sovereignty exception permits a defendant to be placed into jeopardy twice for the same offense, so long as it is by two different sovereign governments (such as a state and the federal government). Prior opinions by Justices Thomas and Ginsburg, as well as a pile of

---

[43] See Oral Argument, *Franchise Tax Board v Hyatt*, No 17-1299, *53–54 (Jan 9, 2019); Oral Argument, *Gamble v United States*, No 17-647, *41–42 (Dec 6, 2018).

[44] *Gamble*, 139 S Ct at 1981 (Thomas, J, concurring); see Part II.

[45] 139 S Ct 2116 (2019).

[46] Id at 2131 (Alito, J, concurring); *Janus*, 138 S Ct at 2470. See Part III.

learned research, had called the doctrine into question, especially on originalist grounds.[47]

In *Gamble*, the Court granted certiorari to decide whether the doctrine should be overruled, and it might have seemed that to agree to ask the question was to foreshadow the answer. But in a 7–2 decision, the Court ultimately decided to retain the doctrine, concluding that the historical evidence against the doctrine was too "feeble" to outweigh other arguments including the Court's many precedents.[48] One of those seven was Justice Thomas, who wrote that "the historical record does not bear out my initial skepticism of the dual-sovereignty doctrine."[49]

Even though his view of stare decisis was no longer relevant to the case, Justice Thomas decided to write at length "to address the proper role of the doctrine of stare decisis," a doctrine which he believed had gone astray from the Court's "judicial duty under Article III."[50] Channeling academic arguments that might once have seemed fringe, Justice Thomas argued that judges have an obligation—not just a *power*, but a *duty*—to disregard and overrule any precedent that is "demonstrably erroneous."[51]

This opinion provided a serious intellectual framework for Justice Thomas's long-standing skepticism of stare decisis. Justice Thomas has aptly been regarded as one of the Justices most willing to overturn incorrect decisions,[52] and has published many separate opinions calling for the reconsideration of settled precedent.[53] In *Gamble* Justice Thomas explained that his long-standing practice of disregarding precedent was not only legitimate, but sometimes obligatory.

---

[47] *Puerto Rico v Sanchez Valle*, 136 S Ct 1863, 1877 (2016) (Ginsburg, J, concurring, joined by Thomas, J); see also Brief of Amicus Curiae Stuart Banner in Support of Petitioner, *Walker v Texas*, No 16-636 (Dec 12, 2016).

[48] *Gamble*, 139 S Ct at 1964.

[49] Id at 1980 (Thomas, J, concurring).

[50] Id at 1981.

[51] Id.

[52] Adam Liptak, *Precedent, Meet Clarence Thomas. You May Not Get Along*, New York Times A13 (March 4, 2019).

[53] For two of many examples, see *Eastern Enterprises v Apfel*, 524 US 498, 538 (1998) (Thomas, J, concurring) (calling for reconsideration of *Calder v Bull*, 3 Dall 386 (1798); *McDonald v City of Chicago*, 561 US 742, 850–58 (2010) (Thomas, J, concurring in judgment) (calling for overruling *The Slaughterhouse Cases*, 83 US (16 Wall) 36 (1873) and *United States v Cruikshank*, 92 US 542 (1876)).

The steps in Justice Thomas's argument are relatively simple: Legal questions can have right and wrong answers. Statutes and constitutional provisions are generally the controlling sources of law in federal courts. Precedents themselves are not law. So to the extent that a precedent reaches the demonstrably wrong answer about a statute or constitutional provision, it is contrary to the law, and judges should follow the law rather than the precedent.[54]

Justice Thomas acknowledged some academic precursors of this argument, especially work by Professor Caleb Nelson.[55] In particular, Nelson had forcefully emphasized the distinction between precedents that were demonstrably erroneous and thus invalid, and other precedents that fell within a plausible range of indeterminacy. But Thomas's variation of the theory brought an important difference: the introduction of discretion.

In cases where a precedent was plausible—that is, it was not "demonstrably erroneous"—Justice Thomas maintained that a judge had discretion. The judge could follow precedent, or not. "[W]hen traditional tools of legal interpretation show that the earlier decision adopted a textually permissible interpretation of the law," then courts "*may (but need not)* adhere to an incorrect decision as precedent."[56] Justice Thomas repeatedly emphasized this point: "Of course, a subsequent court may nonetheless conclude that an incorrect precedent should be abandoned, even if the precedent might fall within the range of permissible interpretations. But nothing in the Constitution requires courts to take that step."[57]

In this respect Justice Thomas's theory departs from the historical approach to stare decisis described by Nelson. On Nelson's account, judicial discretion was more constrained. When the underlying written law[58] was clear, that law constrained judicial discretion. When that law was indeterminate, and thus the precedent was plausible, stare decisis would "restrain the 'arbitrary discretion' of courts" by

---

[54] *Gamble*, 139 S Ct at 1983–84 (Thomas, J, concurring).

[55] Caleb Nelson, *Stare Decisis and Demonstrably Erroneous Precedents*, 87 Va L Rev 1 (2001). See also Gary Lawson, *The Constitutional Case Against Precedent*, 17 Harv J L & Pub Pol 23, 26 (1994).

[56] *Gamble*, 139 S Ct at 1984 (Thomas, J, concurring) (emphasis added).

[57] Id at 1986.

[58] Or in the case of the common law, the "external sources." See Nelson, 87 Va L Rev at 23–27 (cited in note 55), for a complicated debate not important for constitutional purposes.

requiring adherence to precedent.⁵⁹ Justice Thomas abandoned that requirement, without having the boldness to go further and argue that stare decisis was always forbidden. Instead, Justice Thomas created a space where stare decisis produced discretion instead of constraint.

This discretionary departure is especially ironic, because Justice Thomas repeatedly justified his approach on the ground that it was necessary to constrain judicial discretion. He noted that it was "always 'tempting for judges to confuse our own preferences with the requirements of the law,'" and that "the Court's *stare decisis* doctrine exacerbates that temptation by giving the veneer of respectability to our continued application of demonstrably incorrect precedents."⁶⁰ He argued that we should "restore our *stare decisis* jurisprudence to ensure that we exercise 'mer[e] judgment,' ... anything less invites arbitrariness into judging."⁶¹

In fact, however, Justice Thomas was only halfway willing to "restore" this historical account of stare decisis. He proposed a mandatory, historical account of stare decisis for demonstrably erroneous precedents, but a discretionary, novel account of stare decisis for more ambiguous precedents. His approach was therefore only halfway able to fulfill its goals of constraining arbitrariness and judicial discretion.

Moreover, Justice Thomas's approach tries to eliminate arbitrariness, but such arbitrariness also creeps back in through other aspects of the Court's procedures. For instance, the vast majority of precedents are never questioned by the parties. So it becomes very important to know how Justice Thomas's rule of precedent interacts with the traditional rule of waiver. Justice Thomas addressed this issue in a footnote:

> I am not suggesting that the Court must independently assure itself that each precedent relied on in every opinion is correct as a matter of original understanding. We may, consistent with our constitutional duty and the Judiciary's historical practice, proceed on the understanding that our predecessors properly discharged their constitutional role until we have reason

---

⁵⁹ Nelson, 87 Va L Rev at 5 (cited in note 55), quoting Federalist 78 (Hamilton) in Clinton Rossiter, ed, *The Federalist Papers* 439 (1999).

⁶⁰ *Gamble*, 139 S Ct at 1981 (Thomas, J, concurring), quoting *Obergefell v Hodges*, 135 S Ct 2584, 2612 (2015) (Roberts, J, dissenting).

⁶¹ *Gamble*, 139 S Ct at 1981 (Thomas, J, concurring).

to think otherwise—as, for example, when a party raises the issue or a previous opinion persuasively critiques the disputed precedent.[62]

This answer, too, renders stare decisis more discretionary than would application of an ordinary render waiver rule.

Rather than saying that a precedent will not be reconsidered if a challenge to it is waived, Justice Thomas allows only that the Court "may" decline to investigate the correctness of a precedent. There is discretion. And rather than limit those who can challenge a precedent to the parties, Justice Thomas also allows prior opinions to do so, and apparently other unnamed sources ("for example"). This apparently creates discretion to decide when an amicus brief, an academic article, or other source might circumvent the waiver rule. Thus a Justice may, but need not, decline to investigate the validity of a precedent that has gone unchallenged.

A final example of discretion and potential arbitrariness is created by the Court's own certiorari process. The Supreme Court's appellate jurisdiction is largely discretionary, allowing the Court to decide what cases, and what questions presented in those cases, it would like to resolve. Since the parties are supposed to restrict themselves to the questions presented,[63] this means that the certiorari process can filter out most attempts to revisit any of the Court's precedents.[64]

This filtering ability is compounded by a Court-pronounced rule of strong vertical precedent. Lower courts are never supposed to declare the Supreme Court's precedents overruled if the Court has not. No matter how "wobbly" or "moth-eaten" the "foundations" of its precedents, the Court has instructed, "it is this Court's prerogative alone to overrule one of its own precedents."[65] If this rule is followed,[66] then no circuit split emerges about the validity of a Supreme

---

[62] Id at 1986 n 6.

[63] US S Ct Rule 14.1(a); US S Ct Rule 24.1(a).

[64] See Amy Coney Barrett, *Precedent and Jurisprudential Disagreement*, 91 Tex L Rev 1711, 1731–33 (2013); Amy Coney Barrett and John Copeland Nagle, *Congressional Originalism*, 19 U Pa J Const L 1, 16–23 (2016); Frederick Schauer, *Stare Decisis and the Selection Effect*, in Christopher J. Peters, ed, *Precedent in the United States Supreme Court* 121 (Springer, 2012).

[65] *State Oil Co. v Khan*, 522 US 3, 20 (1997). See also *Bosse v Oklahoma*, 137 S Ct 1, 2 (2016); *United States v Hatter*, 532 US 557, 567 (2001); *Agostini v Felton*, 521 US 203, 237 (1997); *Rodriguez de Quijas v Shearson/American Express, Inc.*, 490 US 477, 484 (1989).

[66] To be sure, there have been important cases where it was not, such as the lower-court cases leading up to the recognition of same-sex marriage in *Obergefell v Hodges*, 135 S Ct 2584 (2015), that concluded that the Supreme Court's summary affirmance in *Baker v Nelson*, 409 US 810 (1972), was no longer controlling. See Richard M. Re, *Narrowing Supreme Court*

Court precedent, and circuit splits are one of the primary reasons the Court grants certiorari.[67]

This is how the same Justice who agreed that the Court's qualified immunity jurisprudence should be revisited[68] could nonetheless apply it unblinkingly in subsequent cases.[69] The *duty* to disregard demonstrably erroneous precedents is a lot less powerful if it applies only to precedents that the Justices have chosen to reconsider when exercising their discretion to vote for certiorari. As Judge Amy Coney Barrett and Professor John Nagle have put it: "Institutional features of Supreme Court practice permit all Justices to let some sleeping dogs lie, and so far as we are aware, no one has ever argued that a Justice is duty-bound to wake them up."[70]

III. Justice Alito and Halfway Originalism

While Justice Alito has also described himself as an originalist, his constitutional approach is noticeably distinct from Justice Thomas's.[71] So too, his theory of stare decisis. An interesting illustration of this difference came in Justice Alito's short concurring opinion in *Gundy*.

Gundy was a challenge to a federal statute as violating the nondelegation doctrine. Such challenges are rarely successful, but Gundy concerned a criminal statute—the Sex Offender Registration Notification Act—so there were at least three possible arguments for the challenger to win. One was to convince the Court that the statute lacked an "intelligible principle" and violated the current version of the nondelegation doctrine. A second was to convince the Court

---

Precedent from Below, 104 Georgetown L J 921, 968–71 (2016); Emily Buss, *The Divisive Supreme Court*, 2016 Supreme Court Review 25, 35–64 (2016). Some of those cases specifically relied on the fact that *Baker v Nelson* was a summary affirmance, and arguably subject to a less strong rule of vertical precedent. See *Bostic v Schaefer*, 760 F3d 352, 373 (4th Cir 2014); see also Re, 104 Georgetown L J at 968 n 235 (cited in this note).

[67] US S Ct Rule 10; Barrett, 91 Tex L Rev at 1730 (cited in note 64).

[68] *Ziglar v Abbasi*, 137 S Ct 1843, 1871 (2017) (Thomas, J, concurring in part and concurring in the judgment).

[69] See, for example, *District of Columbia v Wesby*, 138 S Ct 577, 589–93 (2018) (Thomas, J).

[70] See Barrett and Nagle, 19 U Pa J Const L at 20 (cited in note 64).

[71] See Matthew Walther, *Sam Alito: A Civil Man*, American Spectator (Apr 21, 2014), archived at https://perma.cc/XD92-CVGH ("I think I would consider myself a practical originalist."). See also Steven G. Calabresi and Todd W. Shaw, *The Jurisprudence of Justice Samuel Alito*, 87 Geo Wash L Rev 507, 512 (2019) (concluding that a "theme of Justice Alito's jurisprudence is originalism, though not in the traditional sense of the word that one might associate with Justice Scalia").

that a more exacting version of the nondelegation doctrine should be revived. A third was to convince the Court that a more exacting standard should apply in criminal cases, thus making it easier for Gundy to win without threatening the administrative state. Gundy likely hoped to assemble a coalition of votes from among these different theories.

But Gundy did not prevail. A plurality of the Court concluded that the statute contained an intelligible principle and should be upheld under current doctrine.[72] A three-Justice dissent concluded that a more exacting test should be revived, and that the statute would fail.[73] And Justice Alito wrote separately, providing the fifth vote to the majority outcome[74] for his own reasons:

> The Constitution confers on Congress certain "legislative [p]owers," Art. I, § 1, and does not permit Congress to delegate them to another branch of the Government. See *Whitman v. American Trucking Assns., Inc.*, 531 U.S. 457, 472 (2001). Nevertheless, since 1935, the Court has uniformly rejected nondelegation arguments and has upheld provisions that authorized agencies to adopt important rules pursuant to extraordinarily capacious standards. See *ibid*.
>
> If a majority of this Court were willing to reconsider the approach we have taken for the past 84 years, I would support that effort. But because a majority is not willing to do that, it would be freakish to single out the provision at issue here for special treatment.
>
> Because I cannot say that the statute lacks a discernable standard that is adequate under the approach this Court has taken for many years, I vote to affirm.[75]

Justice Alito's approach stands in marked contrast to Justice Thomas's. Justice Alito appeared to maintain that the Court's nondelegation doctrine was erroneous because it permitted excessive delegation to the executive branch, but he nonetheless chose to follow it in *Gundy* because "it would be freakish" to grant relief to sex offenders without also granting it to other regulated parties.

While uncharitable readers might be tempted to see this as an overtly political or results-oriented opinion, Justice Alito in fact

---

[72] *Gundy*, 139 S Ct at 2121.

[73] Id at 2139–44 (Gorsuch, J, dissenting).

[74] Because Justice Kavanaugh did not participate in the decision of the case, Justice Alito's fifth vote was necessary to the publication of the opinions, but not the judgment. Without it, the Court would have affirmed, without opinion, by an equally divided Court.

[75] *Gundy*, 139 S Ct at 2130–31 (Alito, J, concurring in the judgment).

shrewdly identifies a profound problem of constitutional theory. The underlying problem is the problem of constitutional law and the second best. It is not unique to originalism, but it may be especially easy to see for originalists. Suppose the Constitution requires one thing and doctrine requires something different. And suppose that for whatever reason—lack of votes, reliance interests, or something else—the erroneous doctrine is not going to be completely overruled. What should a judge do? Adhere to the Constitution wherever possible, thus minimizing the scope of the doctrine? Adhere to the doctrine until it is overruled? There is a particular dilemma in cases at the border of the doctrine. Extend the doctrine, and you extend the error. Reject the doctrine, and you create a sharp—and perhaps unjustified—difference in two similar types of cases.

Moreover, any approach that sometimes involves considering doctrine will also give rise to the possibility of "compensating adjustments."[76] That is, once doctrine has replaced the otherwise-correct constitutional answer in one area, it is no longer clear what to do in related areas. The most famous example is the argument that we ought to compensate for the unconstitutional expansion of delegated power to agencies by upholding the otherwise unconstitutional legislative veto.[77] One unconstitutional act sort of makes up for the other.

Professor Adrian Vermeule, who has written the most systematic treatment of this problem to date, has concluded that both "the ambitious idea that judges should evaluate global consequences on a case-by-case basis" and the opposite "case-by-case procedure" are suspect on second-best grounds.[78] Most other scholars have grappled with this problem only in the context of individual compensating adjustments to particular doctrines.[79] Perhaps, like *The General Theory of the Second Best* in economics, it has no general solution.[80]

---

[76] Adrian Vermeule, *Hume's Second-Best Constitutionalism*, 70 U Chi L Rev 421, 421 (2003).

[77] Peter B. McCutchen, *Mistakes, Precedent, and the Rise of the Administrative State: Toward a Constitutional Theory of the Second Best*, 80 Cornell L Rev 1, 23–40 (1994); *INS v Chadha*, 462 US 919, 978 (1983) (White, J, dissenting). See also Adrian Vermeule, *Foreword: System Effects and the Constitution*, 123 Harv L Rev 4, 20–23 (2009) (listing this and many other examples).

[78] Vermeule, 70 U Chi L Rev at 436–37 (cited in note 76); see also Vermeule, 123 Harv L Rev at 62–63 (cited in note 77).

[79] Katherine Mims Crocker, *Qualified Immunity and Constitutional Structure*, 117 Mich L Rev 1405, 1442–48 (2019) (official immunity); McCutchen, 80 Cornell L Rev 1 (cited in note 77) (separation of powers and legislative veto). John O. McGinnis and Michael B. Rappaport, *Originalism and the Good Constitution* 94–97 (Harvard, 2013) (expressing skepticism of compensating adjustments by judges).

[80] See generally R. G. Lipsey and Kevin Lancaster, *The General Theory of the Second Best*, 24 Rev Econ Stud 11 (1956).

In any event, Justice Alito's opinion in *Gundy* effectively rejects the simpleminded approach to second-best problems of simply trying to get each case, individually, as close as possible to the correct doctrine. It treats correct constitutional doctrine as something that should be pursued somewhat systematically or not at all.

This is consistent with his opinion the previous year in *Janus*. In *Janus* the Supreme Court held that it violated the First Amendment to force public employees to give a portion of their paycheck to a public sector union. One of the arguments made by the union in its defense was an originalist one: as an original matter, public employees did not have any First Amendment rights, and so First Amendment doctrine should not be extended to give them a new right against compelled subsidies.

Justice Alito, in his opinion for the Court, responded that taking this originalist argument seriously "would mean overturning decades of landmark precedent," and accused the union of "desiring instead that we apply the Constitution's supposed original meaning only when it suits them—to retain the part of *Abood* that they like. We will not engage in this halfway originalism."[81] On its face this was a strange accusation, since the majority itself went on to "retain the part of *Abood* that they like[d]," but the upshot was clear enough: Justice Alito may call himself an originalist, but he did not want to call himself a chump.

Some federal appellate judges have also begun to endorse Justice Alito's skepticism of halfway originalism. In the Eleventh Circuit, litigants asked the en banc court to narrow the scope of *Terry v Ohio*, which authorized frisks without obvious originalist analysis.[82] Judge William Pryor wrote the opinion refusing this request, noting that the well-established exclusionary rule *also* lacked an originalist basis, and concluding: "[W]e cannot use a halfway theory of judicial precedent to cut back on *Terry* while faithfully adhering to the exclusionary rule."[83]

In the Fifth Circuit, the same thing happened in the qualified immunity context. Responding to various criticisms (including by this

---

[81] *Janus*, 138 S Ct at 2469–70 (citation omitted). The Court also went on to dispute the originalist argument on its own terms. Id.

[82] *United States v Johnson*, 921 F3d 991, 1009–11 (11th Cir 2019) (Jordan, J, dissenting), discussing *Minnesota v Dickerson*, 508, 366, 381 (1993) (Scalia, J, concurring) and other originalist critiques of *Terry*.

[83] *Johnson*, 921 F3d at 1002 (en banc).

author) that the doctrine lacked a lawful foundation, Judges James Ho and Andrew Oldham authored a joint dissent invoking the no-halfway-originalism principle. Even if qualified immunity lacked a lawful basis, they wrote, "a principled originalist would not cherry pick which rules to revisit based on popular whim. A principled originalist would fairly review decisions that favor plaintiffs as well as police officers."[84] Hence, the judges asked rhetorically: "Does the majority seriously believe that it is an 'unreasonable seizure,' *as those words were originally understood at the Founding*, for a police officer to stop an armed and mentally unstable teenager from shooting innocent officers, students, and teachers?"[85] No, they declared: "If we're not going to do it right, then perhaps we shouldn't do it at all."[86]

In both cases, the lower-court judges could also reasonably note that they were simply bound to apply Supreme Court precedent regardless of whether it was right or wrong.[87] But they did not stop there, apparently to signal their special skepticism of halfway originalism. Justice Alito is thus hardly a lone voice.

But this call for "principled" rather than "halfway" originalism has problems. The first is that even its proponents do not adhere to it consistently. Consider another example from last Term, the cert petition in *Hester v United States*,[88] where the Court was asked to extend its jury-trial precedents to an order of restitution. Justices Gorsuch and Sotomayor wrote in support of the petition.[89] But Justice Alito wrote to explain his vote against:

> The argument that the Sixth Amendment, as originally understood, requires a jury to find the facts supporting an order of restitution depends upon the proposition that the Sixth Amendment requires a jury to find the facts on which a sentence of imprisonment is based. That latter proposition is supported by decisions of this Court, see *United States v. Booker*, 543 U.S. 220, 230–232 (2005); *Apprendi v. New Jersey*, 530 U.S. 466, 478 (2000), but

---

[84] *Cole v Carson*, 935 F3d 444, 477 (5th Cir 2019) (Ho and Oldham dissenting).

[85] Id at 478 (Ho and Oldham dissenting).

[86] Id. In a subsequent opinion, Judge Ho again voiced these concerns, and clarified that this was not a justification for retaining qualified immunity doctrine in its current form. *Horvath v City of Leander*, 2020 WL 104345, at *13 (5th Cir) (Ho concurring in the judgment in part and dissenting in part) ("We can walk and chew gum at the same time. Courts can faithfully interpret the Fourth Amendment as well as § 1983. We can get *both* prongs of the doctrine right.").

[87] *Johnson*, 921 F3d at 1002; *Cole*, 935 F3d at 477.

[88] 139 S Ct 509 (2019).

[89] Id at 509–11 (Gorsuch, J, dissenting, joined by Sotomayor, J).

> it represents a questionable interpretation of the original meaning of the Sixth Amendment, *Gall v. United States*, 552 U.S. 38, 64–66 (2007) (Alito, J., dissenting). Unless the Court is willing to reconsider that interpretation, fidelity to original meaning counsels against further extension of these suspect precedents.[90]

The principle that "fidelity to original meaning counsels against further extension of ... suspect precedents" may sound reasonable, and it is. But it is the opposite of Justice Alito's injunctions against halfway originalism. The very same argument could have been made of the requests in *Gundy* and *Janus*: *We should not extend our "suspect precedents" permitting delegation to SORNA*, Justice Alito might have said. *We should not extend our "suspect precedents" on compelled spending by public employees to eliminate agency fees*, Justice Alito might have said. One Justice's "halfway originalism" is another Justice's limiting "suspect precedents." Actually, the same Justice's.

This is not meant to score a cheap point in a game of "jurisprudential gotcha,"[91] but rather to demonstrate a broader problem with second-best originalism. The problem is that there is no general solution to the existence of a suspect precedent. It is plausible to say that the precedent should not be extended, because it is suspect. It is plausible to instead say that the precedent should be treated fairly unless and until it is overruled. But if the judge retains discretion to choose either plausible course, then each suspect precedent gives the judge an additional degree of discretion.

Say what you will about the simpleminded approach, but at least it bound the judge. Until there is a general solution to the second-best problem in constitutional law, invoking the problem gives a judge broad discretion to adhere to erroneous—even demonstrably erroneous—precedent.

IV. The Problem with Discretion

These new opinions exploring precedent, while theoretically rich, have exacerbated one of the doctrine's unfortunate features in the Supreme Court—its discretionary nature. This discretion has two aspects. One is the elimination of constraints on the judge's choice

---

[90] Id at 509 (Alito, J, concurring).

[91] Justin Driver, *Judicial Inconsistency as Virtue: The Case of Justice Stevens*, 99 Georgetown L J 1263, 1265 n 7 (2011).

whether to adhere to a precedent or not. Not only do these approaches lack the hard-edged constraints of a rule, but they do not even provide the softer constraint of a guiding standard. They do not contain an internal constraint even for "the puzzled judge" who "would *like* to be able to apply the law without importing nonlegal considerations."[92] The second aspect is that this discretion is not bounded by or derived from law. Taken together, these discretionary features render precedent worse than useless. They make it a tool for evading other requirements of the law, and a threat to certain aspects of judicial neutrality.

Professor Schauer argued in this journal that stare decisis does little to constrain the Justices' decisions, and that this may not be such a bad thing. "[T]he weakness, verging on impotence, of the widely referenced but rarely followed stare decisis norm" may be evidence that we do not actually want or need the stability or authority that the norm promises.[93]

My analysis is less optimistic. It may be true that stare decisis does little to constrain the Justices, for all of the reasons recounted by Schauer and many others. But stare decisis does something else, which is to allow them to escape *other constraints* that might be imposed by law or interpretive methodology. A discretionary doctrine of precedent is not just impotent, but corrosive.

How is it corrosive? For one thing, it is inconsistent with one of the central tenets of judicial review, a tenet that traces all the way back to Chief Justice Marshall's opinion in *Marbury v Madison*.[94] In *Marbury*, the Court had to justify its decision to review legislation duly enacted by Congress. It also had to explain how it could do so without taking on a legislative role, rather than its proscribed judicial role. It did so by emphasizing that judicial review was a *duty*, not a choice. It was "emphatically the province and duty of the judicial department to say what the law is."[95] When the Constitution and a statute conflict, "the court must determine which of these conflicting rules governs the case. This is of the very essence of judicial duty."[96]

---

[92] See William Baude, *Originalism as a Constraint on Judges*, 84 U Chi L Rev 2213, 2223–24 (2017).

[93] Schauer, 2018 Supreme Court Review at 142–43 (cited in note 1).

[94] 5 US (1 Cranch) 137 (1803).

[95] Id at 177.

[96] Id at 178.

If judicial review is a duty, not a choice, then that relieves the Court of a burden of justification. The Court does not need to make its own judgment about which rule is preferable if its choice is forced. This basic account of judicial review is central to a classical conception of the judiciary, one especially revered by formalists, in which the court's job is to simply apply the law in cases that come before it.[97]

To be sure, the true picture is more complicated than a quote from *Marbury*. The law itself may consist of principles or standards rather than rules.[98] The law itself may confer judicial discretion.[99] So the duty to follow the law may require judges to make difficult judgments, and even choices. But these judgments and choices are less of a threat to the law precisely because they are given by, and therefore controlled by, law. This marks the difference between "arbitrary discretion" and "mere legal discretion" that was central to antebellum debates about stare decisis.[100]

To see this distinction, consider why it was plausible for now-Justice Kavanaugh to argue that stare decisis is required by Article III. Article III permits judges to exercise only "judicial" power. If excessive discretion could render judicial activity nonjudicial, and if stare decisis can hem in this discretion, then the doctrine helps to ensure that judges exercise only judicial power.[101] Hence, now-Justice Kavanaugh invoked Federalist No. 78, where Alexander Hamilton wrote: "[t]o avoid an arbitrary discretion in the courts, it is indispensable that they should be bound down by strict rules and precedents which serve to define and point out their duty in every particular case that comes before them."[102] But this structural argument works only if precedent supplements judicial duty rather than undermining it.

The new approaches to precedent come closer to "arbitrary discretion" than "legal discretion." For judges with otherwise formalist commitments, these approaches function to switch off the formalist

---

[97] See, for example, Philip Hamburger, *Law and Judicial Duty* (Harvard, 2008).

[98] See Justin Driver, *Rules, the New Standards: Partisan Gerrymandering and Judicial Manageability After Vieth v. Jubelirer*, 73 Geo Wash L Rev 1166, 1182–85 (2005).

[99] See David L. Shapiro, *Jurisdiction and Discretion*, 60 NYU L Rev 543 (1985).

[100] Nelson, 87 Va L Rev at 9–10 (cited in note 55).

[101] The alternative is that these limits come from written or external sources of law. Id at 9–21, 22–27.

[102] Federalist 78 (Hamilton) in Jacob E. Cooke, ed, *The Federalist Papers* 529 (1961); Kavanaugh Confirmation Hearing at 149, 226, 257 (cited in note 6).

mode. Rather than follow a formalist argument to a politically unpalatable conclusion, a Justice can choose to invoke second-best principles in some cases but not others. Rather than being bound by either precedent or text in cases of ambiguity, a Justice can choose which one to follow, and therefore be bound by neither. Precedent thus operates to negate the legal restrictions on judicial discretion. What good is a doctrine of precedent if it serves to increase judicial discretion rather than to decrease it?[103]

This kind of arbitrary, nonlegal discretion not only permits a judge to indulge nonlegal considerations, but makes it hard for him to avoid it. A legal duty provides some justification for judicial actions that would otherwise be morally suspect. Why may a judge sometimes order the seizure of property, the restraint of liberty, or tolerate bad governmental or private behavior? Because the law says so, and the judge has some duty to apply the law.[104] But once the judge has a choice, he no longer has that excuse.

In other words, once the keys to stare decisis are in the judges' own hands, neither precedent nor nonprecedent can provide an answer to moral dilemmas or to political pressure. Consider the most salient precedent in the country, *Roe v Wade*.[105] In response to growing calls to overrule the controversial decision, the Supreme Court famously relied on precedent to reaffirm its core holding in *Planned Parenthood v Casey*.[106] But the Court did not succeed at its goal of "call[ing] the contending sides of a national controversy to end their national division by accepting a common mandate rooted in the Constitution."[107] The future of the decision remains unsettled.

The same dilemma confronts the current Justices, some of whom may well both believe that *Roe* was wrongly decided, but prefer to narrow it or ignore it rather than overruling it. It is only a matter of time before they are put to the test, and when they do so they may be

---

[103] But see Richard M. Re, *Precedent as Permission* *1 (unpublished article, Nov 11, 2019) ("This essay provides an account of precedent that does not call upon it to do the one thing that everyone expects: constrain judicial decision-making. Instead, precedent is tasked to do something else: identify lawful options. So instead of beginning with precedent's limited ability to constrain, the argument focuses first on what precedent enables.").

[104] On the defeasibility of this duty, see William Baude, *Is Originalism Our Law?*, 115 Colum L Rev 2349, 2395–97 (2015).

[105] 410 US 113 (1973).

[106] 505 US at 854–69 (1992).

[107] Id at 867.

unable to insist either that they were required to overrule it, or that they were forbidden to do so. In the absence of either a clear rule or a legally-sourced standard, the choice whether to follow *Roe* or overrule it will be "arbitrary discretion" in Hamilton's sense. This is precisely the vice that formalist judging is supposed to forswear.

To be sure, discretionary stare decisis is more of a problem for some methods of judging than for others. Some legal theories already assume a great deal of discretion on behalf of the judges. For judges operating under those theories, the additional discretion granted by stare decisis may be nothing new. But Justices Alito and Thomas, like other members of the Court, profess to be originalists, and originalism professes to give judges a source of law outside their own will.[108] Discretionary precedent—neither forbidden nor required—forfeits that justification for originalism.

V. CONCLUSION

The quest for principled judging is in large part a quest for neutral principles.[109] Both originalism and stare decisis derive their enduring popularity from their potential neutrality. And, indeed, at their best they live up to this promise. Originalism can be a neutral principle.[110] Absolute stare decisis is a neutral principle.

There are also some potentially principled approaches for mixing the two, such as a rule that stare decisis controls in cases of indeterminacy and originalism controls in cases of clarity.[111] Or a rule that follows the original understanding of "liquidation," which required indeterminacy, deliberate practice, and settlement—a solution I have suggested elsewhere.[112] Perhaps even a variation on more modern stare decisis doctrine could accomplish this. But if a Justice or a court does not adopt a neutral principle for mixing the two, adopting two neutral principles at the same time is worse than adopting none.

---

[108] See Baude, 84 U Chi L Rev at 2223–29 (cited in note 92).

[109] Herbert Wechsler, *Toward Neutral Principles of Constitutional Law*, 73 Harv L Rev 1 (1959); Robert H. Bork, *Neutral Principles and Some First Amendment Problems*, 47 Ind L J 1 (1971).

[110] Baude, 84 U Chi L Rev at 2223–29 (cited in note 92).

[111] See Randy J. Kozel, *Original Meaning and the Precedent Fallback*, 68 Vand L Rev 105 (2015); Nelson, 87 Va L Rev 1 (cited in note 55). This assumes that clarity is itself a neutral principle, see Richard M. Re, *Clarity Doctrines*, 86 U Chi L Rev 1497 (2019); Ryan D. Doerfler, *Going Clear* (Aug 1, 2019), online at https://ssrn.com/abstract=3326550.

[112] William Baude, *Constitutional Liquidation*, 71 Stan L Rev 1, 42–44 (2019).

The problem of the second best in constitutional law is a harder one, and deserves the same attention that has been given to the topic of stare decisis itself. Without reaching a general solution, however, we can still say it is better to adopt a consistent stance to this problem than an opportunistic one. If a suspect precedent is not revisited, there is a question whether to extend it or to limit it. But a Justice should not pick and choose different approaches for equally suspect precedents.

Modern stare decisis doctrine now does the very opposite of what the doctrine was once supposed to do. It introduces elements of the arbitrary discretion it was once meant to constrain. So while many reports in the coming years will likely assert that the Roberts Court has rendered stare decisis nothing but a pretense, I fear that the truth is actually much worse.

LINDA GREENHOUSE

THE SUPREME COURT'S CHALLENGE TO CIVIL SOCIETY

For organized labor, the significance of *Janus v American Federation of State, County and Municipal Employees*,[1] decided at the end of the Supreme Court's 2017 Term, was obvious. Based on the Roberts Court's new interpretation of the First Amendment's guarantees of free speech and association, *Janus* overturned *Abood v Detroit Board of Education*.[2] *Abood*, decided in 1977 by a vote of 9 to 0, rejected a First Amendment challenge to the system of "agency" or "fair-share" fees that public employees could be required to pay to the union even if they declined to join the union or objected to the union's very existence. By the time the *Janus* court declared by a vote of 5 to 4 that the agency fee system violated the objecting employees' First Amendment rights, *Abood* had come to look like a relic from a different era—as indeed it was, in more ways than one.

Linda Greenhouse is Knight Distinguished Journalist in Residence and Joseph M. Goldstein Lecturer in Law at Yale Law School and a Pulitzer Prize winning reporter for the *New York Times*.

AUTHOR'S NOTE: An earlier version of this article was presented as the Laskin Lecture at Osgoode Hall Law School's 2019 Constitutional Cases Conference. Papers from that conference, including the lecture, were published in Osgoode Hall's *Supreme Court Law Review*: B. L. Berger and S. Lawrence, eds, *2019 Osgoode Hall Law School Constitutional Cases Conference* (2019), 94 SCLR (2d).

[1] 138 S Ct 2448 (2018).
[2] 431 US 209 (1977).

© 2020 by The University of Chicago. All rights reserved.
978-0-226-70856-0/2020/2019-0008$10.00

In tracing the Supreme Court's trajectory from *Abood* to *Janus*, I am not principally concerned with the *Janus* decision's impact on organized labor, although that is likely to be substantial,[3] or with First Amendment doctrine as such. Rather, I will argue that *Janus* exemplifies the Supreme Court's retreat from the notion of the collective good within the framework of civil society. My goal in this article is to situate *Janus* within this wider landscape, and to show how in fostering a constitutional culture that entitles individuals to opt out of duties they find disagreeable, the court is eroding the expectation of collective obligation that civil society requires if it is to thrive.

Two Texts

To frame my analysis, I offer two texts. The first is from Justice Stewart's opinion for the court in *Abood*. He acknowledged that there could be many weighty reasons—political, ideological, even religious—why an employee might object to the union and refuse to contribute to it. He then explained why, nonetheless, the requirement to pay that portion of union dues that supports the collective-bargaining activities that benefit all workers survives First Amendment scrutiny:

> To be required to help finance the union collective-bargaining agent might well be thought, therefore, to interfere in some way with an employee's freedom to associate for the advancement of ideas, or to refrain from doing so, as he sees fit. But . . . such interference as exists is constitutionally justified by the legislative assessment of the important contribution of the union shop to the system of labor relations established by Congress. [Here Justice Stewart quoted from Justice Douglas's opinion in an earlier labor case.] "*The furtherance of the common cause* leaves some leeway for the leadership of the group. As long as they act to promote the cause which justified bringing the group together, the individual cannot withdraw his financial support merely because he disagrees with the group's strategy. . . ."[4]

My second text requires some context. In January 2019, Judge Wendy Beetlestone of the Federal District Court in Philadelphia granted an injunction barring enforcement of new rules issued by the Trump administration for the benefit of employers with either

---

[3] See, e.g., William B. Gould IV, *How Five Young Men Channeled Nine Old Men: Janus and the High Court's Anti-Labor Policymaking*, 53 USF L Rev 209, 234–61 (2019).

[4] *Abood*, 431 US at 222–23 (citing *Machinists v Street*, 367 US at 778, Douglas, J, concurring) (emphasis added).

religious or "sincerely held" moral objections to contraception. These employers were to be excused from the requirement in the Affordable Care Act that all employee health plans cover birth control along with other "preventive" services.[5] As she had done earlier in issuing a preliminary injunction,[6] Judge Beetlestone noted the "remarkable" breadth of this exemption, which applies to for-profit as well as non-profit businesses. She observed that Congress had in fact considered and rejected a broad "conscience" opt-out from the birth control mandate. The new rule thus violated the "plain command" of the statutory text, she concluded, and she noted that if enforced, the rule would cause thousands of women who had the misfortune to work for opting-out employers to lose the insurance coverage to which they were legally entitled.

And now to my text: the response of Caitlin Oakley, the press secretary of the U.S. Department of Health and Human Services, to Judge Beetlestone's ruling. "No American should be forced to violate his or her own conscience in order to abide by the laws and regulations governing our health care."[7]

This article interrogates the space between Justices Stewart's and Douglas's invocation of our "common cause" and Ms. Oakley's seeming obliviousness to the welfare of thousands of American women who happen to work for bosses who object to birth control. These two texts stand as goalposts at either end of a playing field known as civil society. If the two appear asymmetrical—one, a statement by the Supreme Court in a published opinion, the other, a remark by a federal bureaucrat in immediate response to breaking news—the asymmetry is likely to be only temporary. In 2016, following the death of Justice Scalia, the Supreme Court found itself unable to decide the permissible scope of an accommodation for employers unwilling to abide by the birth control mandate. The short-handed Court's stalemate in *Zubik v Burwell*[8] provided the gap that the Trump

---

[5] *Pennsylvania v Trump*, 351 F Supp 3d 791, 816 (E D Pa 2019), aff'd, *Commonwealth of Pennsylvania v President, United States of America*, 930 F3d 543 (3rd Cir 2019). Following five Interim Final Rules, the Final Rule was issued on Nov 15, 2018. 83 Fed Reg 57,536. Petition for cert granted, *Trump v Commonwealth of Pennsylvania*, No 19-454 (docketed Oct 3, 2019).

[6] *Pennsylvania v Trump*, 281 F Supp 3d 553, 577 (E D Pa 2017).

[7] Associated Press, *The Latest: Official Decries Blocking of Birth Control Rules* (Jan 13, 2019), https://www.apnews.com/619b4cb94693436581ff39f8374f296e.

[8] See *Zubik v Burwell*, 136 S Ct 1557, 1560 (2016).

administration's broad exemptions now seek to fill. With the subsequent addition of Justices Gorsuch and Kavanaugh, there is reason to expect that today's Supreme Court will be willing and able, even eager, to decide the question in favor of the conscience opt-outs.

And what would be the harm of that? The United States, after all, has a proud tradition of protecting minorities who assert claims of conscience against mainstream norms that would overwhelm or even crush unconventional practices and belief systems. If the political system has often failed to extend such protections, the courts have done so. Such Supreme Court decisions as *Sherbert v Verner*,[9] which protected a Seventh-Day Adventist from having to work on his sabbath; *West Virginia v Barnette*,[10] holding that Jehovah's Witness children did not have to salute the American flag; and *Wisconsin v Yoder*,[11] which exempted the Amish from having to send their children to high school, are well known to anyone with a passing familiarity with the history of the First Amendment's Free Exercise Clause. These decisions are celebrated as symbols of American society's commitment to freedom of conscience and of the protection of conscience as an essential aspect of civil society. The Civil Rights Act of 1964 protects religious claimants from employment discrimination and requires employers to accommodate the needs of religiously observant employees as long as the accommodation will not impose undue hardship on the conduct of the employer's business.[12]

The conservative writer Ryan Anderson, in an argument against same-sex marriage, observed that "religious liberty plays a crucial role in preserving civil society as something separate from government."[13] Few would argue with that statement as an expression of abstract principle. But given recent developments in our politics and

[9] 374 US 398 (1963).

[10] 319 US 624 (1943).

[11] 406 US 205 (1972).

[12] 42 USC 2000e(j), 2000e2(a)(1). Justice Samuel Alito, in a statement joined by three other Justices, suggested recently that the statutory accommodation for religious employees, as construed by the Supreme Court in *Trans World Airlines, Inc. v Hardison*, 432 US 63 (1977), is insufficiently accommodationist. Assuming that Justice Alito maintains the behavior described in the remainder of this article, we will shortly see cases that raise this long-settled issue making their way onto the Supreme Court's docket. (Statement of Alito, J, respecting the denial of certiorari, *Joseph A. Kennedy v Bremerton School District*, No 18-12, Jan 22, 2019.) On March 18, 2019, the Court requested the views of the Solicitor General on a petition for certiorari that explicitly asks the Court to overturn the 1977 precedent in favor of a broader accommodation requirement. *Patterson v Walgreen Co.*, petition for cert pending, No 18-349.

[13] Ryan T. Anderson, *The Continuing Threat to Religious Liberty*, Heritage Foundation (Aug 4, 2017), https://www.heritage.org/religious-liberty/commentary/the-continuing-threat-religious-liberty.

our law, we need urgently to move from the abstract to the concrete We need to question whether conscience claims, as they are being expressed and honored today, rather than embodying the best of civil society have become a threat to it—and indeed, to the legitimacy of the modern state, where laws of general applicability enacted through democratic politics are assumed to apply to all.[14]

CULTIVATING CHANGE: AN EVOLVING FIRST AMENDMENT

The decision in *Janus*, even its precise vote, surprised almost no one. It was years in the making under the careful cultivation of a single member of the court, Justice Alito. Indeed, by the time *Janus* finally arrived on June 27, 2018, it fit expectations so precisely as to make it difficult to appreciate fully how radical the decision was and how unusual its path to the Supreme Court had been. Resurrecting the fading history of the case allows us to see it as a whole, and helps to illuminate the determination with which the Court is marking the path to the radical individualism that its recent decisions embody.

Since *Janus* is a First Amendment decision, I begin with some First Amendment context. From today's perspective, the mediated view of the First Amendment the Court expressed four decades ago in *Abood*—that the First Amendment provides a framework for balancing the collective interest of the state against the interests of private speakers—seems to come to us from a different era. It was an era when the First Amendment served to enable free and open public discourse. It was an era before, for example, the Supreme Court ruled in the 2011 case of *Sorrell v IMS Health*[15] that Vermont violated the First Amendment rights of pharmaceutical companies when it barred pharmacies from selling doctors' prescription records—records that enabled pharmaceutical sales people to make targeted sales pitches to doctors for expensive new drugs for patients who were being treated with inexpensive old ones. It was an era before the D.C. Circuit ruled[16] that in implementing a 2009 act of Congress,[17] federal regulators could

---

[14] For a powerful explication of this idea, see Robert Post's concluding chapter in the multi-author book of essays, in Susanna Mancini and Michel Rosenfeld, eds, *The Conscience Wars* 473–84 (Cambridge, 2018).

[15] 564 US 552 (2011).

[16] *R.J. Reynolds Tobacco Co. v Food & Drug Admin.*, 696 F3d 1205 (DC Cir 2012).

[17] Family Smoking Prevention and Tobacco Control Act of 2009, Pub L No 111-31 § 201, 123 Stat 1776, 1845 (2009).

not require tobacco companies to display on their cigarette packages disturbingly graphic photographs of what happens to people who smoke—a ruling the Obama administration decided would be counterproductive to appeal to a Supreme Court that was highly likely to affirm it.[18]

And early this year, the U.S. Court of Appeals for the Ninth Circuit, relying on the Supreme Court's most recent First Amendment precedents, granted a preliminary injunction against enforcement of San Francisco's Sugar-Sweetened Beverage Warning Ordinance, which requires soda advertisements to contain a warning that "drinking beverages with added sugar(s) contributes to obesity, diabetes, and tooth decay." The required warning also had to include the notice that "this is a message from the City and County of San Francisco." There is little doubt that a few years ago, this public health measure requiring the inclusion of truthful information in a commercial advertisement would have been upheld. The Ninth Circuit panel's conclusion to the contrary was unanimous.[19]

In other words, *Abood* was the product of an era before the First Amendment was turned into a potent tool of deregulation, before it was, in the words of Justice Elena Kagan's dissenting opinion in *Janus*, "weaponiz[ed]."[20] So when Justice Alito, writing for the majority in *Janus*, said that *Abood* had become "an anomaly in our First Amendment jurisprudence,"[21] it was hard to argue with him.

The shorthand for what Justice Stewart offered as the rationale for *Abood* came to be known as the "free rider" problem—the notion that peace in the workplace would be threatened by the presence of fellow workers who were not paying their fair share. It's worth noting that a series of decisions following *Abood* made clear that the fair-share obligation extended only to the expenses of collective bargaining and representation. Employees could opt out of paying for expenses connected with a union's political advocacy; few questioned that distinction as a matter of law or policy. But the *Janus* majority found any such distinction unworkable as a means of solving what it

---

[18] Brady Dennis, *Government Quits Legal Battle Over Graphic Cigarette Warnings*, Wash Post (March 19, 2013), http://www.washingtonpost.com/national/health-science/government-quits-legal-battle-over-graphic-cigarette-warnings/2013/03/19/23053ccc-90d7-11e2-bdea-e32ad90da239_story.html.

[19] *American Beverage Assoc. v City and County of San Francisco*, 916 F3d 749 (9th Cir 2019).

[20] *Janus*, 138 S Ct at 2501 (Kagan, J, dissenting).

[21] Id at 2483.

viewed as the central problem of coerced speech. As Justice Alito explained: "Petitioner strenuously objects to this free-rider label. He argues that he is not a free rider on a bus headed for a destination that he wishes to reach but is more like a person shanghaied for an unwanted voyage."[22]

The impact of *Janus* is considerable, extending well beyond the labor context. For example, the Court's analysis has invited a new round of litigation against mandatory bar dues and bar membership. The Justices considered one such case last Term, a challenge to mandatory bar membership in North Dakota.[23] That case was filed before *Janus*, clearly in expectation of *Janus*'s outcome. The Justices took the case up in their private conference eight times during the fall and into the winter before finally vacating the Eighth Circuit decision below, which had upheld the compulsory bar membership, and remanding the case to the appeals court for reconsideration in light of *Janus*.[24] While the Court's docket-setting function is notably opaque, it is clear from the many times the Justices are listed as having discussed this petition at their weekly private conference that the disposition was controversial inside the Court. It is highly likely that some members of the Court were eager to take up the bar-dues case immediately, without waiting for the lower courts to decide how to apply *Janus* to related challenges. In any event, other such cases are already in the pipeline; lawsuits challenging mandatory membership in the state bar of Wisconsin were recently filed in both the Eastern and Western Districts of the Federal District Court in that state.[25] Conservative interests are watching these developments closely and cheering the plaintiffs on.[26]

And of course *Janus* will exact a substantial price from public employee unions, which under the legal duty of fair representation[27]

---

[22] Id at 2466.

[23] *Fleck v Wetch*, No 17-886, granted, vacated, and remanded to the Eighth Circuit in light of *Janus*, 139 S Ct 590 (2018). On August 30, 2019, the Eighth Circuit on remand reaffirmed its earlier decision. *Fleck v Wetch*, 937 F3d 1112 (8th Cir 2019).

[24] See https://www.supremecourt.gov/search.aspx?filename=/docket/docketfiles/html/public/17-886.html.

[25] *State Bar of Wisconsin Faces Second Federal Challenge to Mandatory Status*, Wisbar News (Oct 1, 2019), https://www.wisbar.org/NewsPublications/Pages/General-Article.aspx?ArticleID=27249.

[26] See, for example, a *Wall Street Journal* editorial, *After Janus, Free the Lawyers*, Wall St J (April 25, 2019), https://www.wsj.com/articles/after-janus-free-the-lawyers-11556231959.

[27] Grace Shaver Figg, *The Union Duty of Fair Representation: Fact or Fiction*, 60 Marq L R 1116 (1977).

have to continue doing their work on behalf of nonmembers and members alike, even as their dues revenue shrinks. It's no coincidence that public employee unions have been a target of political and judicial conservatives. Even as union membership in the private sector shrinks almost to invisibility, standing now at 10 percent, union membership is actually quite robust in the public sector, where more than one-third of employees are union members.[28] Further, public sector unions tend to skew progressive. They support Democrats.[29]

In the wake of *Janus*, there are lawsuits seeking to claw back agency fees that have already been paid. One such case was recently dismissed in the federal district court in Seattle; the judge declared that the union was entitled to a "good faith" defense, since the dues were constitutional at the time the union collected them.[30] But other such cases are pending, and may find friendlier judicial audiences.

Cultivating Change: One Justice's Project

It began in 2012 with a case called *Knox v Service Employees International Union*.[31] The question was a very narrow one: how the union should have treated a special dues assessment, and what accommodation it should have provided objecting members of the bargaining unit. The objecting employees should have been offered the choice to opt into paying the special assessment, rather than being required affirmatively to opt out. But Justice Alito, in a decision signed by five Justices, went beyond the question presented to place *Abood* squarely in the Court's sights. He wrote that "our prior decisions approach, if they do not cross, the limit of what the First Amendment can tolerate."[32] "The general rule—individuals should not

---

[28] See https://www.bls.gov/news.release/union2.nr0.htm.

[29] Center for Responsible Politics, *Public Sector Unions*, https://www.opensecrets.org/industries/indus.php?ind=P04 (with graph portraying political contributions by individual public sector unions).

[30] *Danielson v AFSCME Council 28*, 340 F Supp 3d 1083 (W D Wash 2018). The Seventh Circuit recently affirmed a District Court decision rejecting the claim by Mark Janus, the named plaintiff in *Janus v AFSCME*, for a refund of his agency fees plus damages. Writing for the panel, Chief Judge Wood concluded that "though Mr. Janus contends that he did not want any of the benefits of AFSCME's collective bargaining and other representative activities of over the years, he received them." She added that "there was no unjust 'windfall' to the union, as Mr. Janus alleges, but rather an exchange of money for services." *Janus v American Federation of State, County and Municipal Employees*, No 19-1553 (7th Cir, Nov 5, 2019).

[31] 567 US 298 (2012).

[32] Id at 314.

be compelled to subsidize private groups or private speech—should prevail."[33]

This was an unmistakable invitation to bring the Court the core issue that Justice Alito had identified. A new case arrived two years later. It was closer to the core, but still not yet the core itself. *Harris v Quinn*,[34] another 5 to 4 decision with a majority opinion by Justice Alito, held that *Abood* did not apply in the context of unionized home health workers, due to an employer-employee relationship that is very different from the relationship in a conventional workplace. Once again Justice Alito went further than necessary to decide the case, his attack on *Abood* becoming even more direct. He offered an extensive inventory of *Abood*'s weaknesses,[35] concluding that the precedent was flawed from the start. Among his many critiques was his assertion that it is not possible to draw a line, as *Abood* purported to do, between a union's expenses for collective bargaining, expenses that are chargeable to objecting employees under the agency fees system, and nonchargeable expenses for activities including lobbying. For a public sector union, it was all politics all the time: "both collective bargaining and political advocacy and lobbying are directed at the government."[36]

Having dismantled *Abood*, Justice Alito did not press in *Quinn* to overturn it. He contented himself with declaring that applying *Abood* in the context of home healthcare aides would mark a "very substantial expansion" of the precedent,[37] so much so, he implied, that overturning *Abood* was not necessary—yet.

Justice Kagan, in an opinion for the four dissenters, saw what lay ahead. There was no principled distinction between this case and *Abood*, she said, and therefore no need for the majority's extended discussion of *Abood*'s supposed deficiencies. "Today's opinion takes the tack of throwing everything against the wall in the hope that something might stick."[38] It would stick soon enough.

The following year, 2015, *Friedrichs v California Teachers Association*[39] reached the Supreme Court. This was the first case since Justice

---

[33] Id at 321.
[34] 573 US 616 (2014).
[35] Id at 633–38.
[36] Id at 636–37.
[37] Id at 638.
[38] Id at 664 (Kagan, J, dissenting).
[39] 136 S Ct 1083 (2016).

Alito began his campaign that squarely presented the issue in a posture that gave the Court a clear choice: reaffirm *Abood* or overturn it. The litigation was financed by the conservative Lynde and Harry Bradley Foundation through its grantee, the Center for Individual Rights; Bradley also financed, at least in part, eleven of the organizations that filed amicus briefs on the plaintiffs' behalf at the Supreme Court.[40]

Friedrichs followed a very unusual path to the Court. In Federal District Court, the plaintiffs did not contest the union's motion for summary judgment.[41] Then, having lost in District Court according to plan, the plaintiffs asked the Ninth Circuit to affirm their defeat. Obliging, as settled law required, the Appeals Court affirmed in a one-paragraph order calling the case "so insubstantial as not to require further argument."[42]

Despite the absence of a conflict in the circuits (the ordinary marker of an appeal deemed worthy of Supreme Court review[43]), the Justices, not surprisingly, agreed to hear the case. Argument took place in January 2016. By the end of the argument, it was perfectly clear that *Abood* would be overturned by a vote of 5 to 4. Justice Alito, we can assume,[44] received the assignment from Chief Justice Roberts. He no doubt turned quickly to the welcome task of drafting his majority opinion, his moment finally at hand.

Then, the next month, shockingly, Justice Scalia died. There would be no majority opinion, not this time. By a 4 to 4 vote, the Justices affirmed the Ninth Circuit in a one-line order, without further discussion or explanation. (A tie vote at the Supreme Court automatically affirms the lower-court opinion, without precedential weight; it is as if the case never reached the Court.) Justice Alito would have to wait just a bit longer, but not very long. Justice Gorsuch joined the Court in April 2017. The National Right to Work Legal Defense Fund filed its certiorari petition in *Janus* in June. The

---

[40] Brian Mahoney, *Conservative Group Nears Big Payoff in Supreme Court Case*, Politico (Jan 10, 2016), https://www.politico.com/story/2016/01/friedrichs-california-teachers-union-supreme-court-217525. See also Senators Sheldon Whitehouse and Richard Blumenthal, brief in support of respondents, *Janus v AFSCME* at 16–17.

[41] 2013 WL 9825479 at *1.

[42] Brief for Pets at *8–, *Friedrichs v California Teachers Ass'n*, No 14-915 (US Sept 4, 2015).

[43] Rules of the Supreme Court of the United States (2019), Rule 10(a).

[44] Justice Alito proved to be the only Justice without a majority opinion from the January 2016 argument sitting.

court granted the petition on its opening day order list at the start of the 2017 Term.

Who is Mark Janus? He didn't start out as the plaintiff in this case. The first plaintiff was the newly elected Illinois governor, Bruce Rauner, a Republican who had run for office on an anti-union platform, backed by millions of dollars in contributions from an Illinois businessman, Richard Uihlein, who also helps fund the Federalist Society, the National Right to Work Legal Defense Fund, and the Liberty Justice Center.[45] With the state legislature controlled by Democrats, Governor Rauner could make no headway with legislation abolishing the agency shop, with its attendant agency fee system. That is a step that is open to the states, and in fact more than half the states had either never instituted or had abolished the agency shop for their public employee unions. Because that option was not politically available to Governor Rauner, he turned to the courts. The Federal District Court threw a wrench into his plans, however, dismissing the governor's lawsuit for lack of standing.[46] The court then permitted Mark Janus, an Illinois state employee, to intervene as the new plaintiff—strange in itself because there was no longer an existing lawsuit in which to intervene. But no matter, the case—*Friedrichs* redux—was soon, after a brief stop at the U.S. Court of Appeals for the Seventh Circuit,[47] on its way to the Supreme Court.

The hurdle that Justice Alito and his five-member majority had to overcome was, of course, stare decisis. Here was a decision, more than four decades old, reaffirmed many times. What to do? Justice Alito did something quite remarkable—he cited himself to show that any reliance interest that attached to *Abood* had been erased—conveniently erased by his own dicta:

> . . . public sector unions have been on notice for years regarding this Court's misgivings about *Abood*. In *Knox*, decided in 2012, we described *Abood* as a First Amendment "anomaly." Two years later, in *Harris*, we were asked to overrule *Abood*, and while we found it unnecessary to take that step, we cataloged *Abood*'s many weaknesses.[48]

---

[45] Noam Schieber and Kenneth P. Vogel, *Behind a Key Anti-Labor Case, a Web of Conservative Donors*, NY Times (Feb 25, 2018).

[46] *Rauner v AFSCME*, USDC ND Ill No 15-cv-01235.

[47] 851 F3d 746 (7th Cir 2017) (affirming dismissal of the amended complaint).

[48] *Janus*, 138 S Ct at 2484.

He went on to describe the fate of the *Friedrichs* case, deriving from the tie vote the conclusion that the world should have discerned that the end of *Abood* was at hand: "During this period of time, any public sector union seeking an agency-fee provision in a collective-bargaining agreement must have understood that the constitutionality of such a provision was uncertain."[49]

In her dissenting opinion, Justice Kagan called Justice Alito out, referring to the court's "six-year campaign to reverse *Abood*"[50] and observing that the majority had found "no exceptional or special reason" for doing so.[51] "It has overruled *Abood* because it wanted to."[52] That is a remarkably explicit statement for one Justice to make about her colleagues. Justice Kagan continued: ". . . the majority has chosen the winners by turning the First Amendment into a sword and using it against workaday economic and regulatory policy. . . . The First Amendment was meant for better things."[53]

I have delved at such length into the history of the *Janus* litigation to make clear the aggressive nature of the Court's attack on the status quo, a status quo anchored in democratic accountability. As I mentioned, states have been free from the beginning either to adopt the agency fee system for their public employee unions or to reject it. Governor Rauner lacked the political power to accomplish his goal by legislation, so he enlisted a friendly Supreme Court.

The disjunction between the Court's decision in *Janus* and the public mood is worth noting. A Gallup poll conducted in early August 2018, about a month after the Court's ruling, showed public support for labor unions at a fifteen-year high, at 62 percent.[54] Support continued to climb the next year, reaching a new fifty-year high by Labor Day 2019, with union support showing significant increases among Republicans as well as Democrats and independents.[55] Schoolteachers in red as well as blue states have staged successful

---

[49] Id at 2485.

[50] Id at 2487 (Kagan, J, dissenting).

[51] Id at 2497 (Kagan, J, dissenting).

[52] Id at 2501 (Kagan, J, dissenting).

[53] Id at 2501–02 (Kagan, J, dissenting).

[54] See https://news.gallup.com/poll/241679/labor-union-approval-steady-year-high.aspx.

[55] Jeffrey M. Jones, *As Labor Day Turns 125, Union Approval Near 50-Year High*, Gallup (Aug 28, 2019), https://news.gallup.com/poll/265916/labor-day-turns-125-union-approval-near-year-high.aspx.

strikes for higher pay and better working conditions.[56] To be sure, the fortunes of organized labor have ebbed and flowed throughout U.S. history, in the courts as well as in politics. Now we have entered an era when anti-union forces that can't prevail in politics will take refuge in the courts.

That's a problem for the legitimacy of the courts, to be sure. But something even deeper is at stake.

THE FADING CONCEPT OF THE COLLECTIVE GOOD

I refer back to Justice Stewart's quotation in *Abood* of Justice Douglas's phrase "the furtherance of a common cause." Setting aside what *Janus* tells us about labor law or the First Amendment, I believe its primary injury is to further constitutionalize the notion that, assuming there is a "common cause," we as a society are not in fact united in pursuit of it; that we can help ourselves to an opt-out of our choice; that we are not all in this together.

There's been much talk about the rise of tribalism in the United States and elsewhere. We retreat to our living rooms where alternate visions of reality greet us from across the airwaves, cable connections, and the internet.[57] It is increasingly hard to sustain the structures of civil society under these conditions. The Supreme Court once had an insight, as embodied by *Abood* and the cases that followed it until recently, that while we may disagree with one another, we are all playing by the same rules of democratic accountability. Somehow American society managed to navigate, through law, what Jeffrey Alexander calls "the seemingly oxymoronic commitment to individuality and collectivity that defines the sphere of civil life."[58]

When did we begin to lose navigational ability, that commitment to the collectivity? It's not possible to pinpoint a moment, but it was certainly well before the 2016 election. The story of the Religious Freedom Restoration Act (RFRA)[59] is instructive. Congress passed

---

[56] Robert Gebeloff, *The Numbers That Explain Why Teachers Are in Revolt*, NY Times (June 4, 2018).

[57] For just one example of American society's divide across the media gulf, see Michael M. Grynbaum, *In Prime Time, Two Versions of Impeachment for a Divided Nation*, NY Times (Nov 16, 2019), https://www.nytimes.com/2019/11/16/business/media/impeachment-media-fox-msnbc.html?searchResultPosition=1.

[58] Jeffrey C. Alexander, *The Civil Sphere* 153 (Oxford, 2006).

[59] 42 USC 2000bb.

RFRA to repudiate the Supreme Court's 1990 decision *Employment Division v Smith*.[60] In *Smith* the Court, by a vote of 5 to 4 and with a majority opinion by Justice Scalia, rejected the argument that the Free Exercise Clause mandates religious exemptions from a law of general applicability.

The case arose when the state of Oregon refused unemployment benefits to two members of the Native American Church who had been fired for using peyote in their religious ritual. Oregon law held that people who become unemployed through violating a criminal statute were not entitled to benefits. The plaintiffs claimed a right to the benefits under the First Amendment's Free Exercise Clause.

Writing for the majority, Justice Scalia acknowledged that the men's claim was a sympathetic one that Oregon might well have chosen to accommodate as, he noted, other states did in similar circumstances. However, he concluded:

> But to say that a nondiscriminatory religious practice exemption is permitted, or even that it is desirable, is not to say that it is constitutionally required, and that the appropriate occasions for its creation can be discerned by the courts. It may fairly be said that leaving accommodation to the political process will place at a relative disadvantage those religious practices that are not widely engaged in; but that unavoidable consequence of democratic government must be preferred to a system in which each conscience is a law unto itself or in which judges weigh the social importance of all laws against the centrality of all religious beliefs.[61]

The decision alarmed and galvanized religious communities across the spectrum from the most liberal to the most orthodox. The result was the Religious Freedom Restoration Act (1993). Liberals were fully on board with this project of congressional triumphalism, as shown by the identities of its chief legislative sponsors. The chief sponsor in the House of Representatives, where it passed unanimously, was Rep. Chuck Schumer. In the Senate, where it passed by a vote of 97 to 3, the chief sponsor was Senator Ted Kennedy. President Bill Clinton signed the bill into law to great acclaim from all religious communities.

RFRA provides that "government shall not substantially burden a person's exercise of religion even if the burden results from a rule of general applicability" unless the government demonstrates that the

---

[60] 494 US 872 (1990).

[61] Id at 890.

policy or practice serves a "compelling governmental interest" by the "least restrictive means." What amounts to a substantial burden, and by what test? How are courts to evaluate whether a challenged policy imposes the least possible burden on religious adherents? Is every religious claim equally weighty? What does the Establishment Clause have to say about this hypervigilant protection of free exercise? These questions went unanswered; in fact, they were scarcely raised in the bipartisan, multifaith fervor to tell the Supreme Court that it was wrong.[62]

But Justice Scalia's warning came to pass. The political context in which RFRA was deployed was transformed during the following decades of what Michel Rosenfeld calls the "dramatic repoliticization of religion."[63] What its sponsors intended as a shield to protect minority religions became, instead, a sword in the hands of powerful forces representing the religious Right and the Catholic Church. What we have now is, indeed, a statute that permits—one might say encourages—"every conscience to be a law unto itself."[64]

The Supreme Court's *Hobby Lobby* decision from 2014 is the case in point.[65] The owner of a national chain of craft stores with thousands of employees claimed entitlement under RFRA to an exemption from the Affordable Care Act's requirement to include contraception coverage in the employee health insurance plan. He raised a religious objection to certain forms of birth control that he deemed, incorrectly, to be "abortifacients."[66] In an opinion by Justice Alito,

---

[62] The Court never subjected RFRA to analysis under the Establishment Clause. In *City of Boerne v Flores*, 521 US 507 (1997), the Court held that RFRA's application to the states exceeded Congress's enforcement authority under Section 5 of the Fourteenth Amendment, leaving the law applicable only to federal action. Many states then enacted their own versions of RFRA. In 2000, Congress supplemented RFRA with the Religious Land Use and Institutionalized Persons Act, 42 USC 2000cc. The Court unanimously upheld the constitutionality of this statute as applied both to the federal government and the states. See *Cutter v Wilkinson*, 544 US 709 (2005).

[63] Susanna Mancini and Michel Rosenfeld, eds, *The Conscience Wars* 58 (Cambridge, 2018).

[64] There is a robust literature on the Religious Freedom Restoration Act, its origins, and its consequences. Two examples, one from early in the post-*Smith* debate, and one more recent, will suffice for our purposes: James E. Ryan, *Smith and the Religious Freedom Restoration Act: An Iconoclastic Assessment*, 78 Va L Rev 1407 (1992); Micah Schwartzmann, Nelson Tebbe, and Richard Schragger, *The Costs of Conscience*, 106 Ky L J 881 (2017–18).

[65] *Burwell v Hobby Lobby Stores*, 573 US 682 (2014).

[66] On the misuse of the concept of "abortifacient" in the context of birth control, see Rachel Frank, *Miss-Conceptions: Abortifacients, Regulatory Failure, and Political Opportunity*, 129 Yale L J 208 (2019).

the Court held by a vote of 5 to 4 that the owner of this for-profit business was entitled to the same accommodation the Obama administration was already offering to religiously affiliated nonprofits. (Churches themselves were completely exempt from the contraception mandate.) The administration was giving these religiously identified organizations the option of simply informing the federal government of their objection to contraception coverage, at which point the government would notify the organizations' third-party insurers to pick up the cost directly. Hands off, in other words. In *Hobby Lobby*, the Court held that the existence of this voluntary accommodation by the administration demonstrated that there was a less restrictive means, within the meaning of RFRA, to address a for-profit employer's religious concerns while still assuring coverage for those employees who did not share his objections.

It is important to underscore exactly what the claim was, both here and in the cases that followed. Obviously, no one was forcing the Hobby Lobby owner—or, in subsequent litigation, the Little Sisters of the Poor, an order of nuns whose chain of nursing homes both employs and serves nonadherents[67]—to buy or use birth control for themselves. Rather, the claim was one of complicity in the sin of third parties—what Douglas NeJaime and Reva Siegel call a complicity-based conscience claim.[68]

There are two points to note about the nature and consequences of this type of conscience claim as it has evolved. One is the increasingly attenuated nature of these claims. Consider Kim Davis, the Kentucky county clerk, who acted under what she called "God's authority" when she refused to perform her duty to issue marriage licenses to anyone legally entitled to marry, including same-sex couples.[69] That was a straightforward complicity claim: my signature would enable your marriage.

The claims put forward in the months and years following *Hobby Lobby*, however, have been much more attenuated: some employers asserted that even submitting the opt-out form to the government

---

[67] See *Zubik v Burwell*, 136 S Ct 1557 (2016).

[68] Douglas NeJaime and Reva B. Siegel, *Conscience Wars: Complicity-Based Conscience Claims in Religion and Politics*, 124 Yale L J 2516 (2015).

[69] See https://www.chicagotribune.com/news/nationworld/politics/ct-kim-davis-kentucky-20181107-story.html. Davis, who became a heroine to the religious Right, was found in contempt of court when she continued to refuse an order to issue the licenses.

made them complicit,[70] while others objected to a proposed workaround by which the government would act to assure contraception coverage even without any formal notice at all.[71] On this logic, it is difficult to say where the chain of complicity would end. It's hard to see why an employer could not claim complicity in sin when issuing a paycheck that a female employee of childbearing age might predictably use to buy birth control products.

The second point to note is the scant regard that the conscience claimants and the Court pay to the harms suffered by third parties from recognition of the complicity claims. While in the *Hobby Lobby* opinion Justice Alito offered the view that the decision's effect on female employees seeking contraception coverage "would be precisely zero"[72] under the accommodation the Court identified, that has proven not to be the case as claimants have rejected one accommodation after another, each more generous. As Professors NeJaime and Siegel point out, accommodation of such claims "does not entail costs borne by society as a whole; instead, accommodation has consequences for the third parties whose conduct is at issue."[73]

This became clear in the *Masterpiece Cakeshop* case, in which a partner in a same-sex marriage left a bakeshop empty-handed after the owner announced that his religious objection to same-sex marriage made him unable to bake a cake to be used in celebration of such a marriage.[74] In other words, the owner of a public accommodation, legally bound under Colorado law not to discriminate on the basis of sexual orientation, claimed the conscience-driven right to be able to pick and choose his customers, on the ground that *his* cake would make him complicit in *their* sin. The Court decided the case in a way that sidestepped the main issue. But other cases are in the pipeline,

---

[70] *Wheaton College v Burwell*, 134 S Ct 2806 (2014).

[71] Brief for petitioners, *East Texas Baptist University v Burwell*, No 14-1418 and consolidated cases, Jan 4, 2016. ("Notwithstanding the various euphemistic labels the government has attached to that regulatory mechanism, there is no escaping the reality that it is a mechanism for petitioners to *comply with*, not avoid, the mandate to which they object . . . because by taking the acts that it requires, an employer would enable the use of its own plan infrastructure to provide 'seamless' coverage to which it holds sincere religious objections." Brief at 42 (emphasis in original).

[72] 573 US at 693.

[73] NeJaime and Siegel, 124 Yale L J at 2542 (cited in note 68). For an extended treatment of the problem of third-party harm, see Schwartzmann, Tebbe, and Schragger, 106 Ky L J at 881 (cited in note 64).

[74] *Masterpiece Cakeshop, Ltd. v Colorado Civil Rights Commission*, 138 S Ct 1719 (2018).

and will multiply in recognition that the Supreme Court's door is open to such claims.[75]

The Trump administration is now testing the boundaries of complicity-based conscience claims with a newly promulgated rule that permits employers to refuse to cover contraception on the basis not only of religious objections but "sincerely held moral convictions" as well. Judge Wendy Beetlestone, in granting a preliminary injunction (before the final order I quoted earlier), marveled at the new rule's "remarkable breadth" and asked: "Who determines whether the expressed moral reason is sincere or not or, for that matter, whether it falls within the bounds of morality or is merely a preference choice?" The administration, she observed, "has conjured up a world where a government entity is empowered to impose its own version of morality on each one of us. . . . That cannot be right."[76]

And that cannot be civil society as we have understood it. That case, too, is now at the Supreme Court's door. In its petition for certiorari, the Trump administration disclaims any responsibility for the third-party harm that would result from the implementation of its rules, asserting that "any loss of contraceptive coverage to women whose private employers invoke the religious exemption would result from decisions of those employers, not the government."[77]

It may seem a stretch to draw a line from *Janus* to wedding cakes to birth control. But these cases all present a similar challenge to the Supreme Court, and to us. They raise the question of whether the Roberts Court will further accelerate the tribalizing of America, or whether this fractured court can find a way to invoke constitutional principles that help to hold us together, all passengers on the same boat in stormy seas.

"A democratic society cannot flourish if its citizens merely pursue their own narrow interests," the political philosopher Robert Audi wrote twenty years ago.[78] And yet the atomistic First Amendment

---

[75] A petition for certiorari in one such case, a claim by a floral designer for the First Amendment right not to provide flowers for a same-sex wedding, was filed in September 2019 after a previous remand from the Supreme Court in light of *Masterpiece Cakeshop*. See 138 S Ct 2671 (2018). *Arlene's Flowers, Inc. v State of Washington*, 441 P3d 1203 (Wash 2019), petition for cert pending, 19-333.

[76] *Pennsylvania v Trump*, 281 F Supp 3d 553, 577 (E D Pa 2017).

[77] *Trump v Commonwealth of Pennsylvania*, petition for cert granted, 19-454, at 26.

[78] Robert Audi, *A Liberal Theory of Civic Virtue*, 15 Soc Phil and Policy 149 (1998).

that the Court appears committed to delivering is enshrining pursuit of narrow personal interests as a constitutional right. Recall that Illinois, through its elected representatives, was perfectly free to abolish the agency fee system for its public sector unions, but the will of the people was otherwise. It was only in that realization that the governor turned to the courts to do his work for him, and to the Supreme Court when the lower courts failed him.

Civil society by definition exists outside the formal structures of government. Judith Shklar defines citizenship in part as having "a sense of obligation to the social environment . . . an internalized part of a democratic order that relies on the self-direction and responsibility of its citizens rather than on their mere obedience."[79]

But neither does civil society exist apart from government, which has the power through law to regulate the structures that sustain it. The Supreme Court, in its role as "republican schoolmaster," in Robert Dahl's classic phrase,[80] is an indispensable partner in the ongoing project of translating into operative law the values that vie for dominance at a given cultural moment. When the Court moves from understanding the First Amendment as furthering a "common cause" to enlisting it as a tool that individuals can invoke to free themselves from the bonds of joint enterprise, we are entering a kind of twilight of democratic legitimacy. When employers and providers of public accommodations are permitted to opt out from meeting their legal obligations without regard to the harm imposed on others, the worn fabric holding society together frays even more. The Supreme Court is necessarily a principal author of the ongoing American story. In the chapter the Court is writing now lies the future not only of civil society but of democracy itself.

---

[79] Judith N. Shklar, *American Citizenship: The Quest for Inclusion* 7 (Harvard, 1991).

[80] Robert Dahl, *Decision Making in a Democracy: The Supreme Court as National Policy Maker*, 6 J Public L 279 (1957).

JAMES T. KLOPPENBERG

TO PROMOTE THE GENERAL WELFARE:
WHY MADISON MATTERS

This essay addresses an aspect of constitutional law that never gets old—the relation between the Constitution and the ideas of James Madison. When I began thinking about writing this essay, I considered addressing the issue of Madison and originalism. But I decided against that. Recent books by Mary Sarah Bilder, Saul Cornell and Gerald Leonard, Jonathan Gienapp, Michael Klarman, Jack Rakove, and chapters of Alison LaCroix's forthcoming book *The Interbellum Constitution* have convinced me that for serious scholars in the field of legal history, the idea of originalism, whether it's 1.0, 2.0, or 3.0, has been so thoroughly discredited that there is little left to say about it.[1]

James T. Kloppenberg is Charles Warren Professor of American History at Harvard University.

AUTHOR'S NOTE: An earlier version of this essay was delivered as the Fulton Lecture in Legal History at the University of Chicago Law School on April 3, 2019. For that invitation, I am grateful to Dean Thomas J. Miles, Professor Geoffrey Stone, and Professor Alison LaCroix, whom I am delighted to acknowledge as the former student who has taught me more about legal history than anyone else. For comments that helped me revise that lecture and clarify my arguments, I am also indebted to Rebecca Brooks, Mary Anne Case, Jonathan Gienapp, Alison LaCroix, Martha Nussbaum, and Geoffrey Stone.

[1] Mary Sarah Bilder, *Madison's Hand: Revising the Constitutional Convention* (Harvard, 2015); Saul Cornell and Gerald Leonard, *The Partisan Republic: Democracy, Exclusion and the Fall of the Founders' Constitution, 1780s–1830s* (Cambridge, 2019); Jonathan Gienapp, *Second Creation: Fixing the American Constitution in the Founding Era* (Harvard, 2018); Jack N. Rakove, *A Politician Thinking: The Creative Mind of James Madison* (Oklahoma, 2017); Alison Lacroix, *The Interbellum Constitution* (forthcoming).

© 2020 by The University of Chicago. All rights reserved.
978-0-226-70856-0/2020/2019-0009$10.00

Instead, this essay examines a way of thinking about the purpose of law and government common to several prominent and influential thinkers in the late eighteenth century. It is a way of thinking that might strike some readers as odd, and others as naive, particularly those whose training came from studying recent work in the mainstream social sciences, especially neoclassical economics, political science, evolutionary psychology, or any field bewitched by the idea of so-called rational choice. I argue that the primary purpose of government, not only for Madison but also for other influential American Constitution writers in the late eighteenth century, John Adams and James Wilson, was not to protect individual rights, or property, or the freedom to do whatever a self-interested individual wants to do. The purpose of government, at least from the perspective of Adams, Wilson, and Madison, was to advance the common good, or, in the words of the Preamble to the Constitution, to "promote the general Welfare." That, I will argue, is why Madison matters.

I will begin with the Constitution of the Commonwealth of Massachusetts, drafted in 1780 by John Adams and still in force today. Adams had earlier provided the template for the first round of state constitutions in an essay he wrote in the tumultuous spring of 1776, *Thoughts on Government*. The framework he sketched there, written in response to a request from William Hooper of North Carolina, served as the model for the state constitutions of North Carolina, New Jersey, and Virginia, and its influence rippled out far beyond those three states.[2] Adams followed that same template when asked to write the Massachusetts Constitution four years later. Voters had rejected the first attempt, but the version Adams proposed became law. Adams wrote to a friend that his Constitution was "Locke, Sidney, and Rousseau and de Mably, reduced to practice."[3]

The presence of Rousseau in that list surprises many people. We often take for granted, mistakenly, that Locke and Rousseau are responsible for two very different traditions of thought and of government, the one liberal and the other, well, *not* liberal but communitarian, or statist, or perhaps proto-totalitarian, if only because Robespierre

---

[2] On the writing and the influence of Adams's *Thoughts on Government*, see James T. Kloppenberg, *Toward Democracy: The Struggle for Self-Rule in European and American Thought* 318–44 (Oxford, 2016) ("*Toward Democracy*").

[3] John Adams, in Charles Francis Adams, ed, 4 *The Works of John Adams* at 216 (Boston, 1850–56).

invoked Rousseau to justify the Terror. Locke is said to have enshrined the rights cherished by Anglo-Americans ever since, and Rousseau is said to have enabled the use of the guillotine. So why did Adams write that both of them had inspired the Massachusetts Constitution? The answer to that question involves reinterpreting both Locke and Rousseau—as well as Sidney and de Mably—and doing that is one of the central challenges I tried to meet in my book *Toward Democracy*. It's a complicated story, which is why the book is so long. Here I will sketch just the contours of a few parts of my larger argument.[4]

I will begin with Rousseau, because it is important to understand that some of his ideas do lie behind the constitutional thinking of Adams, Wilson, and Madison. Since Rousseau savaged the idea of representation in *The Social Contract*, that claim seems counterintuitive. Rousseau pointed to the horribly corrupt system of elections in Britain, where a tiny fraction of the population chose for the House of Commons a few wealthy individuals to "represent" them. He used that example to show the distance between conventional but flawed systems of representative government and his own radical ideal. Rousseau sought a form of government in which all citizens would internalize what he called the general will, his controversial and widely misunderstood concept of the enduring common good. Rousseau denigrated governments that merely added together the particular interests of particular individuals or particular groups. They privileged what he called the will of all, which he contrasted to the general will.[5]

Rousseau credited Denis Diderot with having coined the term *volonté générale*, conventionally translated as "general will," in the article in which Rousseau first discussed—and transformed—the idea. In his article "Political Economy," published in 1755, in volume 5 of Diderot and Jean le Ronde d'Alembert's *Encyclopedia*, Rousseau wrote that the general will "always tends toward the preservation and welfare of the whole and of each part." It is "the source of the laws" and provides "the rule of what is just and unjust." It is quite possible that the

---

[4] See, in *Toward Democracy*, ch 4 (on Sidney and Locke), 5 (on Rousseau and the Enlightenments of England, France, and Scotland), 6–9 (on the American Enlightenment, the American Revolution, and the writing and ratification of the US Constitution), and 11–13 (on the French Revolution and its consequences). *Toward Democracy* at 137–88, 191–251, 252–453, 505–46 (cited in note 2).

[5] On Rousseau's ideas, and for the interpretation of *The Social Contract* that lies behind my claim for his influence on Adams, Wilson, and Madison, see *Toward Democracy* at 212–34 (cited in note 2).

will of any individual, or of any group, might not correspond to the general will. For Rousseau, the general will served as an abstract standard of judgment, an ideal of justice, a principle that provides a norm against which all considerations of individual or group interests must be measured. By definition, "the general will is always in favor of the common good." For that reason Rousseau favored popular government over the monarchies and aristocracies of Europe, but he acknowledged that the problem would persist even in democracies. In any legislative assembly, individuals or groups are likely to try to advance their own interests instead of those of the whole people. Because "personal interest is always found in inverse ratio to duty," narrow self-interest, or the particular interests of particular groups, often masquerade as the general will. Even "the most corrupt men always render some sort of homage to the public faith."[6]

How can this problem be solved? Rousseau's response was disarmingly simple: the first duty of legislators is to "make the laws conform to the general will." Rousseau insisted that "the leaders know very well that the general will is always for the side most favorable to the public interest—that is, for the most equitable; so that it is only necessary to be just and one is assured of following the general will." Remove the filter of self-interest; the luminous truth of justice can shine forth. Since virtue consists in the "conformity of the private will to the general," the objective of government is simply to "make virtue reign." Only if the authority of the general will "penetrates to the inner man," and only if it "is exerted no less on his will than on his actions," can egoism give way to genuine commitment to the common good. "When citizens love their duty," Rousseau concluded, "all difficulties vanish."[7]

In order to understand what Rousseau meant by the general will, his essay "Political Economy" and *The Social Contract* must be read alongside several of his other texts. In his book *Emile*, a book about education that had a powerful impact on Thomas Jefferson and Benjamin Rush, among many others, Rousseau explained why he believed the key to self-government was education. He traced the process by which the protagonist, Emile, was taught by his tutor to internalize his

---

[6] Jean-Jacques Rousseau, "Political Economy," in Roger D. Masters, ed, *On the Social Contract with "Geneva Manuscript" and "Political Economy"* 211–16 (New York, 1978) (Judith R. Masters, trans).

[7] Id at 216–18.

duty. Through careful cultivation, Emile learned to love his duty, and to will what he *ought* to will, rather than simply following his inclinations, thus preparing him for his responsibilities as a citizen in a self-governing polity. More generally, Rousseau believed that such commitment to the common good, inculcated through "public education, under rules prescribed by the government and magistrates established by the sovereign," that is, by the power of the people themselves, "is therefore one of the fundamental maxims of popular or legitimate government."[8]

Rousseau was drawing on a tradition that dates back to the ancient world when he argued that those who follow their animal instincts are slaves to their senses. Only those individuals are free who see beyond their shallow, momentary impulses, or their whims, and act according to the dictates of reason. Rousseau wrote in *The Social Contract* that sometimes people must be "forced to be free," which of course sounds ominous. But he meant by it nothing more sinister than that they must be made to follow the law rather than be permitted, let alone encouraged, to follow their personal preferences. In his words, they must learn to "substitute justice for instinct" and substitute "the voice of duty" for "physical impulse."[9]

Rousseau laid out his arguments in a string of texts. Not only in "Political Economy" and *Emile* but also in the preface to his *Discourse on Inequality*, the preliminary draft of *The Social Contract* known as the Geneva Manuscript, and the constitutions that he was invited to draft for Poland and for Corsica, Rousseau made clear that he saw the value, indeed the necessity, of a properly constituted representative democracy for any population larger than that of a small village. To reiterate the point, in "Political Economy" he described the general will succinctly as "the source of the laws" and "the rule of what is just and unjust." In other words, the general will should be understood as a Constitution.

Most so-called republics in the eighteenth century, including that of Rousseau's native Geneva, were oligarchies. They did not come any closer to what Rousseau was looking for than did the sham of self-government in Britain. Rousseau argued that the people themselves must remain sovereign, not a monarch, or a landed aristocracy, or

---

[8] Id at 223–24. On *Emile* see *Toward Democracy* at 220–21 (cited in note 2).

[9] Rousseau, *On the Social Contract* at 55–56 (cited in note 6).

government officials. The *people* should elect what Rousseau called "the most capable and upright of their fellow citizens" because they would best discern the good of the whole, the *general will*, rather than trying to advance the narrow, partial interests of their constituencies.[10] I am far from the first scholar to argue that Rousseau was offering an updated, secular version of a very old ideal. Present in various forms in the Stoics, Cicero, Augustine, and Calvin, it was the idea that true freedom, as well as civic responsibility, involves learning to channel the will toward the good. Individuals exercise their autonomy not by indulging their appetites but by restraining them.[11]

That, I contend, is why John Adams, good New England Congregationalist that he was, found Rousseau so appealing. Adams owned three copies of *The Social Contract*, and before 1780 he enthusiastically recommended the book to his wife, Abigail, and to his friends. He later changed his mind. After the Terror had transformed the French Revolution, and after the United States had split into rival parties, with Jefferson siding with France and Adams with Britain, Adams criticized everything French, including Rousseau. But that reversal, which you can track if you look at Adams's marginalia in the books in his library, comes in the edition of *The Social Contract* that he bought after the fall of Robespierre.

In the 1770s and 1780s, Adams saw things very differently. He believed that the Massachusetts Constitution, which identified equality and the education of all citizens as necessary for identifying and advancing the common good, should be understood as Rousseau reduced to practice. Adams wrote in his preamble, "It is a social compact by which the whole people covenants with each citizen and each citizen with the whole people, that all shall be governed by certain laws for the common good." Not a compact of the people with their government, as Hobbes and Locke both had it, but of the sovereign people with themselves, and not a compact designed above all to protect individual rights, but instead intended to promote the common good of the whole people.[12]

---

[10] Jean-Jacques Rousseau, *Second Discourse*, in Roger D. Masters, ed, *The First and Second Discourses* 82–83 (New York, 1964) (Judith R. Masters and Roger D. Masters, trans).

[11] See especially Patrick Riley, *The General Will before Rousseau: The Transformation of the Divine into the Civic* (Princeton, 1986).

[12] John Adams, *The Report of a Constitution, or Form of Government for the Commonwealth of Massachusetts*, in Gordon S. Wood, ed, *Revolutionary Writings, 1775–1783* 297–322 (New York, 2011).

This way of thinking persisted through the 1780s. After the new nation had established its independence and John Adams had been sent off to Europe as an emissary, the United States were struggling—and I use the plural deliberately, because that was the standard formulation for decades after independence—to recover from the economic chaos that followed the war. Many Americans in the mid-1780s were uneasy. Would those state constitutions, almost all of them similar to the original framework laid out by Adams in 1776, survive the challenge of independence? Would the Articles of Confederation hold the states together?

Among those who wanted a stronger central government were Virginian James Madison, all of thirty-six years old in the spring of 1787; the Scottish-born attorney James Wilson of Pennsylvania; and that now-familiar (thanks to Lin-Manuel Miranda) "bastard, orphan, son of a whore" Alexander Hamilton. Some of those who feared that the new nation was coming apart managed to engineer what became the Constitutional Convention. It was an audacious gamble. As many readers will know, those who gathered in Philadelphia lacked the authority to do what they did.

Madison arrived at the Convention intent on creating a new form of government. In the weeks before the Convention opened, he wrote for himself a little essay that would serve him as a source book for the next couple of years. He drew on it for his speeches in Philadelphia, for the twenty-nine essays he wrote for the project now known as *The Federalist*, and for his speeches at the Virginia Ratifying Convention. This essay, "The Vices of the Political System of the United States," or "Vices" for short, gives us a look inside Madison's head as he was thinking about a new Constitution. In what follows, I will examine some of Madison's central texts, not only his essay "Vices" but also his speeches and his contributions to *The Federalist*. I will stress dimensions of his thought overlooked by many tour guides who have taken visitors around Madison's world, dimensions that tie his ideas, like those of his friend and closest ally James Wilson, to those of John Adams—and to those of Jean-Jacques Rousseau. I am aware this is an unconventional claim. I can imagine a few readers squirming in their seats and a few eyebrows knitting up. Some readers might even be singing to themselves the closing line from the number in *Hamilton* that Miranda gives King George after being told that John Adams will be the next president: "Gooood luck." But stay with me.

In an article that will become part of her book *The Interbellum Constitution*, Alison LaCroix offers an image of Madison that captures what was distinctive about him: "Madison is often portrayed as a theoretical scientist of politics, but he was also a practical mechanic, sleeves rolled up, tinkering in the works. For him, structure was not an arid set of design sketches but a model of interlocking wheels, cogs, and pistons.... The most pressing issue, as [Madison] saw it, was the debate over the nature of the Union: was it a nation, with a shared set of interests or values, or a collection of states that jealously guarded their borders and powers?"[13] Today I want to show you Madison working to create something more than a collection of states with different ambitions. He sought to bring into being a nation with a shared set of values beyond the narrow interests of its individual citizens.

Madison had studied at the College of New Jersey, later renamed Princeton, under John Witherspoon, a Scottish-born minister and follower of the Scottish moral philosopher Francis Hutcheson. Madison understood the friction between individual impulse and conscience.[14] He perceived the gap between immediate perceptions of self-interest and the dictates of what Hutcheson called rational benevolence. In Madison's essay "Vices," he laid out all the ways in which the people of the United States, like sinful humans always and everywhere, were putting their own interests above the good of the whole. Some commentators, notably Jack Rakove, attribute to Madison early versions of what we now call the problems of collective action and free riders. Madison worried that some states were proving themselves unwilling to shoulder their share of the burdens of being part of a nation.[15] Reading through "Vices," it's hard to see how he thought this experiment in self-government could be saved from chaos.

In "Vices" Madison offered a shrewd—and too seldom fully understood—analysis of social conflict. "All civilized societies," he wrote, "are divided into different interests and factions." Madison listed seven

---

[13] LaCroix, *The Interbellum Constitution*, forthcoming (cited in note 1).

[14] Gideon Mailer, *John Witherspoon's American Revolution* (North Carolina, 2017), stresses the tension between Witherspoon's respect for Thomas Hutcheson's philosophy and the Calvinist emphasis on man's sinfulness. Madison imbibed both, Mailer argues, and that accounts for his belief that it is necessary to acknowledge not only men's ethical nature but also their propensity to sin.

[15] Rakove, *A Politician Thinking* at 47–53 (cited in note 1).

such conflicts, including those between (1) creditors and debtors; (2) rich and poor; (3) farmers, merchants, and manufacturers; (4) members of different religious sects; (5) followers of different political leaders; (6) inhabitants of different regions; and (7) owners of different kinds of property. Madison's understanding of conflict cannot be captured by a simple division between "elites" and the "people." He had seen wealthy and prominent planters disgraced and rejected, as he was in the elections of 1777 and 1785, and as his friend Jefferson was at the end of his term as governor of Virginia. He had seen recent immigrants, such as the Pennsylvanian Wilson and the New Yorker Hamilton, rise quickly from poverty and anonymity to become figures of wealth and power—and then to become targets of public abuse. Madison understood that no single rift, whether of class, or occupation, or religion, or region, captured all the complicated dimensions of human interaction.[16]

The key to Madison's solution lay in harnessing all of these crosscutting divisions and putting them to use. Through political institutions, he believed autonomous citizens could create a culture of democracy devoted to pursuing the common good. How would it work? Madison denied that majoritarianism would be enough. He offered a version of the familiar observation that any group of three can yield a majority of two who can decide to enslave the other one. Madison knew that different regimes had tried to meet these ancient objections to majority rule in different ways. Monarchies relied on the neutrality of the king. Small republics counted on limiting the power government could use against its people. But history showed how frequently such measures failed.[17]

Madison had a different idea, one that resembled those of Rousseau and Adams. He conceived of representative democracy as a process of continuing deliberation and experimental truth testing. He leveraged Aristotle's insight about the moderation of conditions in large states against Montesquieu's admonition that republics must remain small. In a large, self-governing nation, Madison called for, in his words, "such a process of elections as will most certainly extract from the mass of the Society the purest and noblest characters which it

---

[16] James Madison, "Vices of the Political System of the United States," in Jack Rakove, ed, *James Madison: Writings* 71–76 (New York, 1999).

[17] *Toward Democracy* at 386–91 (cited in note 2).

contains; such as will feel most strongly the proper motives to pursue the end of their appointment."[18]

The similarity between that formulation and Rousseau's is uncanny. Also like Rousseau, Madison stipulated the purpose that representatives should keep in mind. This is the issue that I think many commentators on his thought have missed. The goal of government for Madison was not merely to manage conflict or preserve order, as many liberal pluralists and tough-minded political scientists have claimed ever since the 1950s. Instead, in Madison's words, "Justice is the end of government. It is the end of civil society. It ever has been, and ever will be pursued, until it is obtained, or until liberty be lost in the pursuit."[19]

The advantage of a large over a small republic, Madison first argued in "Vices" and then explained in his speeches at the Constitutional Convention and in *The Federalist*, depends precisely on the cross-cutting interests that he had identified. Given the myriad complexities of those conflicts, he judged it all but impossible that any single constellation of interests could form, or mobilize a majority, around any interest other than what he called the "public interest." By the time Madison wrote *Federalist* 51, he had come up with his best formulation of this crucial point: "In the extended republic of the United States," he wrote, "and among the great variety of interests, parties and sects which it embraces, a coalition of a majority of the whole society could seldom take place upon any other principles than those of justice and the general good."[20] Note those words: justice and the general good.

Madison envisioned a system that would do more than balance competing groups, or play off factions against each other, or allow for contests of naked self-interest. Instead, Madison remained committed to an ideal he drew from Witherspoon, and from Witherspoon's teacher Hutcheson. It was an ideal that resembled those of Rousseau and Adams, the ideal that individuals might, through the mechanisms of representative democracy, create laws that would treat all citizens with justice. Not content with the idea of politics as a bare-fisted brawl, a slugfest in which individuals compete by advancing their own

---

[18] Madison, "Vices," in *Writings* at 79–80 (cited in note 16).

[19] Federalist 51 (Madison) in Jacob E. Cooke, ed, *The Federalist* 352 (Wesleyan, 1977).

[20] Id.

narrow conceptions of self-interest, Madison was struggling in "Vices" to find the words to express his alternative.[21]

In April of 1787, Madison had not yet come up with the metaphors of filters and sieves that would become clear to him as he participated in the Constitutional Convention. But he was already trying to explain how the democratic process of multiple elections, the deliberations of representatives, and the two-way communication between representatives and their constituents might—through an endless series of apparently conflict-ridden arguments—bring into being the closest approximation of the common good that flawed human beings could create.[22] Because Madison experienced his share of defeats at the Constitutional Convention, scholars now rarely describe him as "the founder." The Constitution hardly conformed to his model. He opposed the idea that the Senate should represent states rather than population. He rejected that provision as undemocratic, as many of us do now, because it gave disproportionate power to the states with the smallest populations. Like his friend and chief ally, Pennsylvania's James Wilson, he expressed a preference for the direct election not only of congressmen and senators but also of the president. Madison was ambivalent about slavery, which some delegates condemned but which Georgia and South Carolina refused to allow even to come to the Convention floor. Madison wanted the federal government to have a veto over state legislation, just another of his ideas that the Convention rejected.[23]

---

[21] On Hutcheson and eighteenth-century Scottish moral philosophy more generally, see *Toward Democracy* at 241–49 (cited in note 2).

[22] Id at 78–80; see Federalist 51 (Madison) in Jacob E. Cooke, ed, *The Federalist* 352 (cited in note 19). On the related versions of this argument offered by Rousseau and by Thomas Paine, see *Toward Democracy* at 225–35, 319–24 (cited in note 2). See also Robert Burt, *The Constitution in Conflict* 96–98 (Harvard, 1992).

[23] Because Madison was not only a brilliant thinker but also a skilled debater, a shrewd tactician, and a loyal son of Virginia, commentators have long disagreed about what he *really* thought. Michael Klarman, in his recent comprehensive study of the writing and ratification of the Constitution, *The Framers' Coup* (Oxford, 2016), rejects all of Madison's statements of principled commitment to popular government as smokescreens masking his deeper commitment to preventing poor Americans from exercising power and threatening the wealth of the rich. Although this way of reading Madison has a long lineage and many contemporary adherents, I find it unpersuasive for all the reasons offered in this article and in chapters 6–9 of my book *Toward Democracy*. For another recent study of the Constitution-writing process more congenial to my own, see Ganesh Sitaraman, *The Crisis of the Middle-Class Constitution: Why Economic Inequality Threatens Our Republic* (Knopf, 2017). As Sitaraman shows, almost all Americans active in writing and ratifying the Constitution were convinced that popular government could survive in the United States only by preventing precisely the outcome that Klarman claims they had in mind, namely, a polity dominated by the wealthy rather than

But gradually Madison reconciled himself to the compromises necessary to placate the small states and the slave states. When the Constitution was sent to the states for ratification, Madison pocketed his disappointments. He decided to defend it, not as perfect, but as the best the delegates could do. One of the pivotal states, along with his own Virginia, would be New York, which was the seat of the national government in 1787 and contained many Antifederalists who opposed the Constitution. So Madison borrowed money and traveled directly from Philadelphia to New York, where the Congress was meeting, and agreed to cooperate with Hamilton to write the essays we know now as *The Federalist*.

Madison and Hamilton already knew how much they disagreed with each other. Hamilton spoke little in the opening days of the Convention, in part because he was outnumbered on the New York delegation by two opponents of a new national government. His own views were idiosyncratic, which became apparent when he finally did speak. Miranda is right to observe that, in Philadelphia, Hamilton spoke for six hours and proposed his own form of government. He proclaimed himself an outspoken opponent of democracy. He disagreed with Madison and Wilson about popular elections. He wanted a Senate and a president who would serve for life. If Congress had to be elected by the people, he wanted it balanced by a powerful, lifelong executive and a supreme judicial court whose appointed judges would also serve for life. Hamilton's plan, which many delegates thought smacked of monarchy, attracted no support. So when Madison agreed to join forces with Hamilton and John Jay in defense of the Constitution, he already knew that they disagreed about basic issues, including both the mechanics of government and its purpose.[24]

Of the *Federalist* essays, Madison's first contribution to the series, *Federalist* 10, has been enshrined as the classic statement of American political thinking. That is inaccurate for many reasons. First, Hamilton, Madison, and John Jay were writing as Publius. Nobody at the time knew who wrote which essay. Second, their disagreements were real, but in *The Federalist* they were masked. Knowing how *Federalist* 10 came into existence complicates the meaning we attribute to it. In the

---

those who belonged to what Adams, Madison, Wilson, and others of their generation called "the middling sort."

[24] For Hamilton's plan, see James Madison, *Notes of Debates in the Federal Convention of 1787 Reported by James Madison* 129–39 (Ohio, 1966) (Adrienne Koch, ed).

essay Madison developed arguments first sketched in "Vices." He challenged Montesquieu and argued that self-government would work better in a large, heterogeneous nation than in a small city-state precisely *because* of the diversity of people and preferences. As everyone who has studied law or political science in an American university knows, in the final paragraph of *Federalist* 10 Madison described the Constitution as "a republican remedy for the diseases most incident to republican government."[25]

But wait. Just a few months before, in his first speech at the Constitutional Convention, Madison had used different terminology. In that speech, on June 6, he had recommended framing a new Constitution that would be, in his words, "the only defence against the inconveniences of democracy consistent with the democratic form of government."[26] Note those uses of "democracy" and "democratic."

Throughout the Convention, Madison and Wilson had taken the more democratic side on most controversial issues. Wilson argued for direct rather than indirect elections, and for proportional representation in the Senate, because those provisions were, as Madison put it, "consistent with the democratic form of government." Wilson played a much more important role in the Convention than most people realize. In his speech on June 6, 1787, in particular, he advanced an argument on popular sovereignty that proved indispensable for those in favor of the Constitution and a target (then as now) for those who opposed it. Wilson pointed out, accurately, that the only source of power anywhere in the Constitution was the people, "the legitimate source of all authority." Representation was necessary only because "it is impossible for the people to act collectively." By electing their representatives in Congress, and electing those who would choose all other officeholders, the people would see to it that their government would "possess not only firstly the force but secondly the *mind or sense* of the people at large."[27]

Wilson also delivered the most widely reproduced and circulated speech in favor of ratifying the Constitution on October 6, 1787, in

---

[25] Federalist 10 (Madison) in Jacob E. Cooke, ed, *The Federalist* 65 (Wesleyan, 1977).

[26] Madison, Speech in the Federal Convention on Factions (June 6, 1787), in *Writings* 92 (cited in note 16).

[27] James Wilson, Speech in the Federal Convention (June 6, 1787), in *Notes of Debates* 74 (cited in note 24); and on Wilson's role in the debates more generally, see *Toward Democracy* at 398–403 (cited in note 2).

Philadelphia. It was printed in thirty-four newspapers in twelve of the thirteen states. Wilson admitted that the Constitution was *less* democratic than he and some other delegates had wanted. It was imperfect, but the people could make it right because it could be amended. In this crucial speech, Wilson echoed central arguments of Rousseau's *Social Contract*. Under the Constitution, the American people would not alienate their sovereignty. They would retain it and be able to exercise it, just as they had done during the struggle for independence and in the current debate over the Constitution. Their engagement showed their commitment to the common good, which Wilson distinguished from the sum of their individual preferences exactly as Rousseau distinguished the general will from the will of all. The parallel is no accident. Wilson wrote his speeches with a copy of *The Social Contract* at his elbow, the same English translation that John Adams used when he was writing the Massachusetts Constitution.[28]

In a lengthy address Wilson delivered six weeks later, at the Pennsylvania Ratifying Convention, the parallels between Wilson and Rousseau were even more apparent. Wilson asked, why do people leave the state of nature? Although in that condition each individual can act according to the "pleasure of his interest," their "animosities" eventually drive them to form "the social compact." In joining together, each individual surrenders the liberty previously enjoyed, but, in Wilson's words, "it is evident that he gains more by the limitations of the liberty of others, than he loses by the limitation of his own." Wilson declared that "the aggregate of liberty is more in society, than it is in a state of nature," because, precisely as Rousseau had argued, in a properly constituted society individuals are governed by the laws they have made for themselves.[29]

Europeans, Wilson explained, still failed to understand the nature of representation. They still thought in terms of distinct social orders, which played different roles in mixed governments. The entire American citizenry, by contrast, would vote to authorize the creation of the Constitution. Under the Constitution, what Wilson called "the welfare of the whole," his phrase for Rousseau's general will, "shall be

---

[28] James Wilson, Speech at a Public Meeting (October 6, 1787), in Bernard Bailyn, ed, 1 *Debates on the Constitution: Federalist and Antifederalist Speeches, Articles, and Letters during the Struggle over Ratification* 63–69 (New York, 1993) ("*DOTC*").

[29] James Wilson, Opening Address at the Pennsylvania Ratifying Convention (November 24, 1787), in 1 *DOTC* 791–803 (cited in note 28).

pursued and not [merely] a part [of it]." It was for that reason, Wilson concluded, that what he called "the measures necessary to the good of the community," that is to say the law, "must consequently be binding upon the individuals that compose it." When laws emanate from the people themselves, through their elected representatives, and those laws embody the welfare of the whole, then individuals must obey—even if, Wilson might have added, they must thereby be forced to be free. Those at the Constitutional Convention weighed the advantages and disadvantages of various forms of government. In the end they adopted a plan that Wilson characterized as "purely democratical." All the streams of power in the plan can be traced, he concluded accurately, "to one great and noble source, THE PEOPLE." Wilson made clear that the purpose of the framework was exactly the purpose of Rousseau's general will. The processes of representative government, in Wilson's words, by "bringing forward the talents and abilities of the citizens, without regard to birth or fortune," made possible the discovery of the laws that would allow for the maximum enjoyment of individual liberty consistent with the equal enjoyment of liberty by all. Achieving that goal, "the welfare of the whole," was the explicit purpose of the Constitution. That was what made it "purely democratical."[30]

So Madison and Wilson agreed that the Constitution was a "democratic solution," to use Madison's language at the Convention, or "purely democratical," to use Wilson's words. Its purpose was to enable Americans to find the common good, or "the welfare of the whole." The question, then, is why, in *Federalist* 10, did Madison abandon the term "democracy" that he had used in the Convention, the word that Wilson continued to use? I ask readers to consider two possible explanations.

The first explanation, which is the one I offer in *Toward Democracy*, is that Madison was ensnared in an old debater's trick. In *Federalist* 9, the essay published on November 21, 1787, Hamilton as Publius characterized the Constitution, with its reliance on representative government and the indirect election of both senators and the president, as something categorically different from democracy. Adapting the

---

[30] Id; and see Wilson's elaborate closing speeches at the Convention, December 1, 1787, and December 3, 1787, in 1 *DOTC* 820–28, 829–30, 832–68 (cited in note 28). His final speech went on for four and a half hours.

formulation that Madison had used in his "Vices" essay and in his speeches at the Convention about the need for "a defence against the inconveniences of democracy consistent with a democratic form of Government," Hamilton changed Madison's terminology. The institutional architecture of the Constitution, he wrote, provides the "means by which the excellencies of republican government may be retained and its imperfections lessened or avoided."[31]

With that rhetorical sleight of hand, Hamilton distanced Publius—and Federalists more generally—from what Madison had called "the democratic form of government" and instead aligned the Constitution with what he called "the excellencies of republican government." Hamilton's move was so shrewd that he convinced later commentators that the Constitution had somehow been transformed from Wilson's "purely democratical" framework into something else, namely, a "republic" that was distinct from a democracy. Although the Constitution itself had not changed at all, critics ever since have treated it as though it had somehow metamorphosed into a different creature. Federalists like Madison and Wilson became elitists. Antifederalists became democrats, which was even stranger. As Saul Cornell showed in *The Other Founders*, the best book on the Antifederalists, many Antifederalists defended existing arrangements in the states simply to preserve their own positions of authority, arrangements no more democratic than those to be established by the new Constitution, in which all power flowed, as Wilson correctly observed, from the votes of the people, and no wealth or property requirements were stipulated for voters or officeholders.[32]

So when Madison contributed his first essay to *The Federalist*, the celebrated number 10, he inherited Hamilton's rhetorical strategy. Publius had now designated the Constitution "republican" and distinguished it from the popular regimes of direct rule in antiquity, regimes that had proved themselves susceptible to home-grown demagogues

---

[31] Federalist 9 (Hamilton) in Jacob E. Cooke, ed, *The Federalist* 50–56 (Wesleyan, 1977). The authorship of the individual essays has remained a vexed question since the essays' original publication. Even though recent scholarship has resolved most of these disputes, the persistence of disagreements about who wrote which essay suggests how conscious the authors were of making a consistent argument that masked their deep differences. See the introduction to the most comprehensive edition of *The Federalist*, ed Jacob Cooke, xi–xxx (Wesleyan, 1977).

[32] Saul Cornell, *The Other Founders: Antifederalism and the Dissenting Tradition in America, 1788–1828* (North Carolina, 1999); and the discussion of Antifederalists' arguments in *Toward Democracy* at 409–53 (cited in note 2).

and foreign conquerors. Madison was boxed in. Differentiating a "democracy" from a "republic," as John Adams later wrote, made no sense. The "distinction between a republic and a democracy cannot be justified," Adams wrote in a letter to J. H. Tiffany in 1819. "A democracy is as really a republic as an oak is a tree, or a temple a building. There are, in strictness of speech and in the soundest technical language, democratical and aristocratical republics, as well as an infinite variety of admixtures of both." Adams knew, as most later commentators have not, that the two terms were used interchangeably throughout the 1770s and 1780s to designate forms of popular government in contradistinction to monarchy, with different shadings depending on the circumstances in which, and the purposes for which, the terms were used. Adams pointed out, sensibly enough, that the apparently hard and fast categorical distinction in *Federalist* 9 and 10 was inconsistent with common practice in 1787. The widely circulated speeches during the ratification debates by Madison's closest ally at the Convention, James Wilson, with their crescendo of references to the Constitution as "purely democratical," illustrate Adams's point.[33]

How can we explain Hamilton's highjacking of Madison's and Wilson's terminology, which has caused commentators Left and Right to misunderstand Madison? Hamilton's New York City home was on Wall Street, on the block between Pearl Street and William Street. Madison's lodgings, with the Virginia delegation to the Continental Congress, were located at 19 Maiden Lane. The distance between them was about a quarter of a mile, a distance it takes about five minutes to walk. So Madison and Hamilton were in very close proximity to each other. They were able to confer on the essays as they were churning them out— "nonstop," as Miranda has it in *Hamilton*. One can only wonder what Madison said to Hamilton when he read *Federalist* 9, which established Publius as a critic of the democratic principles that Madison and Wilson had defended vigorously, albeit not always successfully, against Hamilton, Robert Morris, and Gouverneur Morris throughout the Convention. We'll never know. To cite Miranda one last time, we'll never be "in the room where it happened."

---

[33] John Adams to J. H. Tiffany (March 31, 1819), in Charles Francis Adams, ed, 10 *The Works of John Adams* 377–78 (Boston, 1850–56).

But now Madison had no choice but to adopt Hamilton's distinction. In *Federalist* 10, published only one day after *Federalist* 9, Madison designated as "pure" democracies the regimes that Hamilton had described as unstable, those with, as Madison put it, "a small number of citizens, who assemble and administer the Government in person." Although it might seem obvious, it is worth emphasizing that no English colony, and no state under the Articles of Confederation, had ever operated in that way. All of them, even the smallest, had relied on representative assemblies since the early seventeenth century. No one in America from the 1760s through the 1780s—not Tom Paine, not any agrarian or urban radical, and certainly not any Antifederalist—ever proposed such a "pure Democracy" as a viable alternative. Hamilton was using one of the oldest rhetorical strategies in the book by creating two straw men and then locating Publius in the sensible, moderate center. Madison was hardly in agreement with Hamilton about the Constitution. All of his writings and speeches before the fall of 1787 showed that Madison, like Wilson, conceived of the Constitution as a democratic solution to the problems of democracy. But in *Federalist* 10 he had no choice but to adopt Hamilton's framework.

Another common interpretation of *Federalist* 10 reflects a different but, I think, related misunderstanding. In perhaps the most familiar sentence in American political thought, Madison wrote "the latent causes of faction are sown in the nature of man; and we see them brought into different degrees of activity, according to the different circumstances of civil society." Only by extinguishing liberty could the causes of faction be removed, and that cure would be worse than the ill. As in "Vices," Madison observed that faction originates in what he called "the diversity of faculties of men, from which the rights of property originate." Because Madison contended that "the protection of these *faculties* is the first object of Government," readers at both ends of the political spectrum have taken him to mean that defending property rights, *not* protecting the faculties from which those rights originate, is the principal purpose of government. But that claim is made plausible only by selective quotation from the essay—and by limited familiarity with Madison. As he did in "Vices" and elsewhere, he noted that there are multiple causes of faction, including not only property but differences of religion, disagreements over politics, local or regional traditions, and one cause that has special salience in 2020, the perennial and sometimes irrational attachments of people to their leaders.[34]

Since these multiple *causes* of faction cannot be removed, Madison continued, we must work against the undesirable *effects* of faction. Governments must find a way, in Madison's words, to prevent legislators from serving as "advocates and parties to the causes they determine." Whatever the issue—indebtedness, domestic manufactures, taxes—responsible government needs what Madison called "the most exact impartiality." Yet there are always powerful temptations for legislators to choose their own or their constituents' "immediate interest," to use Madison's terminology, over what they should be seeking, namely, "justice and the public good."[35]

For Madison, as for Adams and Wilson, faction did not represent a healthy sign of a vibrant culture, as some later pluralists and defenders of limited government have claimed. The causes of faction lay in the human propensity to sin, the inclination to favor one's own interest over the common interest. The solution required cultivating the human capacity for virtue. Madison has long been identified as the epitome of American liberal pluralism, but I think we should reconsider that judgment.

Madison was self-consciously engaged in a strategic project. As the first essays of *The Federalist* were appearing in print, he emphasized in a letter that he was not engaged in writing political philosophy. As was true in Philadelphia, the Federalists had to keep their eyes on the target. "If any Constitution is to be established by deliberation and choice," Madison wrote to Archibald Stuart on October 30, 1787, "it must be examined with many allowances and must be compared, not with the theory which each individual may frame in his own mind, but with the system which it is meant to take the place of and with any other which there might be a probability of obtaining."[36] Much as he

---

[34] For more detailed analysis of *Federalist* 10 and Madison's other defenses of the Constitution, in *The Federalist* and in the Virginia Ratifying Convention, and on the reasons why his and Wilson's expectations for how American democracy would work were unfulfilled in the decades to follow, see *Toward Democracy* at 427–53 (cited in note 2); and the still unsurpassed analysis in Lance Banning, *The Sacred Fire of Liberty: James Madison and the Founding of the Federal Republic* 198–219 (Cornell, 1995).

[35] Federalist 10 (Madison) in Jacob E. Cooke, ed, *The Federalist* 56–65 (cited in note 25).

[36] Madison to Archibald Stuart (October 30, 1787), in William T. Hutcheson et al, 10 *Papers of James Madison* 232 (Chicago, 1962–91).

might have enjoyed writing a *Republic*, a *Utopia*, or an *Oceana*, he had a different objective, and in his next essay, *Federalist* 14, he threw himself into it.

Just two days after Madison's *Federalist* 10 was published, Wilson delivered his great Rousseauean oration at the Pennsylvania Ratifying Convention. Given Wilson's explicit endorsement of Rousseau, and the close parallels between his arguments and Madison's that I have already noted, only the stubborn insistence that Madison must have meant something different from Rousseau has blinded commentators to the similarities between his idea of a public good emerging from the deliberation of representatives and Rousseau's conception of the general will. Given the distinction that he and Hamilton had sketched in *Federalist* 9 and 10, Madison now had to establish the point that Wilson had made so powerfully in Pennsylvania.

In *Federalist* 14, his first essay after Wilson's decisive opening intervention in Philadelphia, Madison replied to Antifederalists anxious that those elected to the United States Congress would be too remote from the people. Their objections foundered on two crucial considerations, the principle of popular sovereignty and the practice of representation. Madison insisted, clearly echoing Wilson's arguments at the Pennsylvania Ratifying Convention, that the entire American political system, from towns through states to the federal government, was founded on the principle of popular government. The old anxiety about a state within a state, *imperium in imperio*, was baseless. All levels of government in the United States stood on a common, but unprecedented, foundation, the will of the people as a whole. Expressing themselves through elections, the American citizenry authorized the power exercised by those they had chosen. The power remained with the people. They could use it whenever they saw fit, simply by replacing one set of elected representatives with another. That was the principle of popular sovereignty.

The practice that Wilson and Madison were pointing to had been going on already for more than thirteen years. Against claims that representatives would be too aloof, or too distant from the concerns of local politics, Madison invoked Americans' experience during the war for independence and under the Articles of Confederation, with the Continental and then with the national Congress. Under the Constitution government would continue as before, with representatives elected to local, state, and national offices to do the work appropriate to their positions, the work they were authorized and selected by the voters to do. Although Madison and Hamilton had now adopted the term "republic" for this system of representative government and confined the use of "democracy" to small polities in which all citizens could gather and vote together, the Constitution they were defending in those terms was of course identical to the one Wilson had defended so eloquently and convincingly in Pennsylvania as "purely democratical." Just as Wilson had insisted that the goal of the representatives deliberating in their assemblies was to broaden the sensibilities of the representatives so that they might come to understand the "welfare of the whole" rather than the narrow interests of a part, and had offered Madison's principle of enlarging the sphere, so precisely had Madison reasoned in *Federalist* 10 concerning the means to the end of justice. Wilson had described "a chain of connection with the people"; Madison in *Federalist* 14 claimed for "America the merit of making the discovery" of popular representation "the basis of unmixed"—that is, nonmonarchical and nonaristocratic—"and extensive republics." Their terminologies now might have differed. Their arguments did not.[37]

Madison's later contributions to *The Federalist* continued to develop these ideas, and they demonstrate his continuing commitment to the ideas of popular sovereignty, republican virtue, and representative democracy, even though Publius's strategic maneuvering required him to locate his arguments between two extremes, both straw men. He turned the open-endedness of the Constitution into a virtue, an illustration of the flexibility that democratic decision making not only made possible but required. He mused on the difficulty of fixing the meaning of words, although he did not use his own shift from democracy to republic to illustrate the point. In response to the anxiety that those elected to the federal government would somehow form an oligarchy, an exasperated Madison pointed out that the entire system was to be in the hands of ordinary voters.

"Who are to be the electors?" Madison asked. "Not the rich more than the poor; not the learned more than the ignorant; not the haughty heirs of distinguished names, more than the humble sons of obscure and unpropitious fortune. The electors are to be the great body of the people of the United States. They are to be the same who

---

[37] Federalist 10 (Madison) in Jacob E. Cooke, ed, *The Federalist* 83–89 (cited in note 25), and see my discussion of Wilson at the Pennsylvania Ratifying Convention above.

exercise the right in every State of electing the correspondent branch of the Legislature of the State." And who are they to elect? Who will be the candidates for the House of Representatives? "Every citizen whose merit may recommend him to the esteem and confidence of his country." Then Madison got to the heart of it: "No qualification of wealth, of birth, or religious faith, or of civil profession, is permitted to fetter the judgment or disappoint the inclination of the people." If Americans could not trust ordinary people to choose the best qualified of their peers to serve in government, then government by the people is impossible. Madison and Wilson realized that the Constitution contained weaknesses; they had struggled against some of those weaknesses in the Convention. But they were puzzled that the advantages of representative democracy itself, advantages they judged self-evident, could be resisted. For more than two centuries, however, critics of the Constitution have contended that a system that provided, as Madison correctly observed, "no qualification of wealth, of birth, or religious faith, or of civil profession" somehow constrained or frustrated "the inclination of the people."[38]

Madison and Wilson instead believed that giving multiple interests a chance to advance their claims would provide an opportunity for genuine democratic debate. They believed that the filtering process of electing representatives would provide the best possible means to reach the goal of justice that all Americans shared. In Madison's words, not the expression or satisfaction of individuals' self-interest or the interest of a single group but "justice is the end of government." Given the size and complexity of the extended republic, "a coalition of the majority of the whole society could seldom take place on any other principles than those of justice and the general good," and variations on that phrase recur several times in Madison's later essays and speeches.

Wilson put it well. When a convention was called in Pennsylvania to debate the 1776 Constitution and consider replacing its unicameral legislature with a bicameral legislature that would bring it into conformity with the rest of the states and the national government, Wilson stated his case for a second legislative body by stressing the creative quality of debate in terms that reminded one of his colleagues of Rousseau. The comparison made sense in light of the close attention

---

[38] Federalist 57 (Madison) in Jacob E. Cooke, ed, *The Federalist* 384–90 (Wesleyan, 1977).

Wilson paid to Rousseau's writings and the similarities between their ideas. Like Rousseau, Wilson had no interest in perpetuating social orders or creating a new hereditary aristocracy. He preferred bicameralism only because he wanted more opportunities for deliberation, which he judged the best way to discern the common good.[39] Just as clearly as Madison, Wilson embraced a vision of popular government—call it republican, as Madison did in *Federalist* 10, or democratic, as Wilson did—committed not to a static ideal of unchanging perfection but to development through time. Wilson described that ideal in the Lectures on Law he delivered in Philadelphia in 1790–91: "This revolution principle," Wilson wrote, that "the sovereign power residing in the people, they may change their constitution and government whenever they please," is "not a principle of discord, rancor, or war; it is a principle of melioration, contentment, and peace."[40]

Given the disagreements that democracy both allows and engenders, and given the bitter conflicts that began almost as soon as the Constitution and the Bill of Rights took effect, that judgment may seem peculiar. But Wilson saw clearly that when no-holds-barred contests occur within the framework of an underlying cultural commitment to individual autonomy and an ethic of reciprocity, such debates do not undercut democracy but enrich and perpetuate it. Instead of allowing discontent to fester and develop into the cancer of civil war, deliberation by democratically chosen representatives can—not must, but can—enable them to reach shared understandings unavailable through any other mechanism. Much as Rousseau had envisioned citizens voluntarily renouncing narrow self-interest and internalizing the general will, as Emile did, so Wilson and Madison both quite self-consciously envisioned the American people embracing the fundamental law they had authorized and that their representatives had brought to life. Government, Wilson contended, "is only the creature

---

[39] In response to Wilson's proposal that both the Senate and the Assembly in Pennsylvania should be elected by the people, Alexander Graydon later wrote that Wilson's conception of popular sovereignty reminded him of Rousseau: "Ces Pauvres Savoyards sont de bonne gens [sic]. As Jean-Jacques says. And who could say less of the good souls of Pennsylvania." See Alexander Graydon, *Memoirs of a Life, Chiefly Passed in Pennsylvania, Within the Last Sixty Years* 198–219 (William Blackwood and T. Cadell, Strand, 1822); quoted in Philip Mead, *Beyond the Federal Constitution: The Creation of the Pennsylvania Constitution of 1790* 40 (unpublished Harvard University seminar paper, Spring 2004).

[40] James Wilson, Lectures on Law, Introductory Lecture: Of the Study of Law in the United States, in Robert Green McCloskey, ed, 1 *The Works of James Wilson* 79 (Harvard, 1967).

of a constitution," and the United States Constitution was the creature of the American people: "in their hands it is clay in the hands of the potter; they have the right to mould, to preserve, to improve, to refine, and to finish it as they please."[41] The structure, with its foundation in the people's will, had the stability of a pyramid, but it would forever remain unfinished, always subject to revision.

Madison did not aim merely at stasis, or moderation, or stability. He did not want just to pit interest against interest, faction against faction, so that they might cancel each other out. He aimed a lot higher, at autonomy, equality, and justice, goals to be achieved through democratic government. The aim, in his words, was "to secure the public good, and private rights, against the danger" of factions, even a majority faction intent on pursuing its own interest against the common interest. Preserving what he called "the spirit and the form of popular government" was "the great object to which our enquiries are directed." Madison's goal remained "the public good," an ideal that lay beyond the interests of any particular group of individuals. How could it be discerned? How could it be achieved?

For Madison, the key to responsible self-government, whether called a republic or a democracy, was deliberation. Representative institutions, in Madison's words, served "to refine and enlarge the public views, by passing them through the medium of a chosen body of citizens, whose wisdom may best discern the true interest of their country, and whose patriotism and love of justice, will be least likely to sacrifice it to temporary or partial considerations." The result, Madison concluded, will be "that the public voice pronounced by the representatives of the people, will be more consonant to the public good, than if pronounced by the people themselves convened for the purpose." When representatives deliberate, Madison argued, they have a better chance to find the common interest, the public good, the spirit beyond faction and self-interest.[42]

---

[41] Id at 304.

[42] Federalist 10 (Madison) in Jacob E. Cooke, ed, *The Federalist* 56–65 (cited in note 25). The commentary on this essay is enormous and continues to grow. An influential early critique of the 1950s liberal pluralist interpretation is Paul Bourke, *The Pluralist Reading of James Madison's Tenth Federalist*, 9 Perspectives in American History 271–95 (1975). Other readings of *Federalist* 10 that I have found particularly helpful include—to cite only a few of many—Marvin Meyers, whose introduction to *The Mind of the Founder* first sparked my interest in Madison as a theorist of justice (see Marvin Myers, introduction to *The Mind of the Founder: Sources of the Political Thought of James Madison* xi–xvvii (New England, 1982)), and with whom I had the good fortune to discuss Madison for many years; Gordon S. Wood's *Is*

That of course was what Rousseau had designated the general will, and Adams the common good. Knowledge of that common good could emerge, as it did for Madison and the other delegates who convened in Philadelphia, only through the process of deliberation, compromise, and creative rethinking. That was why, in *Federalist 55*, Madison wrote that even if every Athenian had been a Socrates, every assembly of the whole citizenry would still have been a mob. When there is no possibility of deliberation, no give and take of arguments but only the choice of voting up or down, yes or no, popular decision making is fatally flawed. That is why plebiscites are problematical, and that is why Madison, like Rousseau, Adams, and Wilson, thought that members of representative assemblies should aim to do more than mirror the self-interested preferences of their constituents.[43]

There a "James Madison Problem"? in Wood, ed, *Revolutionary Characters: What Made the Founders Different* 141–72 (Penguin, 2006), represents a rethinking of his influential argument about what he called "the Federalist persuasion" in *The Creation of the American Republic: 1776–1787* (North Carolina, 1969); David F. Epstein, *The Political Theory of The Federalist* 68–72 (Chicago, 1984); Colleen Sheehan, *The Politics of Public Opinion*, 49 Wm & Mary Q 609–29 (1989); and the still unsurpassed analysis in Lance Banning, *The Sacred Fire of Liberty: James Madison and the Founding of the Federal Republic* 198–219 (Cornell, 1995). Banning emphasizes, as he does throughout this superb book, Madison's dual focus on popular participation and the preservation of liberty. In his discussion of *The Federalist*, Banning offers not only an incisive analysis of Madison's own developing, dynamic ideas but also a clear and fair-minded guide to the voluminous critical debates from Charles Beard through Robert Dahl to Martin Diamond, Irving Brant, and Gordon Wood. Madison's distinction between democracy and republic, although it originates only in *Federalist* 10, rapidly became common among Americans who had not previously differentiated between the two—as indeed Madison himself did not prior to November of 1787. On this broader transformation, see Willi Paul Adams, *The First American Constitutions: Republican Ideology and the Making of the State Constitutions in the Revolutionary Era* 110–14 (North Carolina, 1980) (Rita and Robert Kimber, trans); and see J. G. A. Pocock, *Virtue, Commerce, and History: Essays on Political Thought and History, Chiefly in the Eighteenth Century* 16 (Cambridge, 1985). Ever since Douglas Adair, *"That Politics May be Reduced to a Science": David Hume, James Madison, and the Tenth Federalist*, 20 Huntington Lib Q 343–60 (1957), commentators have debated Madison's debt to Hume's essays, notably "Of the Independency of Parliament," "Of Parties in General," and "On the Idea of a Commonwealth." Hume did indeed discuss the advantages of an extended republic, but so did other writers from Aristotle to James Harrington. More recent scholars have tended to minimize the extent of Madison's debt to Hume. See Drew McCoy, *The Last of the Fathers: James Madison and the Republican Legacy* 42–51 (Harvard, 1989). Given Madison's resistance to Hume's moral psychology and his greater affinity with the ideas of Scottish commonsense philosophy, it makes more sense to align him with Hutcheson, Thomas Reid, or Adam Smith than with Hume. On that issue, see Henry F. May, *Enlightenment in America* 119–20 (Oxford, 1976); Peter Winch, *Adam Smith's Politics: An Essay in Historiographic Revision* 146–63, 178–80 (Cambridge, 1978); and Emma Rothschild, *Economic Sentiments: Adam Smith, Condorcet, and the Enlightenment* 232 (Harvard, 2001).

[43] Federalist 55 (Madison) in Jacob E. Cooke, ed, *The Federalist* 372–78 (Wesleyan, 1977). The point about representation and democracy is crucial. Hamilton and Madison both doubted that a very large body could engage in deliberation, and both of them, for different reasons, considered deliberation crucial. See the discussion in Jack Rakove, *Original Meanings:*

Threats to the common good came from multiple sources. Madison followed his mentor Witherspoon in believing that the dangers of passion and self-interest are ubiquitous, in politics and in the moral decisions that face every individual. Eighteenth-century Scottish philosophers emphasized the capacity of individuals to harness their unruly selves through the disciplined cultivation of conscience to accord with the dictates of benevolence. Madison too believed that the institutions of representative democracy might enable Americans, through their chosen representatives, to identify and defeat schemes running contrary to the common good. Achieving that goal, for individuals and for political institutions, requires that reason constrain impulse.

Decades ago the German historian Willi-Paul Adams showed that in the state constitutional conventions, the words democracy and republic were used interchangeably. But in the 1960s the academic mania for classical republican theory led to its being found everywhere, and then the false binary of republican versus liberal fed into prevailing characterizations of *The Federalist* as a sacred text, even *the* founding text, of American liberalism. That dynamic has caused us to misunderstand what happened in Philadelphia and in the debates that followed. In the Constitution, Madison now proclaimed in *Federalist* 10, "we behold a republican remedy for the diseases most incident to republican government." With a stroke of his quill, Madison reproduced Hamilton's magic trick. Beneath the smoke and mirrors, though, and despite his torching of the straw man of "pure democracy" that no one in America preferred to representative democracy, Madison's commitments to individual liberty, popular sovereignty, and the common good remained intact. He was still defending exactly the same framework that his chief ally Wilson had accurately described as "purely democratical," because there was no source of authority, anywhere in the system, other than the will of the people.

That, then, is the first explanation of the discrepancy between the use of "democracy" in Madison's June 6 speech in Philadelphia and his use of "republic," echoing Hamilton's in *Federalist* 9, in the celebrated *Federalist* 10. Before concluding, however, I want readers to consider an alternative explanation, which comes from Mary Sarah

---

Politics and Ideas in the Making of the Constitution 236–43 (Knopf, 1996): gathering into large assemblies, as ancient Athenians did, meant that passion would rule and rational deliberation would be impossible.

Bilder's provocative book *Madison's Hand: Revising the Constitutional Convention*. Bilder's book was published in 2015, just as the manuscript for my book *Toward Democracy* went into production at Oxford University Press. Bilder's book challenges the conventional understanding of how we should read Madison's *Notes on the Federal Convention*, which has long been considered the most authoritative source for the debates in Philadelphia in the spring and summer of 1787. Even though the *Notes* were published after Madison's death in 1836, most scholars have relied on it as a more or less accurate account. That is how I treat it in *Toward Democracy*. Bilder argues, however, that Madison *altered* the record in significant respects when he revised the *Notes*, first in the late 1780s and then when he returned to the project decades later.

She argues in particular that Madison revised the speech he dated June 6 in the *Notes* and that he inserted into that speech parts of an earlier speech that he gave on June 4. This claim is intriguing because the June 6 speech contains the words "the inconveniences of democracy consistent with the democratic form of government." Bilder found that Madison used different paper for that June 6 speech in the manuscript that eventually became the *Notes*. She contends that he wrote the speech of June 6 later, possibly as much as two years later, between the fall of 1789 and the spring of 1790. That would mean he wrote the speech *after* he had written *Federalist* 10, all the rest of his essays in *The Federalist*, and the speeches he delivered at the Virginia Ratifying Convention.

Now, if that is true, it means that we cannot know exactly what Madison said, if anything, about a democracy or a republic in his opening speech on the Virginia Plan at the Convention itself. If Bilder is right, we can know only that whenever he rewrote his speech, if indeed he did rewrite it for the *Notes*, he was no longer satisfied with the formulation used in *Federalist* 9 and 10, which did not accord with the way he thought the Constitution should be understood. If he did rewrite the speech at a later date, he evidently rewrote it to highlight his commitment to what he chose to call a "democratic form of government" and to distance himself further from Hamilton. If Bilder is right about the timing, Madison would have rewritten the June 6 speech when he was working on two projects. He was drafting the first amendments to the Constitution and mobilizing opposition to Treasury Secretary Hamilton's plan to fund state debts. The tensions between Madison and Hamilton, apparent in the Constitutional

Convention but muted in *The Federalist*, were already coming into the open.[44]

Readers will have to ask themselves which of those two explanations makes more sense. Did Madison abandon his use of the phrase "a democratic form of government" and adopt Hamilton's framework because he had no choice in light of *Federalist* 9, as I argued in *Toward Democracy* and in the first part of this essay? Or, as Bilder contends, did he *later* see the importance of identifying the aim of the delegates at the Convention as a "democratic form of government" after realizing that Hamilton and his cronies in New York had in mind something very different from what Madison, Wilson, Jefferson, and the more democratically oriented champions of the Constitution wanted?

From my perspective, the question remains open. The jury is still out. In either case, however, I believe this brief look at the writings of Adams, Wilson, and Madison shows that they agreed on a fundamental proposition that deserves more attention. The forms of government established in the United States from 1776 through 1787 were, in Wilson's words, "purely democratical" because there was no source of power anywhere, in any of the institutions, other than the will of the people. There was no monarch. There was no aristocracy. There were no inherited privileges. There was nothing but the citizenry. The distinction Hamilton drew between a republic and a democracy was nothing more than a debater's trick, and we should stop seeing it as an important categorical distinction.

In his new book *The Second Creation*, Jonathan Gienapp shows that treating the Constitution as a text with a fixed meaning is a mistake. He makes clear that its meaning was indeterminate, deliberately indeterminate, as both Madison and Wilson insisted during the debates over ratification. Its meanings had to be established in practice, over time, through trial and error. The meanings that developed from those practices were not inherent in the text, nor were they necessary or inevitable. They were contingent products of particular historical controversies and choices made by individuals. An even clearer sense of how that happened will be available when Alison LaCroix completes her masterful book *The Interbellum Constitution*.[45]

---

[44] See Bilder, *Madison's Hand* (cited in note 1).

[45] See Alison LaCroix, *The Interbellum Constitution*, 67 Stan L Rev 397–445 (2015). Madison was well aware, LaCroix shows, that the window in which he could speak to the

Even so, Gienapp concludes, none of us can avoid treating the Constitution as a foundational text, just as judges, attorneys, and legislators have had to do ever since ratification. Even historians certain that it has no singular "original meaning," and that includes me, have to make arguments about why we consider it open-ended, why we think it is "living" rather than fixed or determinate. Our arguments *also* turn on how we interpret the texts left by those who created the Constitution. I think Gienapp is right. That is what I have done in this essay, in which I have tried to show how we should understand Rousseau and Adams and why that understanding should change the way we see Wilson and Madison. The meaning of the Constitution was deliberately, self-consciously, left open for interpretation and debate because only through such open-ended deliberation can "We, the People" govern ourselves rather than allowing a small elite to rule.[46]

The purpose of representation, as Adams, Wilson, and Madison understood it, was to facilitate deliberation, not just horse trading. Their goal was not merely, or even primarily, to defend individual rights, let alone the right to property. Of course their refusal to include women in the ranks of citizens, and the willingness of Madison and other southerners to countenance slavery, mean that they were hardly democrats by our twenty-first-century standards. They detested the idea of parties, for reasons that have become all too clear in our own day: partisanship too often obstructs commitments to the public interest. But in the context of the eighteenth century, Adams, Madison, and Wilson stood on the side of popular government rather

---

public was closing as he approached the final years of his life. Madison in the 1820s was intent on denying what some of his contemporaries and some of our contemporaries claim, that *his* meaning, or the meaning of his generation, must determine the meaning of the Constitution for later generations. Referring to his 1817 veto of an internal improvements bill, the Bonus Bill intended for the construction of roads and canals, he wrote to Martin Van Buren, "I am aware that the document must speak for itself, and that that intention can not be substituted for the established rules of interpretation.... Whether the language employed duly conveyed the meaning of which J.M. retains the consciousness, is a question on which he does not presume to judge for others." As LaCroix puts the point, Madison was writing "to prepare the next generation of Americans to think for themselves in a proper constitutional mode." The contention of certain members of today's Supreme Court, who argue that there is a continuous line from "the Framers" to the present, is clearly erroneous: "the point is that the Constitution of the early nineteenth century was not the Constitution of the twenty-first century, even with respect to provisions of the text that remained the same throughout that time." LaCroix, 67 Stan L Rev at 444 (cite in note 45).

[46] Readers interested in a more detailed presentation of the evidence should read chapters 5–9 of *Toward Democracy* 191–453 (cited in note 2), and the extended notes to the book, available at https://scholar.harvard.edu/kloppenberg/home.

than rule by elites. Their goal was Rousseau's goal, to find a way to advance the public interest over the self-interest of the few.

In conclusion, if you have been thinking of the Constitution as a charter securing individual rights or protecting particular interests against the government, or as a bulwark against efforts to advance the welfare of the public as a whole, I urge you to think again. The Constitution is, above all, concerned with the search for the common good. It establishes a government "to promote the general Welfare." And that is why Madison matters.

KF 4546 .S9 2019
1643150
The Supreme Court review

WITHDRAWN